Unreal Engine 4 Virtual Reality Projects

Build immersive, real-world VR applications using UE4, C++, and Unreal Blueprints

Kevin Mack
Robert Ruud

BIRMINGHAM - MUMBAI

Unreal Engine 4 Virtual Reality Projects

Commissioning Editor: Kunal Chaudhari
Acquisition Editor: Karan Gupta
Content Development Editor: Arun Nadar
Technical Editor: Rutuja Vaze
Copy Editor: Safis Editing
Project Coordinator: Kinjal Bari
Proofreader: Safis Editing
Indexer: Priyanka Dhadke
Graphics: Alishon Mendonsa
Production Coordinator: Arvindkumar Gupta

First published: April 2019

Production reference: 1300419

Published by Packt Publishing Ltd.
Livery Place
35 Livery Street
Birmingham
B3 2PB, UK.

ISBN 978-1-78913-287-8

www.packtpub.com

Table of Contents

`mapt.io`

Mapt is an online digital library that gives you full access to over 5,000 books and videos, as well as industry leading tools to help you plan your personal development and advance your career. For more information, please visit our website.

Why subscribe?

- Spend less time learning and more time coding with practical eBooks and Videos from over 4,000 industry professionals

- Improve your learning with Skill Plans built especially for you

- Get a free eBook or video every month

- Mapt is fully searchable

- Copy and paste, print, and bookmark content

Packt.com

Did you know that Packt offers eBook versions of every book published, with PDF and ePub files available? You can upgrade to the eBook version at `www.packt.com` and as a print book customer, you are entitled to a discount on the eBook copy. Get in touch with us at `customercare@packtpub.com` for more details.

At `www.packt.com`, you can also read a collection of free technical articles, sign up for a range of free newsletters, and receive exclusive discounts and offers on Packt books and eBooks.

Contributors

About the authors

Kevin Mack is a co-founder of *Manic Machine*, a Los Angeles-based development studio specializing in VR and virtual production development using Unreal Engine. *Manic Machine* designs and builds games in VR and provides development services to clients and partners in the film and visual effects industries. Prior to this, he co-founded *WhiteMoon Dreams*, which developed traditional and VR games and experiences. Earlier work includes design on the *Medal of Honor* series for EA, *Fear Effect* series for Kronos Digital Entertainment, and several titles for Disney Interactive. Kevin holds a BFA in film production from New York University and an MFA in film directing from the American Film Institute.

I am deeply grateful to Lorrie for her endless patience and understanding as I spent numerous days and evenings glued to a screen or inside a VR headset. I would like to thank my parents as well for encouraging me always to do what I love and supporting the journey. And for that TRS-80 Color Computer that started it all. Finally, thank you Rob for joining me on this bizarre adventure and being such a fantastic partner through it.

Robert Ruud is a co-founder of *Manic Machine*, where he focuses primarily on the design and development of Manic Machine's proprietary tech and gameplay experiences. Prior to this, he spent six years at *Whitemoon Dreams*, where he designed and engineered gameplay for the successfully kickstarted game, *Warmachine: Tactics*, which was one of the first games to be released to market using Unreal Engine 4, and where he also led the design exploration for the company's location-based VR experiences. Robert holds a BA in philosophy from California State Polytechnic University, Pomona, where his studies focused on cognitive science and philosophy of the mind.

I would like to thank my beautiful, intelligent, and caring girlfriend Hannah for being so incredibly supportive throughout this entire process and life in general. My parents for always believing in me and helping me however they could. My friends for everything they have taught me and the adventures they have joined me in. Finally, I would like to thank Kevin for being an astounding business partner as we explore this new and wonderful medium.

About the reviewer

Deepak Jadhav is a game developer based in Pune, India. Deepak holds a bachelor's degree in computer technology and a master's degree in game programming and project management. Currently, he is working as a game developer at a leading game development company in India. He has been involved in developing games on multiple platforms, such as PC, macOS, and mobile. With years of experience in game development, he has a strong background in C# and C++, and has also refined his skills in platforms including Unity, Unreal Engine, Augmented and Virtual Reality.

I would like to thank the authors, as well as the Packt Publishing team, for giving me the opportunity to review this book.

Packt is searching for authors like you

If you're interested in becoming an author for Packt, please visit `authors.packtpub.com` and apply today. We have worked with thousands of developers and tech professionals, just like you, to help them share their insight with the global tech community. You can make a general application, apply for a specific hot topic that we are recruiting an author for, or submit your own idea.

Preface

Virtual reality (VR) isn't just the media we knew and loved from the twentieth century in a stereo headset. It's much more than that. VR doesn't simply show us images of the world around us in stereo 3D. In a literal sense, sure, that *is* what it does, but that's a little like saying that music just wiggles the air around our ears. Technically true, but too reductive to let us understand it. VR plays with our senses and dances with the cognitive mechanisms by which we think we understand the world. To get VR and learn how to create for it, we have to accept that it is an entirely new medium, and what we don't know about its language, rules, and methods far outweighs what we do know. This is powerful stuff, and, without question, VR or some variant of this technology is likely to be the defining art form of the twenty-first century.

You'd be right to greet this assertion with a bit of skepticism. Given the present state of the technology and of the industry, it takes some imagination to see beyond the horizon of where we are now. And you've probably seen by now that the public's expectations are in a race with the actual state of the technology and the art form. Sometimes, they lag behind its reality, and sometimes they jump ahead. Opinions about VR, therefore, are all over the place. If we're in one of those phases where the tech makes a leap forward, people get amazed and excited by the possibilities and the breathless blogs declare that the world has changed. If we're in one of those phases where the expectations have jumped ahead, suddenly everyone's disappointed that their first-generation Oculus Rift hasn't morphed overnight into the Holodeck and we see a lot of disillusionment on blogs. It's impossible to predict where the pendulum will be in its swing when you read this.

Here's the reality though, and why we believe this medium is worth learning now: VR is coming, it's inevitable, and it changes everything, even if this isn't yet obvious from the rudimentary state of the first-generation technology. This medium carries with it the potential to revolutionize the way we learn, play, engage the virtual world, and so much else. But it's going to take time and imagination.

VR is a medium at a crossroads. The decisions we make now are going to carry us far into the future. The developers working in this medium will be the ones to shape its language and methods for the next generation. To work in VR is to work on a frontier, and that's an exciting place to be.

In this book, we intend to give you a solid set of tools to begin your work on this frontier. This book uses a practical, hands-on approach to teach you how to build VR games and applications using the Unreal Engine. Each chapter walks you step-by-step through the process of building the essential building blocks of a VR application, and we pair these steps with in-depth explanations of what's really going on when you follow them and why things are done the way they are. It's this *why* that matters. Understanding how the underlying systems and ideas work is crucial to the work you'll do on your own after you've finished these tutorials, and, in this book, we've tried to give you both—an understanding of what to do to build a VR application, and the background you'll need in order to use this book as a springboard for your own work in VR.

You should come away from this book with a solid understanding of how VR applications are built, and what specifically you need to know and understand about the Unreal Engine to build them. It's our hope that the work we do together here will set you up to take your exploration into this new frontier wherever you want to go.

Who this book is for

If you're interested in creating VR games or applications, interested in seeing how VR could augment the work you do in your current field, or are just interested in exploring VR and seeing what it can do, this book is for you. You don't have to be an experienced engineer or even deeply experienced with Unreal Engine to benefit from this book; we explain everything as we go. Readers who are entirely new to Unreal Engine will find it helpful to run through Epic's getting started tutorials before diving in here, just so you know where everything is, but this book is entirely appropriate for both experienced Unreal users who need to learn specifically how Unreal works with VR, and for new Unreal users just finding their way around.

Whether you're entirely new to VR development and to Unreal, you've already been working in VR in another engine, or you know your way around Unreal but are new to VR, this book should be able to provide a lot of value. (And we hope even those already well versed in VR creation using Unreal Engine find a few interesting new perspectives and techniques as well.)

What this book covers

Chapter 1, *Thinking in VR*, introduces VR as a medium and discusses a few of the many ways it can be used in a number of fields. We discuss the crucial concepts of immersion and presence, and outline practices for designing and building effective VR experiences.

Chapter 2, *Setting Up Your Development Environment*, takes you through the process of setting up Unreal Engine and setting up to develop for mobile VR, and talks about where to learn about using Unreal and where to get help. For those interested in working in C++, this chapter also shows how to set up your development environment to build C++ projects and to build Unreal Engine from source code.

Chapter 3, *Hello World: Your First VR Project*, shows you how to create a new VR project from scratch, what settings to use when creating for VR and why we use them, and what you need to do differently if you're building for mobile VR. This chapter also teaches you how to get content into your project and work with it, and how to set up a few of the basic blueprints you'll need for VR development.

Chapter 4, *Getting Around the Virtual World*, teaches you how to create and refine navigation meshes for character locomotion, how to build a player-controlled character and set up input handling, and then shows how to build a teleport-based locomotion scheme and how to implement seamless movement for a more immersive VR experience.

Chapter 5, *Interacting with the Virtual World - Part I*, shows you how to add hands to the player-controlled character and use hand-held motion controllers to drive them.

Chapter 6, *Interacting with the Virtual World - Part II*, shows how to set up an animation blueprint to animate the player's hands in response to input, and how to make it possible for players to pick up and manipulate objects in the world.

Chapter 7, *Creating User Interfaces in VR*, shows you how to create interactive 3D user interfaces for VR, and introduces an AI-controlled companion character to be controlled by this interface.

Chapter 8, *Building the World and Optimizing for VR*, teaches you how to use the Unreal Editor's VR Mode to build environments from within VR, and how to find performance bottlenecks in your environment and fix them.

Chapter 9, *Displaying Media in VR*, teaches you how to display video media on virtual screens in VR space, in both mono and stereo. You'll learn how to put 2D and 3D movies onto traditional virtual screens, how to surround the player with 360-degree mono and stereo video, and how to create a media manager to control its playback.

Chapter 10, *Creating a Multiplayer Experience in VR*, teaches you about Unreal's client-server network model, and shows you how to replicate actors, variables, and function calls from the server to connected clients, how to set up a player character to display differently to its owner and to other players, and how to set up remote procedure calls to trigger events on the server from clients.

Chapter 11, *Taking VR Further - Extending Unreal Engine*, shows you how to install and build plugins to extend the engine's capabilities, and how to use Blueprint's powerful debugging tools to dig into unfamiliar code and understand it.

Chapter 12, *Where to Go from Here*, shows you where to get further information as you dive deeper into VR development.

Appendix A, *Useful Mind Hacks*, leaves you with a number of useful *mind hacks* to make your development more effective.

Appendix B, *Research and Further Reading*, provides a few useful starting places for your search that will gradually help accelerate your learning enormously.

To get the most out of this book

You don't need to be an expert Unreal developer to benefit from this book, but it is helpful to have a sense of where things are. If you haven't yet installed Unreal Engine, don't worry—we'll cover this in Chapter 2, *Setting Up Your Development Environment*, but if you've never used it before, it may be helpful at that point to take the time to run through the Unreal getting started tutorials before diving back into this book just so you know where everything is.

All of the projects in this book have been designed to work with the Oculus Rift and HTC Vive minimum specs, so whether you're on a desktop or a laptop, you should be fine provided your system meets these minimum specs. You should, of course, have a VR headset available, and if you're planning to develop for mobile VR, it's still recommended that you have a desktop VR headset available as well, since it will make testing dramatically easier. All of the software you'll be using through the course of this book is freely available online and we'll walk you through downloading and installing it, so there's nothing special you need to have installed on your system before we begin.

This book is primarily written with PC developers in mind, but if you're working on a Mac, your development environment setup will be different, but everything we do in the engine will work the same way.

So that's it. If you have a VR headset, a system that can run it, and internet access (since we'll be downloading the engine and example content), you have everything you need.

Download the example code files

You can download the example code files for this book from your account at www.packt.com. If you purchased this book elsewhere, you can visit `www.packt.com/support` and register to have the files emailed directly to you.

You can download the code files by following these steps:

1. Log in or register at `www.packt.com`.
2. Select the **SUPPORT** tab.
3. Click on **Code Downloads & Errata**.
4. Enter the name of the book in the **Search** box and follow the onscreen instructions.

Once the file is downloaded, please make sure that you unzip or extract the folder using the latest version of:

- WinRAR/7-Zip for Windows
- Zipeg/iZip/UnRarX for Mac
- 7-Zip/PeaZip for Linux

The code bundle for the book is also hosted on GitHub at `https://github.com/PacktPublishing/Unreal-Engine-4-Virtual-Reality-Projects`. In case there's an update to the code, it will be updated on the existing GitHub repository.

We also have other code bundles from our rich catalog of books and videos available at `https://github.com/PacktPublishing/`. Check them out!

Download the color images

We also provide a PDF file that has color images of the screenshots/diagrams used in this book. You can download it here: `https://www.packtpub.com/sites/default/files/downloads/9781789132878_ColorImages.pdf`.

Conventions used

There are a number of text conventions used throughout this book.

`CodeInText`: Indicates code words in text, database table names, folder names, filenames, file extensions, pathnames, dummy URLs, user input, and Twitter handles. Here is an example: "We should take a quick look at your project's `.uproject` file as well."

A block of code is set as follows:

```
html, body, #map {
  height: 100%;
  margin: 0;
  padding: 0
}
```

When we wish to draw your attention to a particular part of a code block, the relevant lines or items are set in bold:

```
[default]
exten => s,1,Dial(Zap/1|30)
exten => s,2,Voicemail(u100)
exten => s,102,Voicemail(b100)
exten => i,1,Voicemail(s0)
```

Any command-line input or output is written as follows:

```
UE4Editor.exe ProjectName ServerIP -game
```

Bold: Indicates a new term, an important word, or words that you see onscreen. For example, words in menus or dialog boxes appear in the text like this. Here is an example: "Select **Window** | **Developer Tools** | **Device Profiles** to open the **Device Profiles** window."

Warnings or important notes appear like this.

Tips and tricks appear like this.

Get in touch

Feedback from our readers is always welcome.

General feedback: If you have questions about any aspect of this book, mention the book title in the subject of your message and email us at customercare@packtpub.com.

Errata: Although we have taken every care to ensure the accuracy of our content, mistakes do happen. If you have found a mistake in this book, we would be grateful if you would report this to us. Please visit www.packt.com/submit-errata, selecting your book, clicking on the Errata Submission Form link, and entering the details.

Piracy: If you come across any illegal copies of our works in any form on the Internet, we would be grateful if you would provide us with the location address or website name. Please contact us at copyright@packt.com with a link to the material.

If you are interested in becoming an author: If there is a topic that you have expertise in and you are interested in either writing or contributing to a book, please visit authors.packtpub.com.

Reviews

Please leave a review. Once you have read and used this book, why not leave a review on the site that you purchased it from? Potential readers can then see and use your unbiased opinion to make purchase decisions, we at Packt can understand what you think about our products, and our authors can see your feedback on their book. Thank you!

For more information about Packt, please visit packt.com.

Thinking in VR 1

"All reality is virtual.
That's a strong statement, and it's not obvious if you haven't thought about it before, so
I'll say it again—the reality we experience is a construct in our minds, based on highly
incomplete data. It generally matches the real world well, which isn't surprising,
evolutionarily speaking, but it's not a literal reflection of reality—it's just an inference of
the most probable state of the world, given what we know at any one time."
– Michael Abrash, Chief Scientist at Oculus

"The most important thing about a technology is how it changes people."
– Jaron Lanier, founder of VPL research, VR pioneer, and interdisciplinary scientist at
Microsoft Research

Welcome to the virtual world. (It's bigger on the inside.)

In this book, we're going to explore the process of creating VR applications, games, and
experiences using Unreal Engine 4. We'll spend some time looking at what VR is and what
we can do to design effectively for the medium, and then, from there, we'll move on to
demonstrate these concepts in depth using the Unreal Engine to craft VR projects that
illustrate and explore these techniques and ideas.

Every chapter will revolve around a hands-on project, beginning with basics such as setting
up your development environment and creating your first test applications in VR, and
moving on from there into increasingly in-depth explorations of what you can do in VR and
how you can use Unreal Engine 4 to do it. In each project, we'll walk you through the
process of building a project that demonstrates a specific topic in VR and explain the
methods used and, in some cases, demonstrate a few alternatives. It's important to us, as
you build these projects, that you come away not just knowing how to do the things we
describe, but also why we do them this way, so you can use what you've learned as a
launchpad to plan and execute your own work.

In this first chapter, we'll look at what VR is and a few of the many ways it's currently used in a wide range of fields. We'll talk about the two most important concepts in VR: **immersion** and **presence**, and how understanding what these are and how they work will help you to make better experiences for your users. We'll lay out a collection of best practices for developing immersive and engaging VR experiences, and talk about some of the unique challenges posed by VR development. Finally, we'll pull this knowledge together and dig into a method for planning and executing a VR project's design.

In brief, this chapter is going to take us through the following topics:

- What is virtual reality?
- What can we do in VR?
- Immersion and presence
- Best practices for VR
- Planning your VR project

What is virtual reality?

Let's start at the beginning, and talk about virtual reality itself. VR, at its most basic level, is a medium that immerses users into a simulated world, allowing them to see, hear, and interact with an environment and things within this environment that don't actually exist in the physical world around them. Users are fully surrounded by this experience, an effect that VR developers call *immersion*. Users who are immersed in a space can look around and often move and interact without ever breaking the illusion that they're actually there. Immersion, as we're going to see shortly, is fundamental to the way VR works.

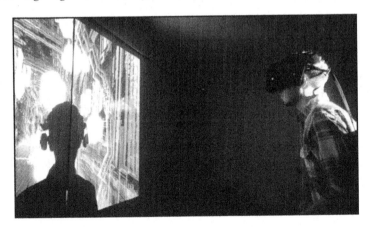

Rob Ruud testing an early build of Ludicrous Speed using an HTC Vive headset

Immersion in VR is a term used to describe a VR system's ability to surround the user with the simulated world. They can look around and, in many cases, move and interact as though they were really there, and because the actual environment is blocked out by the headset, they're given few conflicting cues to remind them that they aren't.

VR hardware

The most common way of immersing a user, and the one we'll be talking about in this book, is through the use of a **Head-Mounted Display** (**HMD**), often just referred to as a **headset**. (There are other ways of doing VR—projecting images on walls, for example, but in this book, we focus on head-mounted VR.) The user's headset displays the virtual world and tracks the movement of their head to rotate and shift the view to create the illusion that they're actually looking around and moving through physical space. Some headsets, though not all of them, include headphones to add to the illusion by enabling sounds in the environment to sound as though they're coming from their sources in the virtual world through a process called **spatialized audio**.

You'll see the terms **HMD** and **headset** used interchangeably throughout this book and in other writing on VR. They all refer to the same thing.

Some headsets only track the direction the user is looking, while others can track changes to the user's position as well. If you're using a headset that tracks rotation but not position, and you lean forward to try to look more closely at an object, nothing's going to happen. The object will seem as though it's moving away from you as you try to lean in toward it. If you do this on a headset that tracks position as well, your virtual head will move closer to the object. We use the term **Degrees of Freedom** (**DoF**) to describe the ways objects can move in space. (Yes, it's OK to pronounce it *doff*. All of the developers do.) Take a look at the following points:

- **3DOF**: A device that tracks rotation but doesn't track position is commonly called a 3DoF device because it only tracks the three degrees of freedom that describe rotation: the degree to which the device is leaning to the side (**roll**), tilting forward (**pitch**), or turning sideways (**yaw**). Up until recently, all mobile VR headsets were 3DoF devices, as they used **Inertial Measurement Units** (**IMUs**) similar to those found in cellphones to detect rotation, but had no way to know where they were in space. The Oculus Go and Samsung Gear headsets are examples of 3DoF devices.

- **6DOF**: A device that tracks position as well as the rotation is a 6DoF device, because it's tracking all six degrees of freedom—roll, pitch, and yaw, but also up and down, side-to-side, and forward or backward movement. Tracking an object's position in space requires you to have a fixed reference point from which you can describe its motion. Most first-generation systems needed additional hardware for this. The Lighthouse base stations for the HTC Vive, or the Constellation cameras for the Oculus Rift provide this postional tracking on desktop systems. Windows Mixed Reality headsets and standalone headsets such as the Oculus Quest and Vive Focus use camera arrays on the headset to track the headset's position in the room (we call this **inside-out tracking**), so they don't require external cameras or base stations. The HTC Vive, Oculus Rift, HTC Vive Focus, Oculus Quest, and Windows Mixed Reality headsets are 6DoF devices.

 3DoF devices track rotation only, so users can look around or point, but can't move from side-to-side. 6DoF devices track position as well as rotation, so users can not only look around, but can move as well.

Headsets can either be tethered to a computer—as is the case with the Oculus Rift and the HTC Vive, which allows the full computing power of the attached PC to drive the visuals – or they can be self-contained devices such as the Samsung Gear, Oculus Go, Oculus Quest, and HTC Vive Focus. At the time of this writing, wireless connections between PCs and VR headsets are beginning to enter the market.

Most headsets also come paired with input devices that allow users to interact with the world, which can act as pointers or as hands. Handheld devices, as with headsets, can be tracked in three or six degrees of freedom. 3DoF devices such as the Oculus Go's controller are essentially pointers—users can aim them but can't reach out and grab something. 6DoF devices act much more like virtual hands and allow users to interact with the world in a much greater variety of ways.

VR isn't just about hardware though

One of the major mistakes many new developers make when first approaching VR is that they try to apply the traditional designs they're used to creating in 2D space to the VR space and, for the most part, this doesn't work. VR is its own medium, and it doesn't follow the same rules as the media that came before it. It's worth it to take a moment to look at what this means.

When most people first consider VR, they see the headset and assume that it's primarily a visual experience—traditional flat-screen media shown in stereo. It's understandable that it would seem this way, but their perception misses the point. Yes, the VR headset is (depending on whether or not it includes integrated audio) either primarily or entirely a display device, but the experience it creates for the user is very different than the experience created by a traditional flat screen.

Let's imagine for a minute that you're looking at a photo or a 2D video looking down over the edge of a tall building. You see the streets far below, but they don't really *feel* as though they're far below you. They're just small in the image. Take the same image, but now present it in stereo through a VR headset, and you'll probably experience vertigo. Why is this? Take a look at the following screenshot:

Non-immersive media, no matter how large or detailed, still leaves the viewer surrounded by reminders that the scene isn't real. Immersive media, on the other hand, seems to surround the user completely. (Scene: Soul:City Environment Pack, by Epic Games)

First, as we mentioned a moment ago, you're *immersed* in the experience. There's nothing else in the surrounding world to remind you that it isn't real. Let's jump back to our previous example—the building edge on your television—turn around and look behind you. Oh. You're just in your living room. Even when you look directly at it, the largest television you could possibly buy still leaves you with lots of peripheral vision to remind you that what you're seeing there isn't real. Everything on a flat screen, even a 3D screen, takes place on the other side of a window. You're watching, but you're not really there. In VR, the window is gone. When you look to the right, the world is still there. Look behind you, and you're still in it. Your perception is completely overtaken by an experience that has become an environment, not just a frame you're looking at.

Second, the stereo image creates a sense of real depth. You can see how far down the drop really goes. The cars in the street below aren't just small, they're far away. In a 6DoF headset that allows motion tracking, your movements in the real world are mirrored in the virtual world. You can lean over the edge or step back. This mixture of immersion, real depth perception, and natural response to your movement comes together to convince your body that what you're perceiving is real. We call this phenomenon *presence*, and it's a sensation that's mostly experienced physically.

Presence in VR refers to the user feeling that they're actually physically in the virtual world, responding to the environment as though they were really there and experiencing these things. Creating an experience of presence is what VR is all about—this is the major thing it can do that other media can't.

The mechanics of immersion and the resulting experience of presence are unique to VR. No other medium does this.

When reading about VR, you'll sometimes see the terms *presence* and *immersion* used interchangeably, but it's generally more clear to think about *presence* as the goal—the sensation you're trying to create in the user, and *immersion* as the mechanism by which we achieve it.

Presence is tough to achieve

While we're on the topic of presence, it's worth pointing out that it's a fragile phenomenon, and the current state of VR technology still faces a few challenges to creating a sense of presence fully and reliably. Some of these are rooted in hardware and are almost certainly going to go away as the technology advances. Users can feel the headset on their face, for example, and on wired headsets, they can feel the cable running from the headset. The current generation of headsets offers a field of view that's too narrow to provide peripheral vision. (The desktop devices offer a 110° field of view, but your eyes, meanwhile, can perceive a field twice as wide.) Display resolutions aren't yet high enough to keep users from being able to see individual pixels (VR users call this the **screen door** effect), and finicky optics can blur the user's vision if they're not perfectly aligned. This means, in practice, that it's hard to read small text on a VR headset, and that users are sometimes reminded of the hardware when they have to adjust it to get back into the *sweet spot* for the lenses.

Looking at the state of things, though, it's obvious that these hardware challenges won't last forever. Self-contained and wireless headsets are quickly entering the market, with increasingly reliable tracking that no longer relies on external equipment. Displays are getting wider, resolutions are getting higher, and optical waveguides show great promise for lighter displays with wider in-focus regions. VR works extremely well already, and it's easy to see how it's going to continue to improve.

There are a few other things that can break presence that we can't do as much about—hitting a desk accidentally with a controller, for example, or running into furniture, losing tracking, or hearing sounds from outside the experience. We can manage these when we have control over the user's space, but where we don't, there's not much we can do.

Even given these limitations, though, think about how profoundly the current generation of VR can create a sense of presence in a user, and realize that it only gets better from here. Users believe what they experience in VR to a degree that simply doesn't happen with other media. They explore and learn in ways that aren't possible in any other way. They empathize and connect with people and places more deeply than they could in any way, other than physically being there. Nothing else goes as deep. And we're only getting started.

What can we do in VR?

So, what can we do with VR? Let's explore this, but before we begin, it's worth it to point out that this medium is still in its infancy. At the time of this writing, we're on the first generation of consumer VR hardware and the vast majority of the population hasn't even seen a VR headset yet, much less experienced it. Try this: the next time you're in a restaurant or a public space, ask yourself how many of the people around you have likely ever seen a VR headset—a handful at best. Now, how many of them have watched a movie (a century-old medium), watched television (three-quarters of a century), or played a video game (just shy of half a century)? VR is that new. We haven't come close to discovering everything we can do with it.

With that in mind then, use these ideas as a map of the current state of things and some fodder for ideas, but realize that there's much much more that we haven't even thought of yet. Why shouldn't you be the one to discover something new?

Games in VR

As we discussed a moment ago, VR at its core creates an experience of presence. If you're developing a game for VR, this means that designs that focus on giving the player an experience of *being* in a place are good candidates for the medium. *Skyrim VR* and *Fallout 4 VR* do a fantastic job of making players feel as though they're really in these expansive worlds. *Myst*-like games that put the player into a space they can explore and manipulate work well too.

The addition of motion controllers to simulate hands, such as those supplied with the HTC Vive, Oculus Rift, and Oculus Quest, enable developers to create simulations with complex interactions, such as *Job Simulator* and *Vinyl Reality*, which wouldn't be possible using traditional game controllers. Tender Claws' *Virtual Virtual Reality* provides a great example, meanwhile, of achieving 6DoF-like control with the Oculus Go's 3DoF controller.

The immersive aspect of VR means that games that surround you with the experience, such as *Space Pirate Trainer*, work well because the player can interact with actors all around them and not just what's in front. This need to watch all around you can be a focus of your design.

The sensation of motion VR evoked in players turns fast-moving games such as *Thumper* and *Ludicrous Speed* into physically-engaging experiences, and games such as *Beat Saber* capitalize on the player's physical movements to turn the game into a fitness tool as well.

Games in VR present a few challenges too, though. This same experience of presence and physical movement that makes the experience so engaging can mean that not every game design is a great candidate for VR. Simply porting a 2D game into VR isn't likely to work. A **Heads-Up Display** (commonly abbreviated as **HUD**) placed over the scene in 2D space won't work in VR, as there's no 2D plane to put it on. Fast movements that could be perfectly fine in 2D may make players motion-sick in VR. The decision to make a game for VR needs to be a conscious choice, and you'll need to design with the medium's strengths and challenges in mind.

When thinking about moving a game or a game design from 2D into VR, there are a few specific areas that need to be considered: will the movement scheme work in VR? How can the UI be designed to fit into the world in VR? Will the game fit within the performance constraints of VR? Does putting this game into VR improve the experience of playing it? We'll address all of these considerations—movement, UI, and performance, in later chapters.

Interactive VR

Interactive VR experiences aren't just limited to games. 3D painting applications such as *Tilt Brush* allow users to sculpt and paint in room-scale 3D and share their creations with other users. *Google Earth VR* allows users to explore the earth, much of it in 3D. Interactive storytelling experiences such as *Colosse, Allumette, Coco VR,* and others immerse users in a story and allow them to interact with the world and characters. Interactive VR applications and experiences can be built for productivity or entertainment and can take almost any form imaginable.

It's worthwhile to keep a few considerations in mind when thinking about creating an interactive VR application. The mouse and keyboard aren't generally available to users in VR—they can't see these devices to use them, so interactions are usually best designed around the controllers provided with the VR system. Text can be difficult to read in VR—display resolutions are improving, but they're still low enough that small text may not be readable. The lack of a 2D HUD means that traditional menus don't work easily—usually, these need to be built into the world or attached to the player's virtual hands (see *Tilt Brush* for an excellent example of this.)

Input and output are the main considerations for interactive VR—how will the user communicate input to the system, and how do they get information back out of it? In both cases, you have to design around the strengths and weaknesses of the system. You don't have a 2D HUD or a mouse, but you do have objects that can be moved and manipulated in space. VR displays can't yet approach the resolution of a desktop monitor, so reading a lot of text may not work. Successful designs in VR take these factors into account and turn them into deliberate design choices.

Interactive VR offers incredible possibilities for entirely new ways of exploring and interacting, and it's likely that we haven't even begun to see the full range of possibilities yet.

VR cinema – movies, documentary, and journalism

The same experience of presence that makes VR so well-suited for certain types of games makes it a powerful medium for documentary and journalism applications. VR is able to immerse users in a circumstance or environment and can evoke empathy by allowing viewers to share an experience deeply. Chris Milk, a pioneering VR filmmaker, has referred to VR as the "*ultimate empathy machine*," and we think that's a fair description. Alejandro Iñárritu's *CARNE y ARENA* was awarded a special Oscar by the Academy of Motion Picture Arts and Sciences in 2017 to recognize its powerful use of the medium to tell a story with deep empathy. VR's capacity to create presence through immersion makes things possible that simply can't be done on a flat screen.

A player experiencing Alejandro Iñárritu's *CARNE y ARENA at Los Angeles County Museum of Art*

Film and video in VR can be presented in several ways, which generally boil down to the shape of the virtual screen on which the images are presented and whether those images are presented in monoscopic 2D or stereo 3D. Flat or curved surfaces are generally used to present media carried over from traditional film or television, while domes, panoramas, or spheres can be used to surround the viewer with a more immersive 2D or 3D experience.

Mono 360° video surrounds the viewer but lacks depth—it's simply mapped onto a sphere surrounding the player. This has the advantage of being easier to produce and requires far less storage and less expensive equipment, and for many scenes, the difference between this and true stereo may be difficult to detect. Most early VR videos were produced this way. Stereo 360° video is similarly mapped to a sphere around the player (we'll learn how to do this in a later chapter), but displays a different image to each eye for true stereo depth. (We'll learn how to do this too.) New approaches to volumetric video that use light fields, **Light Detection And Ranging** (**LIDAR**) and photogrammetry to map real environments into genuine 3D virtual environments are beginning to appear and will likely become more prevalent as technology matures and processing power increases. As of this writing, they're still fairly new, often expensive, and still largely confined to the realms of high-end professionals and academics.

Documentary and journalism pieces are most often filmed as live-action video shot on a 360° camera or rig, in mono or increasingly in stereo, allowing the viewer to look around and become immersed in a seamless sensory environment. 360° cinema is generally intended to be a direct, immersive, and engaging experience, but is usually not interactive. The viewer is generally not able to move freely through the scene except by triggering a cut to a new scene and generally can't affect the events that go on within the scene.

 In planning a cinematic VR experience, two of the primary choices to make are the following: will the experience be presented in mono or stereo, and what's the shape of the virtual screen on which it will be displayed?

Cinematic VR is another area in which simply porting the the language of the flat screen isn't enough. There's no concept of a frame in 360° film, and no concept of a shot size such as a close-up or a long shot. VR filmmakers have to be very careful about moving the camera, as it's very easy to make viewers sick with a moving or shaky camera. Film-making in VR is still in its infancy, and we're beginning to learn the ways the grammar of the language differs from traditional film or television, but still have a long way to go before we'll fully understand the language of the new medium.

This hasn't stopped filmmakers such as Alejandro Innaritu, Nonny de la Pena, Chris Milk, and Felix and Paul from creating astonishing and powerful cinematic experiences in VR, and this highlights what an exciting time it is to be participating in the creation and discovery of a powerful and entirely new art form.

Variants of VR cinema include the following:

- Narrative stories
- Documentaries
- Journalism
- Concerts and happenings
- Sports
- Virtual tourism

Architecture, Engineering, and Construction (AEC) and real estate

VR is ideally suited for **Architecture, Engineering,** and **Construction** (AEC) planning, as it allows designers to explore and iterate quickly on designs, and it serves as an excellent communication tool between designers and clients. VR provides an immersive experience that allows the user to explore and review the space in a real-world scale in a way that simply isn't possible through any other medium.

The **Architecture, Engineering, and Construction** industries are often bundled under the blanket initialism **AEC**.

For the same reasons that VR is such a useful tool for AEC, it's equally useful for real-estate applications, providing prospective buyers an opportunity to tour a home remotely, or to experience a space before it's been built. No medium represents space and scale better than VR.

Unreal Engine, as we'll see, is particularly well-suited for architectural applications, as its physically-based workflow for materials and lighting makes it possible to create surfaces that look real and respond to light the way their real-world counterparts would.

In addition to providing a realistic lighting and shading model ideal for the realistic representation of spaces, Epic Games (the makers of Unreal Engine), also provides a suite of tools designed for non-game uses such as architectural visualization. The most important of these is a toolkit called *Datasmith*, which allows high-detail scenes to be imported from architectural **Computer-Aided Design** (CAD) and 3D packages into Unreal with little or no modification required to reproduce the object placement, lighting, and shading from the original source.

Architectural visualization is often shortened to **archvis** or **archviz**.

In terms of practical workflow, engineering and architecture environments for VR usually begin in a CAD or a 3D **Digital Content Creation** (**DCC**) tool, and are then brought into Unreal either by hand or by using the Datasmith workflow, where it can be made into an environment that can be explored in VR.

For real-estate applications, the environment may be fully modeled in 3D, or may be photographed as a 360° sphere or panorama, which provides less interactivity but is much easier and less expensive to produce. Even though it limits the user's movement, 360° photography can still provide an immersive sense of the space that the user couldn't experience otherwise.

Engineering and design

As with building planning, VR can be an outstandingly effective tool for engineering and other design applications. Designs can be tested in depth and iterated rapidly without requiring physical prototypes to be built and can be placed in virtual environments that allow them to be evaluated in context. Designers can use VR to explore designs and see how parts will fit together and to communicate with stakeholders in an experience that closely replicates the experience of actually handling and interacting with the object.

Education and training

It can be argued that VR began its life in education, in 1929, when Edwin Link created the Link Trainer to train aircraft pilots using an early immersive simulator. The combination of immersion and interaction makes VR a powerful tool for education, learning, and exploration. VR, at its core, is capable of providing a much more concrete and experiential understanding of a subject than other media. Where most other media communicate ideas, VR communicates direct experience.

Traditional education often focuses on communicating facts to students, but facts in isolation can bore or overwhelm them if they don't yet have sufficient context to know what they need them for in the first place. VR, by contrast, can be used to allow students to discover and learn concepts by working directly with materials and representations of ideas they're exploring and learning, practicing real skills and turning abstract ideas into experience. Context is a natural by-product of immersion, and VR's ability to evoke presence can be instrumental in creating a physical, social, or emotional frame for the subject being learned. This can potentially make it meaningful or understandable to the student in ways that may not otherwise have been possible, and can allow students to explore the ways a complex system's parts fit together.

VR also can aid concentration because it isolates the student's senses from distractions that aren't part of the topic being explored and can be effective at creating virtual social learning environments, such as virtual classrooms.

Educational VR can (and should) be made easy to use, immersive and engaging, and meaningful to the student and can allow students to learn at their own pace and use its interaction to fuel their own exploration and discovery.

Commerce, advertising, and retail

VR in commerce (the nickname, **v-commerce**, is sometimes used to describe it) offers a range of new ways for customers to experience products and can create opportunities to connect customers with products they may not otherwise have encountered. Car buyers, for instance, can explore color choices and options in a virtual car configurator that allows them to experience what their chosen options would look and feel like around them. This experience can also be instrumental in moving an aspirational purchase out of the imagination and into the realm of something that feels real.

For retailers, VR offers a way to reach customers who are not able to visit shops, increasing accessibility and the likelihood of sales. Customers can see more clearly and in context what a product is, reducing confusion and returns. VR can give a customer a chance to *try before they buy*, even where the product might be too large, too far away, or too elaborate to demonstrate effectively by other means. Virtual showrooms, for example, can allow customers to place furnishings together into a virtual environment that allows them to see how the pieces would fit together and how they might fit in their own space.

VR can be used as well to facilitate an emotional connection with the brand, placing the customer into a virtual environment or experience that supports the brand's emotional space, such as a mountaintop or a fashion show.

Medicine and mental health

VR offers promising opportunities as well in psychology, medicine, neuroscience, and physical and occupational therapy. VR, for example, can be used in physical therapy by *slowing time* and allowing patients to perform actions slowly and repeatedly and has been used successfully for pain management. VR is also useful for providing simulated virtual patients for medical and emergency training.

In the fields of mental and behavioral health, VR has powerful applications in assessment, training, and the treatment of stress-related disorders. Patients can be exposed to complex stimuli to help to assess and rehabilitate cognitive functions for stroke, traumatic brain injury, and similar neurological disorders.

So much else

The through line through all of the uses of VR described is that VR works especially well to communicate context and create meaning through presence and to allow complex physical interactions with objects that just couldn't be done with a flat screen. Without question, there are still more valuable uses of VR that haven't yet been discovered or considered. The only limit is our own imagination.

Immersion and presence

Now that we've set up a bit of context about what VR is and a few of the many of the things we can do with it. Let's start getting our hands dirty and learn the following:

- What makes VR work
- What can break it
- What we need to do as developers to make sure the VR experiences we build succeed

To that end, let's lay out a few best practices in VR, and then we'll talk about them in depth.

We'll begin by talking about the experience we're trying to create.

Immersion

When VR works, as we discussed earlier, it works through a process we call **immersion**, which we described earlier as a perceived experience of being physically present in a virtual world. For an experience to be immersive, a few things need to be true.

Using all the senses

First, it has to encompass a wide enough range of the user's senses that competing senses from outside the VR experience don't pull the user back out of the virtual space. In practice, this is why VR headsets are designed to block out all other light, and why they usually include headphones or on-board audio. Anything we see or hear that isn't part of the VR experience risks breaking immersion.

While vision and sound are pretty easily communicated through the eyes and ears, physical sensations are more difficult to produce. In VR, we refer to physical sensations as **haptics**. Decades of research have gone into figuring out how to recreate physical sensations, but in practice, it's a tough problem to solve. In the current generation of VR hardware, haptics take the form of a rumble pack in the player's controller that vibrates the controller on cue. While it's limited just to the hand holding the controller, even using such basic haptic feedback as this in your designs is still surprisingly effective for creating a sense of physicality in virtual space. A little vibration when the user's virtual hand contacts an object can go a long way toward making the object feel as though it's physically there and to allow users to sense its boundaries and know when they've made contact with it.

Remember to use all the senses to create an immersive experience, not just the visual. Use sound to involve the ears in the experience and haptic feedback on the controllers to create physical cues.

Make sure sensory inputs match one another and match the user's expectations

Senses need to match the user's expectations, and they need to match one another for an immersive experience to feel real. When the user turns their head, an object they're looking at should move in their view as it would have if it were in the physical world around them. This part is pretty well handled for you by the Unreal engine and your VR hardware, but the next bit, sound, is often overlooked by developers.

Objects that produce sound should use **spatialized audio** to ensure that sounds seem to come from where the objects appear to be. As we mentioned a moment ago, physical objects should produce a tactile response using haptic feedback when the user appears to touch them.

The behavior of visual objects is pretty much taken care of for you by the HMD and Unreal Engine, but make sure you use spatialized audio to localize sounds to their apparent sources, and experiment with haptic feedback to make physical actions feel more real.

Keep latency as low as possible

The quality of the visual and audio experience matters greatly to immersion, and the absolute most important factor driving this quality is the smoothness and responsiveness of the experience. What this means for developers is that frame rate matters above every other consideration in VR. VR developers use the term **latency** to describe the responsiveness of a VR application—the time between the user performing an action, such as turning their head, and seeing the visual result (in this case, the world appearing to rotate around them). Developers call this **motion-to-photon** time, and it's important. If the user turns their head and world lags behind, it won't feel real, and worse, can make them sick. Current VR headsets do quite a lot in hardware and software to minimize and disguise latency, but as a developer, you also have to do a lot as well to keep latency as low as you can possibly get it.

Latency refers to the speed at which a VR application responds visually to the user's actions and is fundamental to immersion in VR. Research suggests that the absolute highest latency you can get away with is 20 milliseconds, but you should be shooting for far less.

In practice, this means that, when you have to choose between detail in your scene and frame rate (and you'll have to make this choice all the time as a developer), choose speed. Users will forgive a lower-resolution texture much more easily than they'll forgive a dropped frame. Much of your work in VR development will focus on getting your scene running at an acceptable frame rate, and we'll talk quite a bit about how to do this in Unreal. For now, make sure you keep this in mind: keeping latency low is absolutely fundamental to immersion in VR, and the choices you make in designing and developing a VR application have to be made with this in mind.

When faced with a choice between image quality and framerate, choose framerate every time. Beautiful textures, high-poly models, and dynamic shadows won't create a convincing experience for the user if they're dropping frames. Users will fill in a remarkable amount of detail in their own minds, meanwhile, if the experience is running smoothly, while they won't believe it at all, or worse, will get sick if latency gets too high.

Make sure interactions with the world make sense

Interactions with objects should be consistent and they should make sense. With the immersive nature of VR comes an increased expectation that objects will behave as they would in real life. In traditional media, delivered on a flat screen and constrained to a frame, the user's eyes and brain are consistently reminded that they're looking at a flat image that isn't real, and they'll forgive a lot. But in VR, the world already surrounds them and seems to be real, and they'll expect it to behave as though it's real too.

Things that don't behave or respond in ways they would in the real world can pull the user out of the experience and break immersion. There's a limit in practice: of course, you can't make every object in the world interactive, but to the degree possible, you should pay attention to what your users' expectations are going to be, and try to meet them. If you put an object in the scene that looks as if it can be picked up, expect users to try to pick it up, and understand that you'll be working against immersion if it doesn't behave as they thought it would. Try to make objects in the scene that *look* interactive *be* interactive, and if they can't be, consider moving them out of the play area or changing their appearance to manage the user's expectation. This is another area where judgment comes into play—not everything can be interactive, and you may not always want it to be, depending on the kind of experience you're trying to create. You should be making conscious choices with immersion in mind when deciding how objects in your world should behave, and those choices should feel consistent with each other within the space of the world and not arbitrary.

Users will try to reach out and touch objects that look as if they can be touched and will try to move them. Try to satisfy their expectations where you can, or design your scene in such a way that these interactions aren't expected.

Explore the unique opportunities for interaction that VR, especially 6DoF VR with hand controllers, gives you. In previous media, users mostly interacted using a mouse, buttons, and joysticks, but in VR, the users hands interact with the world much more directly, and this makes an entirely new range of interactions possible. Where in a traditional game, a watering can might be used by pushing a button, in VR, the user can squeeze the controller grips to pick it up and turn their hand over to use it. Think about what makes sense in your world, and what becomes possible when the user's hands enter the picture, and design to make use of these opportunities. Interfaces don't have to consist of just buttons anymore.

The user's expectations for interaction will vary depending on the type of experience you're creating. If you're making a game that simulates the experience of being in another world, immersion matters a lot. If, on the other hand, you're making a movie viewer, the user probably doesn't really care whether a virtual coffee cup on a table nearby can be picked up, because that's not what they're there for. It's up to you to understand what's going to matter to your users and what isn't and to meet those expectations.

The way you represent the user's hands will drive expectations of how they'll behave as well. If they're modeled as hands, the user may naturally expect that they can pick objects up and move them around. If instead of hands, you display models of the controllers, palettes, weapons, or other tools, you're suggesting a different type of interaction. Users will try to do what it looks like they can do.

Build a consistent world

As we mentioned previously in the discussion about interaction, the whole experience should make sense as it fits together. Users should be able to construct a model of reality, even if it's an abstract or a complete fantasy, from what you give them in the world. The place you're building should feel like a place, with its own language and rules.

The amount of detail you put into your world can have an impact here. The more immersive an experience becomes, the more fragile that immersion becomes. Adding details and immersive elements creates a raised expectation that everything else in the world will live up to that standard too and can pull the user back out of immersion if something doesn't behave consistently with the apparent rules of the world. In many cases, you may want to render your world in a more stylized way to manage the user's expectations. Immersion doesn't require the VR experience to mirror the real world perfectly—it requires the experience to be consistent with itself.

Be careful of contradicting the user's body awareness

Be careful of adding immersive elements that contradict the player's awareness of their body. We all have a natural awareness of where our body is and what it's doing. This is called **proprioception**, and it's the sense that tells you where your arms and legs are even when you're not looking at them. Representing the user's body in ways that don't match this sense can break immersion.

Rendering the user's hands usually works well, as the motion controllers tell us exactly where they are, but this may not be such a good idea to render the rest of the arm, since we have no information about what that arm is really doing. If you guess and get it wrong, it will feel wrong to the user and can break immersion. It's often better not to guess at all, and simply render the hands up to the wrists, leaving the arms, legs, and body imagined. Interestingly, users seem to prefer this. They tend not to notice that the body is invisible until it's pointed out to them, whereas a body that's rendered but wrong calls attention to itself.

For similar reasons, realistic, fleshy hands can make users feel uncomfortable if they don't match their real-world hands. Hands work much better if they're stylized as translucent, cartoonish, or robotic so users don't feel as if they're trying to simulate reality and getting it wrong.

Animators commonly refer to a phenomenon called the **uncanny valley**, which occurs when a simulation gets just close enough to resembling a human that it triggers the viewer's instinctive awareness of everything that's wrong with it. For a simulation to work, it either needs to be stylized enough that viewers don't expect realism, or it needs to get the realism right. Anything in between is creepy. The same principle holds for representations of the user's own body in VR. Don't get it almost right. Get it perfect, or stylize it.

Decide how immersive you intend your application to be and design accordingly

Finally, not every use of VR needs to be equally immersive. Your choices in this really hinge on what your application is intended to do. If it's a tool for visualizing engineering models, you may be most interested in VR's ability to allow the user to manipulate models easily, and it may not matter so much to you whether they really believe they're in another place. If, on the other hand, you're creating an immersive game or cinematic experience, these choices will be critical. It's up to you to figure out which of these rules matters most for your particular application.

Presence

Immersion in VR serves a single goal—the creation of an experience of presence in the user. Presence, as we previously defined it, is a sensation of being in a place, and this is, in large part, a phenomenon perceived physically. Very often, they respond physically and instinctively to things in the world such as heights or objects flying toward them. The body largely believes what it perceives in VR and responds accordingly. If you think of presence primarily in physiological terms, you'll have an easier time understanding how users experience it. What does this experience make your user feel?

A key to understanding presence is to understand that VR doesn't so much work by trying to simulate an environment accurately as it does by triggering and fooling a range of systems that we use to perceive the world. This is one of the reasons why we can get away with low detail in our textures if we get the movement of the world right and keep latency low—our perceptive systems are much more aware of motion than detail. VR doesn't have to fool all the senses—just the right ones in the right ways.

Simulator sickness

A major factor you'll be dealing with quite a lot in VR is **simulator sickness**. This is a form of visually-induced motion sickness that often occurs in VR, and you'll deal with it a lot.

As humans, we spend most of our time walking upright, which takes a tremendously complicated amount of coordination to achieve, and yet we manage to do it without thinking about it. We manage this through a structure in our inner ear called the **vestibular system**, which we use to coordinate movement and keep our balance. This system is extremely sensitive, and it works in conjunction with our vision and our sense of our body (**proprioception**) to understand how we're moving.

You'll hear VR developers talk a lot about the *vestibular system* or the *inner ear*. For our purposes, since the vestibular system is located in the inner ear, we mean the same thing when we use the terms interchangeably. This is one of three systems that tell us whether we're moving and how to keep our balance. The other two are our *visual system* and our *proprioception* (our natural sense of our body's position). Problems arise when signals from these three systems don't agree with one another.

This creates a problem when visual information tells the body that it's moving, but it can't feel that movement in the inner ear. (Researchers call this the **sensory conflict theory**.) Seasickness and carsickness happen for the same reason. When visual movement cues and movement cues coming from the vestibular system in the inner ear don't match, the body can respond by triggering nausea, sweating, and other effects. (Researchers don't yet agree on why this is, but one theory suggests that when the senses don't match, the body may assume that it's been poisoned.)

The challenge with VR is that it does such a good job of simulating movement. The user's mind naturally accepts that the movement they see is really occurring, and runs into problems when the signals from the inner ear don't confirm this. Developers need to be conscious of this challenge and deal with it. We'll talk about ways to do this in a moment. (Be aware that the opposite is true too—always show movement in the headset if the user turns their head.)

Simulator sickness, sometimes shortened to **simsickness**, is a form of motion sickness that can occur in VR. (You'll also sometimes see it shortened to **VIMS** for **Visually-Induced Motion Sickness**.) The most common cause of simulator sickness is poorly-designed locomotion. The second most common cause is high latency. How users move through the world, and how smoothly and consistently it responds to their movements are critical factors in combating simulator sickness.

Safety

Another major consideration is **safety**. Because VR completely overwhelms the user's senses, it's possible to put users into unsafe situations, and it is up to you as a developer to try to avoid this. If you tilt the horizon, for example, there's a high likelihood that your users are going to lose their balance. If you've designed an experience that involves big physical movements, such as swinging a sword or a baseball bat, be aware that your users can't see what's around them and can easily hit objects in the real world. Be conscious as well of factors that can cause eyestrain, such as forcing users to focus on UI elements that are too close to the camera, and photosensitive seizures that can be induced by flashing lights.

With these factors in mind, let's get specific about laying out a few best practices that can help to keep your users comfortable and safe.

Best practices for VR

Now that we've talked a bit about immersion and presence, let's take a look at a few specific practices we can follow to keep our users comfortable and avoid breaking immersion. Don't consider any of these to be set in stone (except the requirements to maintain framerate and to leave the user's head alone)—VR is still a very new medium and there's a lot of room to experiment and find new things that work. Just because someone says a thing can't be done doesn't mean it can't. That having been said, the following recommendations generally represent our current best understanding of what works in VR, and it's usually a good idea to follow them.

Maintain framerate

Are you sensing a pattern here? You absolutely must maintain frame rate. High latency will pull the user right out of immersion, and this is a leading trigger for simulator sickness. Consider the work you're asking the renderer to do in VR, and you'll see that this is going to be a bit of a challenge. The HTC Vive Pro displays a 2,880 x 1,600 image (1,400 x 1,600 per eye), while the original Vive and the Oculus Rift display 2,160 x 1,200 (1,080 x 1,200 per eye), and all of them require this to happen 90 times per second, leaving the renderer 11 milliseconds to prepare the frame. The Oculus Go displays 2,560 x 1,440 pixels (1,280 x 1,440 per eye) 72 times per second, meaning the renderer has about 13 milliseconds to deliver the frame. The Unreal Engine renderer is blazingly fast, but, even so, this is a lot to render, and there is not a lot of time in which to get the frame drawn. You're going to have to make some compromises to reach your target. We'll talk about ways to do this throughout this book.

Here's a list of headsets currently on the market and their rendering demands.

Tethered headsets

HMD Device	Resolution	Target Framerate
Oculus Rift	2,160 x 1,200 (1,080 x 1,200 per eye)	90 FPS (11 ms)
HTC Vive	2,160 x 1,200 (1,080 x 1,200 per eye)	90 FPS (11 ms)
HTC Vive Pro	2,880 x 1,600 (1,400 x 1,600 per eye)	90 FPS (11 ms)
Windows Mixed Reality	It varies. Most display 2,880 x 1,440 (1,440 x 1,440 per eye)	90 FPS (11 ms)

Standalone Headsets

HMD Device	Resolution	Target Framerate
Gear VR	It varies depending on the phone used.	60 FPS (16 ms)
Oculus Go	2,560 x 1,440 (1,280 x 1,440 per eye)	72 FPS (13 ms)
Oculus Quest	3,200 x 1,440 (1,600 x 1,440 per eye)	72 FPS (13 ms)

Bear in mind as well that you should aim for frame rates slightly higher than these targets so hitches don't cause major discomfort.

VR hardware does do a bit of work to reduce perceived latency if the frame rate drops and the new frame isn't ready to be rendered when the headset needs to display it, but it does this by a bit of trickery. In these cases, the hardware will re-render the last frame and adjust it to fit the user's current head movement, so what the user sees isn't an exactly correct frame—it's just better than dropping the frame altogether. (Oculus calls this process **Asynchronous Time Warp (ATW)**, and on the Vive it's called **Asynchronous Reprojection**.) Don't use time warp or reprojection as a crutch, though—they're there to keep the user comfortable when your application hitches, but it's still a degraded experience for the user. Don't let your application miss the target frame rate for extended periods.

Also be sure to test your application on the minimum spec hardware you intend to support, and give your users ways to scale the rendering demands so they can meet the frame rate target on the hardware they're running.

Never take control of the user's head

Beyond dropping frames, the next most common cause of simulator sickness is the sensory conflict we mentioned earlier—a mismatch between motion perceived visually and motion felt in the inner ear. There are two major types of motion you're going to need to accommodate in VR:

- Movement of the player's avatar (walking around, teleporting, or piloting a vehicle)
- Movement of the player's head relative to their avatar

Movement of the player's avatar is handled by the locomotion system you implement for your experience. You really don't have a choice here—you're going to have to create movement that isn't happening in real life, but there are things you can do to make this less of a problem and we'll talk about them shortly.

The word *avatar* originated in Sanskrit and referred to the embodiment of a deity in human form. In its current usage, it extends this metaphor to refer to the embodiment of a human user in a virtual world. You'll hear the term commonly used to refer to a character in a simulated world under the control of a human player. Its companion term, *agent*, refers to a character under the control of an AI routine.

You should never interfere, however, with movement of the player's head.

What this means in practice is: never move the camera in a way the user didn't cause by their own actions. If you're making a game and the user's avatar dies, don't leave the camera bolted to the head as the body falls. You will almost definitely make users sick if you do this. Consider cutting to a third-person view instead or handling the action in some other way. Never move the camera to force the user to look around in a cinematic, and don't apply a **walking bob** or a camera shake. The user should control their head always.

 Never move the camera separately from the user's head, and never fail to move the camera when the user's head is moving. You should always maintain a 1:1 correlation between head movement and camera movement relative to the user's avatar.

This applies both ways. If the player moves their head, the camera must move, even if the game is paused or loading. Never stop tracking.

If you need to teleport the user to a new location or change cameras for any reason, consider using a fast fade to black or white to cover the transition. People instinctively blink when they turn their heads quickly, and it's a good idea to mimic this behavior.

In-game cut scenes need to be handled differently in VR than they would be on a traditional flat screen for the same reasons. Ordinarily, in authoring a cut scene, you would take control of the camera, moving and cutting from shot to shot, but you can't do this in VR. You can't control where your user is going to look, and you need to be careful moving them around. This leaves you with a few options. First, if your scenes are pre-rendered, then you really have no choice but to map them on to a screen in the virtual environment. This breaks immersion, but is no more difficult for the user than watching a movie in real life. If you're doing them in-engine, you need to think about how you're going to handle the player's point of view.

For a first-person point of view, it's probably best to stage the cinematic scene around the user and allow them to look and move freely within it. You can't cut away to another shot when doing this, and you can't guarantee that your user will be looking where you want them to look when a key moment occurs, but it's the most immersive approach you can take.

Cut scenes can also be handled in the third-person, in which you pull the user's viewpoint out of their body and allow them to view the scene unfolding, but you need to do this carefully—the out-of-body experience can be disorienting for your player and can weaken immersion and the player's identification with the character.

For film-making in VR, be very careful of the ways you move the camera. Even very small moves may induce sickness. Users will tolerate forward movement more easily than side-to-side or rotational movement and seem to tolerate movement more easily if it's justified by a visible vehicle or some other way of explaining why it's happening.

Thinking about how to use the camera in VR isn't just about managing user discomfort either. This is new territory, and the rules you learned from film and gaming work differently here. You're designing to recreate the user's eyes, not a camera, and this has far-reaching implications for your compositions. How does the user move? Do they know where you want them to look? What do they see when they look at their hands? What about a mirror? How does surrounding the user with a world (instead of making them watch it through a window) change their relationship to it? All of these factors require a conscious choice as you develop your work.

Do not put acceleration or deceleration on your camera

Depending on the type of application you're creating, you're probably going to need to give your users a way to change their location, either by teleporting or moving smoothly. (We'll dig into this in depth in a later chapter.) If you do choose to implement a smooth movement method though, don't accelerate or decelerate as the player starts and stops moving. Start the movement at full speed, or if you opt to smooth your starts and stops at all, keep them very short. (And, of course, never do a start-moving or stop-moving animation that takes control of the user's camera.)

Do not override the field of view, manipulate depth of field, or use motion blur

We mentioned a moment ago that VR mimics the user's eyes, not a camera. For this reason, don't do things in your simulation that eyes don't do in real life. Never change the focal length of the camera lens or its depth of field. The eyes' focal lengths don't change the way cinematic zoom lenses do, and you're very likely to make your user sick if you change this.

Manipulating the depth of field isn't a good idea in current-generation VR, as we don't yet have a reliable way to know what the user is actually looking at within the view. In the future, as eye-tracking improves, this will likely change, but for now, don't make this choice for your user.

Motion blur shouldn't be applied to your camera or objects in the scene. This is an artifact of the way film photographs a static frame for a fixed period of time, smearing the motion within that frame, but that's not the way eyes work, and it will look unnatural in VR.

While we're on the topic, steer clear of other camera-mimicking effects, such as lens flares and film grain. Again, these mimic the behavior of film, not the eyes, and we're not trying to mimic film in VR. Filmic effects such as these can also cause unwanted physical side effects in the user, contributing to simulator sickness if the effects don't line up between the eyes, and they cost precious frame time to render. Don't use them.

Minimize vection

Have you ever looked out the window of a car sitting still, and watched a large vehicle such as a truck or bus moving, and felt as if you were moving in the opposite direction instead? This phenomenon is called **vection**, and it refers to the illusion of self-movement produced by optical flow patterns. If a large portion of your view is moving, this can produce sensations of movement in your body, and as we discussed earlier, sensations of movement that don't match the signals from the inner ear can trigger simulator sickness.

Vection is the illusion of movement produced when large parts of your field of view move. **Optical flow**, or **optic flow**, refers to the pattern of movement of the contents of your view, and it's these patterns of movement that cause vection.

What this means in practice is that, if a big chunk of your user's view is moving, you're at risk of inducing simulator sickness. We've talked about this already with regard to moving the user's head (don't do it), and we've touched on some of the ways we can handle this in your locomotion system, but you'll also want to be aware of other circumstances that can cause vection.

Be aware of moving patterns that fill large parts of the frame—whether or not they're part of your locomotion system, they can still create an illusion of motion, which may be a problem for your users.

Several games and applications have experimented with a **tunnel vision** effect to reduce vection when users need to move quickly through the environment—when the player's avatar runs, an iris closes in from the edges of the view to reduce peripheral vision.

Users seem to be much more tolerant of forward movement than they are of **strafing**—moving side-to-side. This may in part be because, in real life, we move forward far more than we move sideways, but it may also be because the optical flow the user sees when moving forward still has a relatively fixed point at the center, whereas in sideways movement, everything in the view moves.

 When you're trying to figure out whether a particular movement in VR is likely to cause simulator sickness, it can be useful to think about the kind of optic flow that movement is going to create. Optic flows with relatively fixed reference points, such as the horizon when running forward, may be fine, while flows that move everything in the view, such as sideways movements, may not.

Rotating the player's view is especially problematic. It moves pretty much everything in the view, and the vestibular system is especially tuned to detecting rotation. Be very careful here. Smooth rotations are generally not a good idea, but developers have found that **snapping** the user to a new rotation works well to reorient the user without making them sick. It turns out that the brain is very good at filling in interruptions in perception, so snapping to a new rotation or "blinking" the view during a large movement can be very effective at disrupting the perception of motion without distracting the user.

Many developers have also found that giving users a visible vehicle that moves with them, such as an aircraft cockpit, can mitigate the effect of vection when rotating. Whether this is an appropriate solution for you depends on the type of experience you're creating, but the takeaway here should be that users seem to be less prone to simulation sickness if they're given fixed points of reference in their view. Where this is appropriate, consider factoring it into your design, and where it isn't, consider other ways of breaking the optic flow if you have to do large smooth movements such as blinking or snapping.

Avoid stairs

If you're allowing your user to move smoothly through your environment, be aware that certain features of environments can provoke simulator sickness when users navigate them. Stairs are especially bad. Stairs that provide collision for every step so the view bounces when user navigates it are worse. Environment features such as these that create a sense of vertical movement when traversed can be difficult because the inner ear is very sensitive to changes in altitude.

Avoid stairs if you can. If you can't avoid them, be conscious of how steep they are and how fast you're letting your user move over them. You'll have to test a bit to get it right.

Use more dimmer lights and colors than you normally would

Be careful of using bright lights and strong contrasts in your scene. Bright lights contribute to simulator sickness in some users, and strong contrasts can increase the user's sense of vection as the world moves across their view. Also, with current hardware, bright lights can often create a flare on the headset's fresnel lenses, which can pull users out of immersion by reminding them of the hardware they're wearing. In general, it's recommended that you use cooler shades and dimmer lights than you normally would.

Keep the scale of the world accurate

VR communicates the scale of objects in the world in ways that flat screens simply do not. Each of us sees the world in stereo vision through a pair of eyes that are a fixed distance apart. This distance, called **Interpupillary Distance (IPD)**, contributes to our sense of how large or small objects in the world appear. Most VR headsets can be adjusted to match the interpupillary distance of their user and should be adjusted correctly to minimize eyestrain.

> The distance between the pupils of the user's eyes is called the *interpupillary distance* and is a major contributor to a user's sense of how large or small objects in the world are.

What this means for you as a developer is that the scale of objects in your world matters. On a flat screen, the user is limited to comparing the size of an object to another object to determine how large it is, but in VR, the user's IPD drives an absolute sense of scale. An object that's too large or too small on a flat screen will still appear normal if it's alone on the screen. The same object in VR, even if there's nothing to which it can be compared, will look wrong to a viewer in stereo 3D.

Some users may be prone to simulator sickness if the scale of the world feels wrong, and even those who aren't will still likely feel that the world feels "wrong," without necessarily knowing why.

Make sure objects in your world are scaled correctly. In Unreal, by default, one **Unreal Unit (UU)** is equal to one centimeter.

Be conscious of physical actions

Your users in VR are moving around the real world wearing electric blindfolds. Respect this, and be careful what you ask them to do in VR. Take care when asking users to swing their arms, run, or strafe, as they can easily run into obstacles or walls in the real world. For headsets with cables, don't ask users to turn repeatedly in the same direction and tangle themselves in the cable. Be conscious as well of asking users to reach for objects on the floor or outside their normal reach area—this may not be easy or possible in their real-world physical environment. As mentioned earlier, avoid shifting the horizon in ways that could cause your user to lose balance. Remember that nearly all of the user's information about the world is coming from the VR simulation while they're in it—be conscious of how this information lines up with or contradicts what's in the invisible physical world around them.

Manage eyestrain

The eyes use muscles to focus on objects and orient the eyes, and these muscles, like any other, can get fatigued. We call this **eyestrain**. Symptoms of eyestrain can include headaches, fatigue, and blurred or double vision. As a designer, there are things you can do to minimize eyestrain in your users, and understanding a little about what causes eyestrain will help you do this.

First, eyestrain can be caused by flickering. We've already talked a lot about the importance of keeping latency low—this is another reason to keep low latency a priority. Don't create purposely flickering content, as this can produce eyestrain but could also trigger photosensitive seizures.

 Flickering caused by high latency can cause eyestrain. Keep your latency low.

Second, the eyes need to do some physical work to focus on an object in 3D space. They have to adjust the shape of their lenses to focus on the object (this is called **accommodation**), and they need to aim themselves so their lines of sight converge at the object. This is called **vergence**. We naturally have a reflex that correlates these two actions with each other, so the eyes naturally want to converge to a depth plane that matches the depth to which their lenses are focusing, and the lenses naturally want to focus in a way that matches where the eyes are converging. The problem comes in VR, where the actual images the eyes are seeing are a fixed distance away, but the content of those images exist at a variety of virtual depth planes, so the eyes still have to rotate so they converge at the objects they're looking at. This creates a conflict, as the focal depth the lenses are accommodating doesn't match the depth at which the eyes are converging, and it can cause eyestrain.

Eyestrain can be caused by two factors in VR: *flickering*, which can be managed by keeping your latency low, and conflict between the fixed distance at which the eyes' lenses need to focus to see the headset screen, and the changing distances at which they need to converge to see objects in stereo depth. This is commonly called the **vergence-accommodation conflict**, and you can manage it by keeping important objects in the virtual world about 1 m away so the vergence and accommodation demands mostly line up.

You can manage this when designing your world by keeping these two demands in mind. The fresnel lenses on the HMD make the headset screen appear to be about 1 m from the eyes, allowing the lenses to accommodate to a focal plane about 1 m away. The user's eyes, then, will naturally find it easier to focus on objects in the virtual world that appear to be about that far away. In practice, objects are most easily viewed at a range of 0.75 m to 3.5 m, with 1 m seeming to be ideal. Avoid making users look for long periods at objects less than half a meter away from the eye.

Put objects you know your user will be fixating on for long times at least a half-meter away from the camera and ideally around 1 m to minimize eyestrain.

Don't force your user to be an eyeball contortionist to view your user interface. Attaching a GUI to the user's face is usually a bad idea—as they turn their head to view a UI element, it appears to "run away" because it's attached to the same head that's turning to try to look at it, so users have to turn their eyeballs alone to focus on it. Don't do this to them. It's irritating to users, fatiguing, and has no real-world analogue. Put your UI in the world so your users can focus on it from comfortable viewing angles and at a comfortable distance. Attaching UI elements to the user's body, such as a wrist, can work well as it allows users to bring it into view when they want to interact with it. Putting GUI elements into a cockpit or vehicle can work well too. UI elements can be placed around the world and revealed when the user looks at them.

Keep GUI elements within the ideal range we discussed and at an angle that allows it to be read without straining, if you do wind up attaching it to the user's head.

Try to avoid creating situations that force the user to change focal distance rapidly and often. If you're making a shooter, for example, that puts critical information on a nearby UI element while the enemies are in the distance, you may be creating a situation that will force your user to change focus frequently to check the UI and focus on enemies in the field. In a flat-screen game, this wouldn't be a problem, but in VR, it will tire them out. Design your UI in such a way that the user can get critical information without focusing on it—easy-to-read graphical elements, for example, or consider putting UI elements over the enemies' heads.

GUI elements can be occluded by objects in the world that are nearer to the camera than the UI element is. Don't try to use tricks from 2D gaming space to change this. In 2D game design, it's common to draw a UI element over a 3D element even if that element would really block the player's view of it. If you do this in VR, however, you'll create a confusing stereo image that won't be at all comfortable to look at. Accept the reality that your UI exists as a physical object in the world and follows the same rules as other physical objects.

Make conscious choices about the content and intensity of your experience

Presence, when it's achieved in VR, produces strong reactions. It's an intimate experience, a visceral experience, and sometimes a fear-inducing experience. Be conscious of what you're doing as you craft experiences—you can easily trigger a fight-or-flight response in some users. This might be exactly what you intend, and we're not suggesting that you shy away from whatever it is you're trying to create. But be aware that you can be playing with strong stuff here and make intentional choices. VR is much more capable of triggering phobias than its flat-screen predecessors because the user is immersed in the space and not being constantly reminded by their peripheral vision that what they're seeing isn't true. Be on the lookout for circumstances that can induce vertigo, claustrophobia, fear of the dark, fear of snakes, spiders, or other phobias. Remember also that users will react more strongly to threats within their personal space.

For those of you deliberately playing with fear in VR, making horror experiences, or therapeutic experiences to treat PTSD, there are meaningful distinctions between film and VR—the user always exists in VR, which isn't the case in film. They have an instinctive sense of personal space that you can use to great effect. Film doesn't have this either. In film, an object that's supposed to seem close is just big on the screen, but it's still whatever distance away from the user that the screen actually is. In VR, this space is real. *It's right behind you* in VR really means that it's right behind you.

Let players manage their own session duration

VR puts demands on the user's body, eyes, and mind that other media don't. They're wearing a device on their head, and often standing or moving physically. Design your experience to let them exit whenever they want to or need to and resume later on. Let them take breaks as they need them.

Keep load times short

In contrast to games and applications on flat screens, users in VR can't do anything else while they're waiting for the application to load. Optimize to keep your load times short. Remember as well that, even during a load, your application must be responding to the user's head tracking.

Question everything we just told you

VR is in its infancy as a medium and an art form. It's far too early to pretend we know what its rules are really going to turn out to be. In the early days of film, actors were always filmed in full-frame, because the conventional wisdom at the time was that audiences wouldn't pay to see *half an actor*. Be equally willing to question the guidelines and advice you receive in VR design. These represent the current best understanding of what seems to work, but that doesn't mean that there aren't other ways to do things that haven't been tried. Be open to them. This is part of the reason why these guidelines were each presented with information about why they exist—so you can understand where they're coming from and make your own choices and try your own experiments. You're on a frontier in VR, part of the creation of an entirely new means of communication. Don't be afraid to explore.

Planning your VR project

We've talked quite a lot about VR in the abstract—what we can do with it, and what we think we know so far about how it works and what works well within it. From here on out, this book is going to get pretty practical and hands-on, and our hope is that, as we go through these projects and learn how to build VR experiences in Unreal, these principles we just talked about stay in your mind and guide your choices.

With that in mind, there's one last topic we should explore before we start getting our hands dirty, which is how to turn an idea into a thing you can actually make.

Clarify what you're trying to do

The first thing to do in developing a design is to decide what it's for. This may sound obvious, but it happens all too often that developers jump right into a project and start building without first taking a step back and figuring out what it is that they're really trying to make and who it's for. The result, more often than not, is either an unfocused experience that doesn't really achieve what it was intended to do because the parts aren't all working together to support a common goal, or a project that takes a long time to complete. This wastes a lot of work, as developers discover things that need to change and have to throw out existing work to make the changes. By taking some time to plan before you begin building software, you can save yourself a lot of effort and make it more likely that the project will succeed.

The first thing to remember in design is that the more you build, the more difficult and expensive changes get, so try to make these decisions as early in the process as you can. The cheapest prototype you can make is in your own mind. The second cheapest is on paper. Once you start building software, start with the bare minimum you need to get your project running—a **gray box** environment, or a simple prototype, and test it to see how it needs to change. You're almost guaranteed to discover a few things you hadn't anticipated, and this is the time to discover these things and change what you need. Once you've gone through this process, discovered what really works and what doesn't, and adjusted your design to respond to what you learned, now you're ready to begin putting expensive art and polish into the work. Too many developers work backward and try to make the final product right out of the gate, and they get locked into decisions that could have been changed more easily if the legwork had been done first.

With that in mind, the first thing to think about is who the project is for and why you're making it for them. Is this a game or an entertainment experience? What do you want the user to feel? What will they be doing while they play or participate in the experience? The same questions apply to cinematic VR—what's this experience about? What story are you trying to tell? Take a moment to write this down.

If you're making a learning experience, what does the user need to learn? What's the best way to teach it?

If you're making an architecture or design visualization application, what's important to your end user? An architect or engineer may want to be able to look inside walls and structures to see electrical and plumbing designs, while a real-estate buyer may care more about the quality of light in the space.

Figure out who your user is, and what's important to them, and clarify what you're trying to create and what's important to you. This should be done on paper. It's very easy for vague design elements to hide in your mental model, only to reveal holes or unexpected questions when you start to write them down.

Is it a good fit for VR? Why?

Pretty much the next thing you should do once you've clarified your design intention for a VR project is to think about how it fits in VR.

Think about your project in terms of what VR allows you to do. Does it rely on immersion and a strong sense of presence to work? Is it about making use of VR's ability to simulate the body or to give context to information? Why does your project work better in VR than it would on a flat screen? What can your user do or experience that they couldn't in traditional media?

Think about the challenges VR imposes as well. As we've seen in the best practices mentioned, VR imposes a different set of challenges than traditional media. Simulator sickness is a major concern—does your project require you to move the camera in ways that are going to be uncomfortable for your users? Does it rely on your users to move in a way that may be difficult or impossible in VR? Are you asking your users to read lots of small text that may not be legible on current headsets? Think about the practices we outlined, and evaluate whether any of them pose challenges to your design. This doesn't necessarily mean your design can't work in VR, but it does mean that you'll have to do some additional design thinking to work through those challenges.

Your choice to put your project into VR should be made deliberately. You should be able to describe why your project works better in VR than in traditional media, and how you plan to handle the challenges VR imposes. This too should happen in writing. You'll probably discover opportunities you hadn't seen, and a few challenges you hadn't realized you'd need to overcome. Writing these down will help you to understand what's important about your project and what needs to happen for it to succeed.

What's important – what has to exist in this project for it to work? (MVP)

Now that you've clarified who your project is for, what you intend it to do, and why it makes sense to do it in VR, you're ready to begin figuring out what it's really going to take to build it. It's helpful to figure this out in terms of a **Minimum Viable Product** (**MVP**). This, simply put, is a version of the product that contains only what's needed for it to satisfy its intention. An architectural visualization project, for example, needs to put the viewer into the building at the correct scale, and give the user some way to move around and see what it looks and feels like from different perspectives. What your MVP contains is your choice as a designer, but you should be clear about whether the thing you're talking about is a thing you need or a thing you want. If the project simply isn't worth doing if you can't get a given feature into it, then it's a needed feature and should go into your MVP. If it would improve the experience but users could still get what they needed without it, it's not part of the MVP.

MVP refers to a version of the project that contains only what's needed to satisfy its goal and little or nothing else. Clarifying your MVP can help you to understand what the *spine* of your project is, which can tell you what to prioritize and gives you a baseline from which to evaluate whether your project succeeds at achieving what it set out to do.

The contents of your MVP will differ greatly between different types of projects—the needs of a cinematic VR experience are substantially different than those of an engineering visualization application, but as a designer, you should know what they are and write them down. You don't need to write a book or an essay here—a list of bullets should be enough, but for each item on the list, ask yourself whether the project could still do what it's intended to do without it, and be clear about your answers. Wants, even strong wants, aren't needs. The point here is to know where your floor is.

Be on the lookout as well for things you missed. Imagine your user using your project—what are they trying to do, from moment to moment, from the moment they start up the application until the moment they shut it down? Use this exercise to discover items you missed, and figure out whether they're wants or needs, and get them on to the list if they belong there.

Break it down

If you've gone through the preceding exercises, you should have a clear idea of what your project is for, why it works in VR, and what needs to be in it for it to work. Now you're ready to figure out how to do it.

For the items in your MVP, what do you need to make them exist? Do you need a UI element to display information to the user? Do you need a way for your user to move around? Does the user need to be able to load or save information, or connect to a server?

For each item in your list, figure out what that item really requires you to build and write it down. You should come out of this exercise with a pretty clear breakdown of the things you need to do to get your project built.

 A **breakdown** is a list of things you need to do or build to get your project made. Use it as a tool to ensure that you haven't missed required elements, or underestimated risks, and to see whether the project you're trying to build is realistically achievable with the time and resources you have. It's a tool for spotting problems early, while you still have a chance to fix them, and then later for tracking your progress as you build.

Look through this list—where are the big jobs, and where are the big risks? Can you achieve all of this with the time and resources you have? Do you need to re-evaluate your scope if it's starting to look too big? Bear in mind that it's almost always better to do fewer things well than to try to do everything and do a poor job of it. It's common, at this point, to discover that the project scope exceeds what you can realistically do well, and this is a good thing. The time to discover this is now while it's still on paper and you can reorganize the work, move items off the MVP, or change your schedule or resources. If you discover these problems near the start, you have a fighting chance of solving them, whereas if you discover them only once you're months-deep into software development, you may discover that you've painted yourself into a corner. Set yourself up for success on paper while you still have the flexibility to do so.

Tackle things in the right order

Some items in your breakdown will be easier to do than others, and some will be more fun. Use your judgement when you figure out the order in which you should do things. In general, it's a good idea to tackle the risky things first. If something's important enough to be in your MVP, and there's a risk that it could go long, or might not work at all, it's often smart to get it out of the way early. Doing this gives you time to iterate on a risky item while you work on other things, or in the worst-case scenario, if you discover that a thing you'd counted on just can't be done, you're still early enough in your project that you may be able to fall back to another plan. Don't leave high-risk, high-priority items to the end—you'll be in trouble if something goes wrong.

Look for dependencies between items. If something can't be done before another thing is done—a character, for example, that can't be animated until the character is built and rigged, then make sure those dependencies factor into your plan. It does you no good to plan to do a thing in a certain order and then discover that you can't because something it depends on isn't ready.

 As you plan how you're going to get through your breakdown, look for items that involve risks or uncertainties, items that are just going to take a long time, and items that depend on other items. Factor these into your plan. In general, where you can, do your high-importance, high-risk work early in your project so you have time to handle things if something goes wrong.

A word about project management—there's a forest of literature out there about planning and tracking projects, and discussing them in depth falls outside the scope of this book. Broadly, these fall into two major schools of thought: **waterfall** and **agile**. Waterfall project management methods lay out tasks in a rigid order that assumes that, once one task is done, the next can begin. This works well when the things you're doing are well-defined and don't entail much risk, such as painting a house, but VR design and development rarely works out like this. You simply may not know whether a feature is *done* until you see it running alongside other systems, and you may have to loop back at that point and change something or rework it entirely. Agile methods, such as **Scrum**, take this reality into account, and are intended for design and development projects where things are going to need to be revisited as the project evolves and reveals new information. In general, agile methods work much better for software development than waterfall plans.

Depending on the scope of the project, you may not need to apply a formal project management method, but even if you're planning loosely, there should still be a plan, and you should make sure the plan accommodates the reality that you're going to have to loop back and iterate on features and design, that some items are going to depend on others, and that some things are going to take longer than you thought.

Test early and often

Test your designs as early as you can. VR especially is a very new medium, and people respond to it in very different ways. Test with as diverse a range of subjects as you can, as early as you can, so you can spot things you need to change while they're still relatively easy to change.

Remember as well that VR developers make terrible test subjects. We use VR far, far more than other users and tend to be much more comfortable with VR interfaces and much less prone to simulator sickness than typical users. Test VR with users who are new to it as well as with users who are comfortable with the medium.

Test with as diverse a population as you can. VR embodies the user in ways that previous media don't, and this can matter to your users. Hands that look fine to you may feel alien to a user whose hands look different. Make sure your test population isn't limited to just people like you.

Look for opportunities to test as early in the process as you can make them happen. Even long before you've reached your MVP, test elements such as locomotion systems that may need design iteration. Put users into a gray-box environment and have them navigate through it, and watch what they do and where they get stuck. The more testing you do, the better your project will get, and the earlier you test, the easier it is to act on what you've learned.

Design is iterative

Lots of people assume that finished products somehow spring fully-formed from the minds of genius designers or developers. It doesn't work this way. Anything worth making takes iteration to get there.

Prepare yourself now for the reality that the first iteration of your design isn't going to be everything you wanted it to be, and that's the point. The purpose of the first draft of anything is to show you what's really important about the thing you're building and how it needs to fit together. Plan for this. Design is a process, and time and iteration, more than anything else, are the key elements of that process.

This is why we so strongly advise designing on paper first and testing prototypes in software as early as you can. Each time you give yourself something tangible to respond to, you're going to discover something about it and probably discover a way to make it better.

Summary

In this chapter, we looked at what VR is and some of the ways it can be used in the real world. We talked quite a bit about immersion and presence. Let's recap for a moment here.

Presence, we said, is a physiological sensation of *being* in a place, and is really the point of VR. We create VR to create presence. Immersion is the means by which presence is brought about, and involves taking over the user's senses completely enough that they can begin to believe the virtual world around them.

We discussed a number of currently-held best practices for creating good VR. The most important of these was the need to keep latency as low as possible and the need to be very careful of how you move the user's viewpoint. Simulator sickness is largely caused by conflicts between a visual sense of motion and the lack of motion felt by the inner ear. Breaking up movement and being aware of the types of movement most likely to trigger simulator sickness are important for keeping your users comfortable in your experience. We also talked about safety—the need to be conscious of the kinds of movement you're asking your users to perform, about designing to avoid eyestrain, and the need to be careful about triggering photosensitive seizures.

Finally, we outlined a process for planning a VR project and iterating on its design to make the best project you can and ensure that it succeeds at what you intended it to do.

In the next chapter, we're going to dive in and start getting our hands dirty with the Unreal Engine, and from here on out, the rest of this book will be hands-on. We hope that the ideas outlined in this chapter will stay with you as you develop, and help you to succeed, not just in making running VR applications, but in making them well.

With that out of the way, let's get to work.

Setting Up Your Development Environment

2

The goal of this chapter is to get you set up to develop in Unreal Engine. Even if you've already installed and started working in the engine, you may still find it worthwhile to take a look through this chapter, as there are a few details of the installation process that might be useful to you.

We're also going to take a look at the Epic Games launcher. It's easy to get into the habit of looking at it just as a way of updating the engine and launching projects, but there's a huge collection of useful resources for learning and development there too. It would be a mistake to ignore them.

For those planning to develop for mobile VR on Oculus Go or Samsung Gear, we'll walk you through the process of setting up the Android SDK and setting up a project for deployment to the device, and finally for those interested in C++ development, we'll show you how to set up Visual Studio 2017 for use with Unreal and for those interested in working on the bleeding edge, how to download the Unreal Engine source code and build it yourself.

Through out the course of this chapter, we're going to learn about the following topics:

- Installing Unreal Engine using the Epic Games launcher
- Setting up your development environment to build a project for mobile VR
- Learning more about Unreal Engine, and where to get help
- Setting up your development environment to build a project in C++
- Downloading and building Unreal Engine from source code

Prerequisite – VR hardware

If you're planning to develop for desktop VR hardware, such as the Oculus Rift or HTC Vive, we're going to assume here that you've already set up your headset and ensured that it's working. If you haven't, now's a good time. Head on over to `https://www.vive.com/eu/setup/` or `https://www.oculus.com/setup/`, and run through the guided installation and setup operations there.

Remember that your VR headset driver software, Oculus Home or Steam VR, needs to be running when you use the headset.

If you're going to be developing for mobile standalone VR, your setup process will involve a few other steps, which we'll walk you through after we get Unreal Engine installed. We do recommend even for those developing for mobile VR that you have a desktop VR headset available as well. It dramatically speeds up debugging to be able to launch your software right into the headset without having to cook it and deploy it to the device every time. It's not required, but you will find it helpful.

Either way, test out your headset, make sure it's working, and then let's get our development environment ready.

Setting up Unreal Engine

If you're going to develop VR applications using Unreal Engine, the first thing you'll need, of course, is the engine. Let's walk through the process of setting it up.

What it costs

A natural question to start with when considering Unreal Engine is what it costs. The news here is good. Unreal Engine is free to download and use, and if you use it commercially, the terms are reasonable.

When you download the engine, you'll be asked to agree to one of two license agreements, depending on what you're going to be using it for. If you're a game developer and you make a game or application using Unreal and sell it, you'll pay a 5% royalty on gross sales over $3,000 per calendar quarter. If you don't sell your game or app, or it earns less than that per quarter, Unreal is free to use.

If you're using Unreal for something that isn't intended to be sold to the public (training simulations, architectural visualization, or anything else), Unreal is entirely free under the terms of the Enterprise license agreement. For most businesses, the standard Enterprise **End User License Agreement (EULA)** will be fine, but if you do need to make changes, you can contact Epic to set up an enterprise license with different terms here: `https://www.unrealengine.com/en-US/enterprise/contact-us`. Epic will work with you.

What this boils down to for now is that you can download Unreal and use it for free, and if you start making money with it, the terms are reasonable and clear.

 While we're on the topic, it's worth mentioning that the version of Unreal you get when you download the engine is the same version professional developers use, including the devs at Epic. There's no split between a "pro" version and everything else: everything's included and everything's turned on.

Creating an Epic Games account

Let's get started, then. We're going to begin by heading over to `https://www.unrealengine.com` and hitting the download link. If you've already created an account with Epic, sign in here. If you haven't, now's the time to create one.

After you've signed up or signed in, you'll be asked which license you need to agree to—the **Game Developers license** or the **Enterprise license**. Choose the one that fits your case. Next, select whether you're downloading for Windows or Mac, download the appropriate Epic installer, and run it.

This will install the **Epic Games Launcher**, which you'll use as a hub for managing engine versions, plugins, library content, and learning resources. There's useful stuff here.

The Epic Games launcher

Once you've downloaded and installed the launcher, open it up. It's going to ask you to sign in using the same account you just used to log into the Epic website. (The Launcher can be used offline as well, so you can still run the engine without an internet connection, but of course you have much more useful stuff available to you if you're online.)

Once you're logged in, look at the set of tabs along the left edge of the launcher. There's a tab for Unreal Engine, and then a series of tabs for Epic's store, your game library, and your friends. Select the **UNREAL ENGINE** tab. We'll be spending all our time here:

The Epic Games Launcher as of version 4.22: its layout changes fairly frequently, but the principles remain the same

Across the top of the Unreal Engine tab, you'll find four additional tabs:

- Unreal Engine
- **Learn**
- **Marketplace**
- **Library**

We're going to look at these tabs in a moment, but first, find the **Install Engine** button to the right of them. By default, this button installs the latest stable version of the engine. Let's do this.

Installing the engine

When you hit the **install** button, the launcher will switch to the **Library** tab if it's not already selected, and it will ask you to choose an install location. The default location is usually a good choice here, but you can browse to a new location if you'd like to install the engine somewhere else.

There's also an **Options** button on this page, and we should take a moment to talk about the choices it offers:

Unreal Engine Preview 4.21.0 Installation Options

Component	Size	
Core Components (Required)	9.70 GB	☑
Starter Content	867.29 MB	☑
Templates and Feature Packs	585.28 MB	☑
Engine Source	131.12 MB	☑
Editor symbols for debugging	19.95 GB	☐

Download Size: 7.52 GB

Required Storage Space: 22.03 GB

Apply

Installation options allowing you to determine which components of Unreal Engine are set up on your machine

- **Core Components** have to be installed—that's the bare minimum required to run the editor.
- **Starter Content** includes a number of useful assets to get you started, including a number of materials and models, and the Advanced Lighting Map. We'll be using these assets for the projects in this book, so you should install it.
- **Templates and Feature Packs** give you a range of excellent projects to use as starting points for your game projects, including the VR Template, which we'll use for a few projects in this book. You should install this too.

- **Engine Source** is one of the things that sets Unreal Engine apart from the others: Unreal Engine gives you the entire C++ source code for the engine. This can be a great way to begin learning about C++, and can be a lifesaver when you really need to understand how something works or need to figure out why something is behaving unexpectedly. You don't need to install the engine source, and whether you do is up to you, but it doesn't take up a lot of room so there's really no reason not to. If you anticipate doing any C++ development, you should install it. Once installed, you'll find the source code in the directory where you installed your engine version, under `\Engine\Source`.

- **Editor symbols for debugging** is something you'll need if you plan to debug in C++. Without it, you'll be unable to set breakpoints in the engine source code or trace execution through it. These editor symbols take up a lot of space though, so if you don't plan to develop in C++ or debug using Visual Studio, you can skip it, and you can always install it later if you realize you need it.

These options can be changed after you've installed an engine version, so it's not a problem if you change your mind later on about whether you want an option installed. You can add or remove any of them at any time. Also, if you're keeping older versions of the engine, which developers often do if they're maintaining a legacy project, it's not a bad idea to save space by using the options to uninstall everything but the core components.

For the projects in this book, the default options are fine—**Core Components**, **Starter Content**, **Templates**, and **Engine Source**. If you anticipate developing or debugging in C++, install the editor symbols as well.

Let's hit **Apply** after we've set our options, and install the engine. It's going to take a while. (If you'd like to jump ahead to the *Learning about unreal* section while you wait, you can jump back here when the install finishes.)

Editting your vault cache location

Depending on how your system is set up, you may want to change the location where Unreal stores its vault cache. The vault cache stores assets that you've downloaded from the marketplace, such as projects and asset packs. By default, it lands at `C:\Program Files (x86)\Epic Games\Launcher\VaultCache`. You should be aware that it can get pretty large, so if you're running out of space on your system drive, you may want to put it somewhere else.

If you'd like to do this, from the Epic Games launcher, select **Settings | Edit Vault Cache Location**, select a new location, and hit **Apply**. Then, exit **Settings** and quit the Epic Games launcher (find its icon in the system tray, right-click it, and select **Exit**—simply closing the launcher window will minimize it without quitting it). When you restart the launcher, it will create the cache in the new location. Remember to delete your old `VaultCache` directory from its old location. (While you could copy the cache to the new location, it's often a better idea to force the system to create a new cache, as this will eliminate a lot of leftover stuff you're probably not using anymore.)

Setting up a Derived Data Cache (DDC)

There's one additional bit of setup we recommend you do. As you use the editor, Unreal will compile assets into a form that's ready for use by your local machine's hardware. Rather than forcing the engine to do this every time, it's a good idea to give it a place to stash these compiled assets so that everything loads faster after the first build.

You don't have to do this, but it's a good idea. Materials especially will compile much faster if you do. If you're seeing messages such as the following, you definitely want to set up a DDC:

If you see this warning, be sure to set up your DDC as directed here. It will make a big difference.

Unreal calls this facility the **Shared Data Cache (SDC)**, or the **Derived Data Cache (DDC)**. (This is a different cache than the vault cache we just mentioned a moment ago.) Everything in the DDC is generated, which means that it's fine to clear out its content anytime. New data will be generated in its place. If you change your video card, it's a good idea to empty your DDC, as it will contain a ton of assets compiled for the old card.

You have two options in setting up a DDC: if you're working in a studio environment, you can set up a *shared DDC* in a network-accessible location. To do this, follow the instructions here: `https://docs.unrealengine.com/en-us/Engine/Basics/DerivedDataCache`.

What we're going to talk about here is the other option: setting up a *local DDC* for solo development. If you're in a studio that already has a shared DDC set up, you can and should skip the local setup.

Setting up a local DDC

Open your Windows **Control Panel** | **System and Security** | **System**, and then hit the **Advanced system settings** link:

You can also get here by right-clicking **This PC** on any Windows Explorer pane, and selecting **Properties**.

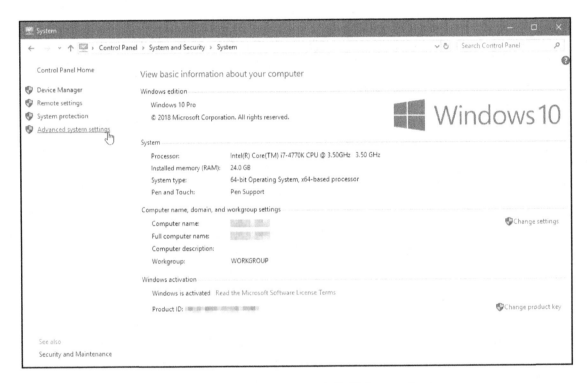

Look for the Advanced system settings link on the left side of the System control panel

In your **Advanced system settings** pane, hit the **Environment Variables** button:

The Environment Variables button is found in System Properties | Advanced. You'll need admin privileges to edit it.

In the **Edit** environment variable dialog that appears, hit **New** to create a new system variable either in your **User** variables, or in the **System** variables section. (If you use the former, the DDC will work for your login, but not for others who log into the same machine. If you put the variable in your system variables, it will apply to all users.)

Enter `UE-SharedDataCachePath` as the variable name, and for its value, browse to a directory where you'd like to stash your derived data. If you're building projects with lots of art, your DDC can take up well over 10 GB, so put it on a drive where you'll have space:

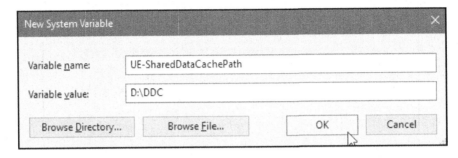

Create a variable named UE-SharedDataCachePath and set it to the location where you'd like to store your DDC.

Hit **OK** to save it. *You'll need to restart your PC before this will take effect.*

If your DDC starts to accumulate lots of stray assets from projects you're no longer working on, or if you change your video hardware, it's safe to clear out its contents entirely; the editor will regenerate the cache.

Launching the engine

Once the engine has been installed, let's launch it to verify that everything is working.

Hit the **Launch** button on the left-hand side of the Epic Games launcher, or the **Launch** button on the **ENGINE VERSIONS** in your **Library** tab:

The Library tab shows your installed engine versions, projects, plugins, and asset packs.

If you've never launched Unreal Engine before on your machine, it may ask you to allow it to install a few prerequisites. Let it. The engine may also ask for permission to communicate through your Windows Firewall. Let it do that, too.

If everything is running as it should, you should see a window that looks something like this:

The Unreal Project Browser appears any time you launch the engine without specifying a project to load.

Let's create a blank blueprint project just to make sure everything's working. (We're going to look at creating projects in depth in the next chapter, but, for now, we just want to test everything out.)

Select the **New Project** tab. Under the **Blueprint** tab, select **Blank**, and leave all the options at their defaults. Give it a reasonable location, and hit **Create Project**.

The editor should open into your new project and you should be ready to go.

If you're developing for desktop VR (rather than a mobile device), let's do a quick test to be sure everything's working. If you're developing for mobile VR, we'll cover that in the next section.

Find the drop-down to the right of the **Play** button in the editor toolbar. Pull it down and select **VR Preview**:

Once you've selected a play mode, this will become the Play button's default behavior until you change it.

 If VR Preview is disabled, check to be sure that your headset is properly connected and that the Oculus or Steam VR software is running and not displaying any warnings or errors.

Once you launch in VR, you should see your scene in the headset. It may not be the world's most exciting scene, and you'll be floating unexpectedly high above the floor (we're going to learn how to set a scene up correctly for VR in the next chapter), but you should be in it. Congratulations! Everything's working!

Setting up for mobile VR

Mobile VR headsets such as Samsung Gear and Oculus Go are separate devices from your PC, so you can't simply launch into a VR preview the way you can with a desktop headset. Instead, you need to package the project and deploy it to the device so you can run it directly on the headset. You'll have to set up a few things to make this possible.

Creating or joining an Oculus developer organization

First, if you're going to develop for Oculus-based mobile VR platforms, you need to register with Oculus as a developer. We're assuming here that you've already created an account with Oculus since you would have needed to do this to use the headset at all. If you haven't yet done so, do that first and log in.

Now, navigate to `https://dashboard.oculus.com/organizations/create/` and run through the steps to register as a developer. If you're joining an existing organization instead of creating your own, contact its administrator to be added to the list of registered developers.

Setting your VR headset to developer mode in Oculus Go

Once you've registered as a developer, you'll be able to use the Oculus mobile app to set your headset to developer mode. You'll need to do this before you can deploy your own projects to the device.

In the app, navigate to **Settings** | **[Your headset]** | **More Settings** | **Developer Mode**, and turn **Developer Mode** on.

If you're unable to do this, confirm that your Oculus account is associated with a developer organization.

Installing Android Debug Bridge (ADB)

Samsung Gear and Oculus Go both run on Google's *Android* operating system. You need to install drivers to allow your PC to communicate with Android devices. To do this, we're going to install the **Android Debug Bridge** drivers.

Navigate to the ADB 2.0 download page at `https://developer.oculus.com/downloads/package/oculus-go-adb-drivers/`, download and extract the `.zip` file, and then right-click `android_winusb.inf` and select **Install**.

For additional information about ADB and how to use it to talk to Oculus Go and Samsung Gear headsets, check here: https://developer.oculus. com/documentation/mobilesdk/latest/concepts/mobile-adb/#mobile-android-debug-intro.

Let the installation complete, and then we're going to install the Android SDK.

Setting up NVIDIA CodeWorks for Android

In order to develop software for Android, you need to install a number of **Software Development Kits (SDKs)** and other resources, and configure them to work with one another. Fortunately, there's an easy way to do this using NVIDIA's **CodeWorks for Android** installer.

Epic includes the required installer with your engine installation. Navigate to the directory where you installed Unreal Engine and look for Engine\Extras\AndroidWorks\Win64. Run the **CodeWorksforAndroid** installer found there:

```
C:\Program Files\Epic
Games\UE_4.21\Engine\Extras\AndroidWorks\Win64\CodeWorksforAndroid-1R6u1-
windows.exe
```

Accept the default options, and when it's finished, *restart* your computer.

Verifying that the HMD can communicate with your PC

Once you've returned after the computer has been restarted, we want to check that your PC can communicate with your Android headset.

Navigate to the location where you just installed Android SDK. By default, this will be C:\NVPACK\android-sdk-windows. Look for the platform-tools directory.

From within this directory, *Shift + right-click* to open a context menu that includes the Open PowerShell window here command. If you right-click without holding *Shift*, your context menu won't include PowerShell. If you're using an older version of Windows 10, or you have PowerShell disabled, *Shift* + Right-Click will open a command line instead.

From within PowerShell, type ./adb devices.

If you're using PowerShell, you must precede any call to launch a program with `./`. (Requiring `./` before an executable call is a safety feature that's standard on Unix-based systems to prevent you from accidentally launching an executable when you didn't mean to. Windows now follows this convention as well.) If you're using the legacy command prompt instead, you simply type the name of the executable: `adb devices`. It's a good idea to get into the habit of using PowerShell instead of the legacy command prompt. It's safer and you can do more with it.

Take a look at the following screenshot:

```
Windows PowerShell
PS C:\NVPACK\android-sdk-windows\platform-tools> ./adb devices
List of devices attached
                 device
PS C:\NVPACK\android-sdk-windows\platform-tools> _
```

The adb devices command lists your currently-connected Android devices.

If the Go or Gear appears as *Unauthorized*, that means your PC was able to see it, but the headset hasn't yet given the PC permission to talk to it. Put on the headset and accept the confirmation dialog that should have appeared there. Run `adb devices` again and confirm that the headset now appears as a device.

Generating a signature file for Samsung Gear

You do not need to create a signature file to deploy to Oculus Go or Quest.

For a Samsung Gear device, you'll need to create an **Oculus Signature File (osig)**.

Follow the directions at `https://dashboard.oculus.com/tools/osig-generator/`, and place the resulting file in your Unreal install directory, under `\Engine\Build\Android\Java\assets`. If the assets directory doesn't yet exist, create it.

For more information on signature files, check here: `https://developer.` `oculus.com/documentation/mobilesdk/latest/concepts/mobile-` `submission-sig-file/.`

Deploying a test project to the device

Now that we've installed all the required software and verified that our PC can see our Android headset, let's create a project and deploy it to the device to make sure everything is working correctly.

Setting up a test project

Launch Unreal Engine from the Epic launcher, and in the **Projects** browser, select **New Project**. Select the **Blueprint** tab, the **Blank** template, and set your project settings to **Mobile/Tablet, Scalable 3D or 2D, No Starter Content**. Choose a location for the project and create it:

The options you set here determine what your project's starting settings will be. but you can change them later.

Checking that your OculusVR plugin is enabled

Once the project has launched, select **Settings** | **Plugins** | **Virtual Reality**, and verify that the **OculusVR** plugin is enabled. (It should already be.)

Setting a default map

Since we're going to be running this project as a standalone executable on our Gear or Go, we need to tell it what map to open when it starts up. Save *the empty map* that was created when the editor started, and give it any name you want.

Select **Settings** | **Project Settings** | **Project** | **Maps & Modes**, and set the map you just saved as **Editor Startup Map** and **Game Default Map**.

Clearing the default mobile touch interface

Ordinarily, mobile applications assume you'll be touching the screen to operate them, but of course this isn't going to happen in your headset, so we need to clear that default setting from our project.

From **Project Settings**, select **Engine** | **Input** | **Mobile**, and from the **Default Touch Interface** drop-down, select **Clear** to set it to **None**.

Setting your Android SDK project settings

Now, we need to configure our project for deployment to our Android headset.

Under **Platforms** | **Android** | **APK Packaging**, hit **Configure Now**, and **Accept SDK License** (you'll only need to accept the license once):

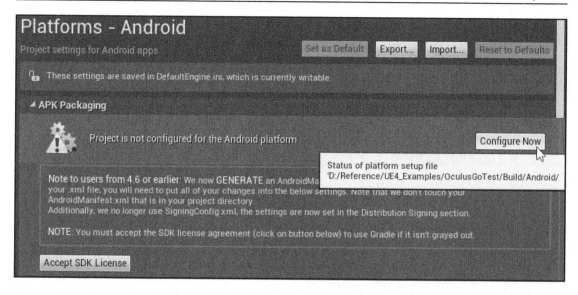

Hitting the Configure Now button will write a project.properties file to your project's Build/Android directory.

We need to set a few settings under this category as well:

- **Minumum SDK Version**: 21
- **Target SDK Version**: 21
- **Enable FullScreen Immersive on KitKat and above devices**: True

You'll see some older documentation tell you to set your minimum and target SDK versions to 19. This is true for Samsung Gear, but for Oculus Go, you must select version 21.

Scroll down to the **Advanced APKPackaging** section and set the following:

- **Configure the AndroidManifest for deployment to Oculus Mobile** to **True**

Older walkthroughs will refer to this setting as *Configuring the AndroidManifest for deployment to Gear VR*. Its name has been changed.

Setting your Android SDK locations

Now, select **Platforms | Android SDK**, and set the following (adjusting for wherever you installed your SDK):

- **Location of Android SDK**: C:/NVPACK/android-sdk-windows
- **Location of Android NDK**: C:/NVPACK/android-ndk-r12b
- **Location of ANT**: C:/NVPACK/apache-ant-1.8.2
- **Location of JAVA**: C:/NVPACK/jdk1.8.0_77
- **SDK API Level**: latest
- **NDK API Level**: android-21

Refer to the following screenshot:

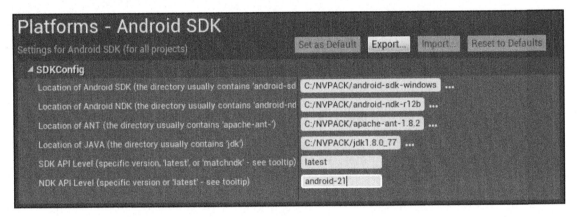

Make sure the directories you specify here point to actual locations on your drive.

Be aware that these directory names are going to change when you update your Android SDKs (which you must remember to do whenever you update your engine version. Make sure you're pointing to the correct directories for each of these after an update, or you'll run into some impressively cryptic errors).

Launching the test project

Close your project settings, and find the drop-down beside the **Launch** button. Open it, and you should be able to see the serial number of your mobile VR headset:

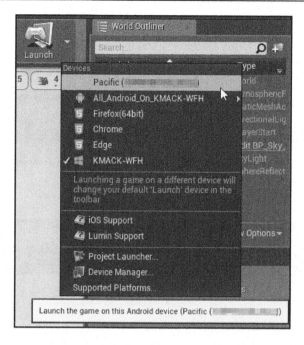

The devices listed here will vary depending on what platforms your project supports and what devices are found.

Select the headset to launch to it. It's totally normal for the editor to become unresponsive for a short time as it gets things ready. Be patient. Once the editor becomes responsive again, you should see something such as the following:

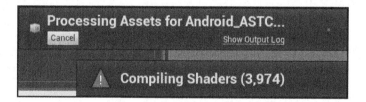

Android asset processing progress indicator

It's not a bad idea to select **Window | Developer Tools | Output Log** so that you can see what it's doing, but this isn't required. Hitting the **Show Output Log** link will do the same thing.

Get in the habit of watching your output log. Lots of developers ignore this, but you shouldn't. You can learn a lot about what the engine is doing by watching the log.

This is going to take a while the first time you run it, because lots of shaders will need to be compiled. Subsequent runs will go much faster.

Once the assets are compiled, Unreal will copy them to your device:

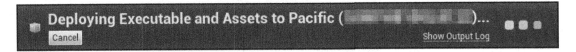

Deployment may take a while depending on how much data needs to be transferred to the device.

Once deployment is finished, the scene should run in your device:

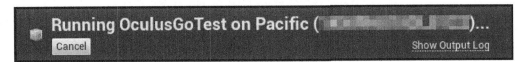

Once this dialog indicates that the project is running on the device, you should be ready to test it.

Put on the headset and you should be in your scene. Congratulations! You've just deployed a project to a mobile VR headset!

Using the Epic Games launcher

Before we go too much further, let's take a look at the Epic Games launcher—there's a ton of useful material here, and this should be a starting place for much of your learning. It's worth it to take some time to look around and see what resources are available to you. It's easy to overlook these resources, but if you get used to understanding where you can learn and find information when you need it, you'll get much further, much faster.

The launcher's Unreal Engine tab is broken into four major sections:

- **Unreal Engine**
- **Learn**
- **Marketplace**
- **Library**

Let's take a look at each of them.

The Unreal Engine Tab

The **Unreal Engine** tab displays featured content and projects, which are definitely worth exploring, but they'll become more relevant to you as you use the engine longer. As a new user, pay particular attention to that row of icons right under the main banner. These are valuable resources:

The Unreal Engine tab as of Unreal 4.22

- The **News** link is a great way to keep up with what's going on; it mostly focuses on new features, events, and interesting ways the engine is being used. This is another one that will get more meaningful to you as you spend more and more time in the engine.
- The **YouTube** link takes you to the Unreal Engine YouTube channel. This is one of the best places to find in-depth tutorials, feature highlights and project spotlights. There's quite a lot of information in the Feature Highlight videos especially that you're not likely to find anywhere else.
- The **AnswerHub** is an essential resource for developers to ask and answer questions. Just about any time you have a question, this should be one of the first places you search for an answer. The chances are pretty high that you'll find what you're looking for. Don't be shy about asking questions of your own, but do try to search for existing questions and answers before you jump in and ask something that's already been answered. Also, try to pay it forward—if you see a question you know how to answer, contribute. This is how the community works.
- The **Forums** are a place for conversations about all topics related to the engine, and are a great place to find out what's going on. Most plugin developers maintain contact with their users on the forums too. There's a forum dedicated to VR and AR development here: `https://forums.unrealengine.com/ development-discussion/vr-ar-development`.
- The **Roadmap** link takes you to a Trello page that describes what's being worked on for upcoming releases and what's planned for the more distant future. Early on in your Unreal development career, this may not be so meaningful to you, but as you get deeper into the engine, those upcoming changes will start to matter.

Learn

This is one of the most important resources on the launcher. You won't regret the time you spend here.

Let's begin by looking at the top bar:

The Learn tab as of Unreal 4.22

- The **Documentation** link takes you to Unreal's documentation home at `https://docs.unrealengine.com/en-us`. The **Get Started with UE4** link on the documentation page is a good place to learn the basics of the art, level design, and programming pipelines. If you're brand new to Unreal Engine, we recommend that you go through these basics so you know your way around the editor. You'll have a much better time building the projects in this book, and you'll get more out of them if you've done this. After you've gotten through the basics, consider this documentation page to be your standard go-to reference any time you need to work with a new tool or system in the engine.
- The **Video Tutorials** link takes you to `https://academy.unrealengine.com/`, an online learning site consisting of tons of detailed video tutorials on topics centered around specific industries, roles, workflows, and concepts. These are worthwhile classes, and are a great way to get an understanding of how the different parts of the engine fit together to allow you to do whatever you need to do.
- The **Community Wiki** page is less useful than the others. As we mentioned previously, the content on this page is not guaranteed to be up-to-date, or even correct. It's worth knowing that it's there, but it's usually a better idea to search for information on the forums and in the documentation than on the Wiki, as incorrect information on the forums will usually be corrected fairly quickly by other users, while it can fester on the Wiki.

The content examples project

Below this bar, we have a few featured links to quick-start guides and blog posts, and then a collection of engine feature samples. The most important of these is the **Content Examples** project. All of the projects here are worth looking at for specific topics, but **Content Examples** should be a regular reference for you. Let's install it now.

Click the **Content Examples** project to open its detail page, and hit the **Create Project** link on the page:

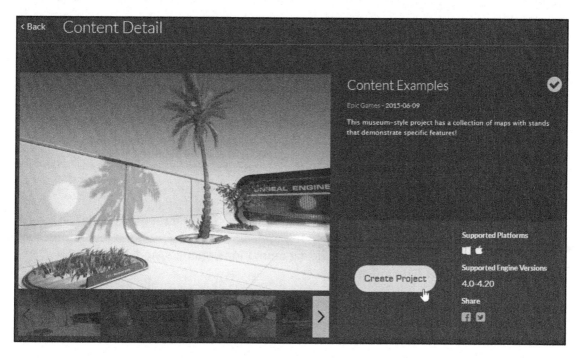

The Content Examples project detail page

You'll be asked where you want to put the project, and what engine version you'd like to use to create it. Put it someplace reasonable (it's not a bad idea to maintain a directory specifically for Unreal reference projects), and select your most recent engine version. Hit **Create** to create the project. The project will launch automatically after you've created it, and later on you can access it from the **My Projects** section of the **Library** tab. Let's allow the project to launch, or launch it specifically from your **Library** tab once it's been created:

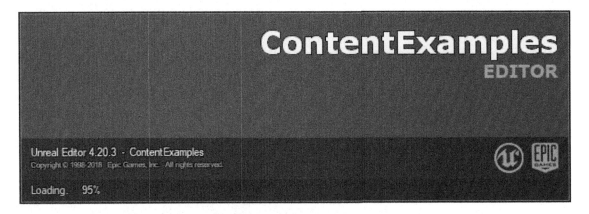

When launching a project, note the Unreal Editor version number and the Loading progress.

It's natural for the project to take a little while to initialize the first time you launch it. Unreal is building assets for your machine. If it appears to be hung up for a few minutes at 45% or 95%, don't worry—it isn't. It's building animations, shaders, and other assets. Subsequent launches will go much faster.

Once the project has opened, hit **File** | **Open Level** (or *Ctrl + O*) to open one of the demo maps. Hit the **Play** button, and use standard **WASD** keyboard controls to move around and look at examples:

One of the demo levels contained within the Content Examples project

Take some time to poke around this project to familiarize yourself with the editor, and get a sense of what Unreal can do. Later on, when you want to include something in your project, make it a habit to check to see whether there's an example in Content Examples that can give you a head-start on figuring out how it's done.

Seriously, this is one of the most useful and often overlooked resources available to you. There's a ton of good stuff in the Content Examples project.

Gameplay concepts and example games

At the bottom of the **Learn** page is a series of projects illustrating specific gameplay concepts and a series of example games. These are incredibly valuable resources for learning more advanced topics and for learning what finished projects in Unreal Engine look like. The content of these projects tends to be more advanced, however, as these mostly represent finished games in a releasable state. You may want to spend some time in the engine before you download them and start to explore. For now, you should know that they're there. Feel free to dig around if you're curious and want to look ahead.

Marketplace

We're going to make use of free assets from **Marketplace** in this book, so you should take some time to look at this tab:

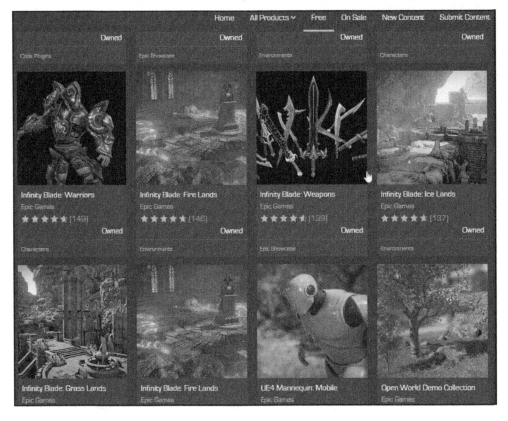

Marketplace content as of Unreal 4.20

Epic provides an astonishing amount of high-quality free material in the **Marketplace**. Often, if Epic cancels a game that it was developing internally, it'll make the game assets available for free on the **Marketplace**. Make use of this, especially when building your learning projects. Assets from *Infinity Blade* are especially useful for projects in VR, as they were originally intended for a mobile game, so they're optimized reasonably well for VR's stringent demands. We'll see how to add **Marketplace** content to existing projects as we start building in the next chapters. Don't ignore the paid material on the **Marketplace** either. Much of it is excellent, and it can give you a huge leg-up in building your projects, whether you use it for prototype, or in your released title.

Library

The **Library** tab is where you maintain your installed engine versions, open your projects, and access your vault of plugins and content packs that you downloaded from the **Learn** tab and **Marketplace**:

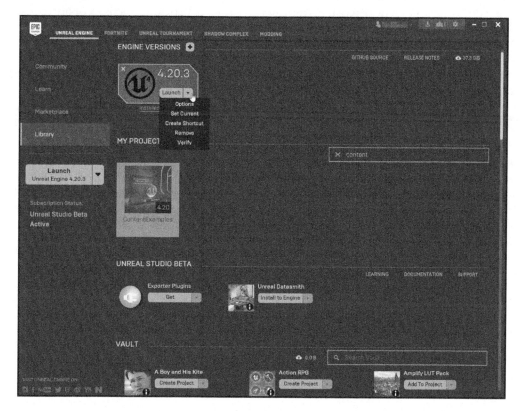

The Library panel as of Unreal 4.20

Use the **ENGINE VERSIONS** section to update your installed engine versions, install new engine versions, and modify their options.

A quick word about engine versions: If you see an indicator appear on an installed engine version indicating that it can be updated, you should update it. Updates to engine releases, such as going from 4.20.2 to 4.20.3, are generally safe to apply, as they involve bug fixes but don't change the way anything works in ways that could break your project.

In addition to updating your currently installed engine version, you can also use the **+** sign beside the **ENGINE VERSIONS** label to add additional installed versions. This allows you to install older versions if you need to open older content that hasn't yet been updated to the current version, or to install preview versions if you'd like to test something that's coming in the next release.

Use caution when working in preview versions. They're intended to allow you to look ahead, but they aren't guaranteed to be stable. Don't put mission-critical work on a preview version. Work in release versions, and use previews to see what's coming or to see how you might need to update your project when you move to the new version.

The **My Projects** section allows you to launch your projects. Project thumbnails are marked with the engine version number for which they're currently set up. You can update a project to a new engine version by launching the newer version, and then opening that project into the newer version. When you do this, you'll be presented with a dialog asking whether you'd like to copy the project or convert it in-place. Converting in place is dangerous; it's recommended that you perform your updates on a copy to be sure nothing in your project conflicts with the update. (That's why the option to convert in-place is buried under the **More Options...** link.) If you have a really old project that's a few versions behind, you're generally going to have better luck converting it a version at a time than trying to jump a few versions. It can work, but whether it does will depend entirely on how many versions you're trying to skip and what's in your project:

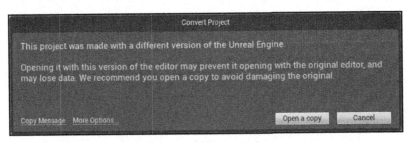

The Convert Project dialog gives you a few options to determine how you want to handle an engine update.

You don't have to launch your projects using the Epic Games Launcher; you can always navigate to where you saved the project and double-click the `.uproject` file directly to launch it in its associated engine version.

The **Vault** section contains everything you own—learning projects, plugins, and content packs. You can add plugins or content to existing projects and create new projects here.

Most of the time, the **Library** tab will be your default tab, since you'll be using it to launch projects, but as we mentioned a moment ago, don't forget about the others.

Setting up for C++ development

This section is entirely optional. None of the projects in this book will require you to develop in C++, but we will occasionally highlight items in native code for those interested in going deeper. If you don't anticipate working in code, or if pages of code give you the screaming heebie-jeebies, it's completely fine to jump over this section and the one that follows it.

 It's absolutely not required to use C++ when developing in Unreal. The Blueprint visual scripting language is incredibly expressive, and there isn't much that it can't do. Most applications, including pretty advanced projects, can be built entirely in Blueprint. Many new Unreal users see the C++ support and worry that they'll have to learn the language to use the engine. You don't. (If you are interested in learning C++ though, this can be a great way to do it.)

Still here? Excellent. The first thing you'll need if you plan to develop in C++ is an editor and compiler with which to build your code. This type of application is called an **Integrated Development Environment (IDE)**. For development in Unreal 4.20 and beyond in Windows, you should be using Microsoft's **Visual Studio 2017 (VS2017)**. Visual Studio comes in several flavors, but for development in Unreal, you don't need any of the professional or Enterprise edition features. The free Community edition has everything you need.

Installing Microsoft Visual Studio Community

Head to the **Microsoft Visual Studio Community** page, `https://visualstudio.microsoft.com/vs/community/`, to download the installer. When you run the installer, you'll be presented with a few options:

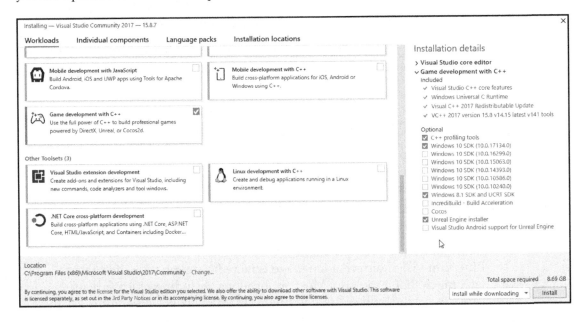

The Visual Studio Community 2017 Setup dialog determines which languages and development tasks your installation will be configured to handle.

Under the **Workloads** tab, select **Game development with C++**, and then on the **Summary** sidebar on the right, make sure you've checked the following:

- **Unreal Engine installer** (required)
- **Windows 10 SDK** (required—should already be checked by default)
- **Windows 8.1 SDK** (required on VS 2017—should already be checked by default)
- **C++ profiling tools** (optional but useful)

If you're going to be developing for Samsung Gear or Oculus Go, make sure you also include this:

- **Android support for Unreal Engine** (required for Gear or Go development)

This installs the Java development kit and the Android tools you're going to need to talk to the Gear and the Go:

∨ Game development with C++ *
  Included
    ✓ Visual Studio C++ core features
    ✓ Windows Universal C Runtime
    ✓ Visual C++ 2017 Redistributable Update
    ✓ VC++ 2017 version 15.8 v14.15 latest v141 tools

  Optional
    ☑ C++ profiling tools
    ☑ Windows 10 SDK (10.0.17134.0)
    ☐ Windows 10 SDK (10.0.16299.0)
    ☐ Windows 10 SDK (10.0.15063.0)
    ☐ Windows 10 SDK (10.0.14393.0)
    ☐ Windows 10 SDK (10.0.10586.0)
    ☐ Windows 10 SDK (10.0.10240.0)
    ☑ Windows 8.1 SDK and UCRT SDK
    ☐ IncrediBuild - Build Acceleration
    ☐ Cocos
    ☑ Unreal Engine installer
    ☑ Visual Studio Android support for Unreal Engine
∨ Individual components
    ☑ Just-In-Time debugger

The Visual Studio 2017 Installation details panel allows you to determine which options are installed.

By setting these options, you've told Visual Studio to include C++ language support, and to include the necessary supporting files to run and develop for Unreal.

These settings are important. Visual Studio 2017 no longer automatically assumes that you're going to be developing in C++, so you need to select which languages you want it to support when you install it. If you realize later on that you missed something, use your **Add and Remove Programs** control panel to modify your VS2017 installation options.

Recommended settings

There are a few things you'll want to change in Visual Studio before you start working. These aren't required, but do make it play more nicely with Unreal. They're documented in depth here: `https://docs.unrealengine.com/en-us/Programming/Development/VisualStudioSetup`. Run through this page and make the recommended changes.

Here's a quick overview of the changes the page is going to ask you to make:

- Increase the width of the **Solution Configurations** control on the **Standard** toolbar because Unreal solution configuration names can be too long to read otherwise.
- Ensure that the **Solution Platforms** control is shown on the **Standard** toolbar. It should already be by default.
- Ensure that **Tools | Options | Projects and Solutions | Always show Error List if build finishes with error** is turned off.
- Set **Tools | Options | Text Editor | C/C++ | View | Show Inactive Blocks** to False.
- Ensure that your **Intellisense** options under **Tools | Options | Text Editor | C/C++ | Advanced** are not disabled. Older instructions would have told you to disable **Intellisense**, as it used to work poorly with Unreal's source code. This is no longer the case, and instructions that tell you to turn it off are now out of date. If you turned **Intellisense** off in the past, turn it back on now.

The UnrealVS plugin

Now that you have Unreal Engine installed and Visual Studio set up, we're going to want to install the UnrealVS plugin to Visual Studio in order, to simplify a number of common tasks you'll be performing in Visual Studio while working with Unreal.

Installing the UnrealVS plugin

Make sure Visual Studio is closed, and navigate to the location where you installed your current Unreal Engine version, and under `Engine\Extras`, find the `UnrealVS` directory. Open the directory corresponding to your version of Visual Studio (in our case, this is VS2017), and run the `UnrealVS.vsix` installer to install the plugin.

 For Unreal 4.20, install it in the standard location. For example, you'll find the plugin here:
`C:\Program Files\Epic Games\UE_4.20\Engine\Extras\UnrealVS\VS2017`.

Turning on the UnrealVS toolbar

Once you've finished running the plugin installer, open Visual Studio, and right-click an empty area of the toolbar to set your active toolbars. Turn on the `UnrealVS` toolbar:

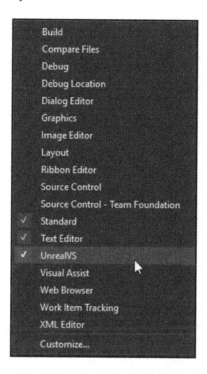

Right-clicking an empty toolbar area in Visual Studio 2017 allows you to select which toolbars are visible.

There's additional documentation on configuring and using UnrealVS here: `https://docs.unrealengine.com/en-us/Programming/Development/VisualStudioSetup/UnrealVS`. By installing it and turning on the toolbar, you've done everything you need to get it running, but it's worthwhile to take a look at this page to get a sense of what UnrealVS does for you and how you can use it.

Unreal debugging support

There's one more thing we need to do before we're ready to go, and that is to install a debugging support file for Unreal in Visual Studio.

Navigate to your engine install directory and find
`Engine\Extras\VisualStudioDebugging`. Look for the `UE4.natvis` file there and copy
it.

Paste it into one of two locations.

You can either install it to your Visual Studio install location, in the following path (you'll
need admin rights on your machine to do this):

- `[VisualStudioInstallPath]\Common7\Packages\Debugger\Visualizers\UE4.natvis`
- **Example:** `C:\Program Files (x86)\Microsoft Visual Studio\2017\Community\Common7\Packages\Debugger\Visualizers`

Alternatively, you can install it to your personal `Documents` directory. If you check within
your user profile's `Documents` directory, you should find a Visual Studio 2017 directory
that was automatically created for you when you installed the IDE. If a visualizers
subdirectory already exists inside this directory, paste `UE4.natvis` inside it. If not, create
the directory and put the natvis file there:

- `[UserProfile]\Documents\Visual Studio 2017/Visualizers/UE4.natvis`
- **Example:** `D:\OneDrive\Documents\Visual Studio 2017\Visualizers`

A `.natvis` file contains instructions to help Visual Studio display the
contents of native data types defined within your particular solution.
Unreal defines its own custom string type (`FString`), custom array types
(`TArray`) and many others. `UE4.natvis` tells Visual Studio how to
display the data contained within these types in a readable way when
you're debugging.

Test everything out

Now, we're ready to verify that we've set everything up correctly. From the Epic Games
launcher, launch your current engine version. Under the **New Project** tab, select **C++**.

If you see a warning such as the following, make sure you've installed Visual Studio 2017,
and that you installed it with the game development with C++, and the recommended
settings were selected:

! No compiler was found. In order to use a C++ template, you must first install Visual Studio 2017.   Install Visual Studio 2017

If you see this warning, you either haven't yet installed Visual Studio, or haven't set up the required installation options.

If you've installed VS2017 and you do see a warning, it means you're missing one of the required options we just mentioned. Use your **Add and Remove Programs** control panel to modify your VS2017 install and add these options.

If you don't see any warnings, you're ready to create a quick test project. Let's select a **Basic Code** template under the **C++** tab, with the default options, and choose a location and name for it:

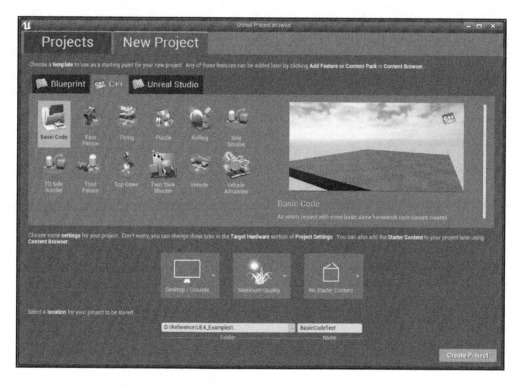

Creating a C++ project works similarly to creating a Blueprint project.

Hit **Create Project**, and allow the tool to create a new project for you. Give it a moment. If you've set everything up correctly, Unreal Editor should open your newly created project, and Visual Studio 2017 should open to the newly created project solution file. Let's close the Unreal Editor now and build and launch the new project from VS2017 just to see how this is done.

In the **Solution Explorer** tab in Visual Studio, find your new project solution under the **Games** tree. Right-click it and select **Set as Startup Project**:

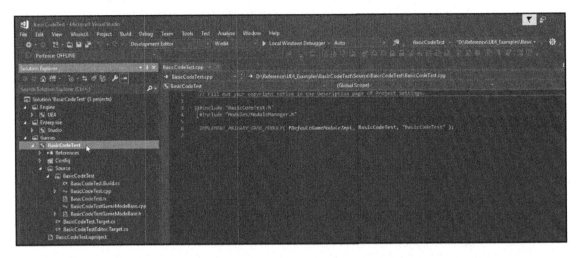

The Solution Explorer on the left side shows you what files are contained in your project. The Workspace on the right shows the contents of the currently-loaded file.

Right-click it again, and select **UnrealVS Quick Build | Win64 | DebugGame Editor**. Your project should begin building.

There are two solution configurations you'll commonly use when developing for Unreal in C++: **DebugGame Editor** and **Development Editor**. Visual Studio is what's called an **optimizing compiler**, which means that it modifies your code somewhat when it compiles it to make it run faster. This has the advantage of letting you write easily readable code that still runs quickly after it's been compiled, but what this means in practice is that if you debug a development build, not every bit of data will be visible, because some variables will have been optimized out.

A debug build leaves everything as you wrote it, so it runs a little more slowly, but you can see exactly what each variable contains. Most of the time, you'll want to use the Development Editor configuration.

You'll see that in addition to DebugGame Editor and Development Editor, you also have DebugGame and Development configurations available. You won't use these when working in the editor; they don't include the editor and require your content to be cooked into a release-ready format. (We'll talk about cooking later on.)

For this example, we selected a **DebugGame Editor** configuration so you'd have a chance to see the compiler build a configuration that hadn't been built yet.

Once your project has finished building, check your output. If it looks something like this, you're good to go:

```
1>Deploying BasicCodeTestEditor Win64 DebugGame...
1>Total build time: 45.92 seconds (Parallel executor: 27.81 seconds)
1>Done building project "BasicCodeTest.vcxproj".
========== Build: 1 succeeded, 0 failed, 0 up-to-date, 0 skipped ==========
```

Now, on your standard toolbar, use the **Solution Configurations** control to select the debug editor configuration you just built:

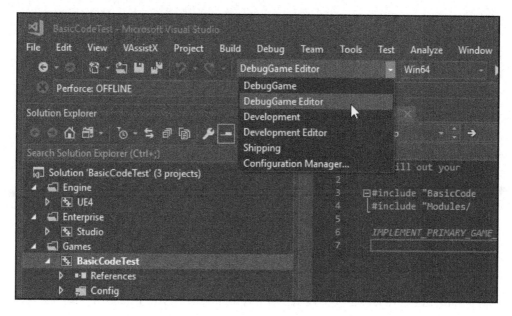

The Solution Configurations control determines what type of build you're going to create.

Hit *F5*, or select **Debug | Start Debugging**, to launch the editor from Visual Studio. If everything is set up correctly, your project should launch, and your Visual Studio window should look something like this:

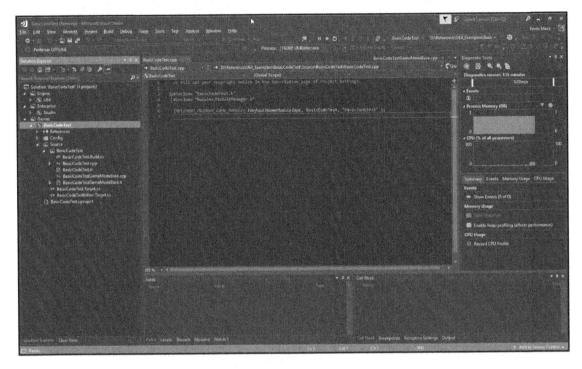

An Unreal C++ project loaded in Visual Studio Community 2017. The orange bar at the bottom indicates that the project is running and Visual Studio's debugger is connected to it.

Congratulations! You're now set up to develop in C++.

Let's take a look at a quick example of why this can be so useful. In the default scene that was automatically created in your Unreal Editor, select **Floor** from your **World Outliner**. Right-click it:

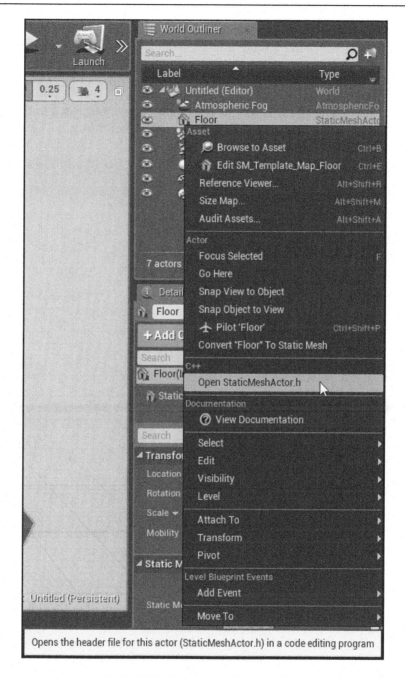

You can open C++ files directly from within the Unreal Editor.

The floor is a Static Mesh actor. Select the option to open `StaticMeshActor.h`. You'll be switched automatically to Visual Studio, and the `StaticMeshActor` header file will be opened:

If you're not able to open `StaticMeshActor.h`, check to be sure you installed the engine source for your engine version. Head to the **Library** tab, find the engine version you're running under **Engine Versions**, and select **Options** from the drop-down to the right of the **Launch** button. Add **Engine Source** if you hadn't already.

```cpp
// Copyright 1998-2018 Epic Games, Inc. All Rights Reserved.

#pragma once

#include "CoreMinimal.h"
#include "UObject/ObjectMacros.h"
#include "GameFramework/Actor.h"
#include "AI/Navigation/NavigationTypes.h"
#include "StaticMeshActor.generated.h"

/**
 * StaticMeshActor is an instance of a UStaticMesh in the world.
 * Static meshes are geometry that do not animate or otherwise deform, and are more efficient to render than other
 * Static meshes dragged into the level from the Content Browser are automatically converted to StaticMeshActors.
 *
 * @see https://docs.unrealengine.com/latest/INT/Engine/Actors/StaticMeshActor/
 * @see UStaticMesh
 */
UCLASS(hidecategories=(Input), showcategories=("Input|MouseInput", "Input|TouchInput"), ConversionRoot, ComponentWr
class ENGINE_API AStaticMeshActor : public AActor
{
    GENERATED_UCLASS_BODY()

private:
    UPROPERTY(Category = StaticMeshActor, VisibleAnywhere, BlueprintReadOnly, meta = (ExposeFunctionCategories = "M
    class UStaticMeshComponent* StaticMeshComponent;

protected:
    virtual void BeginPlay() override;

public:
```

The C++ header file for the StaticMeshActor class describes the class and declares its functions.

This is one of the many amazing things about Unreal Engine—Epic gives you the source code—all of it. For any object, any Blueprint node, anything at all in the editor, you can view the source code underneath. There are no black boxes. Again, this is by no means a thing you have to do in Unreal—the documentation is excellent, but if you're ever facing a mystery and really need to figure out what's going on, being able to read the source code can be a lifesaver.

Building Unreal from source code

You absolutely do not need to download source code and build the engine from scratch for almost anything you'll realistically be doing with it. This section is included here so that you have the freedom to make engine changes if you ever need to, but you can safely skip this. It's rare even for professional developers to work from the bleeding edge source.

This next section is even more optional than the previous. You'll only ever need to do this if you intend to modify the behavior of the engine itself, or if you want to work with a feature that's so new that it hasn't yet been bundled into one of the releases. That's another part of the beauty of this engine though—if you really need it to do something it doesn't already do, you can make the changes yourself. Also, if you make changes that improve the engine or might be useful to other developers, you can use GitHub to contribute your changes to Epic. Lots of developers do, and the net effect of it is that this engine grows and improves at an astonishing pace.

For real though, you can skip this if you don't anticipate needing it. We're going to get a little into the weeds here.

Setting up a GitHub account and installing Git

The source code for the Unreal engine is distributed using a site called **GitHub**. **Git** is a version-control system (a system for managing code revisions and distributing them to users), and GitHub is a centralized location for housing and sharing Git repositories. To download the Unreal Engine source code in a format that allows you to build the engine yourself, you'll need Git and GitHub.

Lots of people confuse Git with GitHub. They're not the same thing. Git is a version control system that allows users to track changes to code, distribute those changes, and manage them in many other ways. GitHub is a website that allows users to store and share Git data. There are other sites that also allow you to do this, though GitHub is the largest, or you could set up a Git repository entirely on your own.

Setting up or logging into your GitHub account

If you do plan to dig into the absolute bleeding edge of Unreal development, the first thing you're going to need is a **GitHub** account. Head to https://github.com/ and sign in, or sign up if you don't already have an account.

Installing Git for Windows

Head to `https://git-scm.com/` and download Git for Windows. Git is a software configuration management tool, which allows you to synchronize your local Unreal source code repository with the source code Epic supplies.

Install it using the default options, with one exception: when the installer asks what you'd like to use as your default editor for Git, the currently selected choice will be **Vim**. Vim is wonderful for those who have gotten used to using it, but for everyone else, it can be pretty counter-intuitive because it follows a completely different set of conventions from pretty much any other application you've used. You'll almost certainly want to select a different text editor if you aren't already one of those people who uses and loves Vim:

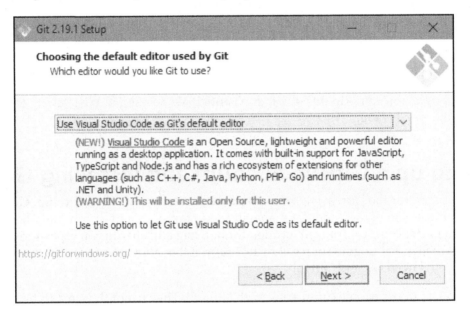

You can choose your preferred text editor as Git's default editor when you set Git up.

It's a good idea to have a robust text editor on your system anyway, as it can be useful for editing config files and a ton of other tasks. Common choices are **Visual Studio Code**, **Sublime Text**, **Notepad++**, or **Atom**. If you have a favorite, feel free to use it. If you don't, Visual Studio Code is a good choice, as it's free and follows the same conventions as Visual Studio. If you need it, grab it here: `https://code.visualstudio.com/`.

Installing Git Large File Storage

Next, you're going to need to install **Git Large File Storage (Git-LFS)**. This allows Git to manage big binary files such as the ones Unreal generates.

Head to `https://git-lfs.github.com/`, download Git-LFS, and install it.

Now, you need to configure Git to use Git-LFS. To do this, do the following:

1. Open Git Bash—a command-line tool for managing Git, which was installed a moment ago when you installed Git for Windows. In Git Bash, type `git lfs install` and hit *Enter:*

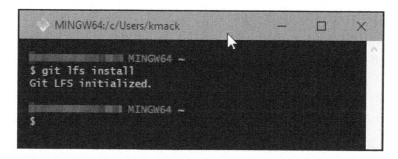

Git Bash is a terminal window specifically used to communicate with Git.

Once you see that Git LFS has been initialized, you can close Git Bash.

Installing a Git GUI

It's not required that you use a GUI to operate Git. Many developers operate Git directly from the command line instead. Certain Git operations are easier to perform this way. The following instructions apply if you'd like to use a GUI for Git.

Head to `https://desktop.github.com/` and download **GitHub Desktop**. There are many other Git GUI applications out there; another popular choice is **Atlassian's SourceTree**, which you can find at `https://www.sourcetreeapp.com/`, but for simplicity's sake for now, we're going to stick with GitHub Desktop. During the installation, the installer will ask you for credentials for the GitHub account you just created. Enter them here.

Once you've finished installing, GitHub Desktop should start up, and you should be looking at a window that looks something like this:

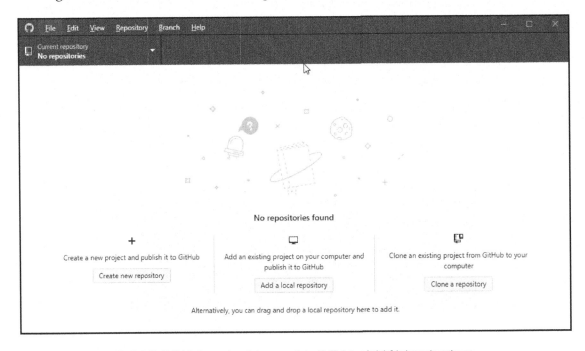

Git GUI's like GitHub Desktop aren't required to communicate with Git, but can be helpful when you're staring out.

Connecting your GitHub account to your Epic Games account

Navigate to `https://www.unrealengine.com` and if you're not logged in yet, log in now. Find your username in the lower-left corner of the page, and hover over it to reveal the drop-down menu. Select the **Manage Account** option:

The account management link as of Unreal 4.22. This opens a browser window to https://www.unrealengine.com/account/personal

Be aware that menus in the Epic Games Launcher change frequently. You can also handle this step by navigating to `https://www.unrealengine.com/account/personal`. Open the **Connected Accounts** tab, find the GitHub icon, and hit **Connect** to connect your Epic account to GitHub. Agree to the EULA if you need to, and sign into GitHub if it asks you to do so. Finally, if the authorization utility asks, click the **Authorize Epic Games** button. You should receive an email confirming that you've done this. If you need further help or if something goes wrong, check the documentation at `https://www.unrealengine.com/en-US/ue4-on-github`.

Confirm that everything is set up correctly by navigating to `https://github.com/EpicGames/UnrealEngine`. If you're able to see the page, you're properly connected. If not, ensure that you've properly connected your account and been authorized to see the UnrealEngine repository.

A word about Git: Git is a phenomenally useful tool, but the work it does can seem fairly complex at first. Detailing all the things you should know about Git falls outside the scope of this book, but we highly recommend that you spend some time to learn what Git is and how it works if you plan to use it. This is a good place to start: `https://git-scm.com/book/en/v2/Getting-Started-Git-Basics`. To understand how GitHub works with Git, start here: `https://guides.github.com/activities/hello-world/`.

Downloading the Unreal Engine source code

Now, you're ready to pull the source. Let's look at how to do this. Navigate to `https://github.com/EpicGames/UnrealEngine`, and take a look around the page. There's a `ReadMe` file on this page as well. It's highly recommended that you read it.

Choosing your source branch

Note that Epic maintains multiple branches of the Unreal Engine repository:

- The **release** branch contains tested source code and is equivalent to the source code you get by downloading the engine using the Epic Games launcher.
- The **promoted** branch contains less-tested code that's used internally by Epic's designers and artists. It's fairly stable and will contain newer, but also less stable, code than that on the **release** branch.
- The **master** branch is the absolute bleeding edge, and contains changes more-or-less the moment Epic's engineers submit them. There's no guarantee that these changes will be stable though, or even compile. If you plan to contribute to the engine though, you should be on this branch:

This view of the Epic Games / UnrealEngine GitHub repository allows you to choose your current branch and download its contents.

For now, let's stick with the **release** branch. Select it using the **Branch** drop-down near the upper-left corner.

Forking the repository

We're going to **Fork** this repository. Forking a Git repository makes a copy of it that allows you to make your own changes without impacting the main repository. Hit the **Fork** button near the upper-right. This will create a personal repository for you containing the source code you just forked.

Cloning the repository to your local machine

Now, you need to get it onto your desktop. Hit the green **Clone or download** button on the right-hand side of the page:

When cloning a repository, you have the option to choose your authentication method and how you'd like the content to be delivered.

You have a few options here.

Option 1 – Cloning using GitHub Desktop

If you're using GitHub Desktop as a GUI, select **Open in Desktop** and allow the page to launch GitHub Desktop. GitHub Desktop will ask you where you want to store the new repository. Tell it where to put it and hit **Clone**:

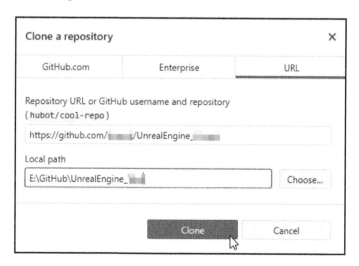

Ensure that the location you choose for your local path has room to hold the engine and its content.

Option 2 – Cloning from the command line

If you're using a command line, hit the **Copy to Clipboard** button to the right of the repository's URL, and then open a Windows Command Prompt and navigate to the directory where you'd like to house your local repository. Once there, type `git clone`, and paste the URL you just copied:

```
git clone https://github.com/yourusername/UnrealEngine_YourFork.git
```

The source code will now be downloaded to the location you specified.

Downloading engine binary content

Navigate to the location where you downloaded the Unreal Engine source just now, and look for the `Setup.bat` file there. Run it:

Unreal Engine content is delivered separately from the source code. You must run this .bat file before the engine can work.

This batch file will now check for engine binary content that's missing or needs to be updated, and will update it. It may take a while the first time you run it.

Generating project files

Next, find `GenerateProjectFiles.bat` in the same directory and run it. This will create the `UE4.sln` solution file for Visual Studio and the required project files for each of Unreal Engine's sub-projects. This should run fairly quickly.

Opening and building the solution

Open the newly generated `UE4.sln` file in Visual Studio. Ensure that the **Development Editor** solution configuration is set, and right-click the `Engine/UE4` project from your **Solution Explorer**. Select **UnrealVS Quick Build | Win64 | Development Editor**:

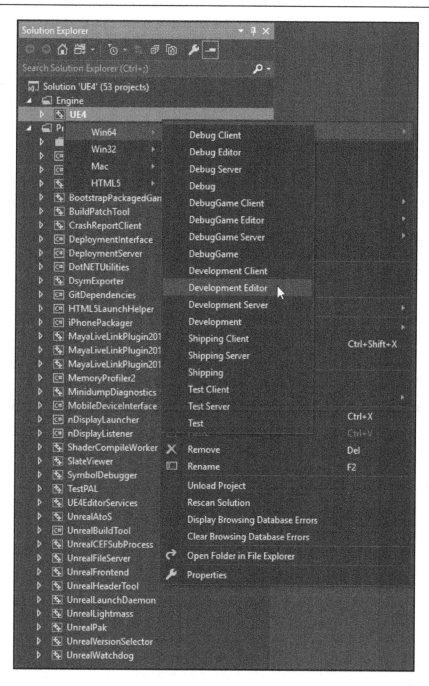

The Quick Build command allows you to select the build configuration you'd like to build. Most of the time, you'll only be interested in Development Editor or Debug Editor configurations.

This build is going to take much longer than the build we ran earlier, as we're now building the entire engine, not just a game.

Once the build completes, ensure that UE4 is set as the startup project (it should be by default), and hit *F5* to launch it in the debugger.

Congratulations! You've now downloaded and built Unreal Engine entirely from source.

Updating your fork with new changes from Epic

Epic will soon release new changes that aren't yet present in your fork. How soon will depend on the branch you're on. If you're on the **release** branch, new changes will come every few weeks. On the **promoted** branch, they will come every day or two. On the **master** branch, they will come every few minutes. In all these cases, you'll need to update your fork to get the new changes.

You can see when new changes need to be merged by looking at the bar below the **Branch** selector. It indicates how many commits have occurred since you last updated your fork:

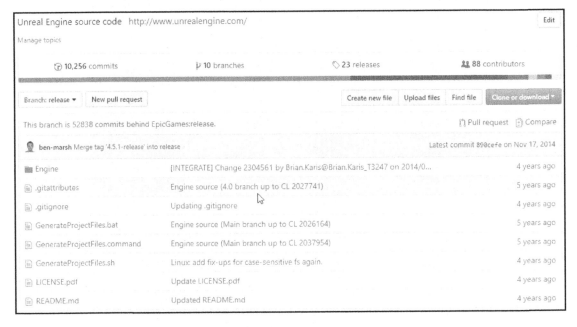

Here's an example of an ancient branch, far behind the current state of the release channel. We can see that it's over 52,000 changes behind. That's old. Dinosaurs roamed the earth when this code was last updated. We'll want to fix that.

Option – Using the command line to sync changes

Keeping your fork up-to-date with changes from the upstream branch is one of those operations that really is easier to do from the command line. We recommend that you do it this way. Let's talk you through the process.

Setting the upstream repository

We've already forked our own repository from the Unreal Engine source repository, and we've cloned it to our local machine. Now, we need to tell our fork how to pull changes from the original project (which we'll call the **upstream** repository). You only need to do this once. In GitHub, open the original Unreal Engine repository page, `https://github. com/EpicGames/UnrealEngine`, and hit the green **Clone or download** button, and then hit the **Copy to Clipboard** button to the right of the URL. Don't open it in desktop or download the ZIP. All you need here is the URL.

Open a Windows Command Prompt (note that you can also use Git Bash for this if you're comfortable with UNIX commands, and if you're going to be using Git heavily, it's recommended that you do), and navigate to the directory where you've cloned your repository. Type `git remote -v` and press *Enter*. You should see your origin repository listed here, but no upstream repository. That's what we're going to set up next:

```
E:\GitHub\UnrealEngine_    >git remote -v
origin  https://github.com/    /UnrealEngine_    .git (fetch)
origin  https://github.com/    /UnrealEngine_    .git (push)
```

The results of a git remote -v command before you've added your upstream repository

Now, type `git remote add upstream` and paste the URL you copied a moment ago:

```
git remote add upstream https://github.com/EpicGames/UnrealEngine.git
```

And let's verify that the upstream repo was properly set up by typing `git remote -v` again:

```
E:\GitHub\UnrealEngine_    >git remote -v
origin    https://github.com/    /UnrealEngine_    .git (fetch)
origin    https://github.com/    /UnrealEngine_    .git (push)
upstream         https://github.com/EpicGames/UnrealEngine.git (fetch)
upstream         https://github.com/EpicGames/UnrealEngine.git (push)
```

The results of a git remote -v command after you've added your upstream repository

Everything looks good—our upstream repo has been set.

For more information on forking a repo and preparing it to pull changes from the upstream depot, have a look at GitHub's documentation here: https://help.github.com/articles/fork-a-repo/.

Syncing the fork

From a command prompt or Git Bash within our repository directory, type `git fetch upstream`:

```
E:\GitHub\UnrealEngine_    >git fetch upstream
remote: Enumerating objects: 16314, done.
remote: Counting objects: 100% (16314/16314), done.
remote: Compressing objects: 100% (3/3), done.
remote: Total 30468 (delta 16311), reused 16314 (delta 16311), pack-reused 14154
Receiving objects: 100% (30468/30468), 47.96 MiB | 3.65 MiB/s, done.
Resolving deltas: 100% (23053/23053), completed with 5458 local objects.
From https://github.com/EpicGames/UnrealEngine
 * [new branch]          4.0               -> upstream/4.0
```

Output from a git fetch upstream operation

Now, *check out* whichever branch you're working in by typing `git checkout`, and the name of the branch. For example, type `git checkout release`, for the **Release** branch, `git checkout promoted` for the **promoted** branch, and `git checkout master` for the **master** branch.

Next, merge the changes from the upstream branch into your local branch by typing `git merge upstream/`, followed by the name of your branch. Again, if you're on the **release** branch, this would be `git merge upstream/release`.

Finally, you need to push your changes from your local machine back to your fork's repository online. Type `git push origin master` to do this.

Reviewing the Git commands we just used

To recap: any time you need to bring your branch up-to-date with the upstream branch, use the following commands:

- `git fetch upstream`
- `git checkout [branch]`
- `git merge upstream/[branch]`
- `git push origin [branch]`

Refer to the following screenshot:

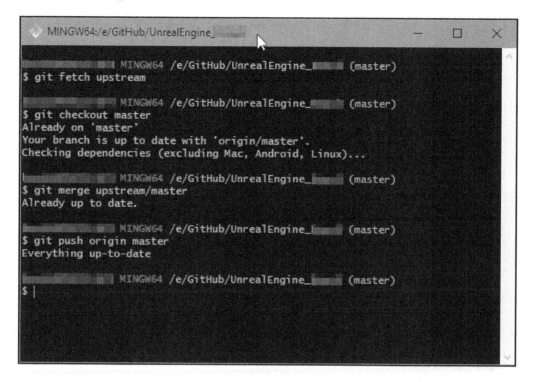

Command outputs in Git Bash.

Option – Using the web GUI to sync changes

If you'd prefer to sync your fork online rather than by using the command line, follow this procedure.

If you're using the command-line procedure for synchronizing your fork, you can skip this part, since it does the same job.

Navigate to your fork's page on GitHub, and hit the **Compare** button on the right-hand side of the bar. If you've made changes locally, they'll appear in the **Compare** window that follows. (Let's assume for simplicity's sake that we haven't, and that we're just trying to get new code from Epic.) To do this, first, hit the **switching the base** link on the comparison page. This will reverse the comparison, so instead of looking for changes on our local fork that haven't gone to Epic, we'll look for changes made by other developers that aren't yet present in our fork:

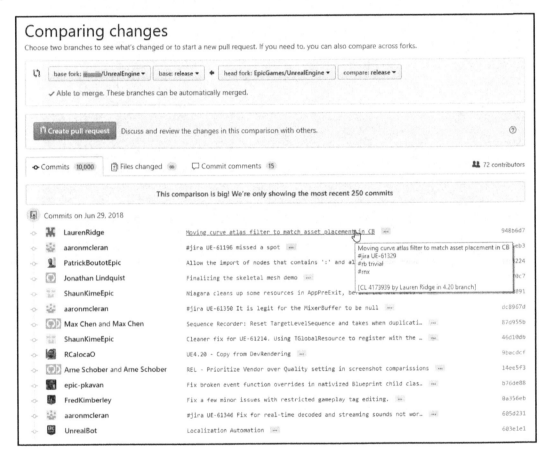

A list of changes on GitHub that haven't yet been merged to your fork

Here, we can see that the new changes can be merged automatically. This is expected because we haven't made any engine changes of our own. (Managing merged changes between your own Unreal Engine fork and Epic's branches is beyond the scope of this book.) In our case, we just want to get up to date.

Creating a pull request

Hit the **Create pull request** button:

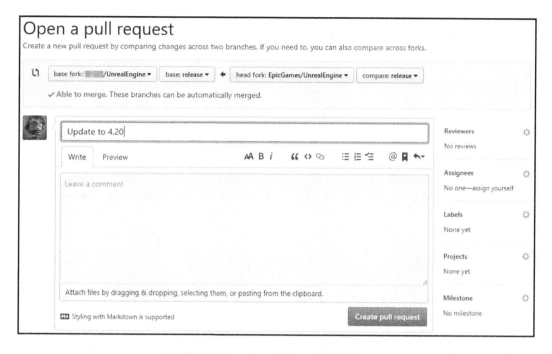

A new pull request to merge changes from the upstream branch to your own

Give your pull request a name, and hit **Create pull request** again to create it.

Your pull request will now be ready for review. In this case, since you initiated it, you can simply accept it:

The pull request confirmation dialog

Merging the pull request

Hit **Merge pull request** to execute the merge and then hit **Confirm merge** to make it happen.

Once the merge is complete, return to your fork, and you should no longer be behind:

Comparison between our branch and the upstream branch. We can see that we're now in-sync.

Pulling the origin to your local machine

Now, you need to update your local copy on your machine.

Head back to GitHub Desktop, and in your Unreal Engine repository, look for the **Fetch origin** button. Hit this to instruct GitHub Desktop to look for changes on the remote repository that you haven't yet copied locally:

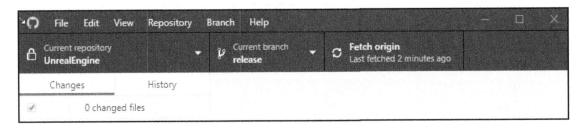

GitHub Desktop before we've fetched the new changes from the repo

In our case, we have a few:

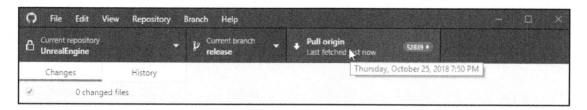

GitHub Desktop ready to pull changes to our local machine

It's time to pull those 52,000 changes down to our local machine. Hit **Pull origin** to do this. GitHub desktop will *check out* the changes, copying them to the local machine. Once this is done, we should see that hitting **Fetch origin** no longer results in any new files to pull—we're current.

Re-synchronizing your engine content and regenerating project files

Regardless of whether you used the command line or a GUI to update your fork, you now need to update your solution file and project files to reflect the new source you've downloaded.

> If you're certain that no source files or assets have been added or removed, you can skip this part. When in doubt, run these operations to make sure your assets are current and that Visual Studio knows about changed files.

With Visual Studio closed, re-run the `Setup.bat` file from your engine directory to update your binary content, and then re-run `GenerateProjectFiles.bat` to update your Visual Studio files. These will run much more quickly than they did the first time, as they're only updating what's changed.

Open the solution, build it, and run it. You should be back in business on the current code.

> Very often, your startup project will change when you regenerate project files. If it does, right-click the project you'd like to launch and select **Set as StartUp Project** to reset it.

Going further with source code on GitHub

There's quite a lot more we could talk about in modifying and building the engine source, but it falls outside the scope of this book. What you've learned here though will allow you to download Epic's most recent Unreal Engine code and build the engine if you need code that's more recent than the current release, or need to modify the engine.

If you do plan to work with Unreal source code from GitHub, it's worthwhile to take the time to learn about it. It's a powerful tool, but it can be mystifying if you're not clear on what it's doing. Help is available here: https://help.github.com/.

Again, most users will not need to do this, but it does sometimes happen that code to support new VR devices appears on the promoted or **master** branches long before it makes it to the **release** branches and the binary release channel through the launcher. You should now know enough to use the latest and greatest, if you ever need to do so.

Additional useful tools

Before we move on from this chapter, let's take a quick moment to talk about other tools you may want to set up to work with Unreal. None of these will be required by the projects in this book, but they're worth knowing about, so you need to know where to look when you need them.

A good robust text editor

Notepad just isn't going to cut it when you need to edit large text files or replace a lot of text in a file. We recommend that you set up a dedicated text editor for this purpose. Here are a few options:

- **Visual Studio Code** (https://code.visualstudio.com/) is a powerful, lightweight text editor that supports lots of languages and contains a number of useful text-editing tools. It's free.
- **Sublime Text** (https://www.sublimetext.com/) is a highly customizable editor with tons of custom integrations for various languages. It is $80, with a free trial.
- **Atom** (https://atom.io/) is a relatively new editor made by GitHub that supports tons of additional package installers for just about anything you could want to do to a text page. Because it's made by GitHub, its Git integration is great. And it's free.

- **Notepad++** (https://notepad-plus-plus.org/) is fast and lightweight and is older than most of the rest, so it has a devoted following. It's free as well.
- **Vim** (https://www.vim.org/download.php) is its own beast. Its user interface conventions bear no resemblance to anything else in Windows, so it takes some significant effort to learn them. Its advantage is that once users learn the keystrokes to operate it, they can navigate through text documents at blazing speed without requiring the use of a mouse. And it runs on nearly anything that computes. We recommend this only if you're already using it and love it or are specifically interested in learning it.

Any of these or any other text editors you know and love will work out fine. Pick one that feels right to you and stick with it.

3D modeling software

Unreal scenes are made of 3D models, and you're going to need to modify them, clean them up, or create them from scratch at various points through your development. (How much you need to do this depends a lot on what you're creating, who you're working with, and the degree to which you're relying on existing art from the marketplace or other sources.) At any rate, it's a good idea to have a tool on your system that can edit 3D meshes.

 You'll commonly hear 3D modeling tools referred to as **Digital Content Creation** tools in the industry, usually shortened to **DCC**. If you hear someone refer to a DCC, they're generally talking about a 3D modeling tool such as Blender, Maya, or 3ds Max.

Here are a few options:

- **Blender** (https://www.blender.org/) is a free and open source 3D modeling program that's heavily used in the independent development community. Lots of tutorials exist to teach you how to create assets in Blender and get them into Unreal. It's free.
- **Autodesk Maya** (https://www.autodesk.com/products/maya/overview) is a professional tool focused on creating content for media and entertainment. Nearly every creature you've ever seen in any movie or game over the past decade was likely modeled and animated in Maya. A Maya subscription costs around $1,500/year, but students are able to use it free for three years.

- **Autodesk 3ds Max** (https://www.autodesk.com/products/3ds-max/overview) is a professional modeling tool focused on creating content for **architecture, engineering and construction** (**AEC**), and product design. It's commonly used in media and entertainment as well, but its animation tools are much more limited than those found in Maya. Pricing for 3ds Max is the same as it is for Maya—around $1,500/year, with a free student license available.
- **Modo** (https://www.foundry.com/products/modo#) is a newer entry to the professional market and is gaining adherents. It's worth a look. A Modo subscription costs $600/year.

The DCC you choose will depend on your budget and what you plan to do with it. Generally, if you're making VR for entertainment, Maya will contain more of what you need, but this is by no means absolute. For architecture and product design, 3ds Max may be what you need. For indie game development, you might be fine with Blender as well. Do some research and find out what's the best fit for your particular needs.

You'll also see a few other tools in your professional travels. You mostly won't see beginners using them, but they're powerful tools and you should know they exist, so you can consider whether they might be a good solution for something you're trying to do:

- **ZBrush** (http://pixologic.com/) is a digital sculpting tool, used for creating highly detailed models and surfaces.
- **Mudbox** (https://www.autodesk.com/products/mudbox/overview), like ZBrush, is a sculpting tool for adding fine detail to models.
- **Houdini** (https://www.sidefx.com/) is a procedural creation tool for 3D geometry and effects. If you need to create a city full of buildings, a forest full of vines, or a churning fireball, Houdini may be what you're looking for.
- **Substance Painter** (https://www.allegorithmic.com/products/substance-painter) is a texture painting tool that allows artists to paint textures directly onto 3D models.
- **Substance Designer** (https://www.allegorithmic.com/products/substance-designer) is a powerful material- authoring tool for creating highly varied and realistic physically-based materials.

These generally are expert and specialist tools, but it's worth knowing they're there and what they do.

Image-editing software

You're often going to need to edit textures and 2D art as well. You'll need a tool with which to do this, and really you have two options you can seriously consider:

- **Adobe Photoshop** (`https://www.adobe.com/products/photoshop.html`) is the standard for 2D image editing. It's worth it. There's a secret to Photoshop's pricing: if you subscribe to it as a standalone app, it costs $20.99 a month, but if you subscribe to the Photography bundle, you get it for $9.99/month instead.
- **GIMP** (`https://www.gimp.org/`) is a free, open source image editing application. It lacks a lot of the functionality of Photoshop, but if you're only occasionally modifying textures, it may be all you need.

Your choice between Photoshop and GIMP will depend on your needs and your budget. If you're working professionally, it's probably best to stick with Photoshop, but if you don't need everything Photoshop does, GIMP might be enough.

Audio-editing software

You're occasionally going to need to edit sounds and music for your games and applications. You have a few options here, too:

- **Audacity** (`https://www.audacityteam.org/`) is a free, open source audio editing solution that's surprisingly good. For much of the sound-editing work you'll need to do, Audacity may be all you need.
- **Adobe Audition** (`https://www.adobe.com/products/audition.html`) is a professional audio-editing tool. Its advantages over Audacity are higher quality effects, and a non-destructive editing workflow, which means that if you apply a filter or effect to your sound, and then want to change it later on, you still can. Audition is available on a monthly subscription, or it can be bundled into an Adobe All Apps subscription.
- **Avid Pro Tools** (`https://www.avid.com/pro-tools`) is the most commonly used audio editing software among professionals, and is available in a free **Pro Tools | First** edition that contains all the features of the professional versions, but limits the number of inputs and audio tracks you can use. Whether this is an appropriate solution for you really depends on how heavily you anticipate editing audio, and what you plan to do with it.

All the options we've mentioned cover sound editing, but for sound creation, there's no shortage of tools and audio libraries available. Cataloging them falls beyond the scope of this book, as sound design is its own art and the rabbit hole goes deep. For most users developing VR applications in Unreal, it's not a bad idea to begin with Audacity, and move on from there when or if you discover you need to do something specific.

Summary

In this chapter, we installed the Unreal Engine and learned about the various options we have available to us when setting it up. We created and launched a simple test project to verify that everything was working. Additionally, for those developing for mobile VR, we learned how to set up the required drivers and software development kits, and set up a mobile test project that we deployed to our device.

Along the way, we learned how to use the Epic Games launcher—not just as a way of keeping engine versions up to date and launching projects, but also as a vital learning and support resource. Through our exploration of the launcher, we learned how to get answers to questions from the **Community** tab and where to find documentation and video tutorials from the **Learn** tab. We explored the incredibly useful Content Examples project and looked at other projects we can use to explore specific topics in the engine. We saw that the **Marketplace** offers a huge range of free and paid content that we can use to accelerate our projects, and we learned how to use the **Library** tab to maintain our projects and engine versions.

For those planning to develop in C++, we learned how to set up our Visual Studio 2017 development environment and configure it to work with Unreal, and then we created a simple test project to ensure that we were able to build and run our own C++ code within Unreal. For the extra adventurous, we learned how to download the Unreal Engine source from GitHub and build the engine entirely from scratch.

Finally, we took a brief look at additional tools that developers may generally find useful when building content for Unreal Engine, including a range of free and paid solutions for various needs.

In the next chapter, we're going to build our first project explicitly for VR. (The quick-and-dirty projects we set up during the course of this chapter allowed us to test that our development environment was properly set up, but they weren't designed specifically for VR.) Now, we're going to learn how to set up a project correctly for VR. Let's jump in!

Hello World - Your First VR Project

3

It's time to start building! Back in Chapter 1, *Thinking in VR*, we learned what VR is and what it can do, and we learned a number of best practices for its design. Then, in Chapter 2, *Setting up Your Development Environment*, we set up our development environment. Now we're ready to start building.

In this chapter, we're going to build a VR project in Unreal from the ground up. We're going to take a different approach, though, from most tutorials. Rather than just give you a list of steps to follow, for each thing we do we're going to talk a bit about what's going on under the hood and why we're doing it this way. This is what's really important. If you understand a bit about how these systems work, you'll be much better equipped to understand what to do when you build your own projects.

As we build our first VR project, we're going to learn a bit about its structure, and we'll learn about the specific project settings that apply most to VR development. We'll also look at those settings and choices that specifically affect mobile VR, and show you what you need to know there. From here, we'll bring a detailed scene into our project and learn a bit about how to move assets safely between projects and how to manage a project's content. Finally, we'll set up the game mode and pawn blueprints we'll need to run a VR project.

This chapter will cover the following:

- Creating a project for VR from scratch
- Understanding important settings and choices you need to make when you start your project
- Setting up a project for mobile VR
- Moving content safely between projects and managing content within your project
- Setting up the basic blueprints you'll need for VR development in Unreal

Creating a new project

All right, let's start creating!

The first thing we need to do is create a new project. We created a few quick throwaway projects in the previous chapter just to make sure everything was working, but now we're ready to begin building for real.

Open your **Epic Games Launcher** if it isn't already open, head to the **Library** tab, and where you see your **Engine Versions**, hit **Launch** on your most current engine version. (You can do this from the **Launch** button on the left side of the launcher as well.)

The **Unreal Project Browser** will appear. Select the **New Project** tab, and let's select the **Blueprint** tab and the **Blank** template to create an empty Blueprint project.

Templates are very useful starting points for Unreal projects. They contain simple and useful working foundations of many game types, and much of the time when you're starting a new project, you'll want to use them. We're beginning with a blank project here so you can see each element as it goes in. You'll probably most commonly use the First Person, Third Person, and VR templates as starting points for most projects.

We have a few more choices to make on this dialog, and we should understand what they mean:

Setting your hardware target

The **Hardware Target** selector gives you two options:

- **Desktop / Console**
- **Mobile / Tablet**

Ordinarily, you should choose the correct option for your target platform, but when developing for VR, it can be a good idea to select the **Mobile / Tablet** option even if you're developing for desktop, as that option will turn off a few rendering options that can be expensive in VR.

Specifically, choosing the mobile target rather than the desktop target will turn off the following rendering options:

- **Separate Translucency**
- **Bloom**
- **Ambient Occlusion**

Setting your graphics target

The next choice you need to make is your **Graphics Target**. Again, you have two choices here:

- **Maximum Quality**
- **Scalable 3D or 2D**

Selecting **Maximum Quality** will turn on all of the default high-end rendering options Unreal Engine offers. As we've mentioned previously, however, in VR, meeting your target framerate is far more important than including detail in your scene. For VR development, it's always a good idea to select the **Scalable** option.

You're better off beginning with everything turned off and turning things on as you need them. If you start the other way, with everything turned on, it can be difficult to figure out what's killing your framerate and figure out what you need to turn off. It's a much better practice to start with your project running at a reasonable speed and keep it running quickly than to build something that runs poorly and hope that you're somehow going to get it running faster later on.

Settings summary

For our project, we're going to go with the following:

- Project Template: **Blueprint - Blank**
- Hardware Target: **Mobile / Tablet**
- Graphics Target: **Scalable 2D or 3D**
- **No Starter Content**

We can leave the **Starter Content** turned off for now, since we can easily add that stuff later when we need it.

Choose where you'd like to save your project and hit **Create Project** to set it up.

Taking a quick look at your project's structure

We've now created an empty project. Let's take a brief moment to take a look at what that actually means.

If you navigate Windows Explorer to the location where you saved your project, you'll see that Unreal has created a file there with your project's name and the .uproject extension, along with four directories:

- **Config**: Configuration files such as DefaultEngine.ini and DefaultGame.ini live here and hold settings for your engine and project.
- **Content**: This is where your project's assets, such as models, textures, materials, and blueprints will live. This is the bulk of your project.
- **Intermediate**: Temporary files created when your project's assets are compiled go here. Everything in here is temporary and will be regenerated if you delete it.
- **Saved**: Log files, screenshots, and save games land in this directory.

If you've generated a C++ project, you'll see three additional directories:

- **Binaries**: Your project's built executable and supporting files live here. When you build your project in Visual Studio, this is where the resulting executable is saved.
- **Build**: Files related to building for specific targets, such as Windows 64 or Android, live here. These include logs are generated as you build, and certain supporting resources such as application icons. You'll rarely touch the contents of this directory.
- **Source**: Your C++ files and the C# scripts that govern building them live here.

The Content directory

For the most part, when you work with an Unreal project, you'll be working with the contents of the Content directory and the Config directory. Generally, you should do all your management of the Content directory from within Unreal Editor, since it can otherwise be easy to break references between objects. We'll talk about ways to do this shortly.

The Config directory

We should, however, take a moment to look at the `Config` directory.

Inside this directory are the config files containing the settings for your project. All of your engine-related project settings, such as choices about rendering quality, are written to the `DefaultEngine.ini` file. When you chose your hardware and graphic targets in the Create Project dialog, you were actually just choosing which default options to write to that file. Similarly, when you change your project settings from the editor, those settings are also written to `DefaultEngine.ini` (or `DefaultGame.ini` for certain game-related settings.)

Your `Config` directory will always contain the following two files:

- `DefaultEngine.ini`: This contains your rendering settings, startup map setting, physics settings, and other options that govern how the engine runs.
- `DefaultGame.ini`: This, for the most part, contains information about your game and copyright information, but it also holds information about how your application will be packaged when you prepare it for release on different platforms

When you make changes to your project settings from within the editor, you're mostly writing changes to these two files.

Other `Config` files may be created depending on what settings you change as you build your project:

- `DefaultInput.ini`: This contains input mappings and settings related to using input devices.
- `DefaultEditor.ini`: This contains settings governing how your editor behaves.
- `DefaultDeviceProfiles.ini`: This contains specific settings for the different platforms to which you might release your application.

You don't have to know about this to use the engine. It's perfectly fine to manage your settings entirely from within the editor, but this is another one of the great things about Unreal Engine - it doesn't scatter important information in weird places. If at some point you do need to figure out what you've set somewhere, you know where to look. It's going to be in one of these files.

If you're not seeing file extensions such as `.ini` in your Windows explorer, open your **File Explorer Options** control panel, and turn off **Hide extensions for known file types**. It's on by default in Windows, but it will hide useful information from you when you're developing.

The Source directory

If you've created a C++ project, your project directory will also contain a `Source` sub directory. Your C++ source files live here.

The Project file

We should take a quick look at your project's `.uproject` file as well. It's actually really just a simple text file with a few bits of information about your project, but if you right-click it in Explorer, you're given three useful options:

- **Launch Game**: This will just open up your project in Unreal Editor. Double-clicking the `.uproject` file will do this too.
- **Generate Visual Studio project files**: This only applies if you've created a C++ project. You'll generally only need to do this if you've cleared the Intermediates directory, which holds your VS project files, or if you've added new source code files from outside the editor.
- **Switch Unreal Engine version**: This changes the engine version associated with your project. Generally, it's safer and more advisable to copy and update your project in the launcher when going to a new engine version, but if you already know it's safe to do, you can switch it here.

A summary of an Unreal project structure

Now that we've taken a quick look at the structure of an Unreal project, we should keep it in the back of our minds as we work.

Again, at its bare minimum, an Unreal project consists of the following:

- The `Project` directory:
  - The `Project` file
  - The `Content` directory
  - The `Config` directory
  - (C++ only) The `Source` directory

If you need to share a Blueprint-based Unreal project with someone, you only need to share the `.uproject` file, the `Content` directory, and the `Config` directory. All the rest are dynamically generated when the project runs.

Depending on what you do with your project, other directories may be created automatically.

That's really all we wanted to do here—just have a quick look around and see the lay of the land before we start adding a lot of content to our project. It can make your life easier later on to know where things are.

Setting your project's settings for VR

Let's jump back into the editor and continue setting up our project. Before we do anything else, we have a few settings we should take a look at.

All of these settings we're about to discuss affect the way your scene is *rendered*:

Rendering is the process of taking the 3D geometry in your scene, looking at it through a virtual camera, and turning that geometry into an image that can be displayed on your screen or in your headset.

As we mentioned in `Chapter 1`, *Thinking in VR*, VR places much heavier demands on the rendering pipeline than traditional flat-screen rendering. Even the lowest-resolution headsets on the current market display quite a lot of pixels and have to update extremely quickly. As if this weren't challenging enough, we also have two eyes to think about, and the views they see aren't exactly the same. This means we're rendering two separate views. That's quite a lot to do and not a lot of time in which to do it.

Because of this, it's important for a VR developer to understand a bit about the rendering options Unreal makes available. Good choices here can get you a long way toward your goal of having something that both looks great and runs fast.

Instanced Stereo

Remember when we mentioned a moment ago that we needed to render two separate views simultaneously in VR? Back in the bad old days (before Unreal 4.11), this was literally true. The engine simply ran the entire rendering process twice – once for each eye. This was hugely wasteful, since the only real difference between the two views was a small shift in the location of the eye looking at it. The full cost of a second render pass was being spent to draw something almost identical to what had just been drawn.

Instanced Stereo rendering improves on this by allowing the scene to be rendered in a single pass. The rendered view is then given to the video hardware along with the information it needs to adjust the view for each eye. It's dramatically faster than running the entire pass twice, and you want to make sure you turn it on. Let's do this now.

 If you create a project using the VR template, Instanced Stereo will already be turned on for you, but if you're creating a project from scratch, or taking an existing project and modifying it to work in VR, you need to remember to do this yourself.

From the editor, open your **Project Settings** either by hitting the **Settings** button on the editor toolbar and selecting **Project Settings...**, or by selecting **Edit | Project Settings**:

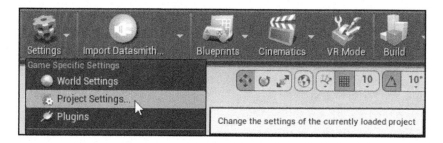

In **Project Settings**, find the **Rendering** item in the **Engine** section. In the **Rendering** page, find the **Instanced Stereo** option in the **VR** section and turn it on:

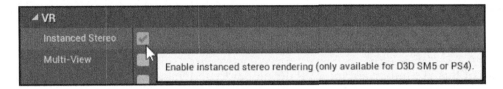

You'll be asked to restart the engine after you do this. This is going to take a little while because your shaders are going to need to recompile.

Round Robin Occlusions

Because we don't have a lot of time available to get our frame on to the headset, we don't want to waste any of it drawing anything we don't need to draw. The engine chooses which objects to draw through a process called **culling**. It uses four main methods to do this, in order, from the fastest and simplest to the most complex:

- **Distance culling** simply ignores any object beyond a certain distance from the camera. This is inexpensive.
- **View frustum culling** ignores objects that aren't in the camera's current view. This is more expensive than distance culling but still pretty cheap.
- **Precomputed visibility** allows designers to set up volumes to tell the engine explicitly what can be seen from certain locations and what can't. For instance, if you know that a player inside a room can't possibly see anything outside, you can use precomputed visibility volumes to tell the engine that it doesn't even need to bother checking.
- **Dynamic Occlusion** tests in real-time to see whether an actor in the scene is blocking another actor. This is relatively expensive, so it's done only with those objects that haven't been culled by the cheaper methods.

For VR projects, Unreal offers an optimized dynamic occlusion culling method called **Round Robin Occlusion**, which only tests occlusion for one eye per frame, rather than both. This saves a considerable amount of time, especially in scenes with a lot of objects, and works well since the views from each eye are nearly identical. The system switches which eye it tests on each frame, which is where the name comes from.

Let's turn it on:

1. In **Project Settings | Engine | Rendering | VR**, check **Round Robin Occlusion Queries**:

Forward and deferred shading

We now need to make an important choice about the rendering method we want to use for our project.

Broadly, there are two ways of drawing a scene, and the difference between them mostly boils down to how the objects in the scene are lit. These two methods are called **forward shading** and **deferred shading**.

You'll sometimes see these as **forward rendering** and **deferred rendering**, or you'll hear people talk about a **forward renderer** or a **deferred renderer**. Epic uses the terms interchangeably in its documentation, but they all refer to the same things. For our purposes here, we'll stick with the term **forward shading**, since that's what the option is called in the editor and it most accurately describes what's really different between the two approaches.

Shading is the process of applying light to geometry. This includes highlights, surface reflections, shadows, and all the various things light does when it hits a material:

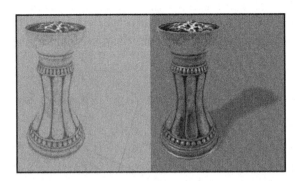

The preceding screenshot shows the same mesh without shading applied, and then with shading applied. In the left-hand image, you can see the shape of the object and its base color (also commonly called **albedo**), but no shadows, reflections, or highlights. The right image has been shaded, so highlights, shadows, and reflections are visible.

We're simplifying things a bit in the descriptions that follow, but, for our purposes, this is fine. You really don't need to know every detail of how a rendering pipeline works to make good decisions about how to use it. It's just important to understand enough to make the right choice for what you need to do.

Forward shading was the original way of drawing 3D scenes through most of the history of real-time 3D rendering. In forward shading, each geometric object in the scene is shaded as it's rendered, and each light in the scene is checked to see how it might affect it. If you have a lot of objects in your scene and a lot of lights, this can turn into a lot of operations. This is why most lighting tended to be baked into static lightmaps, and dynamic lights tended to be so rare in games in the 1990s and early 2000s. Each dynamic light dramatically added to the cost of the scene.

Deferred shading, on the other hand, draws every object in the view, but instead of lighting and shading it right then, it writes out a series of images that contain information about the materials in the scene, the depth of each pixel, and other factors that would affect how the scene is lit. Shading is then performed only once, after all this information has been assembled. This is where the name comes from—the shading pass has been deferred until after the base pass is complete.

This collection of buffers is called the **geometric buffer**, or **G-buffer**, and the process of building them is called the **base pass**. If you're using deferred shading in Unreal Engine (which is the default setting for a new project), you can see the contents of the G-buffer by selecting **View Mode | Buffer Visualization | Overview**.

Take a look at the following screenshot:

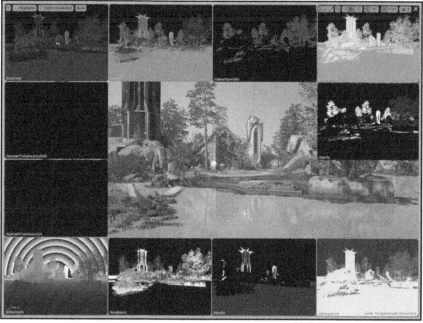

Since the lighting pass happens only once, this is much faster for scenes with a lot of dynamic lights, and also allows screen-space effects such as ambient occlusion to be handled efficiently. It doesn't, however, do as good a job as forward shading with objects that are partially transparent.

Choosing the right rendering method for your project

So, sounds like a no-brainer then, right? Deferred shading seems to offer a lot of advantages. For rendering outside of VR, this is mostly true, and by the late 2000s, deferred shading became the default for pretty much every game engine including Unreal.

VR, however, is a different story. The problem with deferred shading is that because of the way it handles information, it's difficult to turn off individual aspects of the rendering process. For the most part, it's an all-or-nothing deal. This wasn't generally a problem on flat screens—developers were pretty much always going to want everything the deferred shader had to offer. Some of these processes, though, are just too expensive to run efficiently in VR, or they're calculated in screen-space and look bad when they don't match up between the two eyes. In VR, you're often going to want the freedom to turn them off.

When you hear the term *screen-space* what this means is that instead of doing the calculations on the object in 3D space, the part of the scene containing the object is rendered to 2D (this process is called **rasterization**), and then the calculations are performed on the 2D image. This can create a problem in VR, because many screen-space calculations won't match between the eyes. You'll usually want to avoid using screen-space effects in VR.

In Unreal 4.14, Epic added forward shading as an option specifically designed for VR projects. They also introduced a clustering system that reduced the cost of processing lights in the base pass, so it's not nearly as costly as it used to be. For most VR projects, it's a good idea to use forward shading.

There are cases where you may still want to stick with deferred rendering in VR—if your scene needs to support a lot of movable lights, or if you know you'll need very complicated reflections—but you should seriously consider using forward shading for most VR projects.

 You'll almost always want to use forward shading for VR projects. It gives you much greater control over which parts of the rendering process you want to do, and which ones you want to skip; it handles transparency more easily, and supports better anti-aliasing options.

Let's turn it on for our project.

From your **Project Settings** | **Engine** | **Rendering**, find the **Forward Renderer** section, and turn on **Forward Shading**. You'll have to restart the editor after you do this:

 When using forward shading, many expensive material features that would normally be included by default need to be turned on explicitly. This is a good thing in VR, as it gives you the freedom to use expensive features only where they'll be seen. We'll talk later on about doing this when we start creating and modifying materials for VR.

While you can turn forward shading on or off later in your project's development, you'll generally want to make a choice and stick with it, as your project's lighting, materials, and reflections can differ greatly between the two methods. You don't want to put a lot of effort into developing your look, and then make a change like this late in development. You'll wind up redoing a lot of work.

Choosing your anti-aliasing method

One major advantage of using forward shading is that **anti-aliasing** is much easier to achieve than it is when using deferred shading. Let's talk about what this means and why it matters to us in VR.

When the renderer draws a scene onto a flat screen, whether it's a monitor or a VR headset, that display actually consists of a grid of tiny squares, called **pixels** (short for **picture elements**), and the renderer has to decide what color each of them is going to be. This turns into a problem when an object in the 3D scene only partly fills a pixel in the 2D space to which it's going to be drawn. The renderer then has to decide whether the pixel should be filled with the color of the object or the color of the background. There's no in-between—it has to pick one or the other. What this means in practice is that objects can wind up appearing to have jagged edges, especially along diagonal lines that cross over a lot of pixel borders. We call this problem **aliasing**:

A scene rendered with no anti-aliasing

Note the **jaggies** all around the windows in the scene rendered without anti-aliasing. These look bad here and will look worse in VR.

The way we solve this is through a process unsurprisingly called **anti-aliasing**. Different anti-aliasing methods use a variety of techniques to figure out how to soften jagged edges by finding the right color for a pixel to appear to blend between the foreground and background colors. This has the effect of smoothing jagged edges and removing stair-steps from diagonal lines:

A scene rendered using multisampling anti-aliasing (MSAA)

See how much smoother the windows look when this scene is rendered using multisampling anti-aliasing?

This is especially important in VR since headset resolutions are still fairly limited, so users can generally see the individual pixels. Aliasing that would be acceptable on a flat screen may look awful in VR as the user looks around the scene and jagged edges crawl and shimmer all over the place. You want to avoid this.

Fortunately, Unreal Engine gives you three **anti-aliasing methods** to address this:

- **FXAA** stands for **Fast Approximate Anti-Aliasing**. It looks for edges in the scene and blends the colors at those edges, and it is smart enough to avoid processing areas that don't have contrasting edges, so it looks great and runs pretty quickly. This should be your default choice if you're using deferred shading in VR.
- **Temporal AA (TAA)** works by looking at the previous few frames to make decisions about how to anti-alias the current frame. This generally makes it a poor choice for VR as the user's view tends to move quite a lot, and temporal AA can create "smearing" effects on fast movements. Even where smearing isn't apparent, it can appear too blurry to be acceptable on a VR headset. Temporal AA tends to do a fantastic job on flat screens, but it isn't a great choice for VR.

- **MSAA** stands for **Multisampling Anti-Aliasing**. This method is only available when using forward shading, and will give you sharper, better results than FXAA. If you're using forward shading in your project, and you almost always should be, this is the anti-aliasing method you should use.

Let's take care of this in our project:

From your **Project Settings** | **Engine** | **Rendering**, find the **Default Settings** section, and set the **Anti-Aliasing Method** to **MSAA**:

Most of the time, you won't need to change anything about how your anti-aliasing method works, but if you do, read on.

Modifying MSAA settings

This bit is optional. Making adjustments to your anti-aliasing settings is an advanced topic, and for most projects you don't need to do this. If you do wind up needing to adjust your MSAA settings, here's a good way to do it:

Select **Window** | **Developer Tools** | **Device Profiles** to open the **Device Profiles** window:

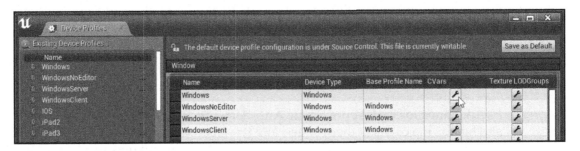

From this panel, hit the **CVars** button in the **Windows** row.

From within the resulting dialog, open **Console Variables** | **Rendering**. From here, you can see all the rendering-related console variables you're currently specifying. If you hit the **+** sign beside **Rendering,** you can type `msaa` in the search window that appears, and add a value for **r.MSAACount**. By default, this value is set to **4**. Reducing it to **3** or **2** will lower the quality of your anti-aliasing but speed it up a bit. Setting it to **1** turns it off. Setting it to **0** turns it off and falls back to temporal anti-aliasing:

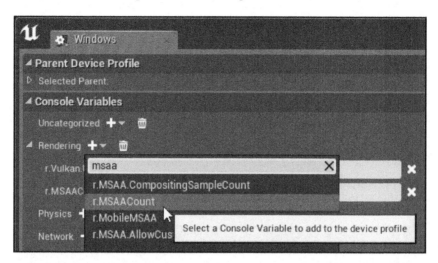

If you've made changes here, hit **Save as Default** on your **Device Profiles** window to save these settings. They'll be written to a new config file in your project's `Configs` directory called `DefaultDeviceProfiles.ini`.

Again, changing these values is an advanced topic. We don't advise that you modify these until you're comfortable that you understand what they do.

Starting in VR

It's also important to tell our project to start in VR when we run it. You do have the option, if you want to build a project that could be run both in VR and on a flat screen, to leave this turned off and use the `-vr` command line argument when you launch it. Our project is a VR-only project, though, so we want to turn this on.

Head to **Project Settings** | **Project** | **Description** | **Settings**, and set **Start** in VR to **True.**

Turning off other stray settings you don't need

In your **Rendering | Default Settings**, turn off **Ambient Occlusion Static Fraction**. Ambient occlusion is a method for creating those subtle shadows that appear where objects touch each other, but they're expensive to calculate and can look awful in VR because they're calculated in screen-space. We're not going to go into depth on this topic here. You already turned off ambient occlusion when you set your project to mobile, scalable 2D/3D, so this is just a stray setting you should clear.

Turning off default touch interface (Oculus Go/Samsung Gear)

If you're developing for Oculus Go or Samsung gear, you need to turn off the default touch interface. Mobile apps ordinarily assume that you'll operate them by touching the screen, but of course this isn't going to happen inside your headset.

Navigate to **Project Settings | Engine | Input**, and from within the **Mobile** section, grab the drop-down beside **Default Touch Interface** and clear it:

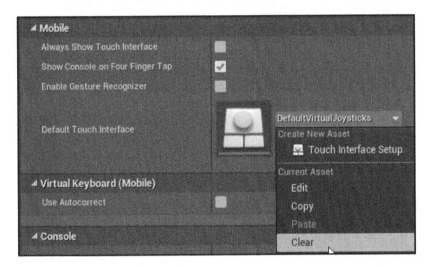

Configuring your project for Android (Oculus Go/Samsung Gear)

We now need to configure the project to use the Android SDK. We went through this process in the last chapter—we just need to set the same settings for this project. Here's a quick reminder of what we need to do.

From **Project Settings** | **Platforms** | **Android**, find the **APK Packaging** section, and hit **Configure Now**. If you already accepted the SDK license in the previous chapter, that button will be disabled – you only have to accept it once:

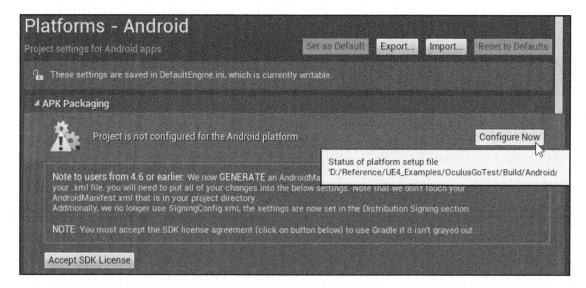

Then set these settings (as we mentioned in the previous chapter, most guides will tell you to use SDK Version 19 as your minimum. This is OK for Samsung Gear, but use version 21 for Go):

- **Minumum SDK Version**: 21
- **Target SDK Version**: 21
- **Enable FullScreen Immersive on KitKat and above devices**: True

Scroll down to the **Advanced APKPackaging** section and set this:

- **Configure the AndroidManifest for deployment to Oculus Mobile** to True.

Verifying your SDK locations

Select **Project Settings** | **Platforms** | **Android SDK**, and make sure your SDK locations are properly set. If you ran through the instructions in the previous chapter, they should be. If not, jump back there and set them up now.

Making sure Mobile HDR is turned off (Oculus Go/Samsung Gear)

Check your **Project Settings** | **Engine** | **Rendering** | **Mobile**, and ensure that **Mobile HDR** is turned off.

Mobile Multi-View (Oculus Go/Samsung Gear)

Remember back in the section on Instanced Stereo rendering when we discussed how wasteful it is to render the entire scene for each eye? The mobile headsets have a solution for this too, called **Mobile Multi-View**. Mobile Multi-View works pretty much the same way Instanced Stereo rendering does – by rendering the scene once for the left eye, and then shifting and adjusting the image for the right eye. We want to turn this on.

In **Project Settings** | **Engine** | **Rendering** | **VR**, set **Mobile Multi-View** to true, and turn on **Mobile Multi-View Direct** as well. Oculus doesn't recommend or support using **Mobile Multi-View** without the **Direct** option. Turn them both on:

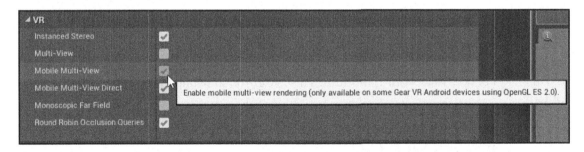

Monoscopic Far Field Rendering (Oculus Go / Samsung Gear)

Here's the thing about stereo depth perception – we can only see it up to a certain distance. Beyond that distance, there's no visible difference between a stereo image and a flat image. They look the same to us. We may as well use that to our advantage.

If we set **Project Settings** | **Engine** | **Rendering** | **VR** | **Monoscopic Far Field** to true, the engine will render any object beyond a specified distance only once, which can save significant time on the right sorts of scenes:

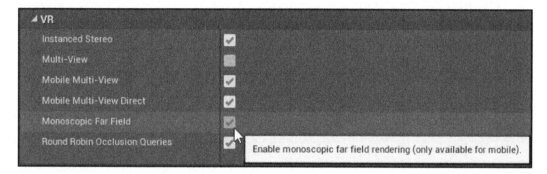

By default, the split between mono and stereo rendering happens at 7.5 meters, but this is set individually on each map. (The location of this split is called the **culling plane**.) This culling plane's distance from the camera is set individually for each map. To adjust it, open **Window** | **World Settings**, and look for the **VR** section on the settings panel that appears. Adjusting the **Mono Culling Distance** will shift the location of the culling plane.

For certain objects in your scene, especially large objects, you may need to force them to render in mono, if their bounds extend close to the camera even though they only ever actually appear far away. In these instances, open the object's **details** and set **Rendering** | **Render in Mono** to true. (This option is hidden in the **Rendering** section's advanced options.)

Project Settings cheat-sheet

We just ran through a number of settings you should modify when setting up your project for VR along with a bit of background for each of them. Just to recap, here's a cheat-sheet of what we changed:

- **Project Settings | Engine | Rendering | VR | Instanced Stereo**: True
- **Project Settings | Engine | Rendering | VR | Round Robin Occlusion Queries**: True
- **Project Settings | Engine | Rendering | Forward Renderer | Forward Shading**: True
- **Project Settings | Engine | Rendering | Default Settings | Anti-Aliasing Method**: MSAA
- **Project Settings | Engine | Rendering | Default Settings | Ambient Occlusion Static Fraction**: False
- **Project Settings | Project | Description | Settings | Start in VR**: True

This is the mobile VR version:

- **Project Settings | Engine | Input | Mobile | Default Touch Interface**: None
- **Project Settings | Platforms | Android | APK Packaging**: Configure and set the settings mentioned
- **Project Settings | Platforms | Android SDK**: Verify that your SDK locations are set.
- **Project Settings | Engine | Rendering | Mobile | Mobile HDR**: False
- **Project Settings | Engine | Rendering | VR | Mobile Multi-View**: True
- **Project Settings | Engine | Rendering | VR | Mobile Multi-View Direct**: True
- **Project Settings | Engine | Rendering | VR | Monoscopic Far Field**: True

Again, don't just follow these blindly. For most VR projects, these are the settings you're going to want, but that doesn't mean they'll apply to every project you ever do.

Decorating our project

Now that we've set up our project's basic settings, let's add some environment art so we have something interesting to look at while we work.

Migrating content into a project

From your **Epic Games Launcher**, open the **Learn** tab, and search for the `Sun Temple` example environment. Hit the **Create Project** button, and choose a location where you'd like to save it:

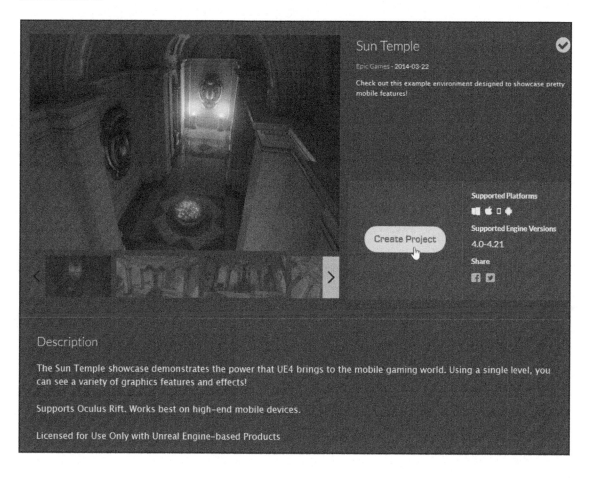

Let it download. Once the project has finished downloading, open it up. It should open up to the **Sun Temple** map. Now we're going to migrate this map into our existing project.

 We could just as easily have downloaded the **Sun Temple** project and then set it up to run in VR. We're doing it this way to give you an opportunity to learn about the **Migrate...** tool. When you need to get assets from one project to another, the Migrate tool is the best way to do it.

In your content browser, select **Content | Maps | Sun Temple**. Right-click it and select **Asset Actions | Migrate...**:

You're now going to be presented with a list of everything that will be copied if you migrate this map. This is the power of the **Migrate...** tool and is why you should use it. When you migrate an asset to another project, Unreal checks for everything else that would be needed for that asset to work, and includes it in the list of assets to be copied. So, for example, if you're migrating a mesh, the materials and textures used by that mesh will be found automatically and migrated too. In our case here, we're migrating a map, so Unreal will bring everything the map relies on into the new project:

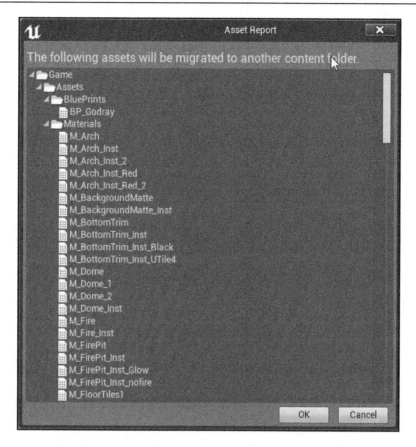

Now you need to choose where you're going to put your migrated content. The destination for a migrate operation always has to be the `Content` directory of the target project. Navigate to that location and select it. (This is why we mentioned at the start of this chapter that it's important to understand the structure of an Unreal project directory. You will occasionally need to know where things live in it.)

Once the migration is complete, let's close this project and re-open the project to which we just added this map.

You should now see a **Sun Temple map** in a **Maps** directory in your **Content** browser. Let's open it up.

Unreal will probably need to compile lots of shaders if this is the first time you've opened this map. (This is one of the reasons why we set up a derived data cache in Chapter 2, *Setting Up Your Development Environment*—once you've compiled your shaders, they'll be stored in this cache so you won't have to re-compile them when you open other projects.)

There's a little bit of extra stuff that came across when we migrated this map. We're going to get rid of it now so we can focus on the new assets we're creating. While we're at it, we're going to take this opportunity to show you a few things about managing assets to the content browser that will be important to you as you continue developing.

Cleaning up migrated content

With the **Sun Temple** map open, open **Window** | **World Settings**, and find **GameMode Override**. (We're going to talk about **Game Modes** shortly.) Clear it by hitting the yellow **Reset to Default** arrow beside the property:

Any time you see a yellow **Reset to Default** arrow, hitting it will restore the property to its standard setting.

Save the map.

Deleting assets safely

Now select the `Blueprints` folder inside your content browser. We're going to make our own blueprints in a moment, so we don't need these. Delete this folder, but pay attention to the confirmation dialog that appears.

If you see a **Force Delete** button with a warning, this means the thing you're trying to delete is still in use somewhere. You should almost never just delete something that's still being referenced. (We say *almost* here because once you really know what the engine is doing, there are certain circumstances where you can push it around a bit, but don't do this until you're really sure you know what's going on under the hood.) Instead, find out where the asset is still in use, and either change the reference to point to something else, or delete the object that's referencing it, or leave it alone:

If it's safe to delete an object, the dialog will just display a **Delete** button. This means that getting rid of it won't break anything else:

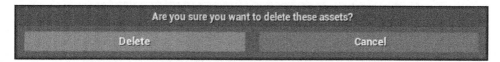

In this case, a force delete warning would mean that you either hadn't cleared out the **GameMode Override** from the map's **World Settings**, or that you hadn't saved the map after you did. If you're looking at a simple **Delete** button, hit it to get rid of the folder and its contents.

Moving assets and fixing up redirectors

Now let's organize what remains. From within your content browser, create a new folder for your project. We can call this folder `HelloVR`.

It's a good idea always to create a folder for your project inside the content browser. This way, as you migrate more content into your project from other sources, or add assets from the marketplace, you'll never be confused about which assets belong to your project and which arrived from outside. Similarly, if you migrate assets somewhere else, they'll all appear together in the new project's content browser. Most developers don't do this. Everybody should. The first time you migrate in a plugin and have it dump assets all over existing folders in your contents, you'll see why. You can prevent a lot of mess by keeping your own project organized.

Since we've gotten rid of our `Blueprints` folder, we still have two other folders from our migrated content that are just sitting out at the content root. Let's move them inside our project folder.

Grab the `Maps` folder and drag it into your `HelloVR` folder. When asked whether you'd like to move or copy it, choose to move it. Now grab the `Assets` folder and do the same.

But what's this? We've moved the folder but the folder in the old location hasn't gone away. Why? The reason for this is that Unreal has left behind a collection of **Redirectors**. You should know about these. Let's make them visible.

From the **Filters** drop-down beside the search bar, select **Filters | Other Filters | Show Redirectors**:

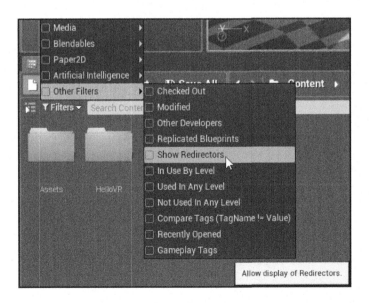

Now let's navigate inside that left-behind `Assets` folder, and jump into its `Blueprints` folder. There's a **Redirector** in there with the name of a **BP_Godray** blueprint that we moved to a new location. Double-click this redirector, and it will take you to the asset's new location. This is what redirectors do. When you move assets in Unreal, it's very likely that something else in your project is using the asset and pointing to it. Rather than force you to change every asset that refers to the thing you're moving right then, Unreal allows you to move it without changing the references, and when other objects try to find it in its old location, the redirector will just point them to the new location, and you can change the location the reference points to later. It's a good system and can save you a lot of hassle on a large project.

You don't want to leave redirectors lying around if you don't need them, however. To clean up a redirector, right-click on it, and select **Fix Up**:

What this is going to do is find every asset that's referring to this asset in its old location, and replace the references to point to the new location. Once this has been done, it deletes the redirector since it's no longer needed.

This can also be done to every redirector in a folder at once. Let's do this next.

First, we'll make it easier to see our content browser's folder structure. Hit the **Sources Panel** button beside your **Filters** drop-down to open your **Sources** panel:

This toggles a tree view of your project's content directory, which can make getting around and moving assets much more convenient:

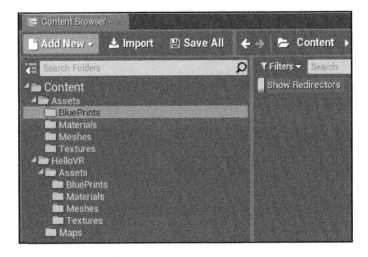

Now that we can see what we're doing, let's select the old `Assets` folder that contains all the redirectors, right-click it, and select **Fix Up Redirectors in Folder**:

Once the operation is complete, you can delete the old `Assets` folder, since it's now empty.

A good way to verify that a folder is empty before you delete it is to right-click the folder in your content browser, select **Show in Explorer**, and from within **Explorer**, select the folder and hit *Alt + Enter* to bring up its properties. If it shows 0 files, it's empty. If there's anything in it, you can dig in and find out what's there and whether it's anything you want to keep.

Our `Content` directory now should be pretty well-organized, with everything we're using consolidated under our `HelloVR` folder. If you get into the habit of keeping your `Content` directory clean while your project is small, you'll have a much easier time once it gets large.

Setting a default map

Now that we've brought in our map and cleaned up the extra Blueprints that came with it, let's set up our project to load **Sun Temple** as its default map.

Under **Project Settings** | **Project** | **Maps & Modes** | **Default Maps**, use the drop-down to set **Sun Temple** as your **Editor Startup Map** and your **Game Default Map**:

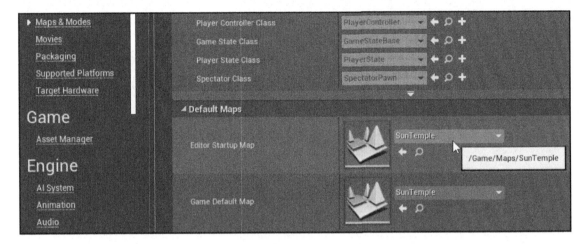

This way, when you start your editor or launch the game as a standalone executable, it will load directly into this map.

Testing our map on desktop

Let's take a look at what we've got so far. If we're working on desktop VR, we can launch the map in VR and look around. Select the drop-down to the right of the **Play** button on your editor toolbar. Select **VR Preview** (if **VR Preview** is dimmed, check to be sure that your VR headset is hooked up and its software is running):

Kinda nice in here, right?

We can't do much yet, and we're not at the right height relative to the floor, but it's running and we're ready to begin setting things up.

Testing our map on mobile (Oculus Go/Samsung Gear)

If we'd like to test the map on mobile, there are a few other things we need to do.

Assuming that we've already set up our project to run on mobile as described, let's check first that our mobile device is connected and can be seen.

Important: If you update your Unreal Engine version, be sure you re-run the **CodeWorks for Android** installer at `<Engine Install Location>\Engine\Extras\AndroidWorks\Win64`. Building with newer Unreal code and out-of-date Android SDK code can create difficult-to-debug errors when you try to run in mobile VR. Remember to keep your CodeWorks up-to-date.

Open Windows PowerShell and navigate to the `platform-tools` directory in your Android SDK directory. By default, this will be `C:\NVPACK\android-sdk-windows\platform-tools`. From here, type `./adb devices`. You should see the serial number of your connected device here with the word `device` beside it. If this reads *unauthorized* instead, you need to accept the connection to your PC from within the headset. If this reads *offline*, you may need to restart your `adb` server. Type `./adb kill-server`, and then run `./adb devices` again:

```
Windows PowerShell
Copyright (C) Microsoft Corporation. All rights reserved.

PS C:\Users\kmack> cd C:\NVPACK\android-sdk-windows\platform-tools\
PS C:\NVPACK\android-sdk-windows\platform-tools> ./adb devices
List of devices attached
* daemon not running. starting it now at tcp:5037 *
* daemon started successfully *
                    device

PS C:\NVPACK\android-sdk-windows\platform-tools> _
```

 If you're working on mobile devices, there's no way around the reality that you're going to spend a lot of time in PowerShell talking to the device. Take the time to learn about ADB especially. When something goes wrong, you're going to use ADB to figure out what's happening. Learn more about it here: `https://developer.android.com/studio/command-line/adb`.

If your `./adb` devices looks good, you should be ready to launch the project to the device.

From your launch drop-down on the editor toolbar, select the Android entry that matches the serial number of your device.

The launch process should begin. As we mentioned in the `Chapter 2`, *Setting Up Your Development Environment*, expect it to take a while the first time you do this.

Setting up a game mode and player pawn

Now that we've set up a basic scene and verified that it runs on the platform, let's get to work on building in some functionality.

Creating a VR pawn

The first thing we're going to need to do is create a **pawn** to represent the player. Pawns are a type of actor that can be controlled by a player or by AI. In our case, we're going to create a pawn that our player can control.

Unreal Engine is an **object-oriented** system. This means that the engine is organized around discrete items called **objects**. An object consists of **properties**, which you can generally see by looking at the **Details** panel of an item you select in the map, and **functions**, which you can often see in the blueprint editor. Objects often **inherit** from one another, so a new class of object might be created using another class as its parent. This means that the new class would take on the attributes and behavior of its parent, but could then change these attributes and behaviors or add new ones. An actor, therefore, is a child of the object class that adds the capability to be placed in the world. A pawn is a type of actor that adds the ability to be controlled by a player or AI. When we create our own class using a pawn as a parent, we're setting up that class to take on everything a pawn can do, and then changing its behaviors or adding our own.

Let's navigate to our `Content/HelloVR/Assets/Blueprints` folder in the content browser, right-click on any empty space in the folder, and select **Create Basic Asset | Blueprint Class**:

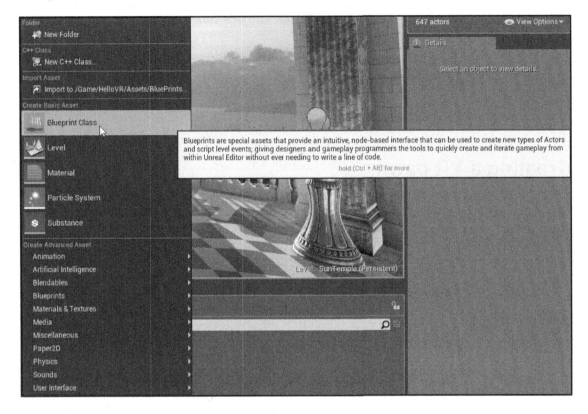

In the dialog that follows, we'll be asked to select our new blueprint's parent class. Select **Pawn**:

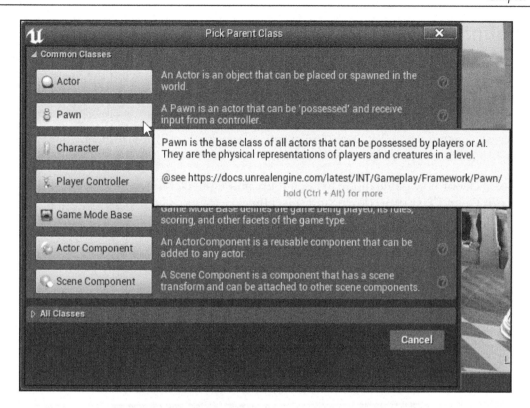

A new blueprint asset will be created in our `Blueprints` directory. Let's name it `BP_VRPawn`.

> It's a good idea to get into the habit of following a **naming convention** when you name your assets. A naming convention is a set of rules you follow when thinking up a name for a new thing you're creating. By following rules when you name objects, you can make it much easier to see what an object is, or to remember what you called it. In this instance, we're using the `BP_` prefix as a reminder that our pawn is a blueprint class. A particularly thorough and well-thought-out naming convention lives here: `https://github.com/Allar/ue4-style-guide`.

In a moment, we're going to start modifying our pawn, but, first, we need to tell our map to use it.

Creating a game mode

Whenever Unreal loads up a map, the first thing it does is check to see what rules govern the behavior of the map. These rules can specify a number of things, but the one we care about right now is what sort of pawn is going to spawn from a `Player Start` object. This collection of rules lives in a class called the **Game Mode**.

Let's create a game mode. Right-click in empty space, create a **Blueprint Class**, and select **Game Mode Base** as its parent. We'll name it `BP_VRGameMode`.

Double-click our new game mode to open it up, and in its **Details** section, select the **Classes | Default Pawn Class** drop-down, and select the `BP_VRPawn` class we just created:

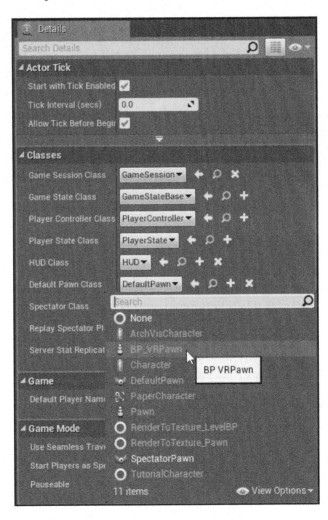

For our purposes right now, this is all we need to do with our game mode. We're just using it to specify the pawn class we'd like to load. Compile it and save it.

 Blueprint is a **compiled** language. Before the code you write can be run by the CPU, it needs to be translated into a language the CPU understands. There are two main ways this can happen. **Interpreted** languages are translated on-the-fly while they're running. This comes with a cost though, since the interpreter needs to be running alongside your code and trying to translate it while it runs. It's much faster to translate everything offline in a separate process so it's ready to go when the CPU needs to run it. This is how compiled languages handle things, and when you compile your blueprints, this is what you're doing.

By default, when blueprints are compiled, they're compiled to a format that's then used by a virtual machine that hosts the blueprint code while your application is running. This system runs fast, but if you want to squeeze even more speed out of it, you have the option to convert them to native C++, which then allows them to be compiled to machine code. At this point, they can run as fast as code written directly in C++.

Assigning the game mode

Now we need to tell our project to use this game mode as its default.

Open **Project Settings**, and under **Project** I **Maps & Modes** I **Default Modes**, set our **Default GameMode** to our newly-created game mode:

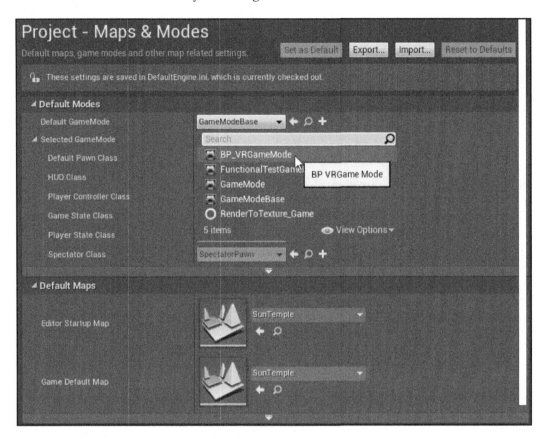

Now any level that loads in our project will use this GameMode to decide what to spawn and what rules to follow when running the scene.

Overriding a GameMode for a specific map

What if we wanted one of our maps to use a different GameMode? For instance, if we set up an entry menu scene, we might want to spawn a pawn designed to interact with the menus in place of our default player pawn. Fortunately, this is easy.

If it isn't already visible, select **Window** I **World Settings** to open up our **World Settings** tab. In **World Settings**, under **Game Mode**, set the **GameMode Override** to the new **BP_VRGameMode** we just created:

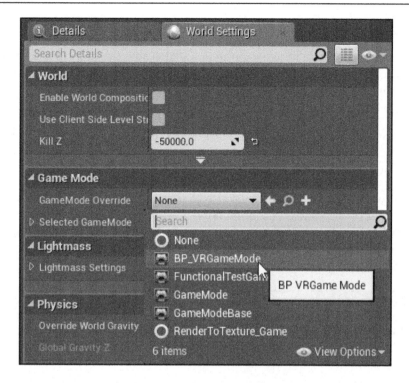

We've just told the engine to use our new game mode when this map loads up, regardless of what GameMode was specified in the project settings.

There are four places where we can specify what game mode to use:

- You can set it in **Project Settings** | **Maps & Modes** | **Default Modes** | **Default GameMode**. A GameMode specified here will load by default anywhere in your project unless something else overrides it.

- You can set the **GameMode Override** in an individual map as we've done here. This will override the global default game mode from your project settings if it's set.

- You can specify a game mode using the *command-line argument* `?game=MyGameMode` when you launch your executable. This, in turn, will override your default game mode, and any override set in your map.

- In your `DefaultEngine.ini`, you can specify specific game modes to load when maps with specific prefixes are loaded. This will override any other specification if it's set.

Placing a pawn directly in the world

While it's generally preferable to use a game mode and a player start object to get your player pawn into the world, you don't have to do it this way, and you'll occasionally run across existing projects, such as the default VR Template project, that don't use a GameMode to set the player pawn.

In these cases, instead of placing a player start object in your scene where you want the player to spawn, drag your pawn blueprint directly into the scene. If your scene has an existing player start, get rid of it.

Remember that we said pawns could be controlled by players or AI? You need to put your pawn under player control since you don't have a GameMode doing the job for you. Select the pawn you just placed in the level, and in its **Details**, find **Pawn | Auto Possess Player**, and set the value to **Player 0**. This will put the pawn under the player's control when it spawns into the world:

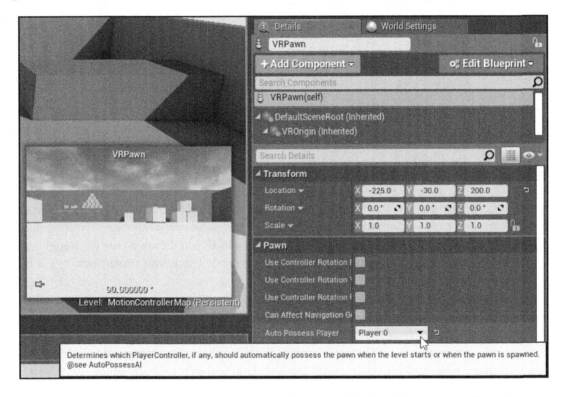

In general, it's better practice to use a GameMode to specify the player pawn class, but you should know that this method exists, because you will see some projects use it.

Setting up the VR pawn

Now that we've created a VR pawn and set up the game mode to use it, let's modify this pawn to set it up appropriately for use in VR. We're going to do this from scratch here. Quite often, you'll use the pawn class supplied with the VR template when you create a simple VR application, but we don't want you to use this as a crutch. It's much better to understand how a pawn is built for VR, so you can build it appropriately for what you need it to do.

The first thing we're going to do is open up our pawn.

Adding a camera

In the upper-left corner of the blueprint editor view, you should see a **Components** tab. Hit the green **+Add Component** button, and in the drop-down that appears, select **Scene** to create a **Scene Component**. Name it `Camera Root`:

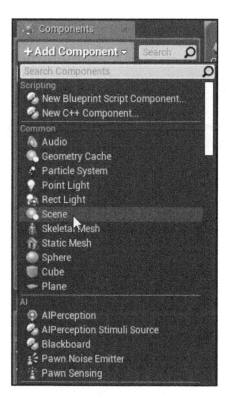

Components are additional elements that can be added to blueprint objects. There's a wide variety of components available to you, and they all do different jobs. Components are organized into a hierarchy, allowing you to attach components to other components. You can do quite a lot with this.

Now, create a new **Camera** component. If the Camera Root scene component was still selected when you did this, the **Camera** component will be created as a child of **Camera Root**. If it isn't, drag it on to **Camera Root** to set **Camera Root** as its parent.

It's often a good idea to set a separate root component as we've done here. This gives you much more flexibility to change the structure of the actor later, or to change rotations or positions of components such as cameras without having to adjust the position of the object.

Adding motion controllers

Next, select the `DefaultSceneRoot` component, and create a `Motion Controller` component. For this one, use the **Search Components** bar at the top of the **Add Component** menu and type `mot` to narrow the search to the motion-controller component. You can save yourself a lot of time by using this search bar. Name this new component `MotionController_L` and make sure it's a child of the `DefaultSceneRoot`, and not a child of the CameraRoot or the Camera.

Select `DefaultSceneRoot` and do this again to create a second motion-controller component. Name this one `MotionController_R` and again make sure it's a child of the `DefaultSceneRoot`, and not any other component:

Your component hierarchy should now look like the preceding screenshot.

Before we move on, we need to set a few properties on our motion-controller components. Select the `MotionController_R` component, and in its **Details** panel, find the **Motion Controller | Motion Source** entry. Set it to **Right** to allow the controller to be moved by the right-hand Oculus or Vive controller. While we're at it, ensure that `MotionController_L` is still set to use **Left** as its motion source. It should be this by default:

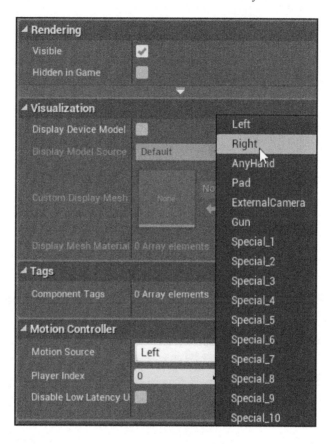

Let's also make both of these controllers visible so we can verify that they're working. From each motion-controller component's **Details** panel, select **Visualization** | **Display Device Model**. Turn this on, and verify that **Display Model Source** is still set to **Default**, which will simply display the model for the motion-controller hardware you're using. We'll replace our motion-controller display later on, but for now, we just want to see them so we can verify that we've set them up correctly:

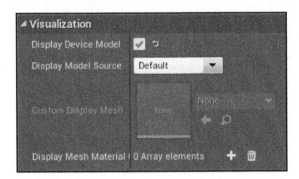

Setting our tracking origin.

Now we need to tell our pawn how it should interpret the location of the headset in the tracked space. Look for the **My Blueprint** tab underneath your pawn's **Components** tab, and if your **EventGraph** panel isn't already visible in the main editing window, double-click **Graphs** | **EventGraph** in the **My Blueprint** tab to display it:

Once you're in your **EventGraph**, find the **BeginPlay** event, or right-click anywhere in the graph editor and type `beginplay` in the search dialog that appears to find or create a **BeginPlay** event. Drag an execution line from the **BeginPlay** event and right-click to create a new node. Find **Input** | **Head Mounted Display** | **Set Tracking Origin**, or begin typing in the search box to find it. Create a `Set Tracking Origin` node, and set its origin to **Floor Level** if you're using a room-scale VR system such as the HTC Vive or Oculus Rift with Touch controllers, or **Eye Level** if you're using a non-room-scale system such as the Oculus Go or older single-camera Oculus Rift.

Adjusting our Player Start location to the map.

Finally, we need to adjust our Player Start position in the map. Find it in your **World Outliner** (you can use the search bar to find it quicker, and then select it and drag it down in the scene until its center intersects the floor (this is a bit of a hacky way to align our pawn, and we'll do a better job of this later, but for now it will work):

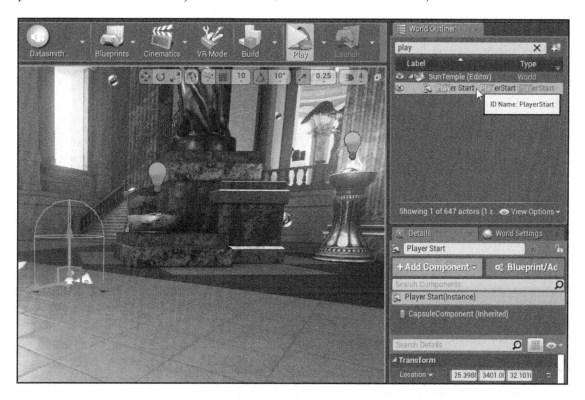

Testing in the headset.

We now have the building blocks we're going to need to create VR experiences in Unreal. We have a project that's been properly set-up to run efficiently in VR, and a pawn that may not do much yet, but is ready to be used as a foundation for the things we really want to do.

Let's test it. Launch the map using VR preview, and verify that your view seems to be at the right height, and that you can see your motion controllers when you move your hands. Framerate should be acceptable as well.

Packaging a standalone build

When we distribute an Unreal application to other users, we generally don't give them the source files for the editor. Instead, we package the project into a stand-alone executable that can be run on the target platform.

Let's create a Windows standalone executable.

Select **File** | **Package Project** | **Windows** | **Windows (64-bit)** to kick off a packaging process. You'll be asked where to put it. Choose a location that makes sense. (Often, creating a `Packaged` directory inside your project directory can be reasonable. You can put your packaged build wherever you want.) When the build status dialog appears, hit **Show Output Log** so you can see what it's doing:

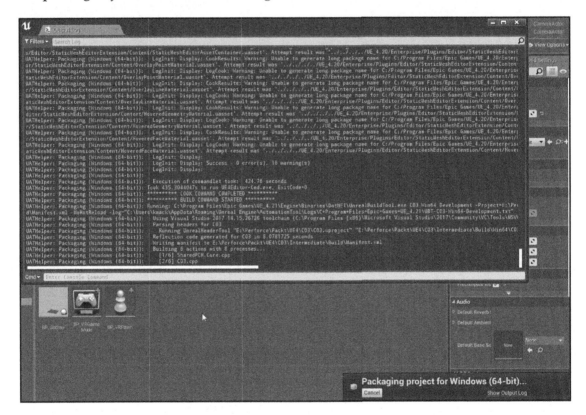

Expect this process to take a while.

Once the process completes, close the editor and check the location where you told the system to build your executable. You should see a `WindowsNoEditor` folder inside it. Inside that, you should see an executable with your project's name. Launch the executable. If you set the **Start in VR** flag in your **Project Settings**, it should launch directly to your headset.

Summary

Congratulations! We covered a lot of ground. In this chapter. We went through the process of creating a starting VR project and set it up properly to run well on the target hardware. We learned how to decide what settings to use when setting up a new project for VR, and how to find our way around inside an Unreal project directory. We also learned about a number of important Unreal Engine features used in VR development:

- Instanced Stereo
- Round Robin Occlusions
- Forward Shading
- Multisampling Anti-Aliasing (MSAA)
- [Mobile] Mobile Multi-View
- [Mobile] Monoscopic Far Field Rendering

We learned how to migrate content from one project to another, and how to clean up our `Content` directory once it arrives.

Finally, we set up a basic VR pawn and set up a game mode to instruct the map to load it. In working with the pawn, we learned about how we can use components to build complex objects out of simple parts, adding a camera and tracked motion controllers. Finally, we set up the first elements of our pawn's blueprint to set our tracking origin appropriately for our VR hardware, and tested our map.

In the next chapter, we're going to make it possible for the pawn we created in this chapter to move through the world. We'll use Blueprints to create a teleport movement scheme, and learn how to set up the environment to support it, and then we'll move on from there to implement a range of immersive movement schemes as well.

Getting Around the Virtual World

4

In this chapter, we're going to take the pawn we built in the previous chapter and get it moving through the world. We'll begin with a commonly employed teleport movement scheme and cover a wide range of tasks that go into setting it up. We'll learn about navigation meshes in our environment, how to set up input events in our project and use them in Blueprints, and how to build a player pawn Blueprint and get it moving around the world. Finally, we'll also explore an immersive seamless locomotion scheme that you can use to allow your players to move through the world without teleporting.

Throughout the course of this chapter, we'll be discussing the following topics:

- Navigation meshes—what they are, how to set them up in your level, and how to refine them
- How to set up a Blueprint for your player pawn, and how to create input events that your pawn can use
- How to perform traces, using both straight lines and curves, to find legal target locations in your environment
- How to create simple in-game indicators to show players what's going on
- How to implement a seamless locomotion scheme to provide immersive movement for projects where teleportation wouldn't be appropriate

This is going to be a lot of ground to cover, but it should be fun, and you're going to come away with a good grounding that's going to help you to figure out how to develop the things you want, and how to understand what other developers are doing when you see their Blueprints. We're going to take a slightly different approach in this chapter from the way most tutorials are done. To be an effective developer, it's far more important to learn how to think about a problem than simply to memorize a series of steps that may not apply to the next problem you face. In this chapter, we're going to walk through the processes of building elements and then, in some instances, *discover* bugs in them. Afterward, we'll need to change things to fix these bugs. This is where the real value in this approach lies—you'll begin to get a sense of how to develop software through iteration, which is the way it's really done. The goal here isn't to make you good at building these tutorials—it's to help you to become a developer who can make whatever you dream up on your own.

With that being said, let's get building!

Teleport locomotion

As we discussed in `Chapter 1`, *Thinking in VR*, one of the biggest challenges we face in VR is motion sickness that's triggered when the user tries to move around. One of the most commonly used solutions for this is to *teleport* the user from place to place rather than to allow them to move smoothly through the space. This breaks immersion, but avoids the problem of motion sickness entirely because it doesn't create a sense of motion at all. For applications where immersive movement isn't a priority, such as architectural visualization, this may be an ideal scheme to employ.

Creating a navigation mesh

The first thing we're going to need for a teleport-based locomotion scheme is a way to tell the engine where players are allowed to move and where they aren't. We can use a *navigation mesh* to do this job.

A **navigation mesh**, often shortened to **navmesh**, is an automatically generated set of surfaces indicating walkable floors in an Unreal level. AI-controlled agents use the navigation mesh to find their way around the world, but it can also be used as a way to identify safe destinations for the player pawn to land, as we're doing here in our teleport system.

Creating a navmesh in Unreal is fairly simple. From your **Modes** panel, select the **Volumes** tab, and find the **NavMesh Bounds Volume**. Drag it into your scene, as shown in the following screenshot:

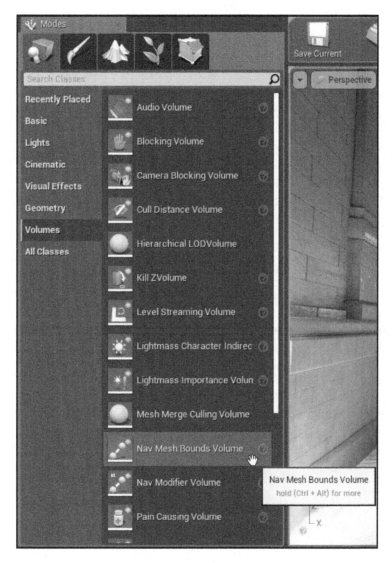

Select the Nav Mesh Bounds Volume from Modes | Volumes

Moving and scaling the Navmesh Bounds volume

The NavMesh Bounds volume needs to surround any floor where you'd like the player to be able to teleport. Let's make our navmesh visible so that we can see where the walkable floors are being set up:

1. Hit the *P* key to toggle navigation visibility or, from the viewport menu, select **Show | Navigation**:

Use the P key or Show | Navigation to display the generated navmesh in the environment.

If you don't see any navigable space after you've placed a NavMesh Bounds volume, make sure it's intersecting a walkable floor. The volume sets the boundaries for the navmesh generation, so if it's above the floor, it won't generate anything.

Of course, this NavMesh Bounds volume we just placed is far too small. Let's extend it to cover the space in which we'd like to move. We're going to do this by scaling the volume.

2. Hit the *R* key to switch to scaling mode, or just tap the *spacebar* until the scaling gizmo appears.

We could scale the volume from the perspective view, but for this kind of operation, it's often a good idea to go to an orthographic view so that we can really see what we're doing.

3. Hit *Alt + J* or use the viewport's view selector to switch to a top view:

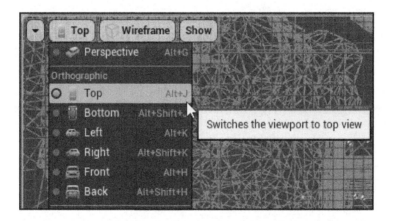

Switch to an orthographic top view using the menu or its associated shortcut key.

4. Scale the navmesh to surround the walkable area of the building.

With your navigation visible, you can see where it's generating navmesh surfaces and whether it's doing a sensible job of it:

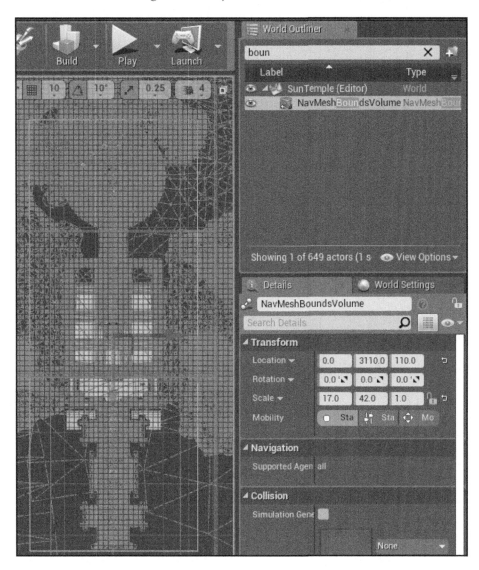

A top view of our level showing the extents of the NavMesh bounds volume

In our case, parts of the building that we expect to be walkable aren't yet covered. This is because we haven't yet done anything with the height of our bounds volume, and these areas are too high or low to fit inside it. Let's jump to a side view to fix that.

5. Hit *Alt + K* to jump to the left view, or select **Left** from your viewport view selection.

6. Scale the bounds volume to a scale that reasonably covers the floor:

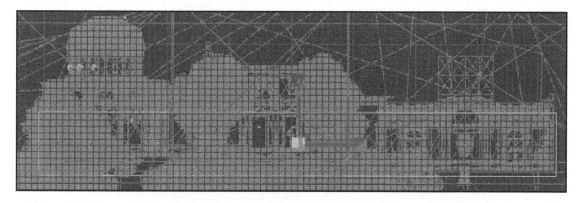

Side view of the level. You can see here that we're scaling the navmesh bounds volume to encompass the floor

7. Hit *Alt + G* to jump back to a perspective view and see how we're doing. Alternatively, you can select **Perspective** from your view selector.

It's worth memorizing these keystrokes for changing views. You'll use them all of the time, and it's handy to be able to switch quickly. *Alt + J, K,* and *H* switch view angles. *Alt + 2* switches to a wireframe view, and *Alt + 4* switches back to a shaded view. There are plenty of other hotkeys, but you'll use these the most.

If we fly to the back of the temple, we can see that we have a problem here. Our navmesh didn't generate as expected in the back corridor. Let's figure out what's going on here:

Here we can see that part of our level hasn't been properly covered by the navmesh.

Fixing collision problems

There are almost always two reasons why a navmesh isn't generating where you expect it. Either your volume isn't surrounding the area where you're trying to generate the mesh, or there's something wrong with the collision in the area. Let's take a look:

1. Hit *Alt + C* to view the collision in the back hall, or hit **Show** | **Collision**.

   It doesn't appear that there's any stray collision encroaching into the hall, so it's probably a missing collision on the floor.

2. Select the floor in the bad area.

3. In its details, find its **Static Mesh** and double-click it to open it up:

Use the Details panel to find the static mesh for the bad floor region.

4. In the Static Mesh Editor, select the **Collision** toolbar item and make sure that **Simple Collision** is checked:

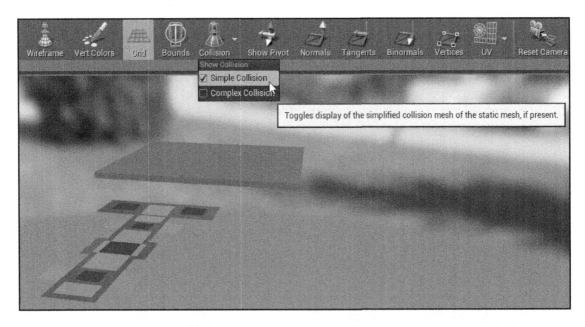

View simple collision for the static mesh

Sure enough, our simple collision is missing. Let's fix this.

5. Select **Collision** | **Add Box Simplified Collision** to add a simple collision plane to our floor.

That's much better. We should now see that the navmesh we expect has been generated back in our main level:

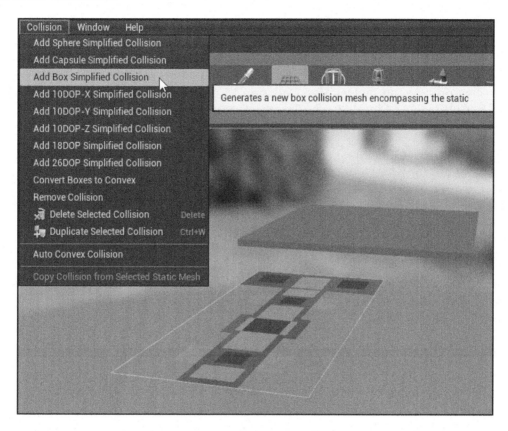

Simplified collision created for our floor mesh

Before we move on, let's take a second to talk about what's going on here. A very common thing we need to do in real-time software is figure out when an object has hit another object. Unreal uses *collision meshes* to do this. A collision mesh is simplified geometry that's used to check for intersections with other collision meshes in the world.

Actors have two of these:

- A **Complex Collision** mesh. This is simply the model's visible mesh.
- A **Simple Collision** mesh. This is a much less detailed convex mesh that surrounds the object. These are often generated when an object is imported, or can be created explicitly in the DCC where the model was created. If it's missing, you can create a simple collision in the editor, like we've done here. As a last resort, you can set **Details** | **Collision** | **Collision Complexity** to **Use Complex Collision As Simple** to use the object's visible mesh for all collision calculations. Don't do this for a mesh with a ton of polygons, though. It's expensive.

Collision detection and handling is its own fairly deep topic and beyond the scope of this book, but for our purposes in VR development, we're going to care a lot about the simple collision meshes of our objects, because we'll use these as walkable surfaces to detect when another object hits them, to detect whether we can grab them, and for many other purposes.

Excluding areas from the navmesh

Looking around our map, we have a few more problems we need to fix. Our Navmesh Bounds Volume is generating a navmesh in a few areas where we don't want our players to teleport. Let's fix this, too:

1. Hit *Alt + 2* to switch to a wireframe view, or use the viewport's View Mode selector to switch to wireframe.

We probably have a few problems we can fix just by adjusting the scale of the NavMesh Bounds volume. If we have navmesh generating on rooftops or window sills, let's reduce our Bounds volume's vertical scale to exclude these areas if we can. This is an area where hitting *Alt + K* to jump to a side view can help.

If our NavMesh Bounds volume is spreading further outside the building than it needs to, we can jump to a top view using *Alt + J* and adjust it to fit better.

We're still going to have a few leftover stray areas that we'll want to exclude, and that can't simply be fixed by scaling the volume. For these, we'll use **Nav Modifier Volumes**. Refer to the following steps:

1. Grab a **Nav Modifier Volume** from your **Modes** palette and drag it into the scene.
2. Move and scale it until it surrounds an area where the unwanted navmesh is being generated.

You'll see the navmesh in this region disappear when the nav modifier volume surrounds it. Take a look at the nav modifier volume properties in your **Details** panel. Do you see that **Default | Area Class** is set to **NavArea_Null**? This tells the navmesh generator to omit generating a navmesh in this region. You can see from the pulldown menu that it can also be used to mark obstacles and crawlspaces, but for what we're doing here, we don't care about these. We're just interested in using it to clear out unwanted navigation.

3. Drag as many of these into your scene as you need to clean up the stray bits. You can hold down the *Alt* key while dragging a modifier volume to duplicate it, or hit *Ctrl + W* to make a copy:

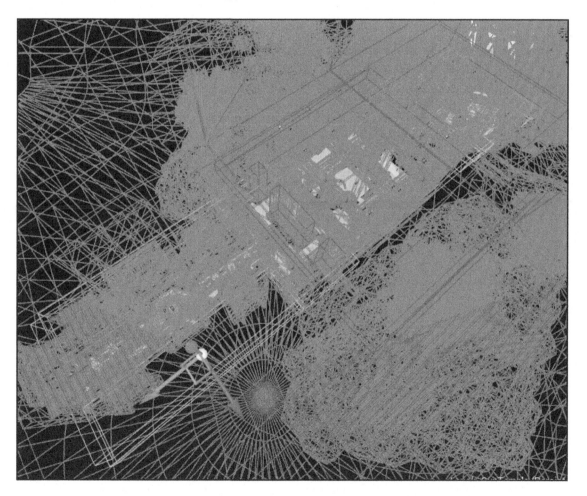

A perspective wireframe view can be useful for finding problems with your navigation coverage.

You'll find it helpful to memorize the transform hotkeys as you're moving objects around. *W* activates the **Translate** tool, which allows you to slide an object around. *E* activates the **Rotate** tool, and *R* activates the **Scale** tool. Tapping the *spacebar* also cycles through these tools. *Ctrl + W* duplicates an object, and holding *Alt* while dragging an object also copies it.

When you're done, you should have a collection of Nav Modifier Volumes blocking off areas you don't want your player to stand on.

Fly through your level and make sure you don't have any weird navmesh where you don't want it. Where you find problems, fix them by scaling your navmesh bounds volume, or adding nav modifier volumes.

Modifying your navmesh properties

There's one other thing you should know about before we move on, and that's where to adjust the properties for the navmesh you've just generated.

If you need to change anything about its behavior, select the `RecastNavMesh` object, which will have been created in your level. In its **Details** panel, you can see properties governing its generation, querying, and runtime behavior.

We're not going to go into these here except to call attention to one of these properties: if you wanted to adjust the size of an area into which your player could fit, you can adjust the Agent Radius to do so. Making this smaller will allow your player to fit into tighter spots. Similarly, you can adjust the Agent Height and Max Height to determine acceptable ceiling heights under which navigation should be generated. Generally, you'll want to make changes to these values before you go crazy fine-tuning your nav modifier volumes since changes here will change where your navmesh is generated. For our purposes, we're going to leave these values alone.

Setting up the pawn Blueprint

Now that we have our navigation built and tuned in our scene, we can turn off navigation visualization by hitting *P*, and start working on our locomotion behavior.

To implement a teleport locomotion scheme, we need to do three jobs:

- Figure out where the player wants to move
- Figure out where the player is actually allowed to move
- Move the player to the new location

Let's get to work.

Iterative development

We're going to develop this method iteratively, the way you really would if you were developing it from scratch. Most tutorials simply walk you through the steps to build a finished method, but the problem with this approach is that it doesn't teach you *why* you're doing the things you're doing. As soon as you want to do something similar, but not exactly the same, you're back to square one.

Instead, we're going to work in stages.

Kent Beck, a pioneering software developer, gives this advice to developers: *Make it work, make it right, make it fast.*

What's important here is the order in which you do things. It seems almost obvious at first, but few developers get it right when they're starting out. You'll save yourself a lot of heartache if you work in this order.

Make it work

Build a rough assembly of what you're trying to do. Test it early and often. Build it to be easy to test and easy to change. Change things around until you're satisfied that it's doing the right work.

Make it right

Now that you know what your code needs to do, figure out how you should really organize it. Are there better or cleaner ways to do what you're trying to do? Are there parts that can be reused? Will this code need to be used anywhere else? Could you debug it if you had to? Use the work you did in the *make it work* phase as a starting point, but now that you understand what you really need to do, write it correctly. It's okay to make a mess in the first stage (in fact, you're probably doing it wrong if you're not making a mess), but clean that mess up in this phase.

Make it fast

Once you have reasonably clean code that's doing the right job, look for ways you could get it running faster. Is there a result that you're generating more than once that you could cache to a variable and reuse? Are you checking conditions repeatedly, even though you know they can only change when certain things happen? Are you copying data that you could just read from its original location? Figure out what you could be doing more efficiently, and speed things up where you can. Be careful here, though. Some optimizations are so minor that they may not really make a noticeable difference to the running application. Go for the big ones, and use profiling tools to understand where your problems really are. You want to make sure you're optimizing things that are really going to make a difference. Also, be careful about making your code more difficult to read or debug as you optimize it. A change that shaves a tiny amount off of your frame time but makes a class difficult or impossible to update or maintain might not be worth it. Use judgment when optimizing.

Do things in order

Many new developers mess this order up, and start trying to optimize their code before they've really made sure they're doing the right thing. This just wastes time, as there's a high likelihood that some of that code will be thrown out. Other developers skip the *make it right* phase, and consider their work done as soon as it seems to work. This is a mistake too, as 80% of the life cycle of a piece of code is spent maintaining and debugging it. If your code works but it's a mess, you're going to burn a lot of extra time trying to keep it running later on.

Problems that are created by rushed or sloppy work early in development are often referred to as *technical debt*. This is stuff you're going to have to fix later because, even though it runs, it may not be flexible or robust, or might just be an unreadable shambles. The time to clear your technical debt is right after you've finished your *make it work* phase, and before you've moved onto other things and started to build more code on top of something that needs to change.

Working in this order and thinking of these as discrete stages will make you a more effective developer.

Setting up a line trace from the right motion controller

Let's begin with the first thing we need to do to get our teleport running—figuring out where the player wants to go:

1. Open up our **BP_VRPawn** Blueprint, and open **My Blueprint | Graphs | EventGraph**, if it isn't already open.

   We should still see the `BeginPlay` event in our Event Graph where we set our tracking origin. Now, we're going to add some code to our **Event Tick**.

 The **Tick** event is called every time the engine updates the frame. Be careful about putting too much work into your Tick events, as they can eat performance.

2. If you don't already see an **Event Tick** node in your Event Graph, right-click anywhere in the graph, type `tick` in the search box, and select **Add Event | Event Tick**. If you already have a Tick event defined, this won't add a new one—it'll just take you to that node in the event graph. If you don't, this will create one now.
3. Right-click to the right of **Event Tick**, and add a **Line Trace by Channel**.

When you perform a line trace, you supply a *start* point and an *end* point, and tell it what *collision channel* you're looking for. If an actor with a collision set to the supplied collision channel intersects the line between the start and end points, the trace will return `true`, and will return information about what it hit. We're going to use this behavior to find our teleport destination.

Let's start our trace at the location of the right motion controller:

1. From your components list, grab `MotionController_R`, and drag it into your event graph.
2. We want to start our trace at the motion controller's location, so let's drag a connector out from the `MotionController_R` return value and release.

3. In the dialog that appears, type `getworld` into the search bar and select **GetWorldLocation**:

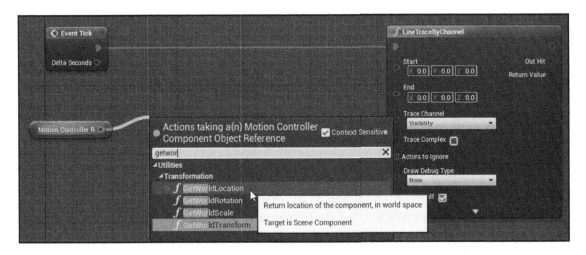

Blueprint node creation is context-sensitive by default. This means that if you're dragging a connection from another object, you'll only be shown actions that would be appropriate for that object.

4. Drag the result of `GetWorldLocation` into the Line Trace node's **Start** input pin.

Now, let's set the trace end point. We're going to end our trace at a point 10,000 units away from our start location, in the direction the controller is facing. Let's do a bit of simple math to figure out where that point is.

5. From the `MotionController_R` output, create a `Get Forward Vector` node.

This will return a vector with a length of 1 that aims in the direction the controller is facing. We said we wanted our end point to be 10,000 units from the start, so let's multiply our **Forward** vector by that value.

6. Drag the `Get Forward Vector` return value out and type `*` into the search bar. Select **vector * float**.

Now, drag a connector out from the float input to the multiply action, and select **Promote to Variable**:

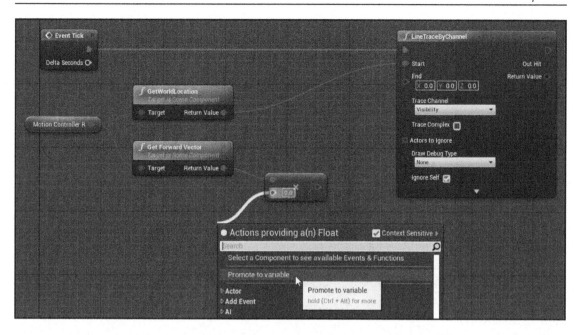

This is a fast way of creating variables in Blueprint. You can simply drag out from an input, select Promote to variable, and a variable will be created with the correct type for the input

7. Name the new variable `TeleportTraceLength`, compile the Blueprint, and set the variable's value to `10000`.

You could have simply typed `10000` directly into the multiplication action's float input, but it's bad practice to do so. If you start hiding values all over the place in your Blueprints, you'll have a hard time finding them later on when you need to change them. Also, a number typed into an input doesn't do anything to explain what it is. A variable, on the other hand, can be given a name that describes what's actually going to change if its value is changed. Numbers buried without explanation in your code are called *magic numbers* by developers, and they're an example of *technical debt*. They're just going to turn into a hassle for you later on when you need to maintain or debug your code. Unless the use of a value is absolutely obvious in its context, use a variable instead, and give it a meaningful name.

We now have a vector that's 10,000 units long, aiming in the controller's forward direction, but right now it would be running 10,000 units from the world's center, rather than from the controller, as we intend. Let's add the controller's location to this vector to fix that:

1. Drag another connector from the controller's `GetWorldLocation` call, and type + in the search bar. Select **vector + vector**.

2. Drag the output from our forward vector multiplication into the other input.

3. Connect the output of this addition to the **End** argument of `LineTraceByChannel`:

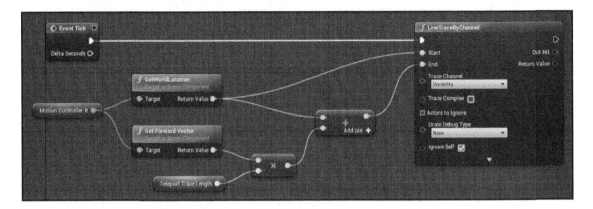

Before we move on, let's set up some debug drawing to see whether everything is behaving as we expect so far.

4. Hold down the *B* key and click on the open space to the right of the `Line Trace` node to create a `Branch` node. (You can also right-click and create a **Branch** node the way you usually do, but this is a useful shortcut.)

5. Drag a connector from the `Line Trace` node's Boolean **Return Value** to this branch's **Condition**.

The trace operation will return `True` if it hits something, and `False` if it doesn't. We're only interested in debug drawing the result if it hits something, so we're just going to use the `True` output from our branch.

If we did hit something, we need to know where the hit occurred.

6. Drag a connector from **Out Hit** and select **Break Hit Result** to see the members of the hit result struct.

A **struct** is a bundled collection of variables that can be given a name and passed around as a single unit. The `Hit Result` struct is a commonly used struct that describes the properties of a detected collision, telling you where it occurred, what actor was hit, and many other details. Calling **break** on a struct allows us to see its contents.

Now, let's draw a debug line representing our trace:

1. Drag an execution line from our `Branch` node's `True` output, and create a `Draw Debug Line` action.
2. Drag the **Location** from the `Hit Result` struct into the **Line End** input on the `Debug Line` call.
3. Drag the hit result's **Trace Start** to the **Line Start**.
4. Set the line's thickness to `2`, and set its color to anything you like.

While we're at it, let's draw a debug sphere at the hit location:

1. Create a `Draw Debug Sphere` node.
2. Connect its execution input to the debug line's output.
3. Set its **Center** to the hit result's **Location**:

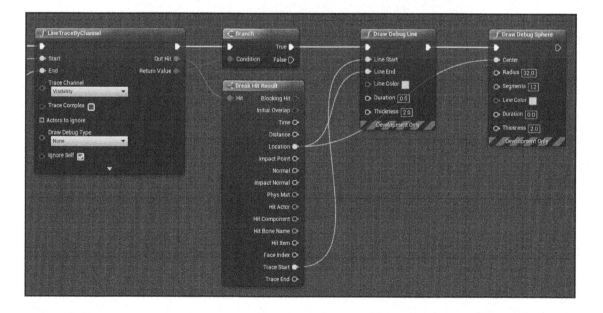

Be aware that `Draw Debug` calls only work in development builds. They're useful for understanding what's going on, but they're just debugging tools and need to be replaced with real visualizations for your actual software. We'll do that shortly.

4. Let's test it. Your result should look something like this:

Good. So far, it's doing what we expect—casting a ray from the controller, and showing us where it hits a surface. The problem, though, is that it's just as happy to hit a wall as a floor. We need to restrict it to valid teleport destinations. Let's do that.

Improving our Trace Hit Result

We're going to do this first by setting up a simple test that only accepts surfaces facing upward. We'll do this by using a vector operation called a *Dot Product* to compare a surface normal with the world's up vector. Follow these steps to get started:

1. Right-click somewhere to the right of our hit result breakout, and create a **Dot Product** node.
2. Drag the **Normal** from the hit result into the first input, and set the second input's **Z** value to **1.0**.

A *normal* is a vector that's perpendicular to the surface from which it extends. A *dot product* is a mathematical operator that returns the cosine of the angle between two vectors. If two vectors are exactly parallel, their dot product will be 1.0. If they're facing exactly in opposite directions, their dot product will be -1.0. If they're exactly perpendicular, the dot product is 0.

Since the vector (0,0,1) is the world's up vector, by testing the dot product of a surface normal against this vector, we can find out whether or not the normal is facing upward by checking whether the dot product is greater than 0.

3. Drag a connector from the result of the dot product, and select the > operator.
4. Create another branch operator using this result as its **Condition**.
5. Press *Alt* + click the execution input to the **Draw Debug Line** node to disconnect it.
6. Drag a new execution line from the return value's branch to this new branch.
7. Connect the **True** output from the dot product's branch with our **Draw Debug Line** node:

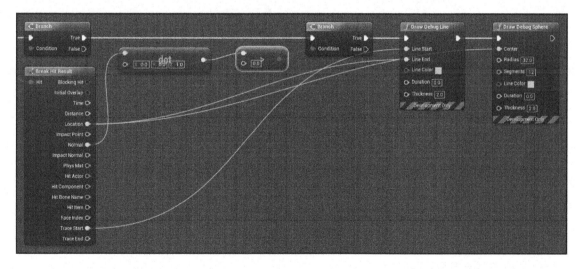

Let's test it. We'll see that we now see the debug sphere drawn when our ray hits a floor, but not when it hits a wall or a ceiling. As we mentioned a moment ago, this is because the dot product of a wall's normal versus the world's up vector will be 0, while the dot product of a ceiling against the world up is -1.

This is better, but what about the places we decided we didn't want the player to go? We spent all of that time setting up our navmesh bounds and navmesh modifiers, and we're not using them yet. We should fix this.

Using navmesh data

Now, we're going to take our test a step further, and look for the nearest point on the navmesh to wherever our pointer is pointing:

1. Right-click in our graph, and create a **Project Point to Navigation** node
2. Connect our hit result's **Location** output to this new node's **Point** input
3. Connect the node's **Projected Location** output with the debug line's **Line End** and the Debug Sphere's **Center**, replacing the location inputs that we'd previously been using there:

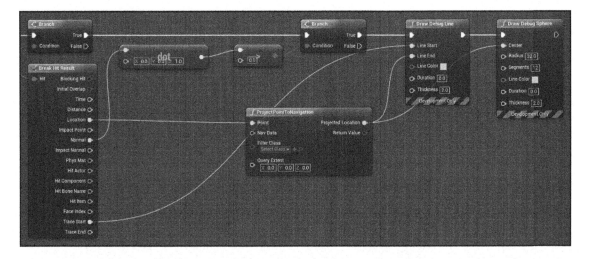

What we're doing here is querying the navmesh we created to find the closest point on the mesh to the location we supplied. This will prevent a location from being selected that we'd excluded from our mesh.

As we look around the scene, though, we can start to see that we're going to have a problem. Casting a ray straight from the controller isn't going to allow us to teleport onto higher locations than where we're currently standing, because the ray won't be able to hit the higher floor. This is a flaw in our system, and we're going to need to rethink this.

This is why it's so important to stick to our guns and do a *make it work* phase before we put a ton of work into cleaning up. It often happens that your first running prototype will reveal things you need to rethink, and it's better to discover these things early, before you've burned a ton of effort.

Changing from line trace to parabolic trace

Thinking it through, it becomes clear that we're going to need a curved path to reach points that are higher than our current viewpoint. Let's modify our trace method to make this possible. This is the result we will get:

The math used to calculate a parabola is actually fairly simple, but we have an even easier option available to us. The `Predict Projectile Path By TraceChannel` method already handles the math for us and can save us some time. Let's use this now:

1. Disconnect our **Event Tick** from the old **Line Trace By Channel** node.
2. Right-click in our graph and create a **Predict Projectile Path by TraceChannel** node.
3. Connect it to our **Tick**.
4. Set its **Trace Channel** to **Visibility**.

5. Next, connect the output from the **GetWorldLocation** of **MotionController_R** to the **Start Pos** input.

To get our **Launch Velocity**, we're going to take the **Forward Vector** of **MotionController_R**, and multiply it by an arbitrary value:

- Disconnect the old `TeleportTraceLength` variable from the **Multiply** node.
- Drag out a new connector from the **Multiply** node's float input and promote it to a variable. Let's name it `TeleportLaunchVelocity`.
- Compile our Blueprint, and give it a value of **900**.
- Connect the result to the **Launch Velocity** input:

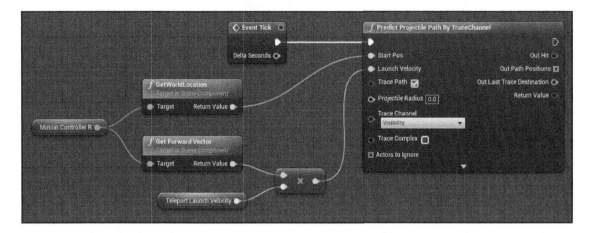

Now, let's draw the resulting path so that we can verify that it's doing what we expect.

Drawing the curved path

The `Predict Projectile Path By TraceChannel` method is going to return an array of points describing the path of the parabola. We can use these points to draw our targeting indicator. Let's get started:

1. Just as we did previously, connect a **Branch** to our **Return Value**. We're only interested in drawing anything if we got a good result.

   Now, to draw the curved path, we're actually going to have to draw a series of debug lines instead of just one.

2. Let's drag a connector from **Out Path Positions** and create a **ForEachLoop** node:

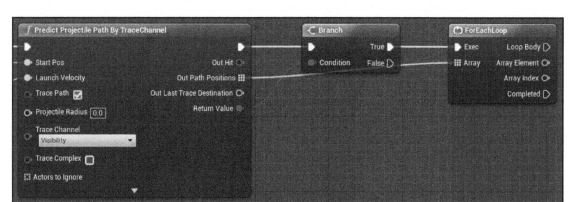

We should take a moment to talk about what we're doing here, since this is a concept you'll use quite a lot.

So far, all of the variables we've handled in our pawn Blueprint have contained single values—a number, a true or false value, and a vector. The connector for **Out Path Positions**, however, looks different. Instead of a circle, it's a 3 x 3 grid. This icon indicates that this is an **array**. Rather than holding a single value, an array contains a list of values. In this case, those values are a list of points that make up the curved path we're going to draw.

A *For Each Loop* is a programming structure called an **iterator**. Iterators loop through collections of values and allow you to perform operations on each element in the collection.

Let's take a quick look at the ForEach Loop's outputs:

- The **Loop Body** will execute once for each item it finds in the array.
- The **Array Element** is the item it found.
- The **Array Index** is where it found it. Arrays are always numbered from zero, so the first item will have an index of **0**, the second will have an index of **1**, and so on.
- The **Completed** execution pin will be called when it reaches the end of the list.

We're going to use this loop to draw the line segments of our curve, but we're going to need two points for each segment, which means we can't draw anything until we reach the second point in the array:

1. Drag a connector from the **Array Index** output and connect it to an **integer | integer node**. Leave the second value as **0**.

2. Connect its output to a **Branch**, and connect the **Loop Body** to the **Branch** input. This will allow us to skip the first value in the array.

3. Create a **Draw Debug Line** node, and connect the **Array Element** to the **Line End** input. Since we're starting with the second value of the array, the point at that location is the end of our line. We're going to get the line start by getting the point before it:

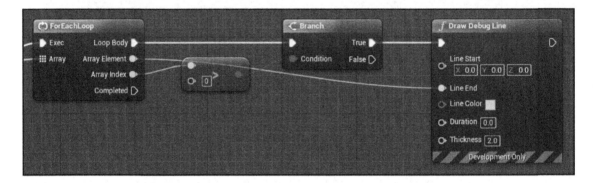

4. To find our **Line Start**, drag another connector from the **Array Index**, and *subtract 1* from it.

5. Now, drag another connector from **Out Path Positions**, and type Get into the search box. Select **Get (a copy)**:

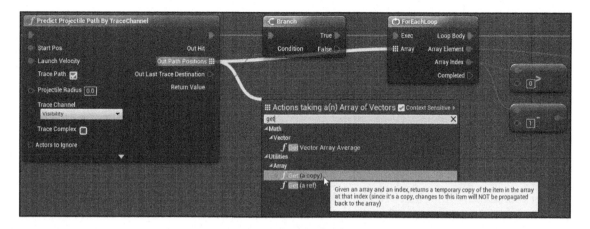

This will get the element stored at the location in the array corresponding to the index we give it.

6. Connect the result of our **Array Index -1** subtraction to the **Get** node's integer input. This will retrieve the value before the one we're currently iterating on.

7. Connect the output from this **Get** node to the **Line Start** of **Draw Debug Line**:

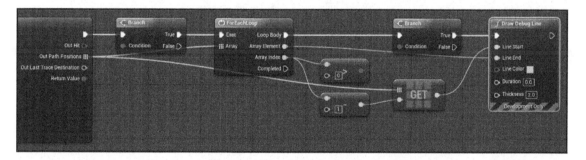

When you're finished, the drawing routine should look something like what's shown in the preceding screenshot.

What we've just done here is looped through each of the path position vectors in **Out Path Positions**, and for each one after the first, we drew a line from the position before it to the current one, until we reached the end of the list.

Drawing the endpoint after all the line segments have been drawn

Finally, let's draw a debug sphere at the trace endpoint. We can reuse the nodes we were previously using to draw the sphere at the end of our straight line trace:

1. Just as we did before, **break** the **Hit Result** struct from **Out Hit**.
2. Take its **Location** and feed it into a **ProjectPointToNavigation** node.
3. Connect a **Branch** to its **Return Value**, and feed the **True** branch's execution into a **Draw Debug Sphere** node.
4. Use the **Projected Location** as the debug sphere's **Center**.

Rather than calling this right after the **Draw Debug Line** node, however, call it from the **Completed** output of **ForEachLoop** instead, since we only need to draw the sphere once after all of the line segments have been drawn.

Your graph should now look like this:

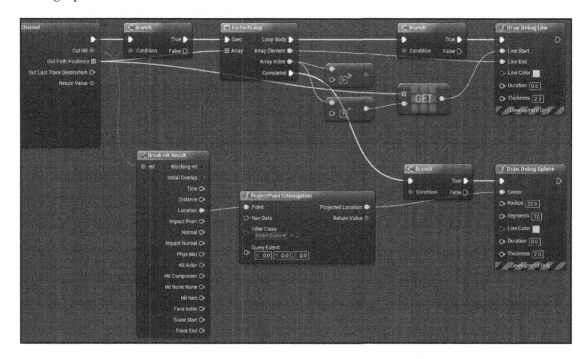

Let's test it and see what happens when we run it:

Great! We're now projecting a curved path that will allow us to get around the map much more easily, and we've used debug drawing to verify that it's giving us good results.

 The Draw Debug methods we're using here will only work in debug and development builds. They aren't included in shipping builds. The correct way to draw this path would be to use the collection of points in **Out Path Positions** to change the shape of a spline mesh, but doing this is beyond the scope of this book. There's a good example, however, in the VR Template, and the work we've done here is a good starting point for understanding what they're doing in that project's Blueprints.

Next, let's take care of the next job and allow our player to teleport to the destination they've chosen.

Teleporting the player

The first thing we need to do in this instance is give the player a way to tell the system when they intend to teleport.

Creating Input Mappings

We're going to use our Engine Input Mappings to set up a new named input. Let's get started:

1. Open your **Project Settings** and navigate to **Engine | Input**.
2. Hit the **+** sign beside **Bindings | Action Mappings** to create a new action mapping:

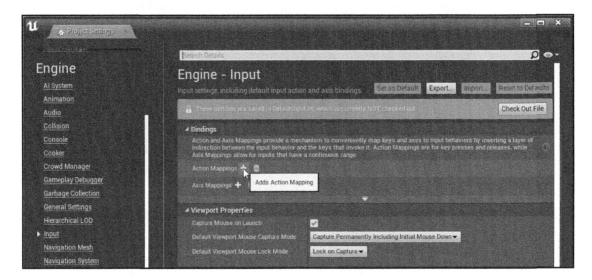

3. We're going to name it `TeleportRight`.

What this is going to do is create an input event with this name that we can then respond to in our event graphs.

You may have already discovered that you can set up events in your event graphs directly to listen to controller inputs and keystrokes. For most projects, though, it's a better idea to map your inputs here as it gives you a central location from which to manage them.

Now, let's indicate what inputs should trigger this teleport action. A drop-down menu has appeared beneath the new action mapping with a **None** indicator displayed. (Hit the expander arrow beside the action mappings if the drop-down menu isn't visible.) Let's carry on:

1. Under **TeleportRight**, use the drop-down menu to select **MotionController (R) Thumbstick**.

    This will handle our Oculus Touch controller mappings, but doesn't help us on the HTC Vive, which doesn't use thumbsticks.

2. Hit the **+** sign beside the **TeleportRight** action to add another mapping to the group.

3. Select **MotionController (R) FaceButton1** for this one:

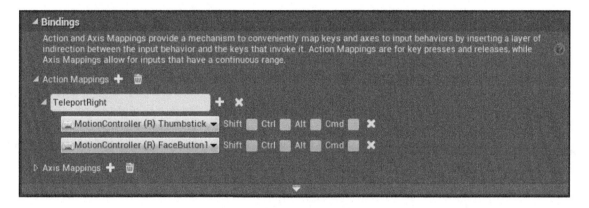

Your bindings should now look like what's shown in the preceding screenshot.

Now, we've told the input system to send a **TeleportRight** input event, regardless of whether the player is using a motion controller with a thumbstick or one with face buttons.

These bindings are stored in `DefaultInput.ini` and can be edited there, but it's generally more convenient to set them up here in the **Project Settings** UI. If you need to copy a bunch of input bindings from one project to another, however, it can be convenient to copy the contents of `DefaultInput.ini` from one project to another. Not every project will have `DefaultInput.ini`. If yours doesn't, you can simply add it and the engine will use it.

Let's close **Project Settings** and return to our VRPawn's event graph. You'll find that you can now create a **TeleportRight** event here, since we defined it in our input settings. Let's do this, as follows:

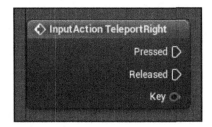

Caching our teleport destination

Now, before we do anything with this event, we need to store the location we found in our trace method previously so that we can use it here when the player tries to teleport:

1. Under **My Blueprint | Variables**, hit the **+** sign to create a new variable.
2. Set its type to **Boolean**, and name it `bHasValidTeleportDest`.

> Variable names are important. They tell the reader (who might be another developer maintaining your code or might be yourself in the future) what a variable represents. Your variable names should accurately reflect what they contain. In the case of True/False Boolean variables, make sure your name describes what question it's actually answering. So, for instance, in this case, *Teleport* would be a poor choice for a name, as it doesn't indicate whether the variable's value means that the player can teleport, is teleporting, has recently teleported, or just enjoys daydreaming about teleporting. Be clear about these things. `bHasValidTeleportDest` clearly indicates what it means.
>
> Prefixing Boolean variable names with *b* is a practice mandated by Epic's coding style guide for C++, but it's a good idea to follow it in Blueprint development as well. (If you plan on developing in C++, you should know and follow the Unreal style guide, which can be found at `https://docs.unrealengine.com/en-us/Programming/Development/CodingStandard`.)

3. Create another variable and name it `TeleportDest`.
4. Set its type to **Vector**.

Let's populate these variables. The location we care about is the **Projected Location** found by the Project Point to Navigation method we're calling at our hit location. Let's store whether we've found a valid location. You'll probably want to drag the **Draw Debug Sphere** node a bit to the right to give yourself some room since we're about to add a few nodes before we call it:

1. Drag your `bHasValidTeleportDest` variable onto the event graph, and select **set** when asked.

   Do you see where the **Completed** output from the ForEach loop runs into the **Branch** statement coming out of our Project Point to Navigation method?

2. Press *Ctrl* + drag the execution input into that **Branch** node to move it onto the `CanTeleport` setter. (Notice that the *b* prefix on Boolean variables is automatically hidden when the variable is used in a graph.)
3. Feed the **Return Value** from the Project Point to Navigation method into this variable. You can press *Ctrl* + drag to move this too.
4. Drag an execution line from **Set bHasValidTeleportDest** to the Branch input, and use the output of the setter to drive the branch.

Let's set our **TeleportDest** to the Project Point to Navigation method's projected location if it returns true:

1. Drag our `TeleportDest` variable onto the event graph and choose to set it.
2. Take the execution line running from our **Branch** node into our **Draw Debug Sphere** node, and press *Ctrl* + drag it to move it into the **Set Teleport Dest** input.
3. Feed the **Projected Location** output into the `TeleportDest` variable.
4. Now, just because it's cleaner, let's feed the output from the `TeleportDest` setter into the **Center** input on our **DrawDebugSphere** node.

> It's worth learning about Blueprint shortcuts. Pressing *Alt* + clicking on a connection disconnects it. Pressing *Ctrl* + dragging a connection allows you to move it somewhere else.

5. From the **False execution** pin of **Branch**, let's set **TeleportDest** to (0.0, 0.0, 0.0).

Your graph should now look like this:

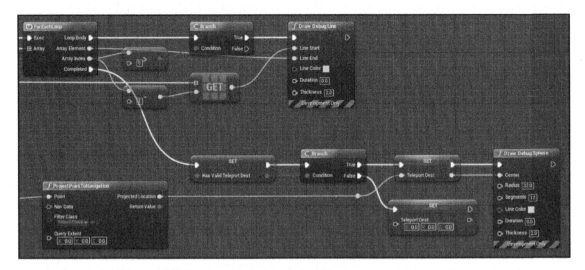

Can you see the extra pin on the connection between **Projected Location** and **Set Teleport Dest**? That's a **Reroute Node**. You can create one by dragging a connection out and selecting **Add Reroute Node** from the creation dialog, or by *double-clicking* on an existing connector. These are useful for organizing your connections so that you can easily see what's going on in your graphs. In general, try to avoid allowing connectors to cross underneath nodes they're not connected to, as this can mislead someone reading your Blueprint. You can also feed multiple inputs into a reroute node or branch multiple outputs from it.

Now, on every tick, we have either a true or a false value in bHasValidTeleportDest, and if it's true, we have the location to which we could teleport.

Executing the teleport

Let's use the value we've just stored in the bHasValidTeleportDest flag to see whether we have a valid destination, and teleport the player pawn to the TeleportDest if we do:

1. From the TeleportRight input action we created a moment ago, we'll connect an execution line from its **Pressed** output into a **Branch** node.

 Remember that you can hold down *B* and click to create a Branch node. Take a look at the other shortcuts found on Epic's Blueprint Editor Cheat Sheet here: https://docs.unrealengine.com/en-us/Engine/Blueprints/UserGuide/CheatSheet. They'll save you a lot of time.

2. Grab your bHasValidTeleportDest variable and drag it onto the **Branch** node's **Condition** input.

3. From the **True** execution output, create a **SetActorLocation** action, and drag your TeleportDest variable onto its **New Location** input:

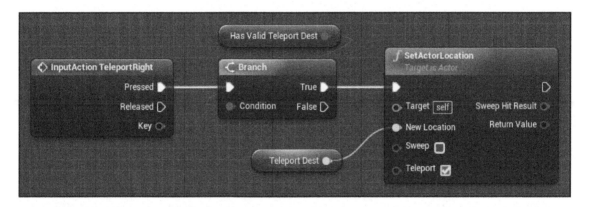

Launch it into a VR preview and give it a shot. You should now be able to teleport around the map. It's nice to be able to explore, right?

Now that we have everything working, let's do some work to improve things.

The first thing we'll notice when we start jumping around the map is that we don't have any way to change the player's orientation at their landing position. We can definitely improve this.

Allowing the player to choose their landing orientation

If we want our player to be able to specify their facing direction when they land, the first thing we're going to need to do is give them a way to tell the system where they want to be looking.

Mapping axis inputs

Let's add an input to give our player a way to do this:

1. Open up **Project Settings | Engine | Input**.

   Do you see the section in **Bindings | Action Mappings** where we set up our **TeleportRight** input? Right below it is a list of **Axis Mappings**.

2. Hit the **+** button beside **Axis Mappings** to add a new mapping.
3. Use the expansion arrow to open it up, and name it `MotionControllerThumbRight_Y`.
4. Map it to **MotionController (R) Thumbstick Y.**
5. Set its **scale** to **-1.0.**
6. Create a second mapping, named `MotionControllerThumbRight_X`.
7. Map it to `MotionController (R) Thumbstick X`, and leave its **scale** as **1.0**.

 Unreal's input system handles two kinds of mappings: **Action Mappings** and **Axis Mappings**. Action mappings are discrete events, such as button or key presses and releases. Axis mappings give you continuous information about an analog input, such as a joystick or a trackpad.

You may have noticed that we scaled the Y input from our motion controller thumbstick by -1.0. This is because the **Y** input from that device comes in reversed, so we need to flip it. Multiplying it by -1 simply inverts the input:

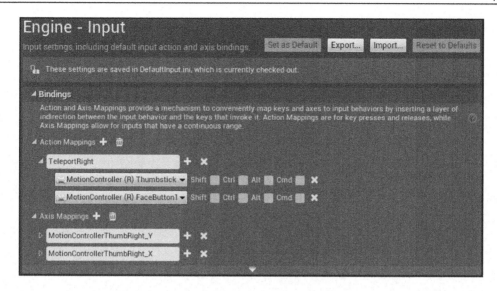

Your input mappings should now look like what's shown in the preceding screenshot.

Now that we've added our new input mappings, we can close our project settings.

Cleaning up our Tick event

Let's jump back to our pawn's event graph.

Since we want to check the player's thumbstick position continuously while we're setting up a teleport, we're going to need to put this on the **Event Tick**. Our **Tick** event is getting a little crowded, though. Let's clean it up before we start adding more:

1. Drag a marquee over the current contents of your **Tick** event:

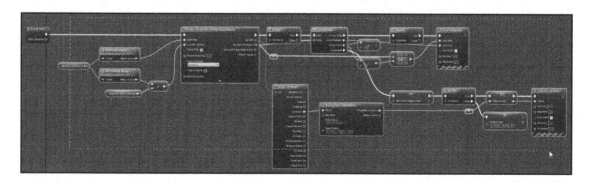

Select all the nodes connected to your Event Tick.

2. Right-click anywhere on the selected nodes and select **Collapse to Function** from the context menu:

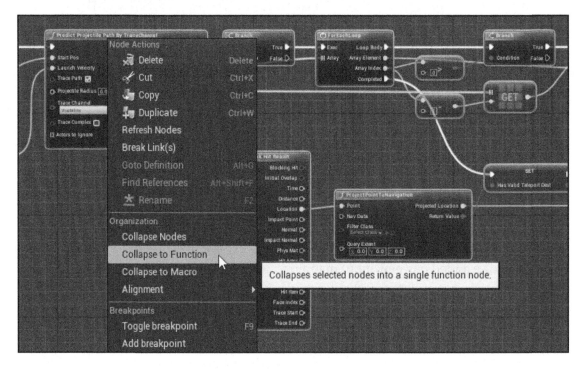

Right-click any of the selected nodes and select Collapse to Function.

3. Name the new function `SetTeleportDestination`.

That's much cleaner, isn't it? Take a look at the following screenshot:

In general, it's a good idea to use functions as a way of organizing and reusing your code, rather than leaving things strewn all over your event graph. Remember that 80% of the life cycle of any piece of code will be spent in debugging and maintaining it, so organizing your code early can save you quite a lot of work later on.

The names you give your functions should be descriptive and they should be accurate. Think of them as a promise to the reader that the contents of the function really do whatever the name suggests they do. That reader might be you in the future, debugging or updating your code, or it might be another developer altogether. If you've named your functions clearly, everyone's going to have a much easier time understanding what your code is doing. If you modify a function in a way that changes what it does, change its name too. Don't let a legacy name mislead your reader.

Using thumbstick input to orient the player

Let's create a new function to handle our teleport orientation:

1. Hit the + button in **My Blueprint** | **Function**s to create a new function.
2. Name it `SetTeleportOrientation`.

   A new tab will automatically open, showing you the contents of your function. Right now, it just contains an entry point with an execution pin.

3. Right-click anywhere inside the function's graph and type `thumbright` into the context menu's search box. You'll see that the two Axis Mappings you created in your input settings are now visible here as functions.
4. Add the **Get MotionControllerThumbRight_Y** and **Get MotionControllerthumbRight_X** nodes here:

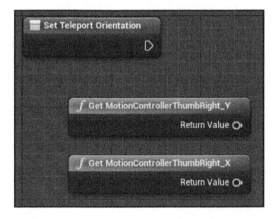

5. Create a **Make Vector** node.

6. Feed the return value from **Get MotionControllerThumbRight_Y** into the **Make Vector** node's **X** input. (This may seem backward, but it's correct—we need to transform this input to use it to drive our rotation.)

7. Feed **Get MotionControllerThumbRight_X** into the new vector's **Y** input.

8. Normalize the new vector by adding a **Normalize** node to the Make Vector's Return Value:

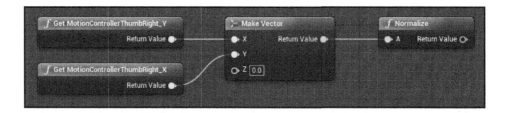

Normalizing a vector scales it to a length of 1. A vector whose length is 1 is called a **unit vector**. Many mathematical operations on vectors will return incorrect results if they're called on vectors with arbitrary lengths. A general rule of thumb is that, if you're doing vector operations to figure out rotations or angles, make sure you're using unit vectors.

Now that we've normalized our input vector, we need to rotate it so it's aiming in the direction the player intends.

Here's the thing about designing locomotion systems for VR: when you present the player with a rotation, you have to decide what its basis is going to be. When the player pushes a stick forward or touches forward on a trackpad, how do we translate that into a real-world rotation? If you've operated a remote control car or been playing games long enough to remember the old *tank-style* controls in *Resident Evil* and *Fear Effect*, you have some notion of what we're describing here. *Forward* in those systems meant the direction the car or character was facing, and if the character was facing the camera at the moment, those controls were going to feel backward.

In traditional first-person designs over the past two decades, this isn't a problem we've had to address. There was no difference between the direction the character was facing and the direction the player was looking, so using the camera's look direction as a forward direction was an obvious choice.

In VR, on the other hand, we have several options:

- We can base our rotation on the *pawn's rotation*, but that's not a great idea in room-scale VR, as the player can turn around in the tracking volume without necessarily rotating their pawn. You don't want to orient a control based on something the player may not be able to see.
- We could base it on the player's *look direction*, which is a better choice since it's consistent from the player's perspective, but creates funky behaviors as the player looks around:

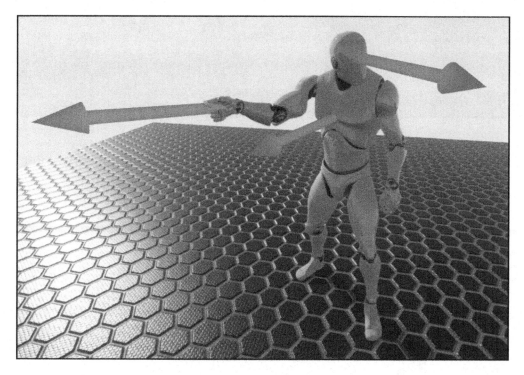

A character in VR can have several transforms at the same time - head, body, and hands.

In VR, a player's head, hands, and body can rotate independently of each other, so it's no longer always obvious where *forward* is.

The best choice, though (and as we'll discover later on when we handle seamless locomotion), is to base it on the *motion controller's orientation*, since the player's already using it to provide input, is aware of its orientation, and can change its orientation easily.

Let's set our system up this way:

1. Add a **RotateVector** node to our **Normalize** node's return value.
2. Drag a reference to **MotionController_R** onto the graph.
3. Drag a **GetWorldRotation** node from **MotionController_R**:

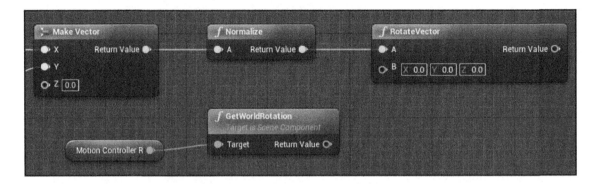

This will get us the right controller's orientation in the world, but we're only interested in the side-to-side rotation (Yaw). We don't want any Pitch or Roll information.

4. Right-click the **Return Value** from **GetWorldRotation** and select **Split Struct Pin**:

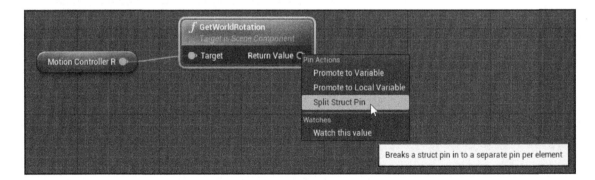

5. Do the same for the **RotateVector** node's **B** input.
6. Connect the **Yaw** output from **GetWorldRotation** to the **Yaw** input to **RotateVector**. Leave **Roll** and **Pitch** unconnected:

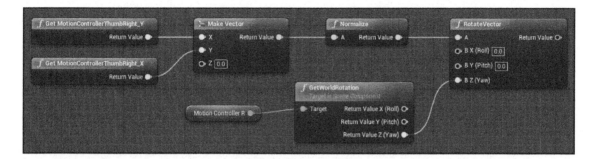

 Splitting struct pins in Blueprints is often cleaner than using **Break** and **Make** nodes to split them and reconstruct them. They do the same thing. It's purely a question of what makes your Blueprint more readable.

Now, we need to turn our rotated vector into a rotator we can use.

7. Add a **RotationFromXVector** node to the **RotateVector**'s return value.

Finally, we need to store this vector so that we can use it later.

8. Drag the **RotationFromXVector** node's return value out and select **Promote to variable.**
9. Name the new variable `TeleportOrientation`.
10. This will create a **Set** node for the new variable automatically. Drag an execution line from your function's entry point to this setter.

11. Drag an execution line from your setter and select **Add Return Node** to add an exit point to your function.

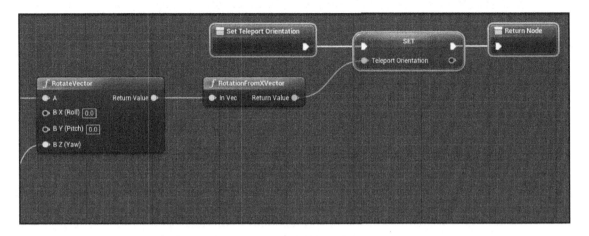

We're now converting the return value from our RotateVector node to a rotator and using it to populate Teleport Orientation.

Adding return nodes to functions that don't return values isn't required, but it's good practice to do it because it makes it clear to someone maintaining or debugging the code where the exit points are. Nothing will break if you don't do this, but your code will be easier to read if you do. We're not going to do this with every method in this book, just to avoid adding extra steps, but it's a good idea to make this a habit.

12. Return to your event graph's **Event Tick**, and drag the **SetTeleportOrientation** function onto the outgoing execution pin from **SetTeleportDestination**:

Set Teleport Orientation will now be called on every frame after **Set Teleport Destination** finishes.

Let's use this new information:

1. In your event graph, find the **InputAction TeleportRight** event, where we're setting our actor location.
2. First, let's collapse this into a function as well. Leaving it out on the event graph is sloppy. Select the nodes to the right of our input action, right-click, and *collapse* them into a new function.
3. Name the new function `ExecuteTeleport`:

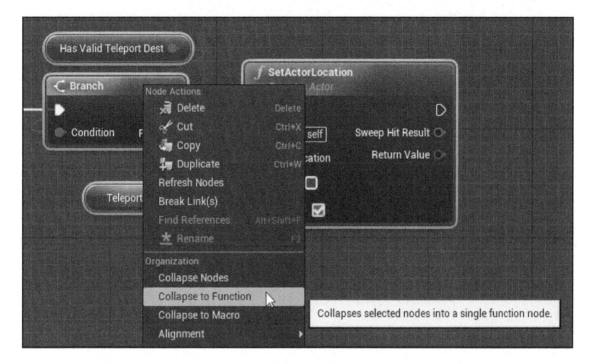

Since we now have a teleport orientation value we need to accommodate, **SetActorLocation** is no longer enough for us, since it only sets location and not rotation. We could call a `Set Actor Rotation` method right after it, using the value stored in our **TeleportOrientation** variable, but there's a cleaner method available to us.

4. Select the **Set Actor Location** node here and **delete** it.
5. Right-click in the graph and create a **Teleport** node.
6. Connect the **True** branch from our Branch statement to its execution input.
7. Connect the **TeleportDest** variable to its **Dest Location** input.

8. Grab the **TeleportOrientation** variable from our **Variables** list and drag it onto the **Dest Rotation** input pin:

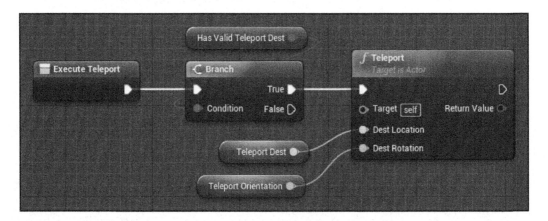

Let's try it out. Much better. Now, the position of our thumb on the trackpad or the orientation of the thumbstick affects our teleport orientation. We can look around much more easily.

There's still one more thing we need to fix though. Our teleport orientation works fine if the player is still looking in the same direction as the pawn's rotation, but becomes confusingly inaccurate if they aren't. Let's accommodate this.

What we're going to want to do here is find out where the player is looking relative to the pawn's orientation, and then combine this difference in rotations with our selected teleport orientation so that when the player lands there, they're looking in the direction they selected.

1. Right-click and create a **GetActorRotation** node.
2. We're only going to want the Yaw value from this rotation, so right-click the node's **Return Value** and select **Split Struct Pin** to break out the rotator's components.
3. From your **Components** list, drag a reference to the **Camera** component onto the graph.
4. Drag its output and call **GetWorldRotation** on it.
5. Right-click its **Return Value** and select **Split Struct Pin**.

6. Right-click in the graph and create a **Delta (Rotator)** node. Split its A and B input struct pins.

7. Connect the **GetActorRotation** node's **Return Value Z (Yaw)** output to the **Delta (Rotator)** node's **A Z (Yaw)** input.

8. Connect the Camera's **GetWorldRotation** node's **Return Value Z (Yaw)** output to the **Delta (Rotator)** node's **B Z (Yaw)** input.

9. Right-click in the graph and create a **CombineRotators** node.

10. Feed the **Teleport Orientation** variable's value into the **CombineRotators** node's **A** input.

11. Feed the **Return Value** from the **Delta (Rotator)** node into the **CombineRotator** node's **B** input.

12. Feed the **Return Value** from the **CombineRotators** node into the **Teleport** node's **Dest Rotation** input.

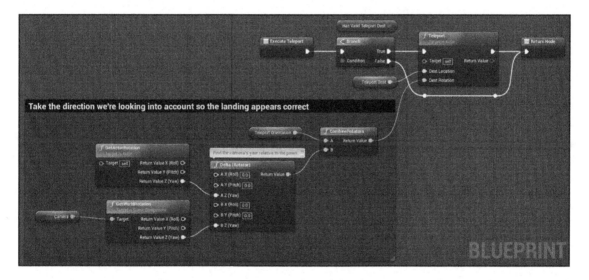

Now when the player lands at the selected teleport spot, they'll be looking in the direction they expect. If you're coming from traditional flat-screen game development, this is a thing you're going to have to get used to accommodating as a VR developer: the pawn's rotation is not synonymous with the look direction. Players in VR can look around without affecting the pawn's orientation, so you'll always need to keep both orientations in mind when handling rotation in VR.

The problem now is that we can't see where it's going to aim us when we land. Let's improve our target indication.

Creating a teleport destination indicator

We'll create a simple Blueprint actor to act as our teleport destination indicator:

1. In your project's Blueprints directory, right-click and create a new blueprint class with `Actor` as its parent class.
2. Name it `BP_TeleportDestIndicator`.
3. Open it up.
4. In its **Components** tab, hit **Add Component**, and add a **Cylinder** component.
5. Set the **scale** of the **Cylinder** to (`0.9, 0.9, 0.1`). (Remember to unlock the uniform scale lock to the right of the **Scale** input.)
6. Under the Cylinder's **Collision** properties, set **Can Character Step Up On** to **No**, and set its **Collision Preset** to **NoCollision**. (This is important—this indicator will interfere with the pawn if it has a collision.)
7. Add a **Cube** component.
8. Set its **Location** to (`60.0, 0.0, 0.0`).
9. Set its **Scale** to (**0.3, 0.1, 0.1**):

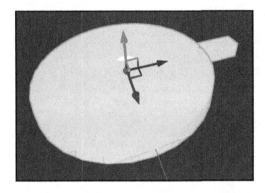

Our indicator should look something like this.

10. Compile it, save it, and close it.

Giving it a material

If the blank white material isn't doing it for you, we can create something a little nicer. We're not going to go crazy on this one, but we can improve its look with some quick work:

1. From your project directory in your **Content** browser, create a **new directory** called `MaterialLibrary`.

2. Right-click inside it and select **Create Basic Asset** | **Material**.
3. Name your new material **M_TeleportIndicator**.
4. Open it up.
5. In the **Details** | **Material** section, set its **Blend Mode** to **Additive**.
6. Set its **Shading Model** to **Unlit**.
7. Hold down the 3 key and click anywhere in the graph to create a **Constant 3 Vector** node. This is how colors are represented in materials.
8. Double-click the node and choose a primary green: **R=0.0, G=1.0, B=0.0**.
9. Drag the output of our color node into the **Emissive Color** input.
10. Right-click anywhere in the graph and create a **Linear Gradient** node.
11. Drag the **VGradient** output into the material's **Opacity** input:

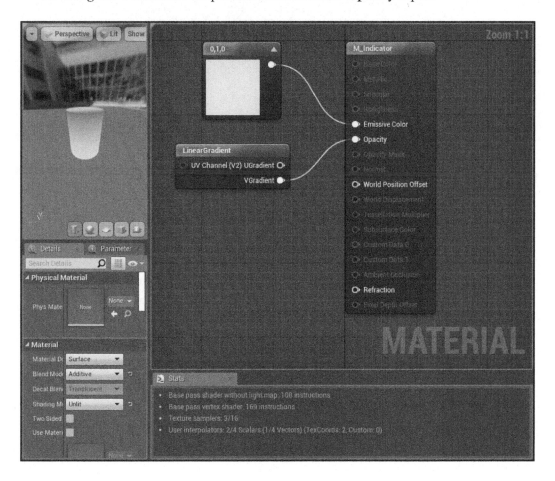

12. Save and close the material.
13. Open your **BP_TeleportDestIndicator** Blueprint and select the **Cylinder** component. Under its **Details | Materials**, set its **Element 0** material to the material you just created.
14. Do the same for the **Cube** component:

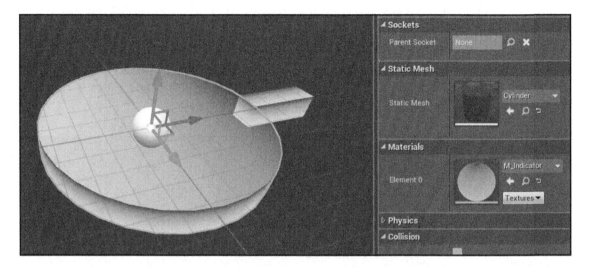

Nice! This is a very simple material, and if we really wanted to, we could spend a lot of time designing something wonderful, but for what we're doing now, this is entirely fine.

Adding the teleport indicator to the pawn

Now, let's add this new indicator to our pawn:

1. In our VRPawn's **Components** tab, add a **Child Actor** component.
2. In its **Details | Child Actor Component | Child Actor Class**, select the new **BP_TeleportDestIndicator** actor we just made.
3. Rename the **ChildActor** to `TeleportDestIndicator`. (You can use the *F2* key to rename objects.)

Let's create a new function to set its position and orientation:

1. Create a new function in the pawn's **Functions** collection, and name it `UpdateTeleportIndicator`.
2. Drag the **TeleportDestIndicator** into the function's graph.

3. Drag the output from **TeleportDestIndicator** and create a **SetWorldLocationAndRotation** node, using it as its **Target**.
4. Drag your **TeleportDest** variable onto the **New Location** input.
5. Drag your **TeleportOrientation** variable onto the **New Rotation** input.
6. Give it a return node:

7. Return to your event graph, and drag an instance of the `UpdateTeleportIndicator` function onto your **Event Tick** after **Set Teleport Orientation**:

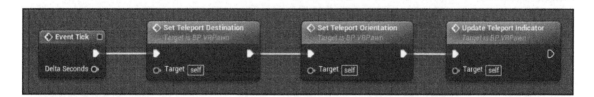

Let's try it out. That's better! Now, we can see where we're going to be facing when we land. While we're at it, let's get rid of that **Debug Sphere** we were using as a temporary solution earlier on.

8. In the **Set Teleport Destination** function, find the **Draw Debug Sphere** call and **delete** it.

Optimizing and refining our teleport

Let's finish things up with a bit of refinement, where we're still seeing some rough edges.

Displaying UI only when teleport input is pressed

First off, we're running the teleport indicators all of the time, regardless of whether or not the user is actually trying to teleport. Let's activate these interfaces only when the user is pressing the teleport input:

1. Add a new variable to our player pawn. Set its type to **Boolean**, and name it `bTeleportPressed`.
2. Press *Alt* + click on the execution line from **InputAction TeleportRight** to the `ExecuteTeleport` function call to disconnect it.
3. Drag the `bTeleportPressed` variable onto the **Pressed** execution pin from **InputAction TeleportRight** to create a setter. Set it to True here.
4. Drag another instance of `bTeleportPressed` onto the **Released** execution pin. Set it to **False**.
5. Connect **ExecuteTeleport** to the setter that's clearing **TeleportPressed**, so the teleport will happen when the user releases the input:

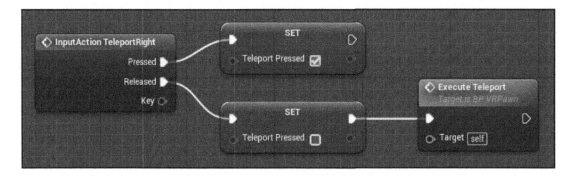

Now that we have a variable that will be true when the teleport input is held, and false when it isn't, we can use this to manage what happens on our Tick event.

6. Disconnect **Event Tick** from **SetTeleportDestination**.

7. Add a **Branch** node here, and use `bTeleportPressed` as its condition.

8. Feed the execution line from **Event Tick** to the **Branch** input, and feed its **True** branch to `SetTeleportDestination`. This way, the teleport UI will only be updated or displayed when the user presses the teleport input:

Let's try it out. This is better, but our destination indicator is still visible while the input isn't pressed, and it's not updating. We need to hide it when we're not using it:

1. Select the **TeleportDestIndicator** component from your pawn's **Components** tab.
2. In its **Details**, set **Rendering | Hidden in Game** to **True**.
3. Drag your **TeleportDestIndicator** component onto the graph.
4. Drag a connector from it and call **Set Hidden in Game** on it.
5. Drag an instance of **bTeleportPressed** onto your graph and **Get** its value.
6. Drag a connector from it and type `not` into the search bar. Select **NOT Boolean**.
7. Plug this value into the **New Hidden** input in your **Set Hidden in Game** action.

This will cause the indicator to be hidden when **Teleport** is not pressed, and not hidden when it is:

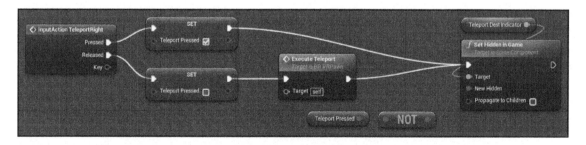

Let's try it again. Much better. The UI is only displayed when we need it.

We would still need to replace the teleport arc we're currently drawing with debug methods before we could ship. We're not going to run through that process here, though, because it's a bit too involved for the scope of this chapter. Basically, what you would do here is create a spline component on the pawn and attach a mesh to it. Instead of using a ForEach loop in `SetTeleportDestination` to draw a series of debug lines, we would save the path positions to a variable. In `UpdateTeleportIndicator`, we would then use these positions to set the points on the spline. If you'd like to give this a shot, there's a good example in the VR Template.

Creating a deadzone for our input

As we jump around the map, it's also becoming clear that we haven't given the player an easy way to teleport without changing orientation. Our system works well when they want to look around, but doesn't give them a way to opt out.

Let's open up `SetTeleportOrientation` and fix this:

1. Create a new variable in **BP_VRPawn**. Set its type to **Float**, and name it `TeleportDeadzone`.
2. **Compile** the Blueprint and set its value to **0.7**. This will accept input at 70% of the trackpad or thumbstick's radius.
3. Drag a second output from the **Make Vector** node that's combining the two Get **MotionControllerThumbRight** input values, and create a **VectorLengthSquared** node from it.
4. Drag the `TeleportDeadzone` variable onto the graph and **Get** its value.
5. Square the value of **Teleport Deadzone**.
6. Drag the output from **VectorLengthSquared** and create a >= node.
7. Drag the squared **Teleport Deadzone** value into its other input:

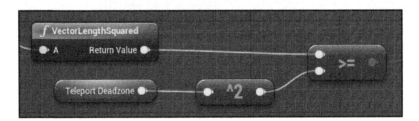

What's going on here? We're interested in finding out whether the user's input is more than 70% of the way toward the edge of its range. We could find this by getting the vector length and comparing it with the **Teleport Deadzone**, and this would give us a correct answer, but finding the actual length of a vector involves a square root, which is expensive. Squaring a value, on the other hand, just involves multiplying it by itself, which is cheap. In our case, since we don't care what the real vector length is—just how it compares with the deadzone. We can skip the square root on our vector length and just compare it with the squared target length. This is a common way of optimizing vector length comparisons. You'll see it a lot.

> Using squared vector lengths to test input deadzones will give you a properly round test region, so you'll get consistent results at any input angle.

Now, let's use the result of this comparison to pick which rotation value we will use:

1. Place a **Select** node in the graph, and connect the output of the >= test to its **Index** input.
2. Disconnect the **RotationFromXVector** node's output from the **Set Teleport Orientation** node.
3. Connect the **RotationFromXVector** node's output to the **Select** node's **True** input.
4. Create a **GetActorRotation** node and connect its output to the **Select** node's **False** input.
5. Connect the **Select** node's **Return Value** to the **Set Teleport Orientation** node's input:

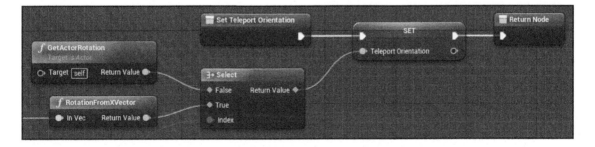

What we're doing here is using the result of our deadzone check to decide whether we should use the rotation value from the thumbstick inputs or just stick with the pawn's existing rotation. If the input is at 70% of the range or greater, we'll use the input. If not, we just use the pawn's rotation.

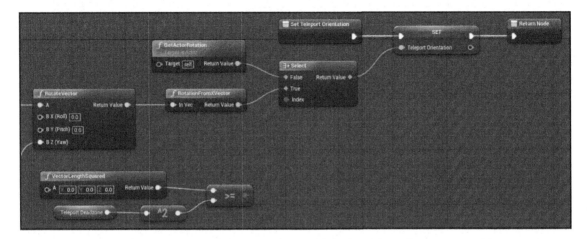

Let's run it. Now, you'll change orientation if you're hitting the edge of the trackpad or pushing the thumbstick a fair distance, but if they're closer to the center, you'll just retain your current orientation when you teleport.

Fading out and in on teleport

Our system is starting to work pretty well, but our teleport can feel a little jarring. Let's fade out and back in to make a more pleasant transition:

1. Open our pawn's event graph.
2. Near our **InputAction Teleport Right** event, create a `Get Player Camera Manager` node.
3. From this node's **Return Value**, create a `Start Camera Fade` action.
4. Set its **To Alpha** value to **1.0**.
5. Drag out its **Duration** input and promote it to a variable. Compile and set its value to **0.1**.

   This will fade the scene camera to black over a duration of one tenth of a second.

6. Disconnect the **input** to the `Execute Teleport` function call.

7. Connect the execution output from the **Teleport Pressed = False** node to the new **Start Camera Fade** action.

8. You'll probably need to drag a few nodes off to the right to make some room.

Now, we're going to call **Start Camera Fade** after the user has released the teleport input, since we've cleared the `bTeleportPressed` flag:

1. Drag an execution line from the **Start Camera Fade** node's execution output and put a **Delay** on it.

2. Set the **Delay duration** to your **Fade Duration** variable.

3. Drag from the Delay's **Completed** output into your `Execute Teleport` function call so that the function will be called after the fade and delay have occurred.

   When the user releases the teleport input, we're fading out over a tenth of a second, waiting another tenth of a second, and then executing the teleport. Now, we need to fade back in once the teleport is done.

4. Create another **Start Camera Fade** node, and connect the **Execute Teleport** output to its execution input.

5. Connect the output from **Get Player Camera Manager** to this node's **Target** input.

6. Set its **Duration** to your `Fade Duration` variable.

7. Set its **From Alpha** value to **1.0** and its **To Alpha** value to **0.0**.

8. Connect the output from this node to the input of your **Set Hidden in Game** node of **Teleport Dest Indicator**:

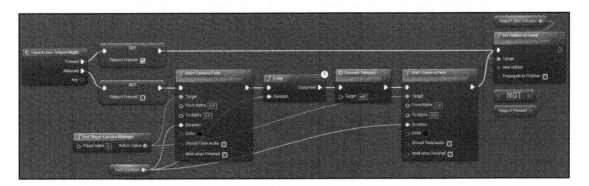

Your graph should now look like this.

Let's test it in-game. This is much nicer. We now have a fast fade out and in when the teleport action occurs. It's subtle, but adds a bit of polish to the application and makes the teleport less jarring.

Since this action takes time, however briefly, we should ensure that the player can't trigger a second teleport while one is already underway:

1. Create a new Boolean variable and name it `bIsTeleporting`.
2. Drag an instance of it onto your graph and **Get** its value.
3. Insert a new **Branch** node between **InputAction TeleportRight** and set **Teleport Pressed** to **True**.
4. Use `bIsTeleporting` as the **Branch** node's **Condition**.
5. Connect its **False** output to the set **Teleport Pressed** to **True** node, and leave its **True** output unconnected.
6. Do the same for the input action's **Released** execution:

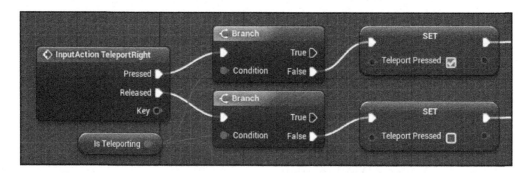

This way, a **Teleport Pressed** or **Released** event will only be processed if `bIsTeleporting` is **False**.

Now, we need to set `bIsTeleporting` to **True** when we start a teleport action, and then set it to **False** again when the action finishes:

1. After the **Set Teleport Pressed = False** node coming from the input action's **Released** output, insert a setter to set `bIsTeleporting` to **True**.
2. Connect its output to the **Start Camera Fade** node.

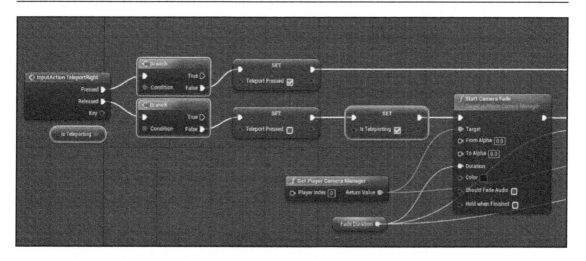

3. After the second **Start Camera Fade** node, add another setter to set `bIsTeleporting` to **False**.

4. Connect the output of that node to the **Set Hidden in Game** input for the Teleport Dest Indicator:

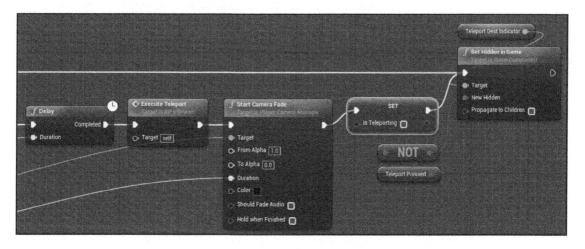

Now, when we execute a teleport by releasing the input, `bIsTeleporting` will be set to true until the teleport action has finished, and a new teleport action won't be accepted.

Teleport locomotion summary

We've covered a lot of ground here and created a pretty comprehensive teleport locomotion scheme. Let's go over the scheme:

- It's bound to the navmesh, so it won't allow players to teleport into illegal locations
- It's using a parabolic trace so that the player can teleport to destinations higher than their current position
- It allows the player to choose their target orientation when teleporting
- It does a decent job of indicating where the player is going to go and where they'll be facing
- It includes a few bits of polish, such as an input deadzone and a camera fade

There's more we could do with this, but it's a reasonably complete solution. If we were to improve it further, we would likely want to allow it to work with either hand, and we would certainly need to replace our debug-drawn teleport path with something that will work in a shipping build. If you choose to explore further from here, the VR Template included with the engine is a great next step. Many of the methods we just wrote here are similar to the methods used in that template, so you should find that you're standing on good ground to understand what you see when you start digging around in there.

Teleportation is an effective solution for getting around in VR because, as we mentioned earlier, it doesn't try to represent movement, so it doesn't generally trigger motion sickness in users. It works pretty well for applications that don't rely on a high degree of immersion in the ways players move through the world.

For games and applications that want to maintain a higher level of immersion, teleportation may not be what you want, as it doesn't behave the way movement in the real world does: it creates a discontinuous sense of space, and introduces interface elements that clearly don't exist in the world. There's no way around the reality that it's an immersion-breaker.

Next, we're going to take a look at an immersive movement scheme that allows players to move smoothly through the world. Very sensitive players or those who are new to VR may not find immersive movement comfortable, so in some circumstances, it may be appropriate to offer teleport locomotion as an option on an application that also offers seamless movement.

Let's take a look at how it works.

Seamless locomotion

If you're making an immersive game or experience, that experience is going to be much more convincing to the player if their sense of the space around them isn't constantly being broken up by teleport actions. Let's take a look at a way to handle seamless locomotion in space.

Setting up inputs for seamless locomotion

Ordinarily, we would probably allow users to select the sort of locomotion scheme they're comfortable with in an options menu, but since our current character doesn't do anything but move around, and we haven't done anything with the left controller yet, we can use it to drive our seamless locomotion scheme.

Let's add a pair of input axis mappings for the left controller's thumbstick:

1. Open **Project Settings** | **Engine** | **Input**.
2. Hit the **+** button beside **Bindings** | **Axis Mappings** twice to add two new axis mappings.
3. Name them `MoveForward`, and `MoveRight`.
4. Bind **MoveForward** to **MotionController (L) Thumbstick Y**.
5. Set its **Scale** to **-1.0**.

6. Bind **MoveRight** to **MotionController (L) Thumbstick X**, and leave its **Scale** at **1.0**:

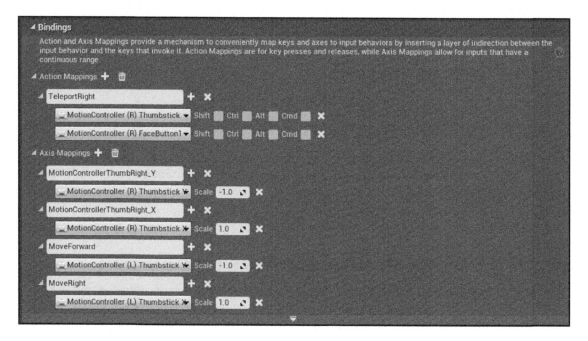

We're all set with our input bindings for the moment, so we can close our project settings.

Changing the pawn's parent class

For our pawn to move smoothly, we're going to need to give it a way to handle its movement input. There are two ways we could do this. We could write our own input handler on our Tick event, but this is a fairly involved process, and unnecessary if we're interested in implementing a straightforward movement scheme.

An easier way is to add a **Movement Component** to our pawn. In Blueprint, however, there's no way to add a movement component (in C++, there is), so instead, we're going to have to change our pawn's parent class to a class that contains the component we need, along with several others we're also going to want. Let's get started:

1. Open your Blueprint of **BP_VRPawn**, and hit **Class Settings** on the toolbar:

 We mentioned earlier that Unreal Engine is an **object oriented** system. An **object** is an instance of a **class**, and classes **inherit** from other classes, taking on their abilities and characteristics as they do. This is where that becomes important. We're going to change the capabilities of our **BP_VRPawn** by changing its parent class to a child of the **Pawn** class that contains the component we need.

2. Under **Details | Class Options**, change **Parent Class** from **Pawn** to **Character**:

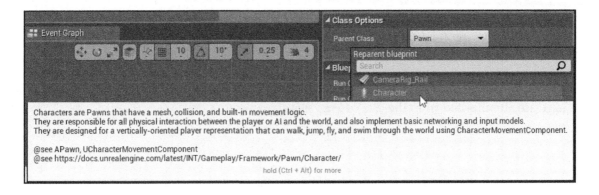

If you look at your **Components** tab, you'll see that a few new components have appeared:

In addition to the components we created earlier on, we now have the following:

- A **Capsule** component
- An **Arrow** component
- A **Mesh** component
- A **Character Movement** component

These are all inherited from the `Character` class.

This is useful. We need the Movement component to allow us to move around, and we need the Capsule component to keep us from walking through walls. We don't really need the Mesh component, since we're not rendering the player pawn's body, but it doesn't hurt us in this instance to have it here and just leave its Skeletal Mesh property empty for now.

Be careful when changing an object's parent class. If the class you're changing to is a child of the previous parent class, that's generally going to be a safe change, because it will add new elements, but the parent's properties and functions will still be there. Going from a child class to a parent class can be riskier, since you may be relying on properties or functions that exist on the child, but don't exist on the parent. Changing to a class that's very different from your current class will probably create problems. It's fine if you know what you're doing, and the engine won't stop you, but you'll probably wind up cleaning up a lot of invalidated function calls or variable references.

Fixing the collision component

If you run the game now, you'll see that we're floating a little higher above the floor than we were previously. This is because our Capsule component is colliding with the floor and pushing us upward. To fix this, open your Pawn's **Viewport** tab. (If you've closed it, you can reopen it by double-clicking the **BP_VRPawn(self)** entry on your **Components** tab.) Let's get started:

- Hit *Alt + K* to switch your viewport to a side view.

- Grab your **Camera Root** and drag it downward until it's sitting at the bottom of the Capsule Component. Its location should now be (0.0, 0.0, -90.0):

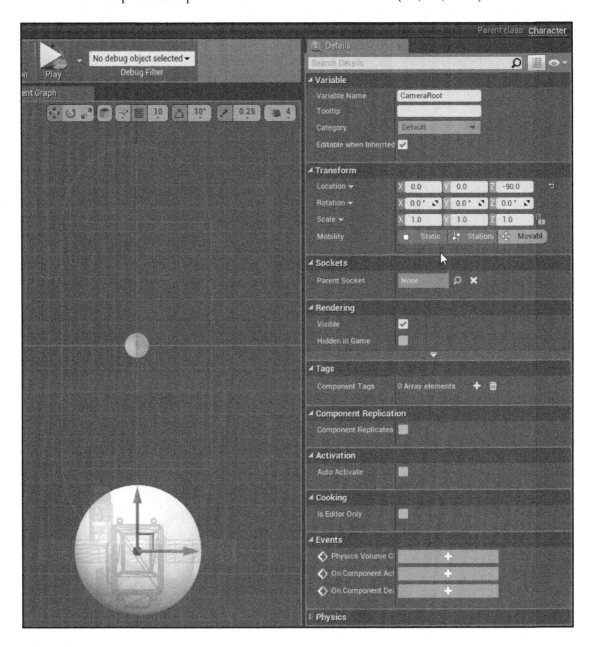

If you run the game again, you'll find that you're properly on the floor.

Handling movement input

Now that we've given our pawn a movement component, let's use the input bindings we mapped a moment ago to allow us to move around:

1. Right-click in your pawn's event graph and create an **Input** | **Axis Events** | **MoveForward** event:

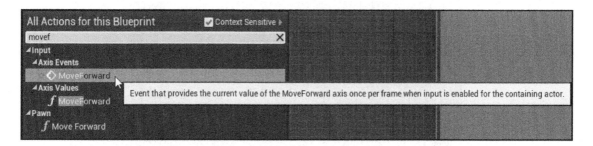

2. Do the same for the **MoveRight** event we created in our axis bindings.

   We now have two events that will run every frame, and allow us to feed movement input to our movement component.

3. Create an **Add Movement Input** node, and connect its execution input to the output of **InputAxis MoveForward**.

4. Feed the **Axis Value** of **MoveForward** into the movement input's **Scale Value**.

5. Repeat this for **InputAxis MoveRight**:

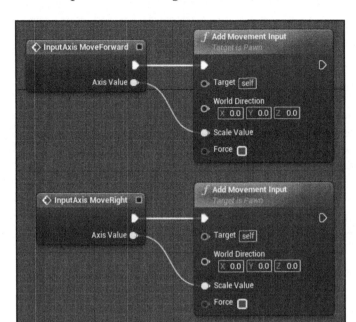

Now, we need to tell it the direction we'd like to move in:

1. Grab your **Camera** component from your components list, and drag it onto your event graph.
2. From its output, create a **GetWorldRotation** node.
3. Right-click on the **GetWorldRotation** output and split the struct pin.
4. Right-click in the graph and create a **Get Forward Vector** node.
5. Split its input pin.
6. Connect the **Yaw** output from **GetWorldRotation** to the **In Rot Z (Yaw)** input in **Get Forward Vector**.
7. Right-click to create a **Get Right Vector** node.
8. Split its input, and connect **Yaw** output of **GetWorldRotation** to its **In Rot Z (Yaw)** input.

9. Connect the output from **Get Forward Vector** to the **World Direction** input to **Add Movement Input** of **InputAxis MoveForward** node.

10. Connect the output from **Get Right Vector** to the **MoveRight Add Movement Input**:

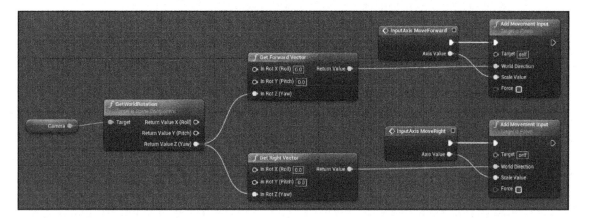

Let's give it a try in-game.

We can still teleport using our right trackpad or thumbstick, but if we use the left input, it slides us smoothly through the world using our camera's look direction as the forward direction.

Gamers that are used to first-person shooters are used to thinking of their camera direction as their forward direction. In VR, this doesn't have to be the case—it's perfectly reasonable for a character to be looking to the right while moving to the left. Our pawn has a concept of *Control Rotation*, which is its actual orientation in space, and is distinct from the direction the camera is facing. In practice, if you're going to drive movement from a pawn's control rotation rather than camera rotation, you need to provide visual cues to make it clear to the player exactly what their forward orientation is, or your movement scheme will just confuse them. To keep things clear in this instance, we've made our movement relative to the look direction.

This works well enough, but it has some problems.

Fixing movement speed

First, we're moving too fast. Let's fix this:

1. Select your pawn's **CharacterMovement Component**, and in **Details | Character Movement: Walking**, set its **Max Walk Speed** to **240.0**

That's a much more reasonable speed for walking through the world.

Letting the player look around without constantly steering

Let's face it. Using the camera forward vector as the basis for our steering feels a little janky. Every time you turn your head to look at something, you have to steer to correct yourself. The world doesn't work that way. Let's use the orientation of the left controller as the basis for our movement instead:

1. Grab the `MotionController_L` component and drag it into the event graph near where we're currently getting the Camera's world rotation.
2. Feed **MotionController_L** component's output into the **GetWorldRotation** node, replacing the Camera's connection:

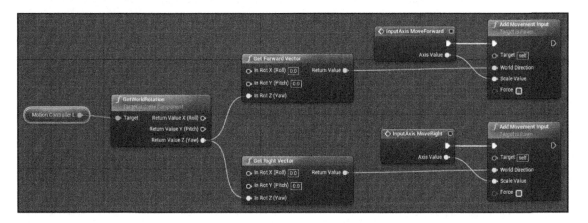

Now, instead of using the Camera's Yaw as our basis for our forward and right world directions, we're using the controller, which makes intuitive sense. Forward is wherever you're pointing the controller, and meanwhile, the player can execute fine movements using the trackpad or joystick. They can steer by pointing in the direction they want to go and can look around without affecting their movement.

Implementing snap-turning

The last thing we need to give the player is a way to change their orientation without having to spin their chair around in the real world.

While it works well to allow your players to move smoothly through the world like we just have, we don't want them to turn smoothly. We discussed the reason for this in Chapter 1, *Thinking in VR*, but to recap here, visually induced motion sickness arises when players see movement that they don't feel. We're especially attuned to movements that appear to be spinning. This likely arises from a number of reasons:

- A sense of spinning is a natural effect of disruptions to the vestibular system from poisoning. Ever had the bed-spins after a rough night out? What happened next? Right. Don't do that to your player.
- Vestibular disconnect is strongest when there's a lot of optic flow in the image. When the player is rotating, nearly everything in the frame is moving to the side. That's a lot of movement.
- In the real world, we naturally blink when rotating our head, or we aim our eyes first at the thing we want to look at (this movement is called a **saccade**), and then turn our head to follow. In the real world, we don't keep our eyes steady while we turn around.

Snapping the player through a turn rather than allowing them to turn smoothly not only avoids creating a huge optic flow that's likely to make your user sick, but it actually does a better job of replicating the way we actually perceive turning in the real world than a smooth turn does.

Let's set up a snap turn.

Setting up inputs for snap turning

Let's add a pair of action bindings to snap right and left:

1. Open your **Project Settings | Engine | Input**.
2. Add two new Action Mappings in **Engine | Input | Bindings**. Name them SnapTurnRight and SnapTurnLeft.
3. Bind **SnapTurnRight** to **MotionController (L) FaceButton2**.
4. Bind **SnapTurnLeft** to **MotionController (L) FaceButton4** and **MotionController (L) FaceButton1**.

We're binding two inputs to **SnapTurnLeft** to accommodate both Oculus and Vive inputs. On Oculus Touch controllers, **FaceButton1** on the left controller is the X button, while **FaceButton2** is the Y button. On the HTC Vive, **FaceButton2** is the left-hand side of the trackpad, and **FaceButton4** is the right-hand side of the pad:

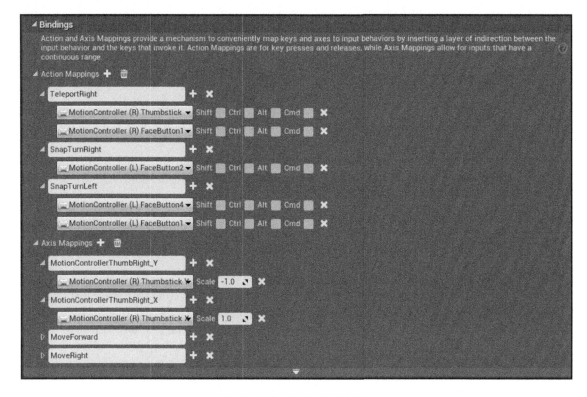

Your input bindings should now look like this.

We can close our project settings now.

Executing the snap turn

Now, let's execute a snap turn when these buttons are pressed:

1. In your pawn's event graph, add input events for your **SnapTurnLeft** and **SnapTurnRight** actions:

2. Create a **GetActorRotation** node and split its output.
3. Drag from the **Return Value Z (Yaw)** output and create a **float - float** node.
4. Drag out from the subtraction node's second input and **promote** it to a variable. Name the variable SnapTurnIncrement.
5. **Compile** your Blueprint and set the **SnapTurnIncrement** value to **30.0**.
6. Create a **SetActorRotation** node, and connect the **GetActorRotation** node's **Roll** and **Pitch** outputs directly to their corresponding inputs.
7. Connect the result of your subtraction to the Yaw input.
8. Connect the **Pressed** execution output from **InputAction SnapTurnLeft** to the **SetActorRotation** node's input.
9. Select these nodes and press *Ctrl + W* to duplicate them.
10. **Replace** the subtraction in the duplicated set with an addition.

11. Connect the duplicated nodes to execution of the **InputAction SnapTurnRight** output:

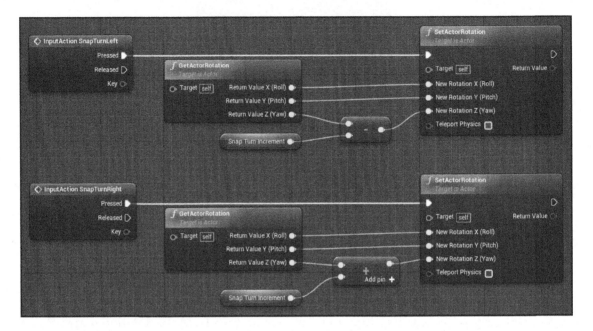

Give it a shot in-game. It's not bad. We could improve it further for sure—right now, snap turning triggers movement as well, but it's a pretty usable solution. If it made sense for our game, we could potentially map down a press on the Vive trackpad or a joystick press on the left Oculus Touch to a 180° turn.

Going further

There are a few ways we could improve the work we've done here, but implementing them fully would fall outside the scope of this chapter. Let's take a brief moment to talk about ways you could improve on this class as you take things further.

Snap turn using analog input

Our current snap turn implementation works reasonably well on Vive wands, but doesn't feel great on Oculus Touch controls. It might feel better for our players to listen to the analog input from one of the thumbsticks and trigger a snap turn if it exceeds a certain threshold. This way, players could flip the thumbstick to the side to execute the snap, or just touch the edge of a Vive trackpad without having to press it.

You could execute this by setting up an input axis binding on a motion controller thumbstick, and testing to see whether the input is greater than a threshold amount (for this test, we used 0.8) for a right turn or less than the negative threshold for a left turn.

You'll need to remember to put a cooldown onto the snap so that it doesn't trigger repeatedly from a single press. In our case, we used a cooldown duration of 0.2.

If you'd like to build this into your pawn, here are the steps:

1. Create an input event handler for your **MotionControllerThumbRight_X** input axis.
2. Create a **Branch**, and only continue if `bTeleportPressed` is **False**. We don't want to process snap turns while we're teleporting.
3. Create a new Boolean variable called `bSnapTurnCooldownActive`.
4. Create a **Branch**, and only continue if `bSnapTurnCooldownActive` is **False**.
5. Create a new float variable called `SnapTurnAnalogDeadzone`, compile, and set its value to **0.8**.
6. Add a >= test to see whether the incoming **Axis Value** from your thumbstick input is greater than or equal to `SnapTurnAnalogDeadzone`.
7. Create a **Branch** from this, and on its **False** output, create another Branch.

8. For this second branch, test to see whether the incoming **Axis Value** is less than or equal to the negative **SnapTurnAnalogDeadzone** (multiply it by -1.0).

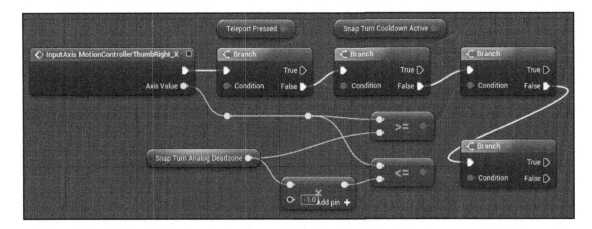

9. Create a new **Custom Event** called **ExecuteSnapTurnLeft**, and feed it into the **SetActorRotation** call you're making from **InputAction SnapTurnLeft**.

10. Create another one called **ExecuteSnapTurnRight**, and feed it in where **InputAction SnapTurnRight** is being handled:

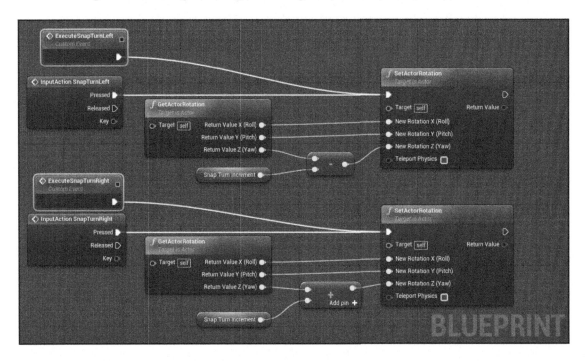

11. Now, back on your **ThumbstickRight** handler, call **ExecuteSnapTurnRight** if the **Input Axis** was >= **SnapTurnAnalogDeadzone**.

12. Call **ExecuteSnapTurnLeft** if the **Input Axis** was <= - **SnapTurnAnalogDeadzone**.

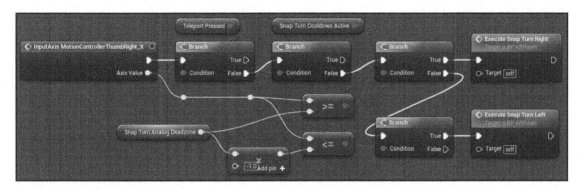

Now, we need to set a cooldown so that we don't get a rapid-fire series of snap turns when the user moves the stick:

1. Add a setter to set **bSnapTurnCooldownActive** to **true**, and call it after both **ExecuteSnapTurnRight** and **ExecuteSnapTurnLeft**.

2. Add a **delay**. The default value of **0.2** is fine here, but if you wanted to tune your cooldown duration, promote this value to a variable.

3. After the delay, set **bSnapTurnCooldownActive** to **False** again.

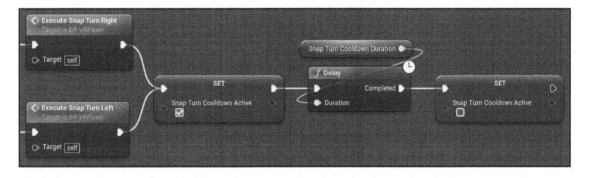

With this Boolean flag and delay, we're simply setting up a gate whereby the snap turn input will be ignored for 0.2 seconds after the last time it was handled, which gives the user time to release the stick once they're oriented where they want to be.

This implementation gives your player a nice natural-feeling snap turn on the right stick while leaving the left stick for analogue seamless movement.

Summary

We did quite a lot in this chapter.

We learned how to set up and refine a navigation mesh in our scene and how to find and fix collision problems with objects in our scene. We learned how to set up input actions and use them to move our player character around, and perhaps most importantly, we learned Kent Beck's mantra for software development: *Make it work, make it right, make it fast*, and learned what it means to follow it as we pursue iterative development. We're going to revisit this a lot. It's a secret to effective software development.

That was a lot of work. The exercises in this chapter covered a lot of ground, but should have left you with a decent sense of how the parts fit together when setting up a player pawn and a locomotion system.

Now that we've given our pawn feet, in the next chapter, we're going to give it hands. We'll learn how to use motion controllers to point, grip, and interact with objects in the world. We'll also build on what we've learned about setting up navigation meshes and drop some AI into the world to use them as well. Now that we can get around the world, we're going to start bringing it to life.

5
Interacting with the Virtual World - Part I

In the previous chapter, we learned how to make our player character move using teleport locomotion and then by adding a more immersive seamless locomotion scheme. We gave our users feet. Now, in this chapter, we're going to give them hands.

We'll start out by creating a new project using assets from the Marketplace to explore another way of starting up a VR project, and then we'll take the VRPawn we built in the preceding chapter and migrate it into this new project. Once we're set up, we'll begin by adding hands to the VRPawn and exploring ways of interacting with objects in the world.

This is important. As humans interacting with the world, we're most conscious of the way things appear as we look around, but we're nearly as conscious of our hands and what they're doing. VR developers call this *hand presence*, and when it's done right, it can contribute significantly to immersion. Think about it for a moment. Your hands are the part of your body that you're probably most aware of most of the time. How well we represent them in VR has a meaningful impact on how *embodied* we feel in the experience.

In this chapter, we're going to learn about the following topics:

- How to create Blueprint-driven virtual hands for our players
- How to use a construction script to customize an object when it's created in the world
- How to use animation blend spaces and animation blueprints to animate our hands
- How to set up new inputs to drive our hands

Let's get to it!

Starting a new project from existing work

Let's begin by creating a new project. We'll migrate the Pawn and game mode we made in the previous chapter into this one, and we'll add some scenery from the Marketplace. As you start to develop a library of elements you've developed yourself, or acquired through the **Marketplace**, this will become a common way of getting a new project going.

Migrating Blueprints to a new project

Launch your current engine version, and in your Unreal Project Browser, create a new project with the following parameters:

- **Blank Blueprint** template
- Hardware target set to **Mobile / Tablet**
- Graphics target set to **Scalable 3D or 2D**
- **No starter content**

Put it wherever you'd like.

Now, let's take the pawn we created in the previous project and add it to this one. To do this, we're going to have to jump back to our previous project to grab the assets we want to migrate:

1. Select **File** | **Open Project** and browse to your previous project's `.uproject` file. Open it up. Your current project will close when you do this.
2. Once in your previous project, find the `BP_VRGameMode` blueprint we created.
3. Right-click it and select **Asset Actions** | **Migrate...**, as shown in the following screenshot:

In addition to the object you select, the **Migrate...** utility collects any other object that your selected object relies on to work. Because our Game Mode uses the VRPawn as its default pawn, the **Migrate...** utility will collect the pawn, as well as the teleport indicator we made for it:

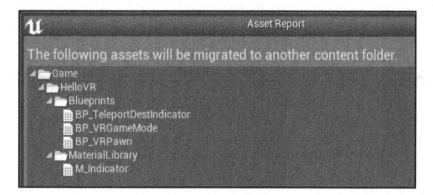

4. Hit **OK**, and when you're asked where to put the new content, select your new project's Content directory.

Great! Copies of your game mode and pawn have now been added to your new project.

We also mapped a few inputs, and we're going to need those too.

Copying input bindings

Remember when we mentioned that input mappings are just text entries in `DefaultInput.ini`? Since we haven't mapped any inputs in our new project, we can recreate the old project's input bindings by just copying the `DefaultInput.ini` file. You could just as easily recreate the inputs using the **Project Settings** menu, but it's faster to do it this way when you can get away with it:

1. Navigate to your old project's `Config` directory.
2. Select `DefaultInput.ini` and copy it to your new project's `Config` directory.

If you open it up, you'll see that it contains the input bindings we created, as shown in the following screenshot:

```
+ActionMappings=(ActionName="TeleportRight",bShift=False,bCtrl=False,bAlt=False,bCmd=False,Key=MotionController_Right_Thumbstick)
+ActionMappings=(ActionName="TeleportRight",bShift=False,bCtrl=False,bAlt=False,bCmd=False,Key=MotionController_Right_FaceButton1)
+ActionMappings=(ActionName="SnapTurnRight",bShift=False,bCtrl=False,bAlt=False,bCmd=False,Key=MotionController_Left_FaceButton2)
+ActionMappings=(ActionName="SnapTurnLeft",bShift=False,bCtrl=False,bAlt=False,bCmd=False,Key=MotionController_Left_FaceButton4)
+ActionMappings=(ActionName="SnapTurnLeft",bShift=False,bCtrl=False,bAlt=False,bCmd=False,Key=MotionController_Left_FaceButton1)
+AxisMappings=(AxisName="MotionControllerThumbRight_Y",Scale=-1.000000,Key=MotionController_Right_Thumbstick_Y)
+AxisMappings=(AxisName="MotionControllerThumbRight_X",Scale=1.000000,Key=MotionController_Right_Thumbstick_X)
+AxisMappings=(AxisName="MoveForward",Scale=-1.000000,Key=MotionController_Left_Thumbstick_Y)
+AxisMappings=(AxisName="MoveRight",Scale=1.000000,Key=MotionController_Left_Thumbstick_X)
```

Setting up new project to use the migrated game mode

Now that we've copied our Game Mode and our Pawn, and our input bindings have been set up, we can return to our new project:

- If you hit **File** | **Recent Projects**, it should be listed there, but if not, use **File** | **Open Project** to navigate to it

Now, let's set up our project to use the game mode we just brought over:

- Open **Project Settings** | **Project** | **Maps & Modes**, and under **Default Modes**, set **Default GameMode** to BP_VRGameMode

This will cause this game mode to be used on any map in our project, unless we override it. As you'll recall, this game mode tells the project to load up our VRPawn.

Additional project settings for VR

Remember to set those other VR-relevant settings we described in `Chapter 3`, *Hello World – Your First VR Project*, as well:

- **Project Settings | Engine | Rendering | VR | Instanced Stereo**: True
- **Project Settings | Engine | Rendering | VR | Round Robin Occlusion Queries**: True
- **Project Settings | Engine | Rendering | Forward Renderer | Forward Shading**: True
- **Project Settings | Engine | Rendering | Default Settings | Anti-Aliasing Method**: MSAA
- **Project Settings | Engine | Rendering | Default Settings | Ambient Occlusion Static Fraction**: False
- **Project Settings | Project | Description | Settings | Start in VR**: True

Also, remember that you shouldn't follow these blindly. For lots of VR projects, forward shading will be the way to go, but you should always put a little bit of thought into whether the particular thing you're doing would work better with the deferred shading model. (This may be the case if you're going to do a lot of dynamic lighting and reflective surfaces.) The same goes for the anti-aliasing method. MSAA is usually what you'll want if you're doing forward shading, but there are instances in which temporal anti-aliasing or FXAA will look better. Instanced Stereo is pretty much always something you'll want, and the same goes for the Round-Robin Occlusion Queries.

Testing our migrated game mode and pawn

Let's test it before we do anything else:

1. Drag a **Nav Mesh Bounds Volume** onto the default map that opened with our project, and scale it to cover the entire floor. (Remember that you can hit *P* to view it.)
2. Launch a **VR Preview** and verify that you can teleport around your map and use seamless movement.

Excellent. This quick test allows us to verify that the game mode we brought over from the other project has loaded and it's spawning an instance of our VR Pawn at the player start.

Test things as you build them, a step at a time. It's far easier to find the source of a bug after a few changes than after a lot of changes.

Adding scenery

Now, let's bring in some scenery so that we have a place to play:

1. Open up your Epic Games Launcher and in the **Marketplace**, search for **Soul: City**. (It's free.)
2. Hit **Add To Project**, and add it to the project you're working on now.
3. Once it's done, reopen your project if you closed it, and open **Content** | **Soul City** | **Maps** | **LV_Soul_Slum_Mobile**.

   Grab a coffee while your shaders compile. Now, we should set up our project to open this map automatically.

4. In **Project Settings** | **Project** | **Maps & Modes**, set **Editor Startup Map** and **Game Default Map** to LV_Soul_Slum_Mobile.

Adding a NavMesh

We're also going to need to add a **Nav Mesh Bounds Volume** to this scene so that we can teleport through it.

As you learned in the previous chapter, setting up a **Bounds** volume can be an involved process if you want to do it right. For our purposes here, we're going to cheat a little and just drop a volume generally over the bulk of the scene. If you'd like to tune the volume further, you can scale it and place it more carefully, and use **nav** modifiers to exclude areas you don't want. If you want to keep it simple, the following settings are good enough for what we're focusing on here:

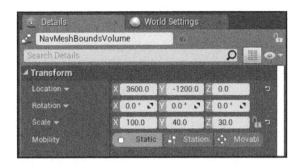

- **Location**: X=3600, Y=-1200, Z=0
- Scale: X=100, Y=40, Z=30

We get the following output:

Our NavMesh is kind of a shambles on this map. If you'd like to clean it up, feel free to apply the methods we talked about in the previous chapter.

Testing the map

Launch a VR preview and explore the scene a bit. Hmm. Something's wrong. Our input isn't working correctly. Because we verified on the previous step that our pawn works and our input mappings are good, we know that's not the problem. Let's make sure we're loading the correct pawn:

1. Open up your **World Settings**, and look at the **Game Mode | Game Mode Override**.
2. Sure enough, there's another game mode being loaded there. Use the reset arrow to clear the overridden game mode.

Let's test again. That's much better. Now, we're able to navigate through the environment.

While we're here and able to walk around, let's point out a few things about this environment. It's not a perfect environment for a virtual reality project, and in this case, that gives us a few useful things to talk about:

- **Scale matters in VR**: First, as we walk around, we can see that the scale of certain objects is inconsistent. Some of the staircases appear to be the correct size, while others are enormous. We're not going to do anything about that here, but this is an important takeaway: the scale of the objects in your world matters a great deal in VR. People have an instinctive sense of how big things are, and VR gives them much stronger cues about the sizes of objects than flat screens do. If your scale is off, they'll notice that in VR.
- **Lights can cause lens flares in VR**: The other potential issue is the bright neon lights. They make for a great-looking environment, but you're probably noticing that they sometimes flare the Fresnel lenses in your headset from certain angles. We're not saying you need to avoid bright lights or contrasts in your scenes, but be aware that they can sometimes call attention to the hardware. The takeaway here is that you always want to check your artwork in the VR headset in addition to the flat screen.

Creating hands

Now that we have a scene to work with, let's get to the meat of this chapter and start setting up some interaction.

Before we do anything else, let's improve the way we're representing the motion controllers in the scene. Currently, we're using debug meshes, which won't render correctly if our user is using a different headset from the one we used when we authored the scene. It was good enough to get us going, but now we need to replace it with something more permanent.

To get a hand mesh we can use, we're going to raid the **VR Template**. It's likely that, for many of your VR projects, you'll simply begin by creating a project based on the VR Template, or you'll migrate the entire **MotionController** Pawn Blueprint into a project you've created, but for our purposes here, we want to build the pawn ourselves so that we understand what's in it.

Migrating hand meshes and animations from the VR Template project

If you already have an example of the VR Template project created, use **File** > **Open Project** to open it up. If you don't already have one, close your current project and from your Epic Launcher, launch the engine and create a new project using the VR Template. It doesn't really matter what other settings you use for this one—we're just here for the meshes:

1. In the **VR Template** project's **Content Browser**, navigate to **Content** | **VirtualReality** | **Mannequin** | **Animations**.
2. Select the three animation assets, right-click them, and select **Asset Actions** | **Migrate**. Ignore the blend space and animation blueprint for now—we're going to learn how to make these ourselves:

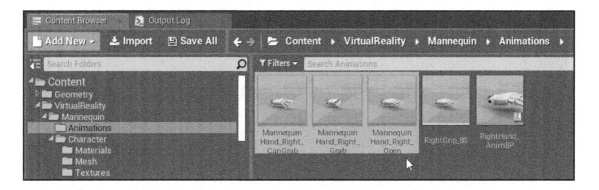

You'll see that the **Migrate** utility has not only collected the animations you selected, but it also found the mesh, its physics asset, and its skeleton, along with its material and the textures that feed into it:

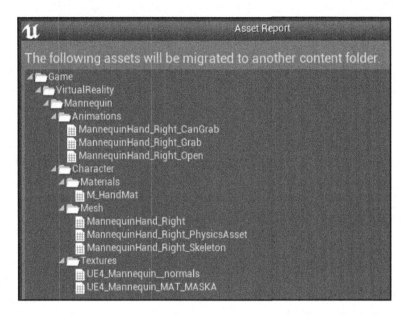

3. Select your current project's Content directory as your destination.

Now that we've collected a few assets we can use, we're ready to return to our project.

4. Hit **File** | **Recent Projects**, and open your previous project. (Use **File** | **Open Project** if it doesn't appear here.)

Adding hand meshes to our motion controllers

Back in our current project, we should now have a VirtualReality directory in our **Content Browser**, with a Mannequin subdirectory containing Animations and the Character folder.

Let's apply these hand meshes to our pawn's motion controllers.

Creating a new Blueprint Actor class

The first thing we're going to want to do is create a Blueprint to represent them, since we want to animate the hands to respond to the player's actions:

1. Right-click in your project's `Blueprints` directory, and select **Create Basic Asset | Blueprint Class.**
2. Select **Actor** as its parent class.
3. Let's name it `BP_VRHand`.
4. Open it up.

We mentioned earlier in this book that a core principle of object-oriented development is that we pull things that belong together into self-contained objects that can handle their own behaviors. This is a good opportunity to do this, since we're about to link animated hand meshes with our motion controllers. We could absolutely get away with just adding a pair of skeletal mesh components to our pawn and attaching them to our motion controller components, but it's going to be much cleaner and ultimately easier to manage if we architect things a little better than that.

Adding motion controller and mesh components

Let's add the components we're going to need:

1. Add a **MotionController** component to your **Components** list.
2. With the new **MotionController** component selected, add a **Skeletal Mesh** component so that it becomes a child of the motion controller:

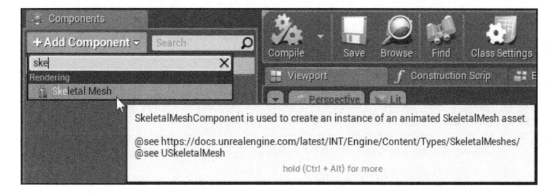

3. Let's name it `HandMesh`.

4. In the **Skeletal Mesh** component's **Details** panel, set its **Mesh | Skeletal Mesh** property to `MannequinHand_Right`:

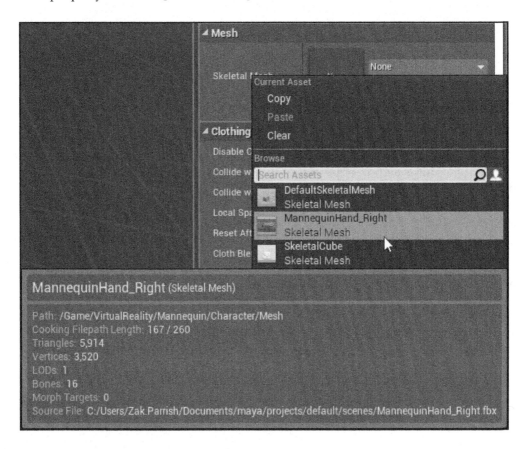

Adding a Hand variable

Since we're going to reuse this VRHand for both the right and left hands, we need to set up a way for the object to know which hand it's representing:

1. Add a variable to the **Variables** list of `BP_VRHand` and name it `Hand`.

2. Set its **Variable Type** to `EController Hand`.

3. Set its **Instance Editable** property to `true`:

 You'll notice that, when you set **Instance Editable** to true, the eye icon next to the variable's name is open. This indicates that this variable is allowed to be set to different values for each separate instance of the object in the world. Since we need one of these objects to be set to the right hand and the other to the left hand, this is what we want here:

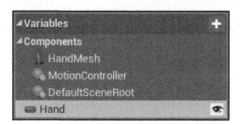

Now that we have an instance-editable **Hand** variable indicating which hand this object is going to represent, we need to tell our **MotionController** component about that too. We're going to do this in the VRHand's **Construction Script**.

Using a Construction Script to handle updates to the Hand variable

If you look at the **Functions** list for your BP_VRHand class, you'll see that a **Construction Script** has been automatically created for you. This is a function that runs when the object is created or updated before gameplay has begun. Construction Scripts are very useful for synchronizing values that need to be lined up before the software runs. In our case, this is exactly what we want. If we change the value of this **Hand** variable, we want the motion controller's motion source to change automatically to match up with it. Let's make that happen:

1. Open up your BP_VRHand's **Construction Script**.
2. Drag a reference to your **Motion Controller** component into the **Construction Script**.
3. Drag out its output and call Set Motion Source on it:

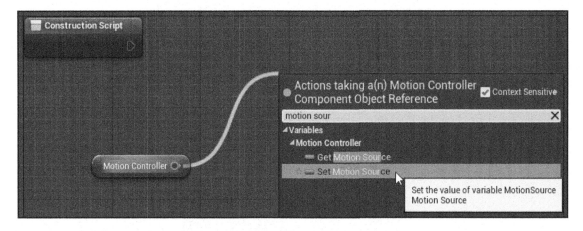

4. Drag a reference to the Hand variable into your **Construction Script**.

5. Drag its output onto the `Motion Source` input. You'll see a `Convert EControllerHand Enum to Name` node appear automatically:

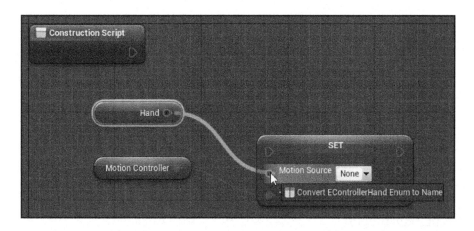

Some data types can be converted easily into other types. In this case, we're converting an enum into a name. **Enum** is short for **enumerator**. An enum is a special data type that allows us to create a predefined list of values and then use that collection of values as a data type. If you have a known set of possible values for a data type, it's far better to use an enum to list them than it is to use a name or a string. This prevents a typo from causing a value to fail, and compares much, much faster than a string comparison. It's generally pretty easy to turn enum values into human-readable values in Blueprint when we need them, as we're doing here.

6. Finally, connect your execution output of **Construction Script** to the `Set Motion Source` input, so that your whole **Construction Script** looks like this:

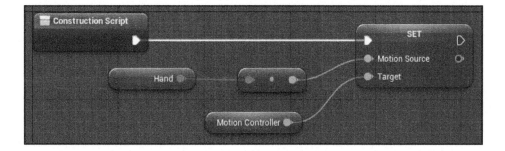

Adding BP_VRHand child actor components to your pawn

Let's return to our BP_VRPawn blueprint now:

1. In its **Components** list, select your **Camera Root** component, and add a **Child Actor Component** as a child.
2. Name it Hand_L.
3. In its **Details**, under **Child Actor Component**, set the **Child Actor Class** to BP_VRHand.
4. Select **Camera Root** again so that it will be the parent of the next component we make, and add another **Child Actor** component.
5. Set its **class** to BP_VRHand, and name it Hand_R.
6. This time, below the **Child Actor Class** property, expand the **Child Actor Template** property.
7. Set **Child Actor Template** | **Default** | **Hand** to Right. (We're able to do this because we made this variable instance editable in the preceding steps.)

Now we need to ensure that the BP_VRHand actors spawned by these components know that this pawn is their owner. This is required for the motion controllers to register correctly.

1. In BP_VRPawn, find **Event BeginPlay** in the **Event Graph**.
2. Drag a reference to the Hand_L component you just created onto the graph.
3. Drag its output and select **Get Child Actor** to get a reference to the BP_VRHand object it contains.
4. Drag the **Child Actor** output and call **Set Owner** on it.

5. Right-click in the graph and select **Get a Reference to Self** to create a **Self** node.
6. Drag **Self** into the **Set Owner** node's **New Owner** input.
7. Drag the execution output from **Set Tracking Origin** into the **Set Owner** node's execution input.
8. Repeat this for the Hand_R component.

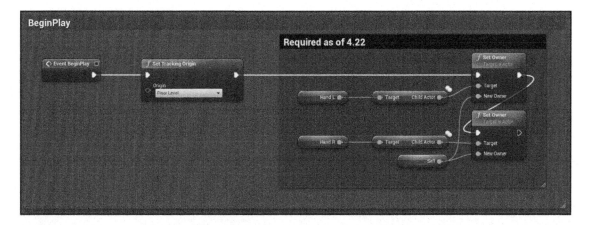

Before we do anything else, let's test it.

We should still see our old motion controllers rendered since we haven't gotten rid of them yet, but we should now see a pair of hands as well, and they should be moving correctly with our motion controllers.

Our hands have a few problems we should fix, though.

Fixing issues with Hand meshes

If we look at our hands as they move with the motion controllers, we can see that they're displaying at an unexpected angle:

1. Let's fix this by setting the `HandMesh` component's **Transform** | **Rotation** to **90°** around the *X* axis:

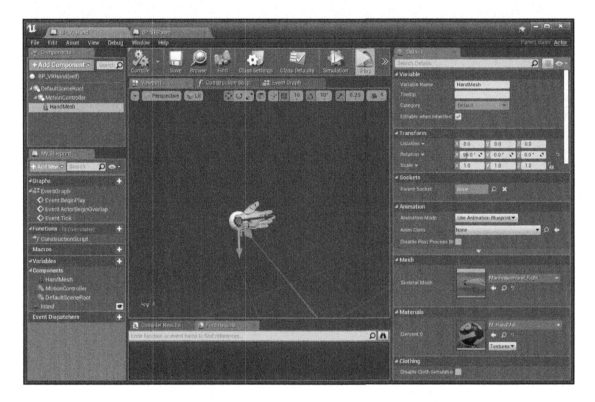

Second, they're both appearing as right hand meshes, even though one of them is bound to the left hand. We can fix this in our construction script too.

2. Drag out an == operator from our Hand variable's output. Test to see whether it's equal to **Left**.

3. Add a **Branch** node using this test result as its condition.

4. Drag a reference to your Hand Mesh into your construction script graph.

5. If **Hand** == **Left**, call Set World Scale 3D on your Hand Mesh to **X=1.0**, **Y=1.0**, and **Z=-1.0**:

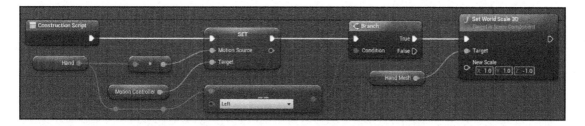

Setting the Hand mesh scale to -1 on its Z axis mirrors it along that axis, which is a spiffy way of creating a left-handed mesh from a right hand without having to create a second mesh.

Give it another try. The hands should now be angled better, and you should now have one left and one right hand. It's still not perfect, though. The hand meshes aren't quite in the right spot, and as a result, they don't quite feel like our own hands:

1. Select the HandMesh component from your **Components** list, and set its **Details | Transform | Location** to **X=-13.0, Y=0.0, Z=-1.8**.

2. Nudge these values around until they feel about right to you.

Getting the angle of the hands right is very important in VR. As we discussed in Chapter 1, *Thinking in VR*, our proprioceptive sense of where our hands are is very strong, and if they look even a little bit out of place, they won't feel real. Take the time to find what feels natural here. It's a subtle detail, but it matters.

Replacing references to our old motion controller components in blueprints

Now that we've got our hands in place, we need to remove the old, redundant motion controller components from our pawn and where we're referring to them, replace those references with references to our new hands. Let's get started:

1. Open up your pawn blueprint and select its `MotionController_L` component.
2. Right-click it and select **Find References** (Pressing *Alt + Shift + F* will do this as well):

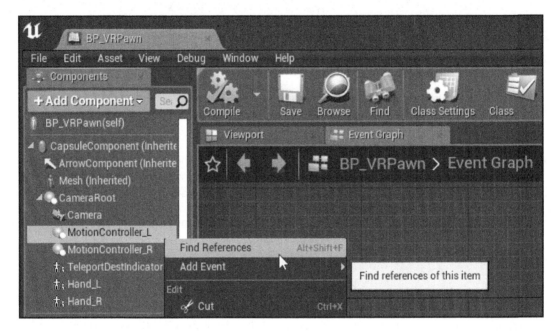

A **Find Results** panel will open and show you where this component is being used in your blueprint. We can see from this list that `MotionController_L` is being used in one place in our graph.

3. Double-click it to jump to where it's being used in our **Event Graph**:

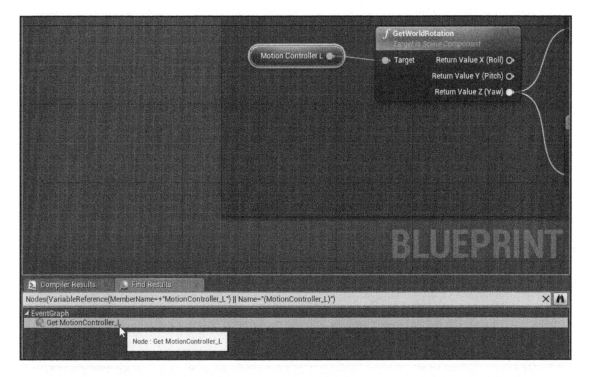

We want to replace our reference to `MotionController_L` with a reference to our newly created `Hand_L`.

4. Drag a reference to `Hand_L` onto your graph.

We can't simply replace a reference to `MotionController_L` with a reference to our `Hand_L` object, because that object itself isn't moving with the controller. It contains a motion controller component, and the visible Hand Mesh is a child of that motion controller. We need to get a reference to that motion controller—or even better since the player can see it—to the hand mesh.

Creating a function to get our hand mesh

The first thing we need to do to get access to the internal components of our VRHand object is to get a reference to the child actor that's contained within our **Child Actor Component**. Let's get started:

1. From Hand_L, drag out a connector and select **Get Child Actor**:

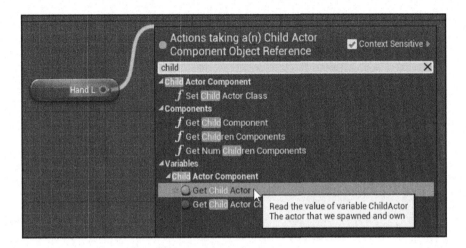

Remember all of the times we mentioned that Unreal Engine is an object-oriented environment? We keep coming back to this because it's important. The **Child Actor** reference we just extracted from our **Child Actor** component is a reference to an Actor class. As we mentioned in the previous chapters, Actor is the parent class for any object that can be placed in the world. The Actor class, however, doesn't have a **Hand Mesh** component. It just has the basic stuff required to place any object in the world. A BP_VRHand object, which is a child of the Actor class, does contain this component. We need to tell Unreal that the actor we're working with in this case is a BP_VRHand. We do this using a Cast operator.

2. Drag a connector from `Child Actor` and select `Cast to BP_VRHand`:

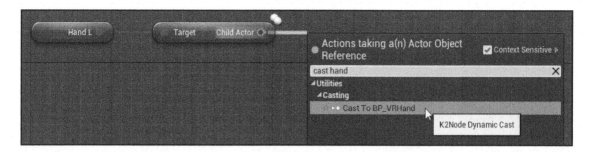

This will create a `Cast` node. `Cast` nodes require an execution input because they're not guaranteed to succeed. If you try to cast some random actor to a `BP_VRHand`, it will fail, because the actor you gave it isn't a `VRHand`. The cast node doesn't turn the object into an actor of that type—it tells the system to treat the reference as the specified type if it actually is an instance of that type.

We're going to deal with this execution line in a moment, but first, let's get the hand mesh from our object.

3. Drag a connector from the `Cast` node's `As BP_VRHand` output and select `Get HandMesh`:

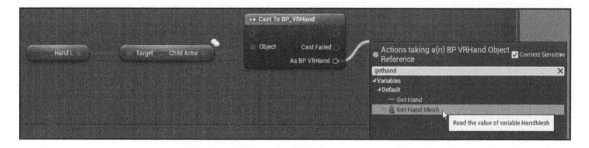

We can now feed this into the `GetWorldRotation` node that's currently reading from `MotionController_L`.

4. Drag the `HandMesh` output into `GetWorldRotation`, replacing the old `MotionController_L` reference:

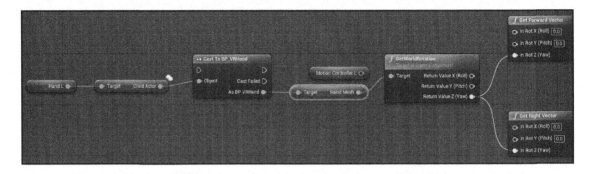

This isn't going to work yet, though, because we haven't connected the execution lines to our `Cast` node yet. If you try to compile this right now, you'll see a warning on the cast node and an error on `Get HandMesh` because of this.

There are two ways we could fix this. We could insert the **Cast** node into the main execution lines from our inputs, and only make the **Add Movement Input** calls if they succeed, but in our case here, there's a cleaner way. We can create a *Pure function* to perform the cast.

A **Pure function** is a function that doesn't change the state of the object that contains it, and because of this, it doesn't need to be placed into an execution line. In our case here, we're just getting a reference to the hand mesh—it doesn't matter when we do this because we're not changing anything. We're just reading a value, so as long as that happens before we need to use it, that's fine.

5. Select the **Hand_L** node, its **Child Actor**, the **Cast**, and the **Get Hand Mesh** nodes.

6. Right-click and select **Collapse to Function**:

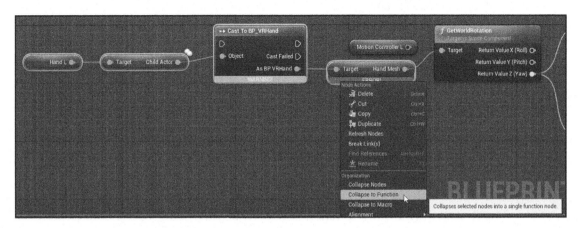

7. Name the function `GetHandMeshForHand`.
8. Set its **Pure** property to `true`:

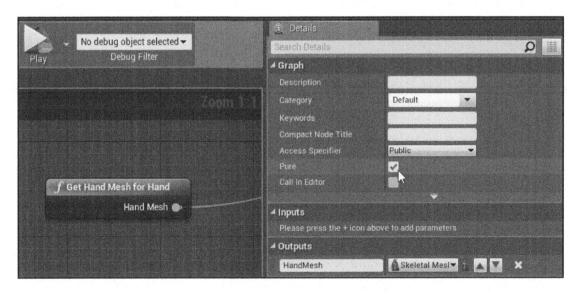

You'll notice that, when you did this, the execution pins went away. Now, we have a simple, clean node we can use to get our Hand mesh.

Let's improve it. We know we're going to need to do the same operation for the right hand, but it would be wasteful to make a second function to do an almost-identical job. Let's set this function up so that it can grab either hand.

9. With the function selected, find its **Details | Inputs list**, and hit the + button to create a new parameter.

10. Set the parameter's type to EControllerHand and name it Hand:

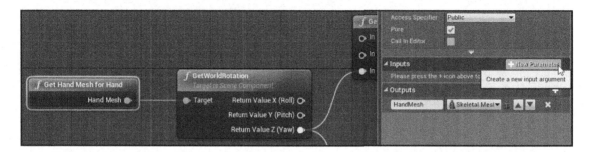

You'll see that your pure function node now has an input selector, and because the input we're using is an enumerator, it already knows what values are available. Useful, right?

This is yet another reason why enumerators are superior to strings as data types. Please, oh please, with very few exceptions, don't use strings as data types. They're slow and massively prone to user error.

Now, we need to update our function to use this new input.

11. Open the Get Hand Mesh for Hand function.

Right now, we're getting a reference to **Hand_L**, regardless of what the user selects for the Hand input. It's time to fix that.

12. Drag a connector from your Hand input and create a **Select** node.

13. Drag the return value from the **Select** node into the **Target** input of **Child Actor**, replacing the input from Hand_L.

14. Take the **Hand_L** reference and feed its output into the selector's **Left** input.

15. Drag an instance of **Hand_R** onto the graph and feed it into the selector's **Right** input.

16. We can leave the rest of the inputs as Null, as we're not using them here:

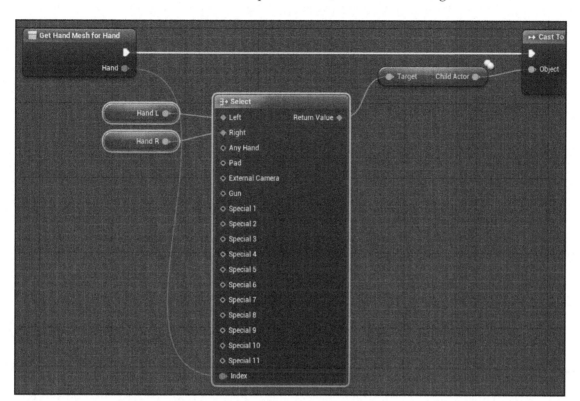

Now, if the user feeds **Left** into the Hand argument, the Hand_L reference will be used, and if they feed in **Right**, it will read from Hand_R. We're not safely handling cases where the user passes in any other value here, so the function would throw an error if the user selected **Gun** or some other input. Technically, this would probably be fine in this case since we know exactly what inputs we plan to give it, but for the sake of good practice, let's make it safer.

If we pass a value into the **Select** node that isn't **Left** or **Right**, it's going to return a Null (empty) reference. Trying to read a value from an empty reference is a bad thing to do. In C++, it will crash your application. In Blueprint, it will just throw an error, but it's still not good practice to let it happen.

17. Drag an output from the **Select** node, and create an **IsValid** node. You have two versions here. Use the macro version (the one with the question mark), as this will give you convenient execution pins you can use:

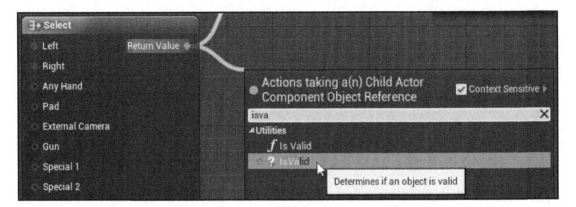

18. Drag the execution pin from the function input into the **Exec** pin on the `IsValid` node.

19. Drag the **IsValid** output into your **Cast** node's input so that the **IsValid** check will happen before the cast is attempted.

20. Drag out from the **Is Not Valid** output and select **Add Return Node**. Don't connect anything to the **Hand Mesh** output here. This will return a Null (empty) value if the user passes a bad input into the `Hand` variable.

21. While we're at it, we should also connect our `Cast` node's **Cast Failed** output to this empty return node, so if the cast fails, it won't try to get the **HandMesh** from a bad object.

The completed function should look like this:

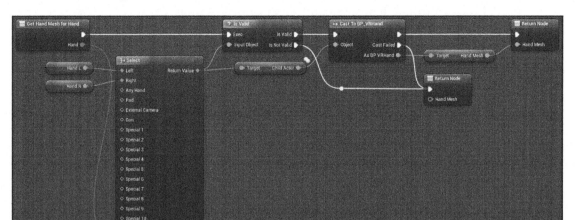

We've now created a pure function that returns the **HandMesh** contained within the child actor component for the supplied hand. Here it is in use:

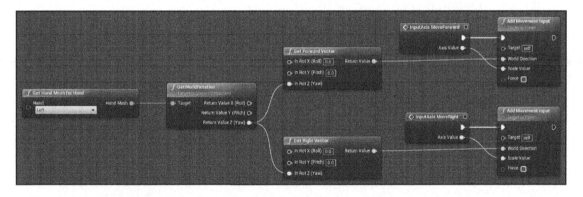

Now that we've created a clean, easy-to-use function to get our Hand mesh, let's use it to replace our `MotionController_R` references as well.

22. From your **Components** list, right-click `MotionController_R` and select **Find References**. You'll see that we're using it in two places.
23. Double-click the first use to jump to that part of the graph.
24. Drag an instance of the `GetHandMeshForHand` function onto the graph where `MotionController_R` is currently being used.

25. From the Hand drop-down menu, select **Right**.
26. Press *Ctrl* + drag the output connection from `MotionController_R` onto the output connection from `GetHandMeshForHand`:

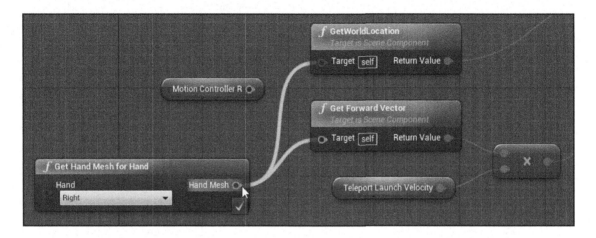

Pressing *Ctrl* + dragging is a fast way to move all of the connections to a Blueprint node from one pin to another.

Your graph should now look like this:

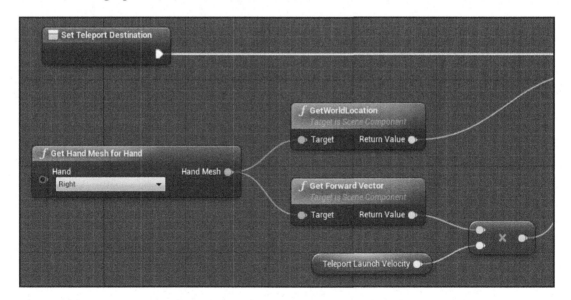

27. Do the same for the other reference to `MotionController_R`.

28. From the **Components** list, delete the `MotionController_L` and `MotionController_R` components.

Test it out. Your motion controllers should be working as they did before, but the hand meshes have now replaced the old controller meshes.

Animating our hands

Now, let's get our hands to change their posture based on the player's input.

The first thing we're going to need to do here is tell the hand when the player wants to do something with it. Let's do this by creating a pair of functions on the `BP_VRHand` that can be called from outside:

1. Open up your `BP_VRHand` Blueprint.

2. Create a new function in its Functions list. Call it `Grab Actor`.

3. Create another function called `Release Actor`.

4. Inside each of these functions, create a **Print String** node with the name of the function in it. Since we're not going to make these functions do anything just yet, we want to be able to see when they're being called:

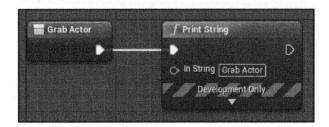

Let's do a better job of organizing our functions and variables. We haven't been doing this yet, but it's good practice.

5. For both of these functions, set their **Details** I **Graph** I **Category** to `Grabbing`. After you've used a category name once, it will appear in the drop-down list for other functions and variables.

A quick word about access specifiers

While we're here, take note of the **Access Specifier** property for these functions. By default, it's set to **Public**. In this case, this is what we want, but let's take a moment to talk about what these access specifiers mean:

- **Public** functions can be called from outside the class. So, if I create a `Foo` class with a public function called `Bar`, I can grab an instance of `Foo` from some other blueprint and call its `Bar` function.

- **Private** functions cannot be called from outside the class. Let's say that the `Bar` function is an internal operation that the `Foo` class uses as part of some other operation, and it shouldn't be called from outside. In that instance, the function should be set to private so that nobody else will try to call it from outside and it won't clutter the list of available actions for the class in other contexts.

- **Protected** functions cannot be called from outside the class, but can be called from within child objects of the class. If the `FooChild` class inherited from the `Foo` class, and the `Bar` function was private in the `Foo` class, `FooChild` would not be allowed to call it. If it was protected, then `FooChild` could call it, but it still couldn't be called from outside the object.

 Your general rule of thumb should be to make every function private unless you intend to call it from outside the class. Unreal defaults to making functions public because this is easy for developers who may not understand access specifiers yet, but now that you do, you should be making everything private unless you have a reason not to. Early on in your development, when your application is still small, this won't make much of a difference, but once it gets big, it will. It's a big time saver and debugging aid to be able to look at a function and know that it's safe to change it because you can be sure that nobody else is using it.

For these two functions we just created, the default `Public` access specifier is correct, because we intend to call them from the pawn.

Calling our grab functions from the pawn

For now, we can close out of `BP_VRHand` and open up `BP_VRPawn`. Before we can do much with our pawn, though, we're going to need to add a few more action mappings to our project's inputs.

Creating new input action mappings

We're going to do this just as we've done previously, using the Input UI in our Project Settings. Keep it somewhere in the back of your mind as well that these settings are just reading and writing your `DefaultInput.ini`. It's pretty much always a good idea to do your work here, but worthwhile to know what's really happening when you make changes in this interface. Let's get started:

1. Open **Project Settings** | **Engine** | **Input**, and expand the **Action Mappings** list.
2. Add a new **Action Mapping** named `GrabLeft`, and bind it to `MotionController (L) Trigger`.
3. Add another new action named `GrabRight`, and bind it to `MotionController (R) Trigger`:

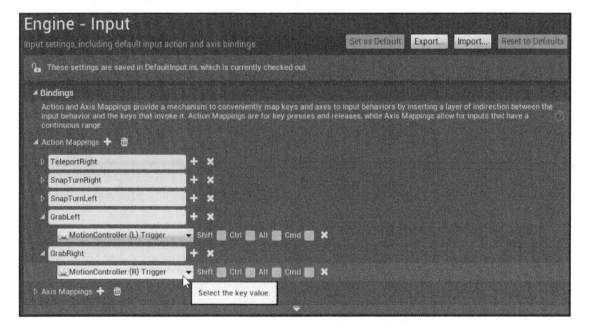

4. Close your project settings and return to your `BP_VRPawn` blueprint.

Adding handlers for new action mappings

Now that we've created new input actions in our project settings, let's get our pawn listening for them:

1. In your pawn's **Event Graph**, add an **InputAction GrabLeft**.
2. Drag a reference to your **Hand_L** child actor component onto the graph.
3. Call `Get Child Actor` on it.
4. `Cast` the Child Actor's output to a `BP_VRHand`.
5. Drag a connector from the **As BP_VRHand** output from the `Cast` node, and call `Grab Actor`. You're able to call this function here because we made it public.
6. Call the `Cast` node from the input action's **Pressed** output.
7. Call `Grab Actor` if the cast succeeds. The blueprint editor will probably connect this for you automatically:

You can see here that we stacked the inputs on top of the Cast node. This is purely a visual organization strategy. It's often a convenient way of organizing your nodes to make it clear that the whole cluster is really just referring to a single object.

8. Drag a marquee over the `Hand_L` node, its `Get Child Actor` call, and the `Cast` to select all three nodes.
9. Right-click them and select **Collapse to Macro**.
10. Name the new macro `GetHand_L`.

The new macro will have automatically inserted itself where these nodes originally stood.

11. Hit *Ctrl + W* to duplicate the macro.

12. Connect the input action's **Released** output to the new macro's input.
13. Call `Release Actor` on the **As BP_VRHand** output from the macro.

If we open up the `GetHand_L` macro, we will see that it contains the nodes we previously had sitting loose in our graph:

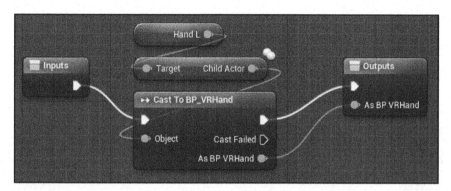

We can see that we're not doing anything if the cast fails, and in this case, that's what we want. If, for some reason, the `Hand_L` class's child actor changed or wasn't set, we don't want to try to make any calls on it.

It's important to make the distinction that *macros are not functions*. They look like functions and can often be used to do similar jobs, but a macro is really just an instruction to the Blueprint compiler to paste its contents into the graph where the macro appears. It doesn't have the ability to house local variables the way a function does. Macros are very simple—just an automated copy and paste. Some developers will advise you to avoid macros outright. This is definitely good advice if your understanding of how macros differ from functions is fuzzy, but if you understand how they work, they can be very useful. As a good rule of thumb, keep your macros very small. If you're doing a lot of work in a macro, you're really telling the compiler to paste a ton of nodes into your graph, and it should probably be a function in that case. Treat macros as a way of making a reusable node that does a simple job. Use them for readability and to make your code easier to modify later on.

Now, let's repeat this for our right controller input:

1. Select your GetHand_L macro from your **Macros** list, and hit *Ctrl + W* to duplicate it.
2. Rename the new macro GetHand_R.
3. Inside it, replace the Hand_L reference with a reference to Hand_R.
4. Drag two instances of GetHand_R onto your graph.
5. Connect them to the **InputAction GrabRight** node's **Pressed** and **Released** pins.
6. Call GrabActor and ReleaseActor on their outputs, like you did previously.

Your completed graph should look like this:

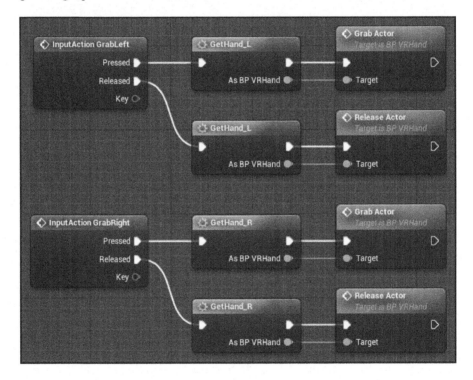

If you're thinking that we could have copied our **GetMeshForHand** function and modified it to return the BP_VRHand reference directly, you're right. We could also have modified that function outright and moved the **Get HandMesh** calls we made in the teleport functions outside. There are often many right ways to do the same job. In this instance, where we're just doing a simple cast, a pair of macros is a nice way of keeping our blueprint readable.

Let's test it. If we've done everything right, we should now see Grab Actor and Release Actor messages appearing in our view when we squeeze and release the triggers.

Implementing grab animations in the Hand blueprints

Now that we've set up our inputs and set up the VRPawn to pass them along to their respective motion controllers, let's get those motion controllers animating when these inputs are received.

Let's jump back into our BP_VRHand Blueprint:

1. In the **Variables** list of BP_VRHand, add a new Boolean variable named bWantsToGrip.
2. Hit *Alt* + drag a setter for bWantsToGrip into the Grab Actor function graph. Set it to **true** when Grab Actor is called.
3. Hit *Alt* + drag a setter for bWantsToGrip into Release Actor. Set it to **false** here:

Pressing *Ctrl*+ dragging a variable automatically creates a getter for that variable. Pressing *Alt* + dragging a variable creates a setter.

Creating an Animation Blueprint for the hand

Unreal uses Animation Blueprints to control animations on Skeletal Meshes. We're going to need one for our hand:

1. In your content browser, right-click in your project's `Blueprints` directory, and select **Create Advanced Asset | Animation | Animation Blueprint**:

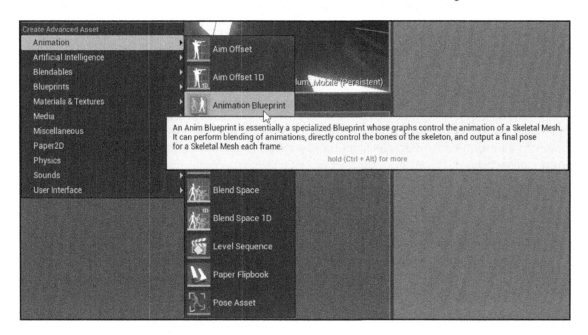

A dialog will appear asking for the animation Blueprint's parent class and for the target skeleton it's going to control:

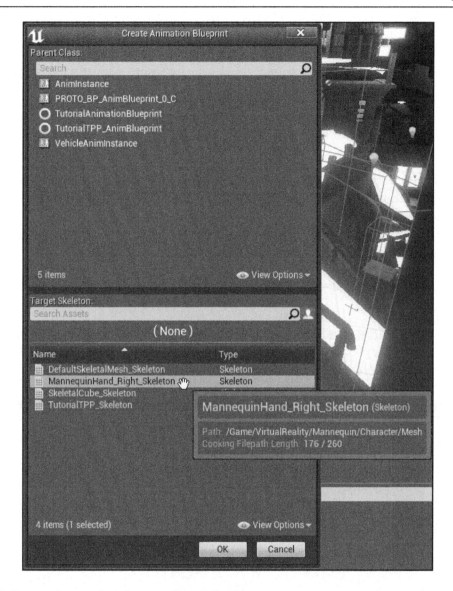

2. Leave the parent class empty, and select MannequinHand_Right_Skeleton as its **Target Skeleton**.

3. Name it ABP_MannequinHand_Right.

Creating a blend space for our hand animations

Now, we want our hand animations to respond to this value. Since we want to be able to blend smoothly between different animation poses, our best tool for this job is a *Blend Space*.

You have two types of Blend Space available to you. There's the standard Blend Space, which blends two different axes (this is commonly used for aiming poses in shooters), and a simpler blend space that just blends along one axis. This is the one we want. Let's get started:

1. Right-click in your `Blueprints` directory, and select **Create Advanced Asset** | **Animation** | **Blend Space 1D**.
2. A dialog will appear asking what skeleton this Blend Space will apply to. Select `MannequinHand_Right_Skeleton`.
3. Name it `BS_HandGrip`:

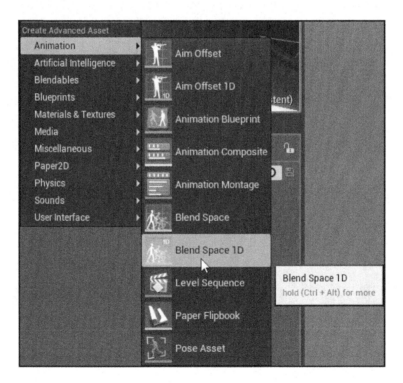

4. Open up the blend space we just created:

The Blend Space editor consists of an Asset Details panel on the left, a preview window, the Sample Point workspace at the bottom, and an animation asset browser in the lower right.

In the lower right-hand corner, you can see the list of animations we migrated from the VR template for our hand. It's simply displaying any animation in the `Content` directories that's mapped to the Hand Mesh's skeleton.

In the bottom center under the preview, we can see the workspace where we're going to construct our blend.

The first thing we need to do here is set up the axis we're going to use for our blend. Let's get started:

1. In the upper-left corner, find **Asset Details | Axis Settings**, and expand the **Horizontal Axis** block.
2. Set its **Name** to `Grip`.
3. Set its **Maximum Axis Value** to 1.0.

    Now, we have a place to put our animation poses.

4. From the **Asset Browser**, drag `MannequinHand_Right_Open` onto the workspace until it snaps onto the 0.0 grid line.

5. Drag `MannequinHand_Right_Grab` onto the 1.0 line.

6. Drag `MannequinHand_Right_CanGrab` into the middle, at 0.5.

Test it out by holding down the *Shift* key and dragging on the workspace. We can blend seamlessly between the three animation poses we applied to the **Grip** axis by changing its value:

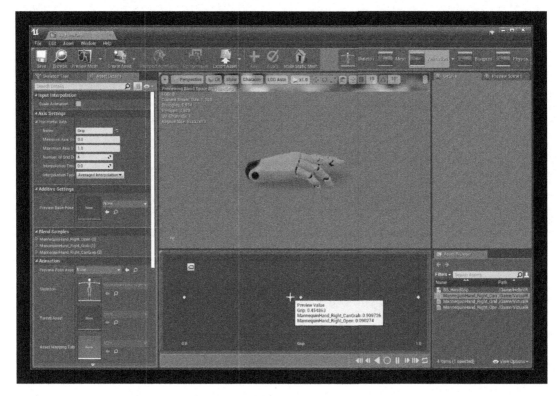

Let's get this working in our Animation Blueprint.

Wiring the blend space into the animation blueprint

We can now use the blend space we just created as an asset in its animation blueprint. The animation blueprint is a powerful tool the allows you to control the way animations are played on a skeletal mesh. It's split into two main sections:

- The Anim Graph, which takes animation inputs and processes them to calculate the mesh pose on every frame

- The Event Graph, which behaves similarly to the Blueprints you've already authored and is used to process the data that the animation blueprint is going to use to decide what animations to play

Let's learn how it works:

1. Open the animation blueprint we created a moment ago.

   Looking at its **My Blueprint | Graphs** block, you can see that in addition to the familiar **EventGraph** we find in all of our blueprint assets, there's a second graph, called **AnimGraph**.

2. Double-click **My Blueprint | Graphs | AnimGraph** to open it:

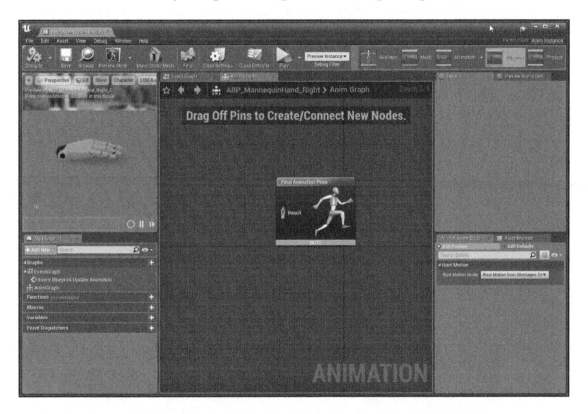

The **Anim Graph** is responsible for determining the animation pose of its controlled skeletal mesh on each tick. We can see here that we have a Blueprint graph, but it's different from the event graphs we're used to. Everything in the Anim Graph leads to that **Final Animation Pose** and is used to decide what it's going to be. We're not going to go deeply into Animation Blueprints here, as their setup is a deep subject and outside the scope of this book but they're worth learning about. The Anim Graph for our hands is going to be fairly simple.

3. From your **Content Browser**, grab the BS_HandGrip Blend Space we created a moment ago and drag it onto the **Anim Graph**.
4. Drag its **Animation Pose** output to the **Result Animation Pose** input on the **Final Animation Pose** node.
5. Drag out a connector from the **Grip** input on your BS_HandGrip node, and promote it to a variable. Name the variable Grip:

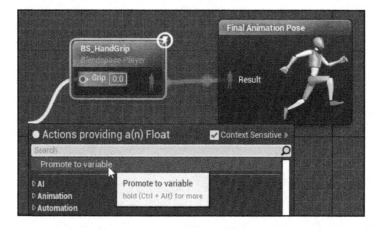

6. Set the Grip variable's **Slider Range** and **Value Range** minimum values to 0 and maximum values to 1.
7. Compile the blueprint:

In the lower-right corner of the window, you will see an **Anim Preview Editor** tab. The variables you create in your animation blueprint appear here, and you can change their values in real time to see how they would affect your animation. (You're not actually changing the default value of the variable here—you're just previewing the system's behavior with different values.) Give it a try. Mouse into the Grip value and drag it around to slide between 0.0 and 1.0. You'll see that it's driving the blend space we created, which in turn is driving the final animation pose. You can close and open the hand by changing the value of the Grip float.

Let's get this responding to our user's input.

Connecting the animation blueprint to our hand blueprint

We need to tell our BP_VRHand actor that the HandMesh component should use our new animation blueprint to drive its animation state:

1. Open up BP_VRHand and select the HandMesh Skeletal Mesh component from the **Components** list.
2. In its **Details** | **Animation**, verify that its **Animation Mode** is set to **Use Animation Blueprint**. (It should be by default.)
3. Use the **Anim Class** drop-down menu to select your new animation blueprint:

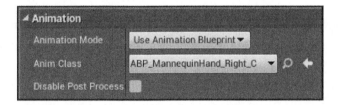

Now, let's drive the **Grip** value on the animation blueprint we just connected.

4. Find the **Event Tick** in event graph of BP_VRHand, or create it if needed.
5. Drag a reference to Hand Mesh onto the graph.
6. Drag a connector from Hand Mesh and call Get Anim Instance on it.

For a Skeletal Mesh being controlled by an animation blueprint, the Anim Instance is going to be a reference to that animation blueprint. Now, since we need to access a specific member of that blueprint, we need to cast the anim instance to the specific animation blueprint class we're using.

7. Drag a connector from the Get Anim Instance return value and cast it to our new animation Blueprint class (ABP_MannequinHand_Right.)

8. From the **As ABP_Mannequin Hand Right** output, call Set Grip.

9. Hit *Ctrl* + drag bWantsToGrip onto the graph to get its value.

10. Drag a connector from bWantsToGrip and create a Select node.

11. Connect the **Select** node's Return Value to Set Grip's Grip input.

12. Set the **True** value on the **Select** node to **1.0**.

Your graph should now look like this:

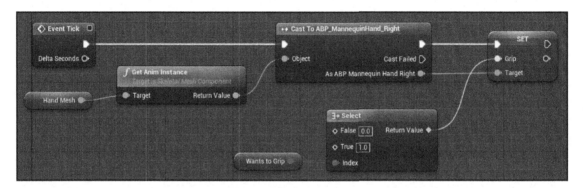

Let's run it and test it out. Okay, good. Our hands are responding to our input. They don't look great doing it yet, but we can see that the basics are working. When we squeeze the trigger on a motion controller, that input sets bWantsToGrip to true, and on the **Tick Event** of VRHand, we're setting the value of the **Grip** variable on our Animation Blueprint to 0.0 or 1.0, based on the current value of bWantsToGrip.

Now, let's improve things a bit and set the system up to be more flexible.

Creating a new enumerator for our grip

Right now, we're just driving the Grip value on the hand's animation blueprint directly, but it really makes more sense to let the animation blueprint handle this, and just tell it what's going on. The system that handles animation, after all, should be responsible for deciding how it wants to do that.

Let's give ourselves an easy way to communicate our grip state to the animation blueprint. An **enumeration** is ideal for this:

1. Right-click in your **Blueprints** directory, and select **Create Advanced Asset** | **Blueprints** | **Enumeration**. Name it `EGripState`:

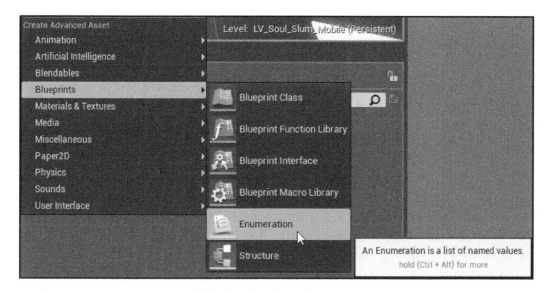

2. Open up the new enumerator.
3. In its **Enumerators** list, hit **New** to create a new entry.
4. Set the new entry's **Display Name** to `Open`. You can leave its description blank:

5. Create another enumerator entry, and name it `Gripping`.

6. Close the enumerator.

Now, we've created a new data type that we can use to store information and pass it in and out of objects. Let's add it to our animation blueprint.

7. Open up your animation blueprint and add a new variable to its **Variables** list.

8. Set its **Variable Type** to `EGripState`, and name it `GripState`.

Remember a moment ago when we noticed that the animation blueprint contained two graphs—the **Anim Graph** and an **Event Graph**? Now, we're going to begin to make use of the event graph. This is a powerful system. It allows us to keep our game logic where it belongs, in the gameplay objects, and keep our animation logic where it belongs, in the animation blueprint. We can pass a value into the animation blueprint, and then in its event graph, determine what we want it to do with that input.

9. In your animation blueprint's **Event Graph**, find the **Event Blueprint Update Animation** node, or create one if it isn't already present. This is the equivalent of a tick event in an animation blueprint.

10. Press *Ctrl* + drag a reference to your new `Grip State` variable onto the event graph.

11. Drag a connector from its output and create a **Select** node.

You'll notice that, when you create a **Select** node from an enum, it's automatically populated with that enum's available values:

12. Hit *Alt* + drag a reference to the `Grip` variable onto the graph to create a setter.

13. Drag the output from the **Select** node into the Grip setter.

14. Set its **Gripping** value to **1.0**.

15. Compile the blueprint.

16. In the **Anim Preview** editor, verify that changing **Grip State** from **Open** to **Gripping** closes the hand:

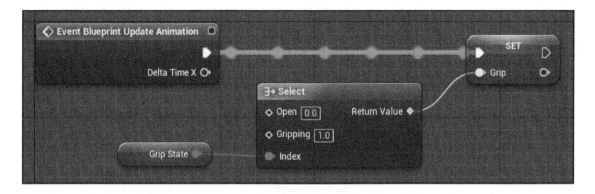

Now, let's update BP_VRHand to send the enum value instead of a grip value:

1. Back in your BP_VRHand's Event Tick, delete the Grip setter and the select node feeding it.
2. Drag out a connector from the Cast output, and select Set Grip State.
3. Drag out a new **Select** node from your bWantsToGrip getter.
4. Drag the **Select** node's output into the GripState setter's input.
5. Set the **True** value of the Select node to Gripping.

Your graph should now look like this:

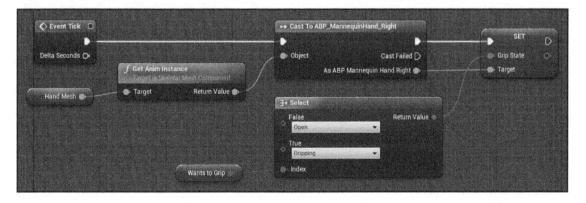

Test it out. There's no visible change, right? What we've done here is set up our graphs so that we can now modify them more easily. Now that we've verified that the new setup is working the same way the old one did, let's jump back into the animation blueprint and improve the way we handle its input.

Smoothing out our grip animation

Snapping between the open and closed animation poses looks awful. Let's smooth this out by transitioning between the values over time:

1. Jump back to your animation blueprint's **Event Graph**.
2. Right-click and add an `FInterp to Constant` node.
3. Drag your `Grip` variable onto its **Current** input.
4. Drag the output of your **Grip State Select** node onto its **Target** input.
5. Drag the **Delta Time X** value from `Event Blueprint Update Animation` into its **Delta Time** input.
6. Drag out a connector from its `Interp Speed` input and promote it to a variable named `Interp Speed`.
7. Compile the Blueprint and set `Interp Speed` to **7.0**.
8. Connect the output from `FInterpToConstant` to the `Grip` setter's input:

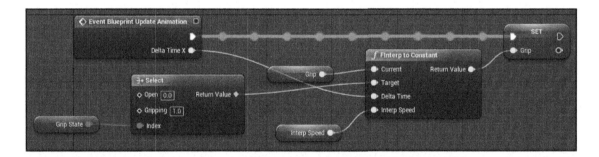

Test it out. That's much better. Now, our hand is interpolating between poses instead of just snapping to the value. What's happening here is the **Interp to Constant** node is managing a smooth transition to a new target value that was selected by Grip State over the duration specified by InterpSpeed. If we want the transition to happen faster, we can just reduce Interp Speed. If we want it longer, just make Interp Speed larger.

As simple as this example is, it begins to show the power and flexibility animation blueprints provide. We can easily communicate state information from the VRHand blueprint, telling the animation blueprint what we're trying to do, and then do whatever we'd like to do to illustrate that state in the animation blueprint.

Summary

This was another involved chapter. We did a lot here. We began by creating a new project and migrating our VRPawn blueprints, along with their required objects, into the new project. We learned a quick way of recreating input bindings by copying the contents of `DefaultInput.ini` to a new project. We then added the **Soul:City** assets and maps to our project and set up a navmesh so that we could explore it.

Then, we got to the meat of this chapter. We scavenged a hand mesh from the **VR Template** project and created a `Blueprint` class to drive their behavior. We learned how to use construction scripts to change objects when they're created, both in the editor and in-game. We learned how to create child actor components inside our pawn and how to use them in blueprints. We learned how to create an animation blend space and an animation blueprint to animate our hand meshes and how to use an enumerator to pass state information into the animation blueprint.

In the next chapter, we're going to learn how to use these hands to pick up objects. We'll learn how to use blueprint interfaces to enable function calls to be made on a wide variety of objects and how to detect actors we can pick up. We'll also learn a bit about using haptic feedback effects to indicate to players when they've made contact with an object they can pick up.

6
Interacting with the Virtual World - Part II

In the last chapter, we set up our hands and learned how to animate them. As we mentioned then, this alone can represent a big step toward establishing presence in our application. Now, let's take things to the next step and start using them.

In this chapter, we're going to learn about the following topics:

- How to use Blueprint interfaces to add functionality to a variety of Blueprints
- How to use attachments to pick up and drop physics actors
- How to indicate to players when they can interact with an object
- How to create haptic feedback effects to provide more tactile feedback to the user

Creating an object we can pick up

We'll begin by making a few objects we can pick up. Let's start with a simple cube:

1. Right-click in your project's `Blueprints` directory in your content browser and select **Create Basic Asset | Blueprint Class**.
2. This time, instead of selecting one of the common classes as its parent class, expand the **All Classes** entry at the bottom of the **Pick Parent Class** dialog.

3. Select **Static Mesh Actor**:

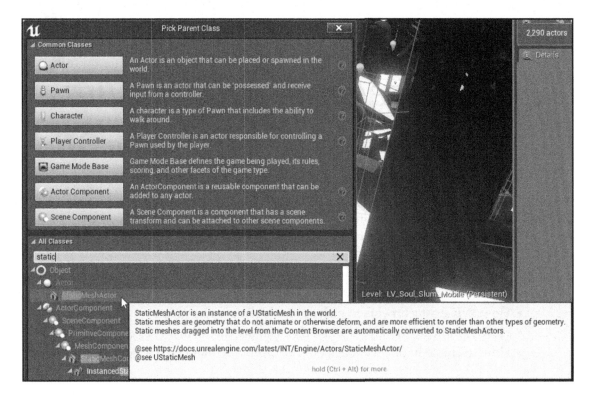

4. Name it `BP_PickupCube`.
5. Open up `BP_PickupCube`.

You can see that it inherited a `Static Mesh Component`.

We could just as easily have created an `Actor` Blueprint and added a `Static Mesh` component, but it's a good idea to get in the habit of choosing your parent classes appropriately when you're building a new asset. Don't reinvent things if you don't have to.

6. Set the **Static Mesh** property of `Static Mesh Component` to `Engine Content/Basic Shapes/Cube1`.
7. Set its **Scale** to `0.2, 0.2, 0.2`.
8. Set its **Materials | Element 0** to `Content/SoulCity/Environment/Materials/Props/MI_Glow`. (Or anything else you like, but this one will be easy to see in the map.)

Now, we want our cube to simulate physics, so let's set a few values to make this happen:

1. Set its **Physics | Simulate Physics** flag to `True`.
2. Set its **Collision | Simulation Generates Hit Events** to `True`.
3. Set its **Collision | Generate Overlap Events** to `True`.
4. Make sure its **Collision | Collision Presets** is set to `PhysicsActor`. (This should have been set for you automatically when you set **Simulate Physics** to true.)
5. Set its **Collision | Can Ever Affect Navigation** to `False`. (This will be hidden in the **Collision** section's **Advanced** properties.)

We've now created a small glowing cube that will respond naturally to physics, but not block our navmesh as it moves around the world.

Now, we're going to need to give it the ability to be picked up. There are a few ways we could do this. We could simply write `Pickup` and `Drop` methods right into blueprint of `BP_PickupCube`, but we're going to need to be able to call these functions from outside.

As we saw previously, if you want to call a function from outside its blueprint, you have to be sure you're talking to a class that contains that function, which we do by casting the reference to that class. This would be fine if we only ever anticipated picking up cubes, but what if we want to be able to make other objects easy to pick up? We don't want to have to rewrite our `BP_VRHand` blueprint every time we add a new type of object that could be picked up, so that's not a great solution here.

We could derive `BP_PickupCube` from a common parent that implemented the `Pickup` and `Drop` methods, and just cast our references to that parent. That's better, but still not perfect. `BP_PickupCube` inherits from `StaticMeshActor`, but what if we want to make it possible for something that inherits from `SkeletalMeshActor` to be picked up? We don't have an easy way to create a common parent class in that instance.

The answer to this dilemma is a *Blueprint Interface*. An interface is a Blueprint object that allows us to define functions that can be called on any object that implements the interface, no matter what class that object derives from. It's a class you can attach to any object, and it acts as a promise that the object to which it's attached will implement each of the functions included in the interface. If I create an interface that declares the `Pickup` and `Drop` functions, for example, and I apply that interface to my `BP_PickupCube`, I can call the `Pickup` and `Drop` methods without having to cast the object first. This is a powerful pattern. You can make your code very flexible and easy to extend by using interfaces smartly.

Don't worry if this isn't completely clear yet. It's going to make more sense once we build it.

Creating a Blueprint Interface for pickup objects

To create a Blueprint Interface, follow the given steps:

1. Right-click in your project's `Blueprints` directory, and select **Create Advanced Asset** | **Blueprints** | **Blueprint Interface**:

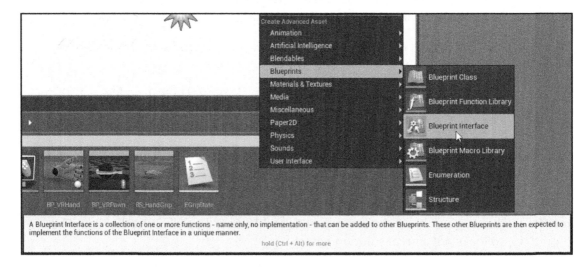

2. Name it `BPI_PickupActor`.

   When you open it up, you'll see that it contains a **Functions** list, and nothing else. You'll notice that the graph can't be edited. This is because the interface is simply a list of functions that the attached object must implement, but those functions don't get written in the interface.

3. By default, it's created a new function declaration for you. Name it `Pickup`.

4. Under the function's **Details** | **Inputs**, add a new input. Set its type to **Scene Component** | **Object Reference**, and name it `AttachTo`:

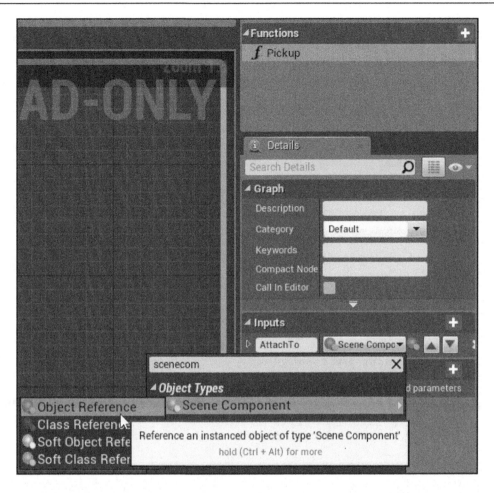

5. Add another function, and call it `Drop`. This one doesn't need any input.
6. Compile, save, and close the interface.

Now, let's apply this new interface to `BP_PickupCube`:

1. Open `BP_PickupCube`, and hit the **Class Settings** item on the toolbar.
2. Under **Details** | **Interfaces**, hit the **Add** button under **Implemented Interfaces**.
3. Select `BPI_PickupActor`.

Implementing the Pickup and Drop functions

Now that we've added this interface to the `BP_PickupCube` class, we can implement the functions we declared in that interface in our event graph. Let's get started:

1. In your **Event Graph**, right-click and select `Event Pickup` to create a Pick up event. This event exists on this Blueprint class now because we've attached an interface that declares it. You'll see that the event indicates that it's an interface event from `BPI_PickupActor`.

2. Create a `Drop` event in the same way.

   Now that we've created handlers for the two events coming from our interface, let's make them work.

   When this object is picked up, we want to turn off its physics simulation so that it doesn't fall out of our hand, and we want to attach it to a scene component on the hand that's picking it up.

3. Drag a reference to the `Static Mesh Component` onto the **Event Graph**.

4. Call `Set Simulate Physics` on it, setting **Simulate** to `False`.

5. Right-click in the graph and select `Get Root Component`.

6. Drag a connector from the **Root Component** reference, and select `Attach to Component`. You'll see that there are two options for this. Roll over them and select the one whose tooltip reads **Target is Scene Component**, since we're going to be attaching to a scene component:

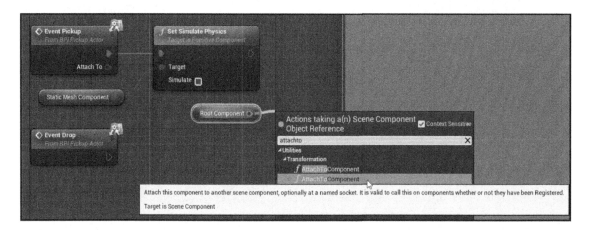

7. Drag the **Attach To** output from `Event Pickup` to the **Parent** input on the `Attach To Component` node.

8. On your `Attach To Component` node, set the **Location**, **Rotation**, and **Scale** rules to `Keep World`, and set **Weld Simulated Bodies** to `False`.

Your completed Pickup implementation should look like this:

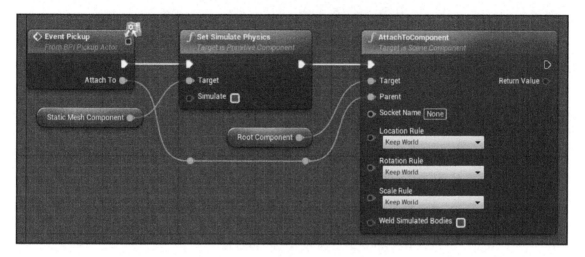

When we drop this object, we want to turn its physics back on and detach it from the scene component we attached when we picked it up.

9. Select your `Static Mesh Component` reference and the `Set Simulate Physics` call, and hit *Ctrl + W* to duplicate them.

10. Connect execution of **Event Drop** pin to the copied `Set Simulate Physics` call.

11. Set **Simulate** to True so that we're turning physics back on.

12. Right-click and create a `Detach From Actor` node.

13. Set the **Location**, **Rotation**, and **Scale** rules to `Keep World`, just as we did on the **Attach** node.

Your completed Drop implementation should look like this:

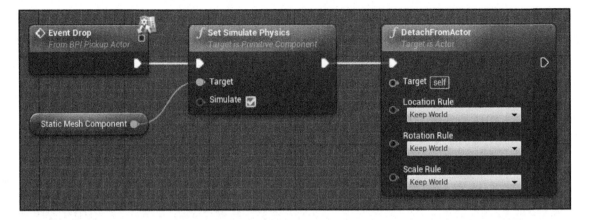

That's it for our `Pickup Cube` actor. We can close the blueprint.

Setting up VRHand to pick up objects

Now, we're ready to get our hands grabbing these objects.

Creating a function to find the nearest pickup object

The next thing we need to do is find out what objects are near enough to our hand to be picked up. Let's create a function to do this:

1. In `BP_VRHand`, create a new function called `FindNearestPickupObject`.
2. Set its **Category** to `Grabbing` and its **Access Specifier** to `Private`.
3. In its implementation graph, right-click to create a `Get All Actors with Interface` node, and set its **Interface** value to `BPI_PickupActor`.

   This is going to give us an array of every actor in the scene that implements the `BPI_PickupActor` interface.

4. Drag a connector from the **Out Actors** output and create a `For Each Loop` node:

We're going to iterate through the actors that could possibly be picked up, ignore any actor that's too far to be considered, and then return the closest remaining eligible actor.

5. From the For Each Loop **Array Element** output, drag out a connector and call Get Actor Location on it.
6. Drag a reference to Hand Mesh onto your graph and call Get World Location on it.
7. Subtract the hand mesh's world location from the array element's actor location:

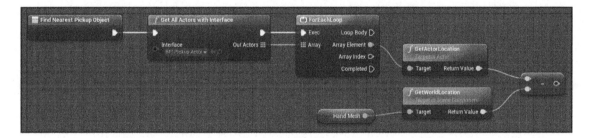

8. Get Vector Length Squared for the resulting vector.
9. Drag out its result and select **Promote to local variable**. Name the new variable LocalCurrentActorDistSquared:

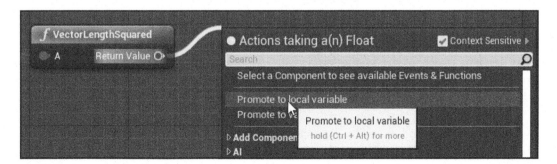

10. Connect the **Loop Body** execution line to the local variable's setter.

11. Drag the output from our local variable setter and create a <= test to see whether it's equal to or shorter than the value we're going to give it.

The reason why we're creating a local variable here is that we're going to need to use this value again if there's more than one grabbable actor in our test radius, and we don't want to waste time recalculating the distance, so we're stashing it here so that we can use it later if we need it.

12. Create a float variable and name it `GrabRadius`. Compile the Blueprint and set its value to **32.0**. (Later on, you can tune this value to whatever feels right for you.)

13. Press *Ctrl* + drag `GrabRadius` onto your graph.

14. Drag a connector from its output and `Square` it.

15. Connect the result of the square to the <= test's second input:

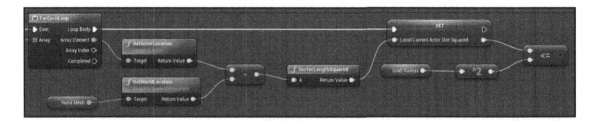

Remember when we mentioned that real distance checks are expensive? This is a place where it matters because we're going to call this function on the `Tick` event. Since we just want to see whether the actor is within the supplied radius, but we don't care how far away it really is, it's cheaper to do this test on the squared values.

16. Create a `Branch` node from our <= test's output.

If our actor passes the <= test, we know it's within the grab range. Now, we need to see whether it's the closest object in that range.

17. In the **Local Variables** list, create a new local variable named `ClosestRange`, and set its **Variable Type** to `Float`. Set its **Default Value** to `10000.0`.

Local variables are variables that only exist within the function in which they're declared. They can't be read from outside the function. It's a good idea to use local variables within functions for values that are only used by that function so that they don't clutter the surrounding object. Local variables are also reset to their default values each time the function is run, so you don't have to worry about strange values hanging around from previous function calls.

18. Press *Ctrl* + drag `LocalCurrentActorDistSquared` onto your graph to get its value.
19. Drag a connector from its output and create a < test from it.
20. Drag the `Closest Range` local variable into the test's second input.
21. Create a `Branch` using the < test result as its condition:

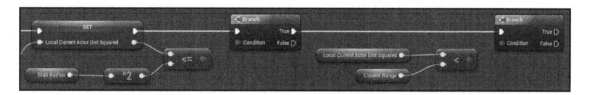

If this test returns true, we've found a new closest actor. We want to save a reference to it and record its distance as the new closest range.

22. Press *Alt* + drag `Closest Range` onto the graph, and drag `LocalCurrentActorDistSquared` into its input.
23. Set this value from the branch's **True** output.
24. Create a new local variable named `NearestPickupActor`, and set its type to **Actor | Object Reference**.
25. Press *Alt* + drag it onto the graph to set its value.
26. Set its value to the `For Each Loop` **Array Element**. (This is going to be a long connection. Consider creating some reroute nodes to make it more readable.)

27. Connect it to the output from the `Set Closest Range` node:

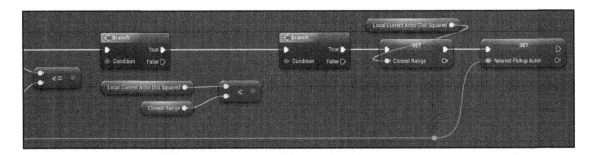

Finally, once we've iterated through all of the possible objects and found our best pickup candidate if one exists, we want to save that value so that it can be used by our pickup method.

28. Create a new variable (not a local variable this time—we want to read this value outside), name it `AvailablePickupActor`, and set its type to `Actor > Object Reference`.

29. Press *Alt* + drag it onto the event graph near the **Completed** output of the `For Each Loop`.

30. Connect the **Completed** output of the `For Each Loop` to the **Set** input of `Available Pickup Actor`.

31. Drag the `Nearest Pickup Actor` local variable onto the setter's input:

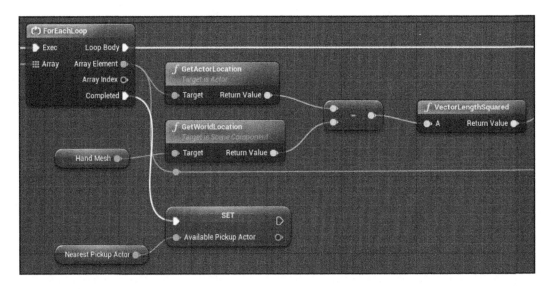

What this is going to do is set an externally readable `Available Pickup Actor` variable to the actor we found when we iterated through the list of possible actors, if we found any. `Nearest Pickup Actor` will be `Null` if we didn't find any.

Calling Find Nearest Pickup Object on the Tick event

Now, it's time to call our new function so that we know when we're able to pick an object up. We don't want to do this, however, if we're already holding an object, so we should store a reference to any object we're already holding. Let's get started:

1. Return to your event graph of BP_VRHand **and find** Event Tick.
2. Create a `Sequence` node near Event Tick.
3. We want to update our hand animation only after we've looked for objects we could grab, so press *Ctrl* + drag the output from execution pin of **Event Tick** onto the `Sequence` node's **Then 1** output.
4. Connect the execution pin of **Event Tick** to the **Sequence** node's input.
5. Marquee select the node network connected to the **Sequence** node's **Then 1** output and drag them down to give yourself some room to work:

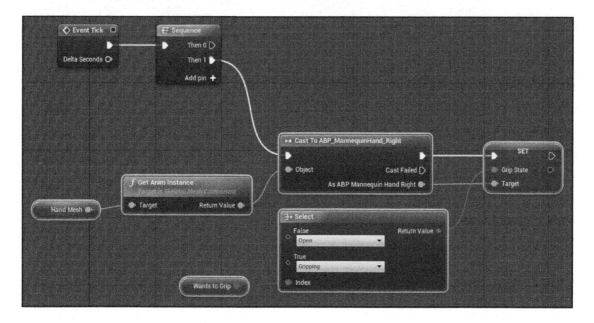

6. Create a new variable, name it `HeldActor`, and set its **Variable Type** to `Actor > Object Reference`.

7. Press *Ctrl* + drag `HeldActor` onto your event graph to get its value.

8. Right-click it and select `Convert to Validated Get`.

9. Drag a call to `Find Nearest Pickup Object` onto the graph, and call it from the `Held Actor` getter's **Is Not Valid** output:

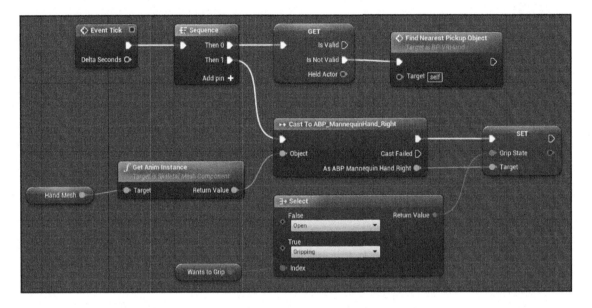

This way, we're only bothering to check for pickup actors if we're not already holding one.

Picking up an actor

Now that we're looking for actors we could pick up, let's make that happen when we try to grab them. Let's get started:

1. Open up your `Grab Actor` function in `BP_VRHand`.

2. We don't need the `Print String` node here anymore, so we can delete it.

3. Press *Ctrl* + drag a getter for `HeldActor` onto your graph, right-click it, and convert it into a validated get.

4. Connect the `bWantsToGrip` setter's execution output to the `HeldActor` getter's input.

5. Press *Ctrl* + drag a getter for `AvailablePickupActor` onto the graph and make this a validated get too.

6. Connect the **Is Not Valid** output from the `Held Actor` get to this getter's input, since we're only interested in picking up an object if we're not already holding one.

7. Drag out a connector from `Available Pickup Actor` and call `Pickup (Message)` on it:

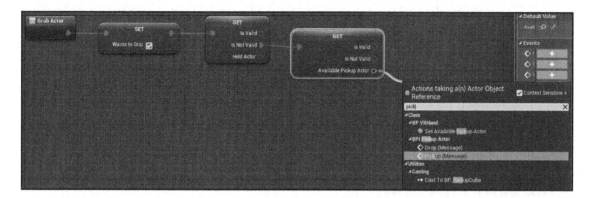

This is why Blueprint Interfaces are so useful. We didn't need to cast the pickup actor to any particular class to call the interface method on it. We can simply make the call, and if the object implements the interface and knows what to do with it, the call will work. If the object doesn't implement the interface, it simply does nothing.

If you need to find out whether a given actor implements an interface, call `Does Implement Interface` on it. This will return true if the interface is found on the object. In this particular case, making this call would be redundant since we know that `Available Pickup Actor` will always implement the **BPI_PickupActor** interface. We used that interface as a filter when we were looking for objects in the `Find Nearest Pickup Object` function.

8. Drag the **Motion Controller** component onto your `Pickup` node's **Attach To** input.

9. Drag the `Held Actor` variable onto the output of `Available Pickup Actor` to set it to that value.

10. Add `Return Nodes` to your exit points. (You don't have to do this, but your code will be far more readable in the long run if you make this a habit.)

Your completed `Grab Actor` graph should look like this:

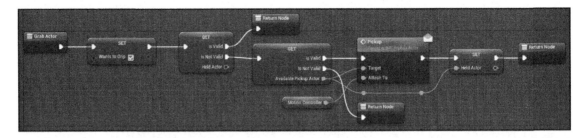

To summarize what's going on here, when `Grab Actor` is called, `bWantsToGrip` is set to true, and then we check to see whether we're already holding an object. We don't do anything more if we are. If we're not, we check to see whether we found an object on `Event Tick` that we could pick up. If we didn't, there's nothing more to do. If we did, we send a `Pickup` message to it through its interface, with a reference to our `Motion Controller` component as the object it should attach to, and we stash it as our `Held Actor`.

Releasing an actor

Since we can now pick an actor up, we're also going to want to be able to drop it again. Let's do this now:

1. Open up the `Release Actor` function.
2. Delete the `Print String` node from it—we're done with it.
3. Press *Ctrl* + drag `Held Actor` onto the graph, right-click it, and convert it into a validated get.
4. Call the validated get after we set `bWantsToGrip`.
5. Connect a return node to its **Is Not Valid** output:

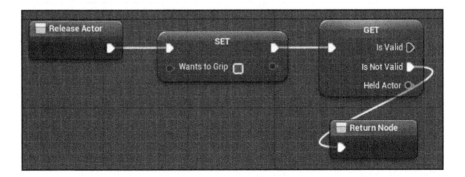

If we're not holding anything, there's nothing more we need to do. If we are, we should make sure that the actor still thinks we're the one holding it (since we could have grabbed it with the other hand) and drop it if it's still our object.

6. Drag a connector from `Held Actor` and get its `Root Component`.
7. Call `Get Attach Parent` on the root component.
8. Drag a connector from **Return Value** of `Get Attach Parent` and create a `==` test.
9. Drag the `Motion Controller` component onto the test's other input.
10. Create a `Branch` using this test's result as its condition:

11. From the Branch's **True** output, call `Drop` on the `Held Actor`.
12. Press *Alt* + drag `Held Actor` onto the graph to create a setter.
13. Connect it to the execution output from the `Drop` call, and to the `Branch` node's **False** output so that we clear the value in either case:

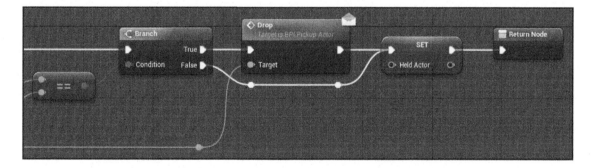

Your completed graph should look like this:

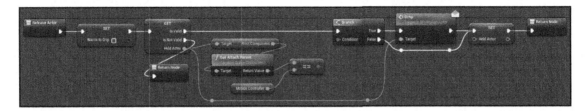

To recap what's going on here, when `Release Actor` is called, we first set `bWantsToGrip` to false. We then check to see whether we're currently holding anything. If we're not, there's nothing more to do. If we think we are holding something, we check to make sure the object we think we're holding still sees our motion controller as its parent, since we could have grabbed it with the other hand. If we really are holding the object, we drop it and clear out the `Held Actor` variable. If it turned out we were no longer holding the object after all, we clear out the `Held Actor` variable so that we no longer think we are.

Test grabbing and releasing

Let's test this in our map:

1. From your editor's **Modes** panel, select **Place | Basic | Cube**, and drag it into your scene. Set its **Location** to **X=-2580**, **Y=310**, **Z=40** so that it's sitting near the player start.
2. Grab `BP_PickupCube` from your content browser, and place it on the cube you just placed. You can use the *End* key to drop it to the surface below it. (`X=-2600`, `Y=340`, `Z=100` is probably a decent location for it.)
3. Press *Alt* + drag a few more of these `BP_PickupCubes` and stack them on the cube:

Launch a **VR Preview**. Walk or teleport up to the objects on the cube and use the triggers to pick them up, drop them, throw them, and move them from hand-to-hand.

Not bad, but there are a few things we need to fix here.

Fixing cube collision

First, and most importantly, they're colliding with the VRPawn's collision capsule and throwing us around. We'd better fix that:

1. Open the `BP_PickupCube` blueprint and select its `Static Mesh Component`.
2. Under its **Details | Collision**, change its **Collision Presets** from `PhysicsActor` to `Custom`.

3. The individual collision response channels for this object are now editable. Set the **Pawn** collision response to `Overlap` instead of `Block`:

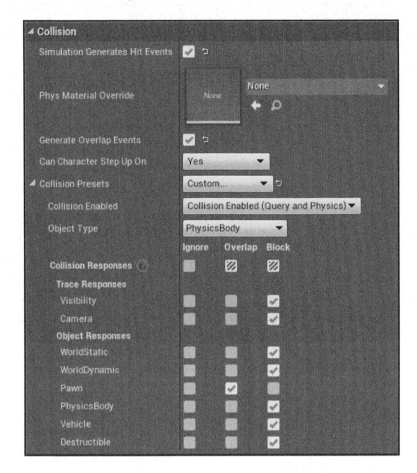

This way, we can still detect collisions with the pawn if we're interested in them, but they're not going to prevent the player from moving around.

Letting players know when they can pick something up

Secondly, we're not giving the player any visual indication that they can pick something up. Let's improve this.

First off, let's add another state to our EGripState enumerator:

1. Open up EGripState from your project's Blueprints directory.
2. Under its **Enumerators** list, hit **New** to add another entry. Name it CanGrab.
3. Close and save it.

   Now, we need to tell our Animation Blueprint what to do with this.

4. Open the ABP_MannequinHand_Right animation blueprint and open its Event Graph.
5. Under Event Blueprint Update Animation, you'll see that the Grip State Select node has been automatically updated to reflect the new Can Grab enumerator we added. Set its value to 0.5:

   Try it out by compiling and then changing **Grip State** in the **Anim Preview Editor**. The hand should go to a halfway-open state when **Grip State** is set to Can Grab.

6. Save and close your animation blueprint.

   Next, we need to get the BP_VRHand blueprint to set Grip State to Can Grab when it detects that the player can grab something. Let's create a pure function to determine what our Grip State should be.

7. Open **Event Graph** of BP_VRHand and find Event Tick.
8. Select the bWantsToGrip reference and the Select node connected to it and collapse them into a function.

9. Name the function `DetermineGripState`, set its **Category** to **Grabbing**, set its **Access Specifier** to **Private**, and set **Pure** to True:

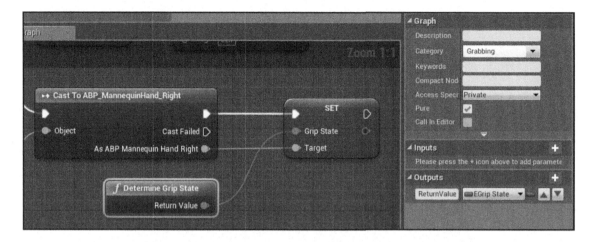

10. Open up `DetermineGripState`.

11. Press *Ctrl* + drag `Held Actor` onto the graph and convert it into a validated get.

12. Connect it to the function input and add a new `Return Node` from its **Is Valid** output.

13. Set this node's **Return Value** to `Gripping`:

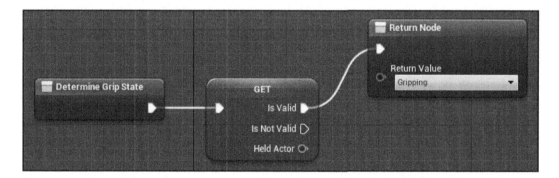

If we're holding an object, we don't care about anything else—we should just animate to the **Gripping** state.

14. Add a `Branch` node to the graph.

15. Drag the `bWantsToGrip` value into its **Condition**.

16. Connect its **True** branch to the `Gripping Return Node` we just created.
17. Press *Ctrl* + drag `AvailablePickupActor` onto the graph and convert it into a validated get.
18. Add another `Return Node` connected to its **Is Valid** output, and set its **Return Value** to `Can Grab`.
19. Add another `Return Node` to its **Is Not Valid** output, with the value **Open**:

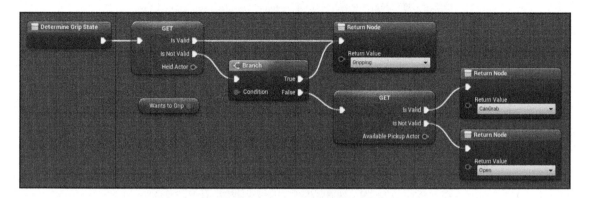

Let's test it out. Now, you should see the hand change its pose when it detects an object it can grab.

Adding haptic feedback

There's one other thing we should be doing, which is adding some degree of feedback to the hand when the player makes contact with an object. This may seem like a small thing, but it's actually significant to the process of evoking presence. We don't have many ways at present to simulate physical sensations, but any sensation at all that's paired to an event or action can go a long way toward making the virtual world feel less "ethereal" and more physical.

Let's learn how to add a bit of rumble to our controllers.

Creating a Haptic Feedback Effect Curve

First, we need to create the haptic effect we want to play:

1. Right-click in your project's `Blueprints` directory and select **Create Advanced Asset | Miscellaneous | Haptic Feedback Effect Curve**:

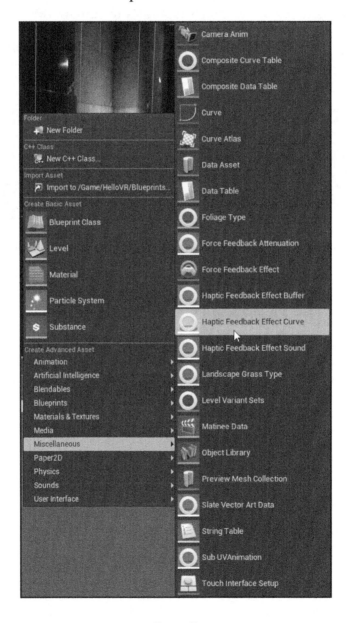

2. Name it `FX_ControllerRumble`.

3. Open the **Haptic Feedback Effect Curve** we just created.

   You'll see that you have two curves under **Haptic Feedback Effect | Haptic Details**: **Frequency** and **Amplitude**. We're going to create a very simple effect here, but it's really worth experimenting with these curves and figuring out how to create convincing feedback effects.

4. Right-click on your **Frequency** curve's timeline near the **0.0** time and select `Add key to None`.

5. Fix its **Time** and **Value** settings to read `0.0` for each:

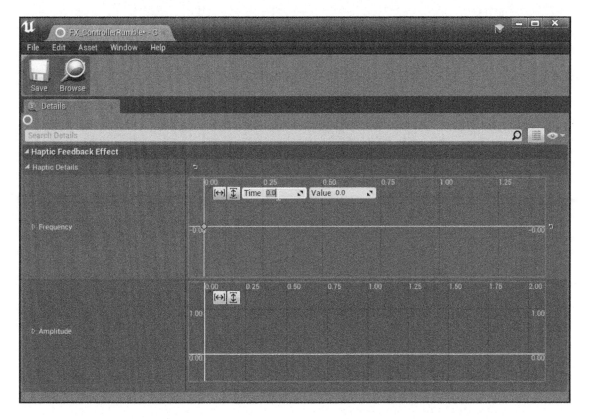

6. Right-click again on the timeline and add another key. Set this one's **Time** to `0.5` and its **Value** to `1.0`.

7. Create a third key on the curve, with **Time** as `1.0` and **Value** as `0.0`.

8. Create the same three keys for your **Amplitude** curve:

Your completed curves should look like what's shown in the preceding screenshot.

9. Save and close your new haptic effect curve.

Playing the haptic effect on command

Now that we've created a Haptic Feedback Effect Curve, let's set up a method to play it:

1. Open **Event Graph** of BP_VRHand and right-click. Select **Add Event | Add Custom Event**. Name the new event RumbleController.
2. Create an **Input** for this event. Name it Intensity, and set its type to Float.
3. Right-click and create a Get Player Controller node.
4. Drag a connector out from GetPlayerController and create a Play Haptic Effect node.

5. Select the **Haptic Effect** we just created.
6. Drag the `Hand` variable into the **Hand** input.
7. Drag the event's **Intensity** output into the **Scale** input:

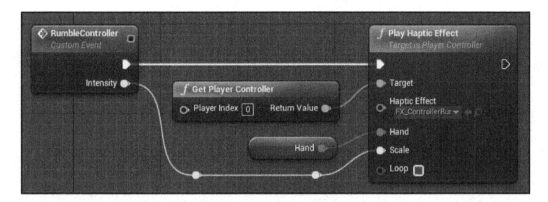

Now, let's call this Gaptic effect whenever we make contact with a new object we could pick up.

8. Open up your `Find Nearest Pickup Object` function of `BP_VRHand`.

   See where we're setting `Available Pickup Actor` to the value we found in `Nearest Pickup Actor`? Let's detect when we're putting a new value in there and trigger the effect when that happens.

9. Right-click your `Nearest Pickup Actor` getter, and convert it into a validated get.
10. Press *Ctrl* + drag the execution input into `Set Available Pickup Actor` onto the `Get Nearest Pickup Actor` getter's execution input.
11. Drag a connector from the `Nearest Pickup Actor` getter's value and create a `!=` (Not Equal) node.
12. Drag a reference to `Available Pickup Actor` from your **Variables** list into the `Not Equal` node's other input.
13. Create a `Branch` from its output.
14. Drag the **Is Valid** execution pin from `Nearest Pickup Actor` into the `Branch` input.
15. Call `Rumble Controller` from its **True** output and set its **Intensity** to `0.8`.
16. Drag the output from `Rumble Controller` into your `Available Pickup Actor` setter's input.

17. Drag the **Is Not Valid** output from `Nearest Pickup Actor` into the setter of `Available Pickup Actor`.

18. Add return nodes after `Set Available Pickup Actor` and from the `Not Equal` test's `False` branch:

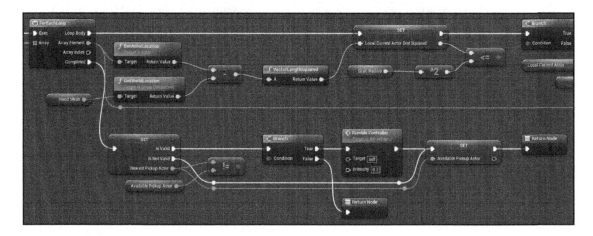

To recap what's going on here, once we've completed iterating through the objects we could potentially pick up, we need to check whether we've found one. If we didn't, we just set `Available Pickup Actor` to the null value so that we're clearing it if it previously contained a value. If we did find an object we could pick up, we check to see whether it's different from our current `Available Pickup Actor`. If it is, we rumble the controller before we set `Available Pickup Actor` to the new value.

Going further

There are a few ways we could further improve on what we've done here:

- First, detecting grabbable objects by distance gives us fuzzy results. It doesn't take the object's size into account. Using a sphere to represent our grabbing hand and testing for overlaps against this sphere is going to give us more accurate results. If you'd like to refactor this code to use that method, the VR Template project contains a good example.
- Second, our haptic feedback effect feels indistinct. It fades in and out evenly, and doesn't provide much of a physical sensation. Editing those curves to provide a sharper attack could make the effect more convincing.

Summary

This chapter picked up where the last one left off and gave us a chance to start picking up objects. We learned how to use Blueprint Interfaces to enable function calls to be made on a wide variety of objects and how to detect actors we could pick up and use attachments to pick them up and drop them. Finally, we also learned how to create haptic feedback effects to indicate to players when they've made contact with an object they can pick up.

As we mentioned at the start of the previous chapter, hand presence is an important factor in driving an overall sense of presence in VR. We're aware of our hands all of the time in real life, and bringing them into the virtual world does a lot to make us feel present in the space as well. In addition, the ability to use our hands to manipulate objects directly is one of the crucial things we can do in VR that we just can't do in any other medium. (For an example of just how well this can be done, check out *Vinyl Reality* by **EntroPi Games** (`https://vinyl-reality.com/`) and then imagine trying to do the same thing with a gamepad or a keyboard.) Hands are important to VR, and they're unique to VR. Take the time to get them right in your applications.

In the next chapter, we're going to learn how to create user interfaces in VR to display information and to make it possible for users to interact in 3D space.

Creating User Interfaces in VR 7

In the previous chapter, we learned how to create virtual hands driven by the motion controllers. This enabled our users not only to look around the world and move through it, but also to begin to interact with it. In this chapter, we're going to take this further, and learn how to create **user interfaces (UIs)** that communicate information and accept input.

 You should seriously consider whether your application really requires a graphical UI. Just because most applications need a GUI doesn't necessarily mean that's the case for all of them. Artificial-seeming UI elements can break immersion. When building UI elements, try to figure out how to fit them meaningfully into the world so that they look as though they belong there. Don't fall too much in love with buttons either. They're commonly used in 2D UI designs because they work well with a mouse, but VR hand controllers offer a much, much wider range of potential actions. Think beyond the button.

Most applications we develop for VR will require a **Graphical User Interface (GUI)** of some sort, but UIs in VR pose new challenges that we didn't have to face on the flat screen. Most of the time, when we're building a flat-screen UI, we can simply overlay 2D UI elements on top of our 3D environment using a **head-up display** (**HUD**) and then read mouse, gamepad, or keyboard input to allow the user to interact with it. This doesn't work in VR.

If we simply draw a 2D interface over each eye's view, its position is going to appear the same for each eye. The problem with this is that our stereo vision scopic interprets an object that looks the same to both eyes as being infinitely far away. This means that, when 3D objects in the world appear behind the UI on the screen, those objects are going to appear to be closer than the UI, even though the UI is drawn over them. This will look terrible and will almost certainly make your user uncomfortable.

The solution to this is to incorporate UI elements into the 3D world, but it isn't enough to simply create an HUD panel in front of the player's face and project onto this, either (we'll talk more about why that is when we get to the player's UI later in this chapter). There's no way around the reality that you have to re-think UIs in VR. Think of what you're doing as re-creating objects you interact with in the real worlds rather than as re-creating 2D metaphors from the flat-screen world.

We need to re-think how we interact with UI in the 3D world as well. We don't have access to a mouse cursor in VR (which wouldn't work for us anyway, because it's a 2D input device), and keyboard commands aren't a great idea, since your user can't see the keyboard. We're going to need new ways to communicate input into the system. Fortunately, Unreal gives us a solid set of tools to handle 3D UIs in ways that will work well in VR.

In this chapter, we're going to run through the process of creating the various elements we'll need to create a functional UI in VR by creating a simple AI-controlled companion character with an indicator displaying its current AI state, and a control interface on the player character that allows us to change that state.

Specifically, we're going to cover the following topics:

- Creating an AI-controlled character and giving it a simple behavior
- Creating interfaces in 3D space using **Unreal Motion Graphics** (**UMG**) UI designer to display information
- Attaching UI elements to objects in the world
- Using widget interaction components to interact with these interfaces and affect objects in the world
- Displaying the widget interaction component to the user

Let's get to it!

Getting started

For this project, we're going to begin by simply taking the previous chapter's project and making a new copy. In previous chapters, we've explored a few ways of creating new projects using material from other projects. Simply duplicating and renaming a project can often be the simplest way to do this, and is appropriate if you're taking the work you've done in a previous project and expanding on it, as we are here. (It's also perfectly reasonable for this chapter's work to keep working from the previous project, if you'd like to.)

Creating a new Unreal project from an existing project

When creating a new project by copying, there really isn't a lot that needs to be done. It's enough to simply do the following:

- Copy the old project directory.
- Rename the new directory and the .uproject file.
- Delete the generated files from the old project.

Let's run through this process using our project from Chapter 5, *Interacting with the Virtual World – Part I,* as a starting point for our work in this chapter:

1. With Unreal Editor closed, find the location of the previous chapter's Unreal project.
2. Make a copy of the project directory and give it a new name.
3. Inside the new directory, rename the .uproject file. You're not required to match the name of the project file to the name of the directory that contains it, but it's good practice to do so.
4. Delete the Intermediate and Saved directories from your new project directory. These will be regenerated when you open the new project, and stray data left over from old projects can cause problems. It's always better to start clean with these.
5. Open up the new .uproject file. You'll see that the Intermediate and Saved directories you just deleted are regenerated for the new project. The project should open to the default map (LV_Soul_Slum_Mobile) we set in the last chapter.
6. Hit the toolbar's **Build** button to rebuild its lighting.

Test the project by launching a VR preview. Everything should work as it did in the previous project.

As we mentioned before, it's also fine simply to continue working from the previous chapter's project. Either way, we're now ready to add the AI character we're going to control.

We're not alone – adding an AI character

Creating an AI-controlled character from scratch would take us into areas that fall outside the scope of this book, so, instead, we're going to repurpose the standard player character from the third-person template and change the way it's controlled.

If you already have a project created using the third-person template available, open it up. If not, create one:

- Select **File** | **New Project**, and create a new Blueprint project using the third-person template. It's fine to leave other settings at their default values – they won't affect anything we're doing.

Migrating the third-person character blueprint

Whether we've taken an existing third-person template project or created a new one, what we want to do now is migrate the ThirdPersonCharacter blueprint:

1. In the third-person project's content browser, navigate to Content/ThirdPersonBP/Blueprints and select the ThirdPersonCharacter blueprint.
2. Right-click and select **Asset Actions** | **Migrate**. Migrate the character into the Content directory for this chapter's project.

   Now, we can close this and return to our working project. A new ThirdPersonBP directory should have been added by our content migration.

3. Navigate to Content/ThirdPersonBP/Blueprints, and find the ThirdPersonCharacter blueprint. Open it up.

Cleaning up the third-person character blueprint

There are a few things we don't need here that we can safely clear out:

1. First, select everything in **Event Graph** and delete it. We don't need any of these input handlers.
2. We also don't need the **FollowCamera** and **CameraBoom** items in the **Components** list, so delete those:

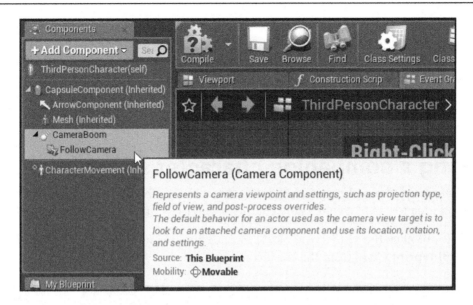

Now, we have a clean character that's going to work out well for what we need it to do.

Examining the animation blueprint

Even though we took a shortcut and migrated our character, it's still not a bad idea to take a look at how it works.

Select the character's `Mesh` component and look at the **Animation** section of the **Details** panel. You'll see that this character is animated using an animation blueprint called `ThirdPerson_AnimBP`. Use the magnifying glass beside the **Anim Class** property to navigate to the animation blueprint and then open it up so we can see what's inside:

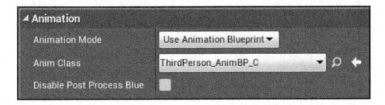

It would take us outside the scope of this book to discuss animation blueprints in depth, but, in general what you should understand about them is that, just as we saw with the controlled hands, they're responsible for determining how a skeletal mesh animates in response to whatever factors govern its animation.

You saw a simple example of an animation blueprint driving the hand pose. This one's doing a similar job, but driving a character skeleton. It's not a bad idea to take some time to burrow through this blueprint to see how it works. You can find further documentation at https://docs.unrealengine.com/en-us/Engine/Animation/AnimBlueprints. When you're done looking around, feel free to close the animation blueprint. We won't need to change anything here.

Creating a companion character subclass

Since we're going to be adding new behaviors and components to this character, it's going to be a good idea for us to create a new character blueprint and derive it from this one:

1. Right-click the `ThirdPersonCharacter` blueprint and select **Create Child Blueprint Class** from the context menu:

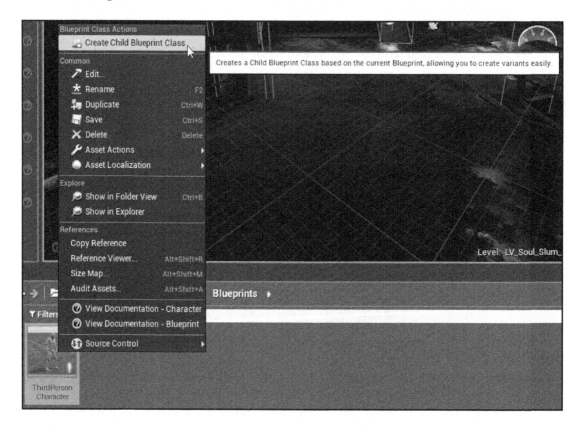

2. Let's name the new class `BP_CompanionCharacter` and move it to our project's subdirectory inside the `Content` folder.

3. Now, we can drag an instance of `BP_CompanionCharacter` into the level:

Place your companion character somewhere that's covered by the navigation mesh. Previously, we used a navigation mesh to allow us to indicate which areas of the map were valid teleport destinations. Now, in addition to this, we're going to use it for its intended purpose. Navigation meshes provide a simplified model of the walkable space of a map that can be used by AI-controlled characters to find their way around. Remember that you can use the *P* key to show and hide your navmesh if you need to check its coverage.

Adding a follow behavior to our companion character

Let's give our character a simple behavior. We'll have him follow the player:

1. Open the `BP_CompanionCharacter` event graph and find or create an **Event Tick** node.
2. Right-click in the graph and create a **Simple Move to Actor** node.
3. Create a **Get Controller** node and feed its output into the **Simple Move to Actor** node's **Controller** input.
4. Create a **Get Player Pawn** node and feed its output into the **Simple Move to Actor** node's **Goal** input:

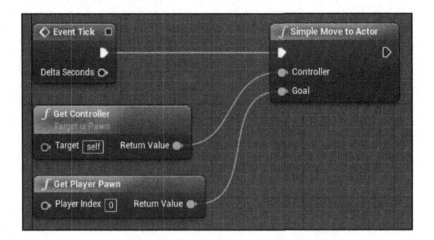

Launch your map. Our companion character should run to your location (if he doesn't, verify that he's starting on the navmesh and that the navmesh section where he's standing can access your **PlayerStart** location).

Examining the AI controller

Let's take a moment to talk about what's going on here:

1. Shut down the gameplay session, select the **Simple Move to Actor** node, and hit *F9* to set a **breakpoint** there.

A breakpoint is a debugging tool that instructs the Blueprint interpreter to pause execution when it hits the point you've set. While you're in the paused state, you can roll over variable and function outputs to see what they contain, and you can step through the code to see how it executes. We'll cover using breakpoints and debugging tools in depth in a later chapter.

Run the map again, but don't bother putting the VR headset on – we just want to see what happens when the breakpoint is hit:

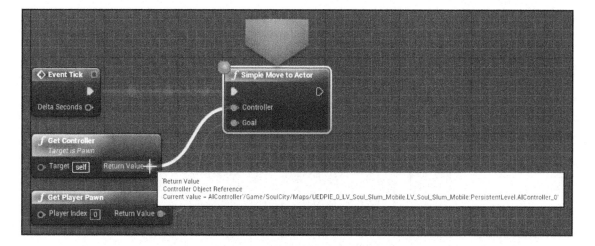

2. When execution stops at the breakpoint, roll over the output from the **Get Controller** node. You'll see that this character is currently controlled by an **AI Controller** that was automatically created for it.

Any pawn or character in your level must be **possessed** by a controller before it can execute commands. The pawn or character you control as a player is possessed by a player controller. Characters that are expected to behave autonomously need to be possessed by an AI controller.

3. Select the **Simple Move to Actor** node again if it's been deselected, and hit F9 to clear the breakpoint.
4. Click on **Resume** on the toolbar to return to normal execution.

The character should run to your location.

Setting breakpoints in your blueprints is a valuable way of debugging them and seeing how they operate. If you're working with a blueprint written by another developer, setting a breakpoint and stepping through the execution can be a valuable way of figuring out how it works. You can set and clear breakpoints by hitting *F9,* and step through execution by using *F10. F11* and *Alt + Shift + F11* allow you to step into and out of child methods in a blueprint. You can view the values currently set in your blueprint by mousing over input and output connectors.

If we take a look at the `BP_CompanionCharacter` class' **Details | Pawn**, we can see that **Auto Possess AI** is set to **Placed in World**, meaning that the specified AI controller will automatically take control of this pawn if it's placed in the world. Other options here allow us to specify that the AI controller should possess the pawn when it's spawned, or should not auto-possess at all. The **AI Controller Class** specifies which AI Controller class will possess this pawn. If we needed to, we could select a new AI controller class here. In our case, we don't need to do this because the default controller can do everything we need it to do:

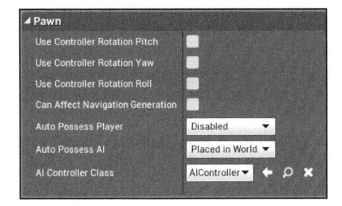

As with the depths of animation blueprints, a deep discussion of AI controllers and decision trees falls outside the scope of this book, but if you wanted to take it further, it's worthwhile exploring the documentation at `https://docs.unrealengine.com/en-us/Gameplay/AI`.

It's worthwhile spending some time poking around with these elements. If you're developing applications that involve visible non-player characters, time spent learning about the animation blueprint and the AI controller is absolutely well spent.

Improving the companion's follow behavior

Now that we've gotten our character following us, let's improve its behavior. It tends to crowd us a bit, and it would improve things if our companion only tried to follow us when we got a specified distance away from him.

First, for the sake of organization, we should bundle our movement behavior into a function:

1. Select the **Simple Move to Actor** node and the **Get Controller** and **Get Player Pawn** nodes feeding it.
2. Right-click and collapse them to a function named FollowPlayer.

Now, let's improve the way it works:

1. Open up the new function.
2. Drag an output from GetPlayerPawn and select **Promote to local variable**. Name the new variable LocalPlayerPawn.

> Use local variables in functions whenever you access a piece of information that would cost time to collect again. Since we know we're going to need to use the player pawn a few times in this function, it's faster to get it once and save the value rather than to re-fetch it every time we need it.

3. Connect the setter that was automatically created for you to the function input.
4. Create a **Get Squared Distance To** node from the **Local Player Pawn** node's output.
5. Right-click, select **Get a reference to self**, and feed **Self** into the **Get Squared Distance To** node's **Other Actor** input:

6. Create a float variable named `FollowDistance`, compile, and set its value to `320.0`. (Feel free to tune this value later on once the behavior is running.)

7. **Square** the `FollowDistance` (remember that the **Square** node will appear in the graph as **^2**), and test to see whether the result of **Get Squared Distance To** is greater than the square of the follow distance. Create a **Branch** node from the result:

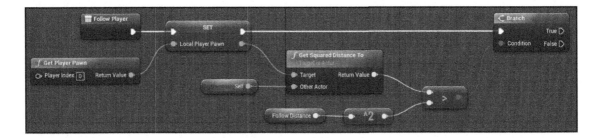

Recall that we mentioned previously that square roots are expensive to calculate, so when you're just comparing distances but don't care what those actual distances are, use squared distances instead.

This **Branch** node will return **True** when we move beyond the follow distance from the companion character, and **False** while we're within that distance.

8. Connect the **Branch** node's **True** output to your **Simple Move To Actor** node.

9. Connect the **False** output to a `Return Node` since we don't need to do anything if we're within the follow distance.

10. Grab an instance of `LocalPlayerPawn` and plug it into the **Simple Move to Actor** node's **Goal** input.

11. `Get Controller` should still be connected to your **Simple Move to Actor** node's **Controller** input.

12. Add a `Return Node` to the **Simple Move to Actor** node's exit:

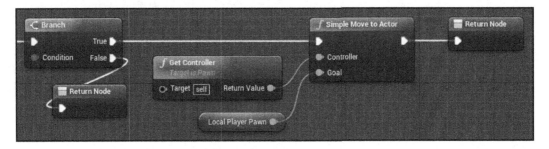

Try it out. The companion pawn should now wait until you get more than 320 units away from him before trying to follow you again:

Not bad. This is a very simple behavior, but it's a good start.

For AI behaviors of any meaningful complexity or behaviors that need to be executed by many characters simultaneously, it's a good idea to implement them using **behavior trees** instead of Blueprint tick operations. Behavior trees allow us to construct very complex behaviors in a clean, readable way, and run much more efficiently than simple Blueprint operations on the tick event. We built our character's behavior in Blueprint here to avoid going too far onto a tangent, but a behavior tree would really be a better structure to use here.

Now that we have our companion character executing behaviors, it's time for us to move on to the real meat of this chapter, which is adding UI elements to the world.

Adding a UI indicator to the companion pawn

Now that our character is moving through the world, we're going to give it another behavior state and allow the player to instruct it to wait.

Before we create this new state, however, we're first going to create a simple UI element to indicate the companion character's current state. We'll build it as a placeholder first, since we haven't yet created its new state, and then, once we have, we'll update it to reflect the real underlying data.

Creating a UI widget using UMG

Unreal provides a powerful tool for constructing UI elements. UMG allows developers to lay out UI elements on a visual layout tool, and to tie Blueprint behaviors directly to the objects in the layout. We call UI elements **widgets**. Let's learn how to create them:

1. In your project's Content directory, right-click to create a new asset. Select **UI | Widget Blueprint**:

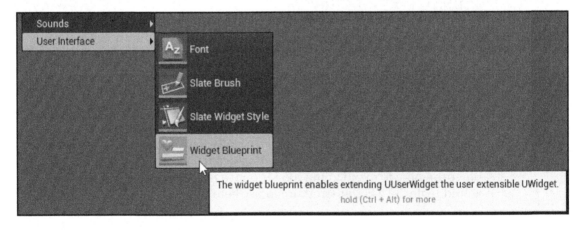

2. Name it WBP_CompanionIndicator and open it up.

You'll be presented with the UMG UI Designer.

Unreal offers two toolsets for creating UIs. The original, called **Slate**, is only usable in native C++. Much of the editor itself is written using Slate, and some of the older game examples, such as ShooterGame, implement their interfaces in Slate. **UMG** provides a much more flexible and user-friendly method of creating UI objects in Unreal, and this is what we'll be using to build our interface elements.

UMG is a very robust and deep system. You can create nearly any sort of interface element imaginable by using it. We're not going to be able to cover everything UMG can do in this example, so, when you're ready to go further, we encourage you to explore the documentation at `https://docs.unrealengine.com/en-us/Engine/UMG`:

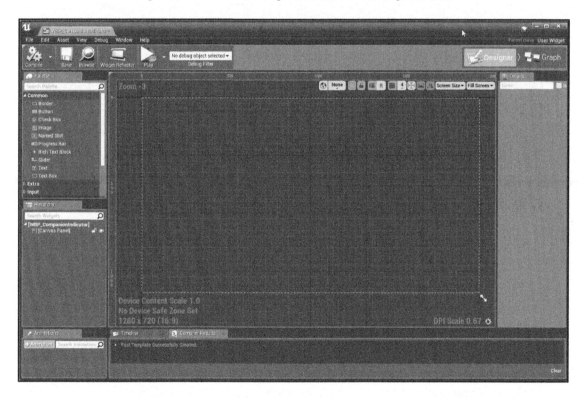

To begin with, notice that the UMG designer consists of two tabs: **Designer**, and **Graph**. The **Designer** tab is your layout tool. The **Graph**, just as with other contexts within Unreal, is where you specify the widget's behaviors.

Let's set up a simple UI to begin with, just so we can get all the parts into place:

1. In the upper-right corner of the **Designer** window, find the **Fill Screen** drop-down menu, and set it to **Custom**.

 It's very common in flat-screen applications to design a UI widget to scale itself with the screen, but this isn't a feasible approach in VR, where our UI elements need to exist in 3D space. Setting this value to **Custom** allows us to specify the UI widget's dimensions explicitly.

2. Set the **Custom** dimension to **Width=320, Height=100** (you can also use the resizing tool to the lower right of the widget outline to adjust this):

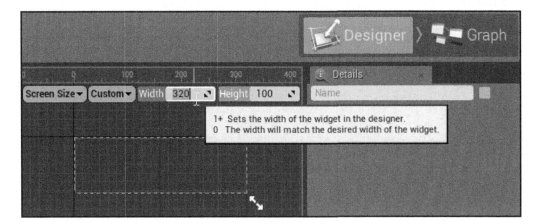

3. Grab a **Common | Text** object from the **Palette** and drag it into the widget's **Hierarchy** panel as a child of the **Canvas Panel**.

 You can add elements to the canvas by dragging them directly onto the designer workspace, or by dragging them into the **Hierarchy** panel.

Let's center this text object in our panel.

4. Select the `Text` object in our hierarchy if it isn't already selected.
5. Set its name to `txt_StateIndicator`.

You're not required to name your widgets, but if you create a complicated UI, and everything is named `TextBlock_128327`, you're going to have an unpleasant time finding what you're looking for in your outline. It's a good practice to name your stuff sensibly when you make it.

6. From the **Anchors** drop-down menu, select the centered anchor and click it:

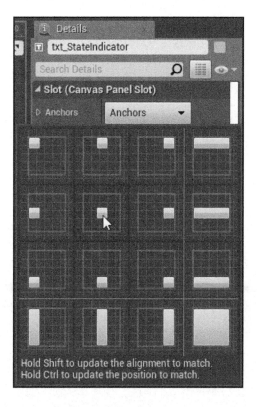

7. Set its **Position X** and **Position Y** properties to `0.0`. You'll see the text object move so its upper-left corner is aligned with the center anchor.

8. Set its **Alignment** to **X=0.5**, **Y=0.5**. You'll see the text object move so that its center is now aligned with the center anchor.

9. Set its **Size to Content** to true.

10. Set its **Justification** to **Align Text Center**.

11. Set its **Text** to read **Following** (we're going to set this dynamically later on).

Anchors are an important concept to get the hang of in building UIs using UMG. When an object is placed on the canvas panel, its position is considered to be relative to whatever it's using as its anchor. For a UI canvas that doesn't change size, this may not matter much – you could simply leave everything anchored to the upper-left corner, but as soon as you start changing the size of your UI, anchors matter. It's a good idea to get used to using the appropriate anchors for wherever you want your object to appear. You'll save yourself a lot of re-working later.

An object's **alignment** determines where it considers its origin to be, on a scale of (0,0) to (1,1), so an alignment of (0,0) places the origin at the object's upper-left corner, while an alignment of (1,1) places it at the lower-right. (0.5, 0.5) centers the origin on the object.

You can use *Ctrl* + click and *Shift* + click when selecting an anchor to set the object's position and alignment values automatically when you select the anchor.

Take a look at the following screenshot:

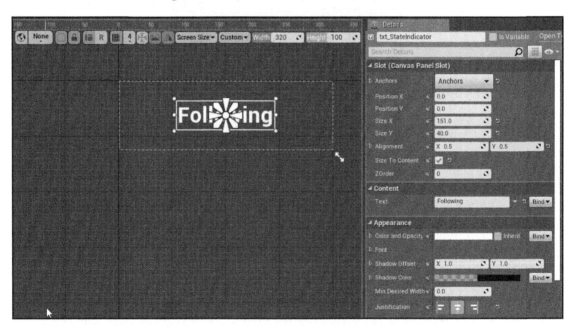

So, to recap, when you're placing an object on a UMG canvas, choose an anchor that determines where the object considers the position (0,0) on the layout board to be. This can differ between objects, and that's a powerful thing. Next, determine where on the object it should consider its own origin to be using its **Alignment** setting. Finally, set its position.

When thinking about designing interfaces in UMG, you'll have an easier time if you think of what you're doing as setting up the *rules by which objects arrange themselves* on the panel, rather than setting their locations explicitly. UMG is designed to make it easy to create interfaces that scale properly with different widget and screen sizes, and respond dynamically to the data that's driving them. It does this very well but it can be confusing to new users, until you shift your mindset away from thinking of static layouts and toward thinking of it as a dynamic system of rules.

We're done with this object for now, so we can close it.

Adding a UI widget to an actor

Now that we've created our indicator widget, it's time to add it to our companion pawn:

1. Open up `BP_CompanionCharacter`, and from its **Components** panel, select **+Add Component** | **UI** | **Widget**.
2. Name the new component `Indicator Widget`.
3. Under its **Details** | **UI**, set its **Widget Class** to the `WBP_CompanionIndicator` class we just created.
4. Set its **Draw Size** to match the custom size we set for our widget layout: (**X=320, Y=100**).
5. Jump over to your Viewport if you're not already in that view.

You should now see your widget displayed along with the pawn, but it's too large and not yet in the right position.

UI widgets displayed in 3D space will tend to look blurry if they're displayed at 100% of the scale at which they were built. It's a better idea to build the widget to be larger than you need it to be and then scale it down when you attach it to the actor. This will cause it to display at a higher resolution than it would if you built the widget to be smaller and displayed at full scale.

6. Set its **Location** to (**X=0.0, Y=0.0, Z=100.0**).

7. Set its **Scale** to (**X=0.3, Y=0.3, Z=0.3**):

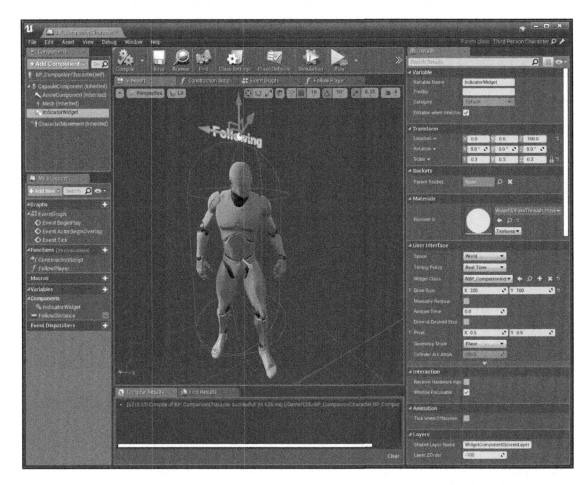

The indicator widget is attached to the pawn's Capsule Component and will move with the pawn.

Let's test it in the level. Not bad, but there's a problem – the indicator faces in the direction the pawn is facing, so it's difficult or impossible to read if the companion pawn isn't facing you. We can fix this.

Orienting the indicator widget to face the player

We're going to create a function that orients the indicator to face the camera.

1. Under **My Blueprint** | **Functions**, create a new function named `AlignUI`.
2. Set its **Category** to UI, and its **Access Specifier** to **Private** (setting categories and access specifiers isn't required, but it's a very good practice to follow. It will make your life easier when your project gets larger).
3. Open it up.

Implementing the Align UI function

Within the body of this function, we're going to find the location of the player's camera and orient the indicator widget to face it:

1. Drag the **Indicator Widget** from the **Components** list into the function graph.
2. Call **SetWorldRotation** on the **Indicator Widget** and connect the function's execution input to this call.
3. Drag another connector from **Indicator Widget** and call **GetWorldLocation** on it.
4. Create a **Get Player Camera Manager** node and call **GetActorLocation** on the result.
5. Create a **Find Look at Rotation** node and feed the **Indicator Widget** component's location into the **Start** input and the **Camera Manager** node's location into its **Target**.
6. Feed its result into the `SetWorldRotation` function's **New Rotation** input.
7. Give the function a `Return Node`:

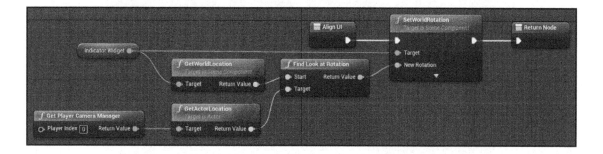

By getting the location of the player camera manager, we've gotten the location from which the player is looking into the scene. The `Find Look at Rotation` method returns a rotator whose forward vector points from the start location, where the widget is, to the target location, where the camera is. Calling `SetWorldRotation` using this rotator causes the UI widget to face the camera.

Calling Align UI from the Tick event

Now let's call the `AlignUI` function on **Event Tick**:

1. Jump back out to your event graph.
2. Drag a new execution line from **Event Tick** and type `seq` on release. Select **Sequence** from the resulting list and create a **Sequence** node.

   The **Sequence** node will interpose itself automatically between **Event Tick** and the **Follow Player** call that was previously connected to it:

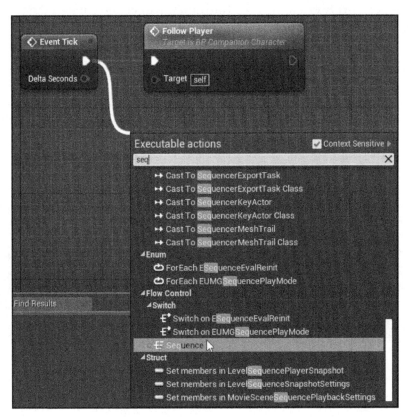

3. Call `Align UI` from the **Sequence** node's **Then 1** output:

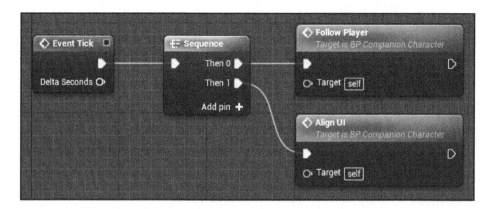

Try it out in the level. The UI indicator should now orient itself to face the camera regardless of where the companion pawn is looking:

Good. We've created a simple UI element for our companion pawn. Of course it doesn't do much yet, since the pawn only has one state, but we're ready to fix that now.

Adding a new AI state to the companion pawn

First, let's give our companion pawn a way to know what state it's in. This information is best stored in an enumeration:

1. In the **Content Browser**, wherever you saved BP_CompanionCharacter, right-click to add a new object, and select **Blueprints** | **Enumeration**. Name it ECompanionState.

2. Open it up and add two items to the enumerator, named **Following** and **Waiting**, as follows:

3. Save and close the new enumerator.

Implementing a simple AI state

Now that we've created an enumerator to name our character's AI states, let's define the behavior we already created as the character's `Following` state:

1. Open `BP_CompanionCharacter` and create a new variable. Set its name to `CompanionState` and its **Type** to the `ECompanionState` enum we just created.
2. Find **Event Tick** in your event graph.
3. Hold *Ctrl* and drag the `CompanionState` variable onto the graph.
4. Drag a connector from its output, and type `sw` in the search box to filter your search to `Switch on ECompanionState`. Add the node.
5. Hold *Ctrl* and drag to move the execution input leading to your `Follow Player` call from that node's input to the execution input to your new switch statement.
6. Connect the switch statement's **Following** output to your `Follow Player` call:

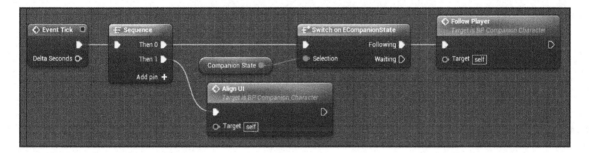

Now, when your companion pawn's `Companion State` is set to `Following`, it will execute the follow behavior, but if that state is set to `Waiting` instead, it won't.

Indicating AI states using the UI indicator

Before we go ahead and create our character's next AI state, let's update our UI element to reflect the state the character is in. We'll want this shortly when we begin changing it.

Since we want our indicator UI to display information about the pawn to which it's attached, we need to tell it about that pawn:

1. Open up `WBP_CompanionIndicator` and select `txt_StateIndicator` from the design panel or from the **Hierarchy** tab.

2. Set its **Is Variable** property to true:

By setting txt_StateIndicator as a variable, we've given ourselves access to the object in this widget's event graph, so we can grab a reference to it and change its value.

3. Flip to the **Graph** tab.
4. Create a new function and name it UpdateDisplayedState.
5. Add an input to the function named NewState and set its type to ECompanionState.
6. Open the function.
7. txt_StateIndicator should now be visible in your **Variables** list. Hold *Ctrl* and drag it onto the function's graph.
8. Drag a connector from txt_StateIndicator and call SetText on it.

9. Drag a connector from your **NewState** input and type se into the search box. A **Select** node should be available. Place it in the graph as follows:

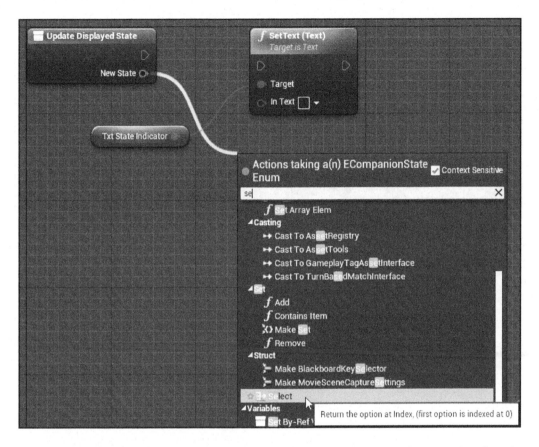

Your newly-created **Select** node will have been automatically populated with options for each of the ECompanionState enum's values. Select statements can be used to select a wide variety of data types. To set its type, simply connect it to any other function or variable's input or output, and it will take on the type of whatever you connect to it.

10. Connect the Select statement's **Return Value** to your **Set Text** node's **In Text** input.

You'll see that the Select statement has now taken on the **Text** data type, and you can now enter values for the **Following** and **Waiting** options.

11. Populate the select statement's text inputs with the names of the appropriate states.

12. Connect the function's execution input with the **SetText** node:

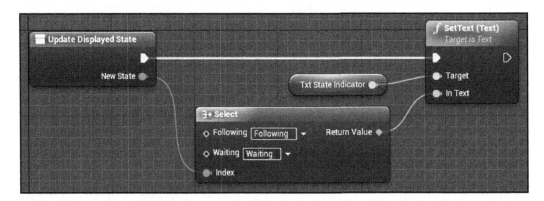

Now, whenever we call `Update Displayed State` on this UI element, it will update the displayed text to whatever we've entered in our `Select` statement for the newly-supplied state.

 You've seen in this example, and the previous how we can use switch statements and select statements with enumerators. These are valuable techniques and worth remembering, as they're easily readable, and will update automatically if you add values to an enumerator or remove them. Enumerators and switch and select statements are your friends.

It's worth noting here that there's another way we could have updated this UI, and it's a method you'll commonly see taught. We could have stashed a reference to the pawn that owns this widget in a variable, and then we could have used the **Bind** method to set up a real-time update for the text element:

This is a good opportunity to talk about a few important considerations in UI development, and explain why we didn't use **Bind** in this instance.

Using events to update, rather than polling

First, the **Bind** method updates with every UI update. For values that change continuously, this is something you'll want, but for a value like the pawn's AI state that only changes only occasionally, and only when you perform an action that changes it, it's wasteful to check on every single tick to see whether it needs to display a new value. Whenever possible, you should favor updating your UI only when you know a value you're displaying needs to be updated, rather than having your UI poll the underlying data to see whether what it's displaying is still accurate. This will really start to matter if you build an interface with a lot of different elements and you have every single one of them updating every frame. Planning for efficiency in your UI pays off.

Being careful of circular references

The other reason we want to be careful about doing this is a bit more subtle, but it's important to know about. If we were to stash a reference to the pawn on the widget blueprint, and simultaneously stash a reference to the widget blueprint on the pawn, we've introduced the possibility of a **circular reference** (sometimes also called a **cyclic dependency**):

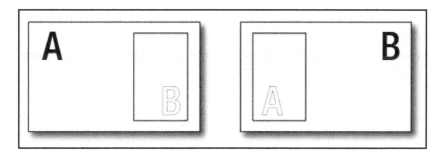

A circular reference: class A can't compile until B is built, but class B can't compile until A is built

A circular reference occurs when one class needs to know about another class before it can be built, but that other class needs to know about the first class before *it* can be built. This is a bad situation that can create very difficult-to-find bugs.

In the event of a circular reference between the widget blueprint and the pawn, the widget blueprint might not be able to compile correctly because it needs the pawn to be compiled first, but the pawn might not compile correctly because it needs the widget blueprint compiled first (we say "might not" because a lot of other factors can affect the order in which objects are built, so it may sometimes work. You may not immediately realize you've created a circular reference because things could work for a while, and then stop working when you change something seemingly unrelated). You don't need to be paranoid about this. Unreal's build system is very good at figuring out how to determine the right order to build things, but if you try to keep your references going in one direction, you'll save yourself what can turn into a very challenging bug-hunt.

Using the event-driven structure we've set up, the widget blueprint doesn't need to know anything about the pawn. Only the pawn needs to know about the widget blueprint, so the compiler can easily figure out which object it needs to build before it can build the other, and no circular reference occurs.

Ensuring that UI is updated when our state is changed

Now, because we've chosen to use an event-driven model rather than a polling model to drive our indicator UI, we have to ensure that any time the `BP_CompanionCharacter` class' `Companion State` changes, the UI is updated.

To do this, we'll want to make the variable private, and force any other object changing this value to use an event or function call to change it. By forcing outside objects to use a function call to change this value, we can ensure that any other operations that need to happen when that value changes will happen by including them in the function or event's implementation. Because we've set the variable to private, we're preventing anybody else from changing it without calling this function.

This is a common practice in software development and a good one to internalize. If there's a possibility that you might need to perform operations in response to a variable's value changing, don't let outside objects change it directly. Make the variable private, and only allow other objects to change it through a public function call. If you make a habit of doing this, you'll save yourself a lot of headaches when your project gets large.

Let's create a function to handle setting the companion state, and make the variable private so that developers are forced to use it when they want to change the AI's state:

1. Select the `BP_CompanionCharacter` class' `Companion State` variable, and, in its **Details**, set its **Private** flag to true.
2. In the event graph, create a new custom event and name it `SetNewCompanionState`.
3. Add an input to this event. Name it `NewState`, and set its **Type** to `ECompanionState`.
4. Hold *Alt* and drag a `CompanionState` setter onto the graph, and connect its execution and its new value to the new event:

Now we need to tell the indicator widget that this state has changed.

5. Drag a reference to the `IndicatorWidget` component onto the graph.
6. Call `Get User Widget Object` on the `IndicatorWidget` reference (remember that `IndicatorWidget` is not a reference to the widget itself, but to the component that holds it).
7. Cast the `Get User Widget Object` component's return value to `WBP_CompanionIndicator`.
8. Call **Update Displayed State** on the cast result:

Now, because `Companion State` is private, it can only be changed by calling `SetNewCompanionState`, and we can be sure that the UI indicator will be updated whenever this happens.

Adding an interactive UI

Now it's time to give ourselves a way to change our companion pawn's state. To do this, we're going to add a widget component to our player pawn, along with a widget interaction component we can use to interact with it:

1. In the **Content Browser**, find the location of BP_VRPawn—our player pawn.
2. In the same directory, create a **UI | Widget Blueprint**, and name it WBP_CompanionController.
3. Save it and open it.
4. In its **Designer** window, change Fill Screen to Custom as we did with our previous widget.
5. Set its size to **Width=300, Height=300**.
6. From the **Palette**, select **Panel | Vertical Box**, and drag it onto your **Hierarchy** as a child of the **Canvas Panel**:

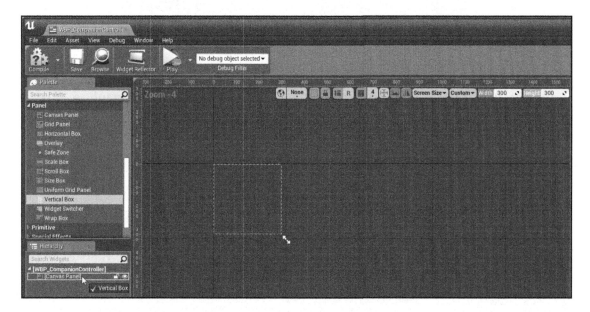

7. Set its **Anchors** to fill the entire panel by selecting the lower-rightmost option (in addition to managing placement rules, anchors can also manage stretching rules):

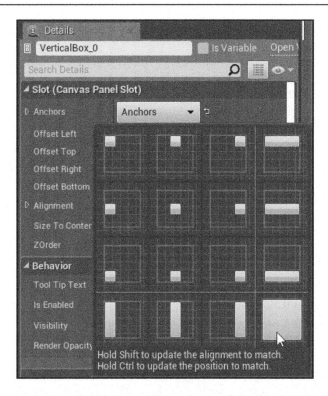

8. Set its **Offset Left**, **Offset Top**, **Offset Right**, and **Offset Bottom** to 0.0.

9. From the **Palette**, select **Common** | **Button**, and drag it onto the **Vertical Box**. Name it btn_Follow.

10. Drag another button onto the same **Vertical Box** and name this one btn_Wait:

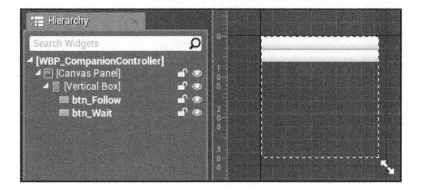

11. Drag a **Common** | **Text** widget onto your btn_Follow. Set its **Text** to Follow.

12. Drag another **Common** | **Text** widget onto `btn_Wait` and set its **Text** to `Wait`.

You may have noticed that we gave our buttons meaningful names when we created them, but we didn't bother to rename our text blocks. The reason for this is that these buttons are variables and we're going to refer to them in the widget blueprint's graph, while the text labels won't be referenced anywhere else, so their names don't really matter. You can apply your own judgment in choosing which items to name explicitly, but generally, your rule should be that if you're going to refer to the object anywhere else, it should have a meaningful name. You don't want to return to a widget blueprint after months of working on something else to find a forest of references to Button376 in the graph.

Our buttons are pretty small, and not well-placed on the widget. Let's do a little bit of layout work to fix this.

13. Right-click `btn_Follow` in the **Hierarchy** panel or on the layout designer, and select **Wrap With...** | **Size Box**.
14. Select the **Size Box** that just appeared in the **Hierarchy** panel, and set its **Height Override** to 80.0:

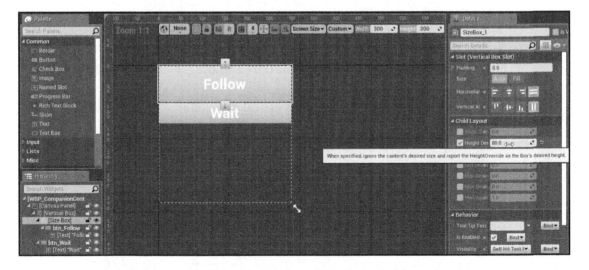

Size boxes are used to set specific sizes for UMG widgets. If you don't use a size box, the widget will scale automatically according to its rules. Wrapping it with a size box allows you to override these rules and set selected dimensions explicitly, while still allowing the rest to scale automatically.

15. Wrap `btn_Wait` with a **Size Box** and set its **Height Override** to 80.0.

    Now, let's center these buttons vertically on the panel. We'll do this by adding Spacers.

16. From the **Palette**, drag a **Primitive | Spacer** onto the **Vertical Box** in the **Hierarchy** panel. Place it before the **Size Box** surrounding `btn_Follow`.

17. Set its **Size** to `Fill`.

18. Drag another **Spacer** onto the **Vertical Box**, after the **Size Box** surrounding `btn_Wait`, and set its **Size** to **Fill** as well:

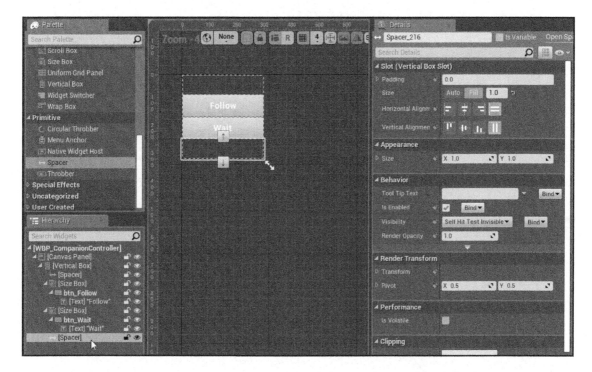

Let's add one more spacer to separate the buttons a little.

19. Drag a **Spacer** onto the **Hierarchy panel** before the Size Box surrounding `btn_Wait`. Leave its **Size** as **Auto**, and set its **Padding** to 4.0.

Here, we've seen an example of using spacers to tell the layout how to deal with space that isn't occupied by other widgets, and also to force some separation between widgets. By placing **Fill** spacers before and after the buttons, we centered them in the vertical box, and by placing an **Auto** spacer between the buttons, we separated them by a fixed amount.

Adjusting the button colors

These default button colors are going to appear too bright to be readable in our fairly dark scene. We can fix this by adjusting their background color properties:

1. Select btn_Follow and hit the color swatch for its **Details** | **Appearance** | **Background Color**.
2. In the resulting color picker's **HSV** input, set its **Value** to **0.05**.
3. Do the same for btn_Wait:

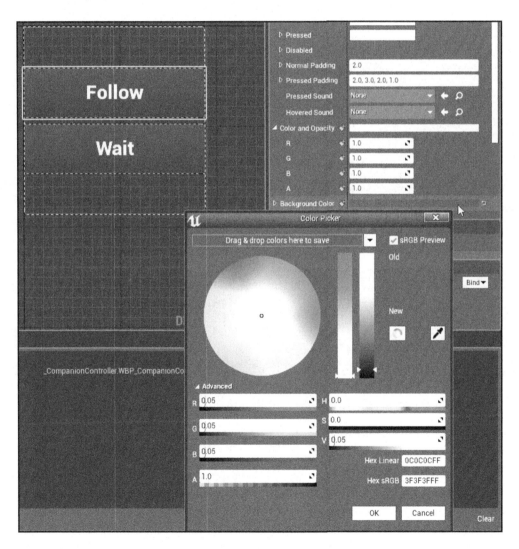

This will dim the button's background enough to allow us to read it clearly under the environment's lighting.

Adding event handlers to our buttons

Now, let's make our buttons do something when they're clicked:

1. Select `btn_Follow`, and from its **Details** | **Events**, hit the **+** button for its **On Clicked** event:

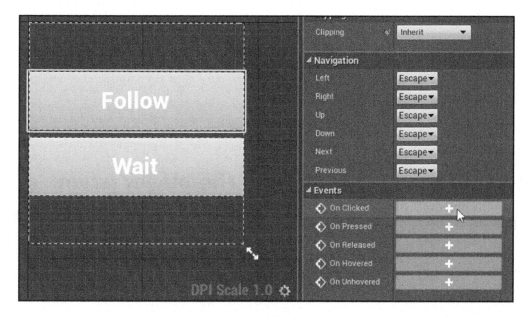

You'll be taken to the widget's event graph, where a new event named `On Clicked (btn_Follow)` has been created.

2. Create a **Get All Actors of Class** node in your graph, and set its **Actor Class** to `BP_CompanionCharacter`.
3. Drag a connector from its **Out Actors** array, and create a **ForEachLoop** from it.

4. Drag a connector from the **Array Element** output of **ForEachLoop**, and make a call to the **Set New Companion State** event we created on **BP_CompanionCharacter**. Set the state to **Following**:

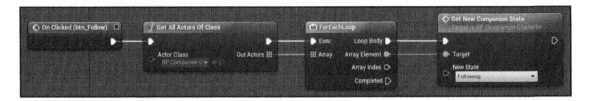

Let's do the same thing for `btn_Wait`.

5. Again, select `btn_Wait` from the **Designer** tab, and create an **On Clicked** event for it.
6. Select the nodes connected to the `On Clicked (btn_Follow)` event, and hit *Ctrl + W* to duplicate them.
7. Change the companion state we're setting to `Waiting`.

Attaching the UI element to the player pawn

Now, just as we did with our companion pawn's overhead indicator, we need to place this UI somewhere in the world.

The natural response for someone used to designing for flat-screen applications would be to follow the design principles they already knew and create some sort of HUD to display in the headset. This isn't such a good idea.

First, any UI you attach to the headset is attached to the player's head. When they turn their head to look at it, it's just going to keep moving away. This gets old fast and can induce motion sickness in some users. This problem is compounded by the fact that the fresnel lenses in VR headsets are much less clear at the edges than they are at the center, so UI elements at the edge of the player's vision are going to be difficult to read. Finally, we face the problem that there's no easy way to interact with a UI element that's been bolted to our forehead.

A better solution is to attach the UI to something the player can control, like their wrist. Let's do this now:

1. Open up BP_VRPawn, and find Hand_L in its components list.
2. Add a **Widget** component as a child of Hand_L. Name it CompanionController.
3. Set WBP_CompanionController as the widget's **Widget Class**.
4. Set its **Draw Size** to (**X=300, Y=300**) to match the size at which we created it.

   Now let's get it attached.

5. Find your BP_VRPawn player's BeginPlay event.
6. Drag a new connector from BeginPlay and create a **Sequence** node. Our Set Tracking Origin call should automatically attach to the **Sequence** node's **Then 0** output.
7. Drag a reference to the CompanionController widget, which we just added to the pawn, onto the graph.
8. Drag a connector from it and create an **Attach to Component** node.

   Remember that there are two variants of this node: **Target is Actor**, and **Target is Scene Component**. Select the node designed to work with a scene component.

9. Drag an execution line from the **Sequence** node's **Then 1** output to the **Attach to Component** node's execution input.

   We could also simply have dragged a connector from **Set Tracking Origin** output to the **GetHand_L** call, but it's a better practice to keep unrelated operations on separate execution lines so it's easier to see what really belongs together. By putting **Set Tracking Origin** on one sequence output, and the **GetHand_L** call on another, we're making it clear to the reader that these are two separate jobs being done.

10. Drag out an instance of the Get Hand Mesh for Hand method we created earlier (if you want to set up for a left-handed player, change its **Hand** value to **Right**; otherwise just leave it at the default **Left**).

11. Feed the resulting hand mesh into the **AttachToComponent** node's **Parent** input:

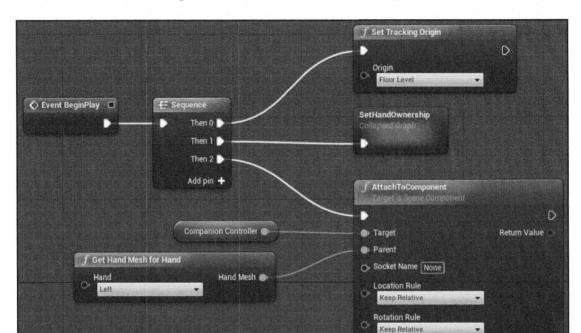

Let's run it. It's tremendous and not yet correctly aligned, but it's moving with the left hand as we intended.

12. Drag another connector from `CompanionController`, and call `Set Relative Transform` on it.

13. Right-click the **New Transform** input and split the struct pin.

14. Enter the following values:

   - **New Transform Location**: (X=0.0, Y=-10.0, Z=0.0)
   - **New Transform Rotation**: (X=0.0, Y=0.0, Z=90.0)
   - **New Transform Scale**: (X=-0.05, Y=0.05, Z=0.05)

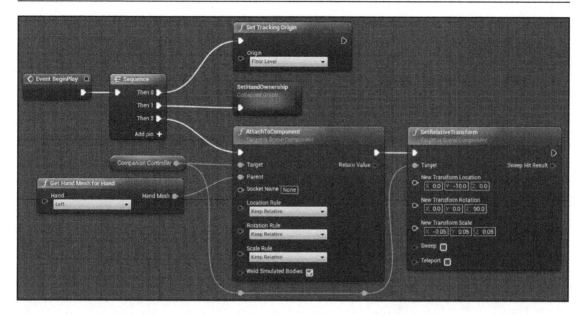

Note that we're negating the Scale's **X** value here. If you recall, we flipped our left-hand mesh by inverting its scale. Since we're attaching to that flipped mesh, we need to negate the scale here too, otherwise our widget will appear mirrored (if we're instead attaching this to the right hand, set the scale's **X** value to positive 0.05 instead, and set the rotation's **Z** value to positive **90.0**).

Run it again and we'll see that the wrist menu is now much better aligned with our wrist.

Now for the next challenge: how do we press one of these buttons?

Using widget interaction components

UIs in virtual reality pose a significant problem: how do we allow the user to interact with them? Early solutions often used gaze-based controls. The user would push a button by looking at it for a fixed amount of time. Yes, it was as clunky as it sounds. Thankfully, with the advent of hand controls, we no longer need to do it this way.

In Unreal, we most commonly interact with UI elements in VR by using a **widget interaction component**, which acts as a pointer in the scene and can simulate mouse interactions when used with UMG widgets.

Let's add one to our right hand:

1. Open up `BP_VRPawn` and add a **Widget Interaction** component to its **Components** list (its default name is fine).
2. In its **Details** panel, set its **Show Debug** flag to `True`.
3. On our **Event Graph**, find the **Sequence** node on our `Begin Play` event, and use the **Add pin** button to add a new output:

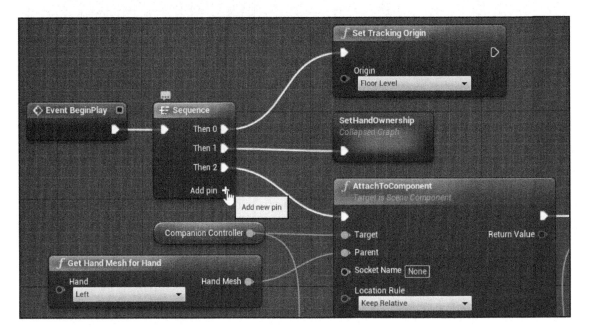

4. Drag a reference to our `Widget Interaction` component onto the graph.
5. Drag a connector from the `Widget Interaction` reference and create an **Attach To Component (Scene Component)** node with `Widget Interaction` as its target.
6. Drag a `Get Hand Mesh for Hand` function call onto the graph, and set its **Hand** property to **Right** (or **Left** if you attached the UI to the right hand).

7. Feed its **Hand Mesh** output into the **Attach To Component** node's **Parent** input:

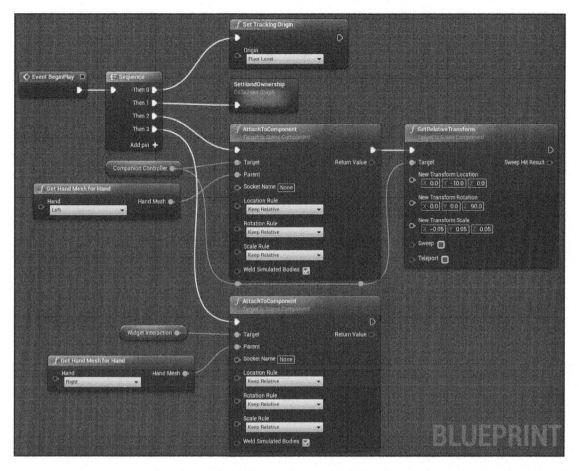

We're now attaching the controller UI to the left hand and the Widget Interaction component to the right hand.

Now, let's test it:

Good. The widget interaction component's default placement and alignment aren't bad. We could adjust it by using a `Set Relative Transform` call if we wanted, but for what we're doing here, this is fine.

Another way of setting the placement of objects we're attaching to another object is to place a socket on the target object's skeleton. If you add a socket to a skeleton, simply put its name in the **Attach to Component** node's **Socket Name** property. In the interest of staying on topic, we're sticking to simple **Set Relative Transform** calls, but if you want to explore using sockets, the directions on `https://docs.unrealengine.com/en-us/` `Engine/Content/Types/SkeletalMeshes/Sockets` will apply.

Now that we have our widget interaction component attached to our hand, we're ready to pass input through it.

Sending input through widget interaction components

First off, we're going to need to choose what input should drive our widget interaction. Since we're only using our triggers to grab objects, it should work out fine to add our widget interactions to these same inputs:

1. Find the `InputAction_GrabLeft` and `GrabRight` event handlers on the `BP_VRPawn` player's event graph.
2. Drag a reference to your `Widget Interaction` component onto the graph.
3. Drag a connection from the `Widget Interaction` component, and call `Press Pointer Key` from the connection. Set its **Key** drop-down to `Left Mouse Button`.
4. Drag another connection from `Widget Interaction` and call `Release Pointer Key`. Set this **Key** drop-down to `Left Mouse Button` as well.
5. If you've attached your `Widget Interaction` component to the right hand, call `Press Pointer Key` from the end of the `InputAction_GrabRight` component's **Pressed** event chain after the `Grab Actor` call (if the interaction component is on the left hand, call it from `GrabLeft` instead).
6. Call `Release Pointer Key` from the `InputAction_GrabRight` component's **Released** chain, after the `Release Actor` call:

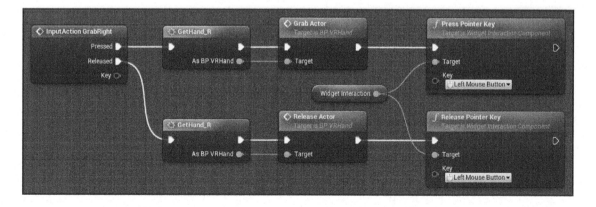

What we're doing here is telling the widget interaction component to communicate with the widget as though the user had moved a mouse pointer over it and pressed the left button. This is a powerful and flexible system—you can recreate nearly any input event and pass it through the interaction component.

Let's test it. You should now be able to point the widget interaction component at your wrist controller and pull the trigger to activate a button. Try running around the level and switching your companion between the **Follow** and **Wait** states.

Making a better pointer for our interaction component

The last thing we should probably improve before wrapping this up is that obtrusive-looking debug beam on our widget interaction component. Let's take a moment to replace it with something better-looking.

1. In BP_VRPawn, select the Widget Interaction component and turn off its **Show Debug** flag.
2. In the **Components** panel, add a **Static Mesh** component as a child of WidgetInteraction. Name it InteractionBeam.
3. Set its **Static Mesh** property to /Engine/BasicShapes/Cylinder.
4. Set its **Location** to (**X=50.0, Y=0.0, Z=0.0**)
5. Set its **Rotation** to (**Roll=0.0, Pitch**=-90.0, Yaw=0.0). Remember that Pitch is mapped to **Y** in the UI.
6. Set its **Scale** to (X=0.005, Y=0.005, Z=1.0).
7. Set its **Collision | Can Character Step Up On** to No, and its **Collision Presets** to NoCollision.

> If you add a UI or other attached element to a hand and you suddenly find that your movement is blocked, check to see whether you've turned its collision off.

Try it out. We now have a gray cylinder indicating our interaction component. We should give it a more suitable material.

Creating an interaction beam material

We're going to give our interaction beam a simple translucent material. We want to be able to see it in the world, but we don't want it to be so obtrusive that it distracts our attention from the world:

1. Find the location in our `Content` directory where we saved the `M_Indicator` material we used for teleportation.
2. Create a new material in this directory and name it `M_WidgetInteractionBeam`.
3. Open it up and set its **Blend Mode** to `Translucent`. (Remember: to set material properties, select the output node.)
4. Hold down the *V* key and click to create a **Vector Parameter** node. Name it `BaseColor`.
5. Set the **BaseColor** node's default value to pure white – (**R=1.0, G=1.0, B=1.0, A=0.0**).
6. Feed its output into the **BaseColor** and **EmissiveColor** material inputs.
7. Right-click in the material graph and create a **Texture Coordinate** node.
8. Right-click and create a **Linear Gradient** node with the texture coordinate's output feeding into its **UV Channel** input.
9. Hold the *M* key and click to create a **Multiply** node.
10. Drag the **LinearGradient** node's **VGradient** output into the **Multiply** node's **A** input.
11. Hold *S* and click to create a **Scalar** parameter. Name it `OpacityMultiplier`.
12. Set its **Slider Max** to **1.0** and its **Default Value** to **0.25**.
13. Feed its output into the **Multiply** node's **B** input.

14. Feed the result of the **Multiply** node into the material's **Opacity** input:

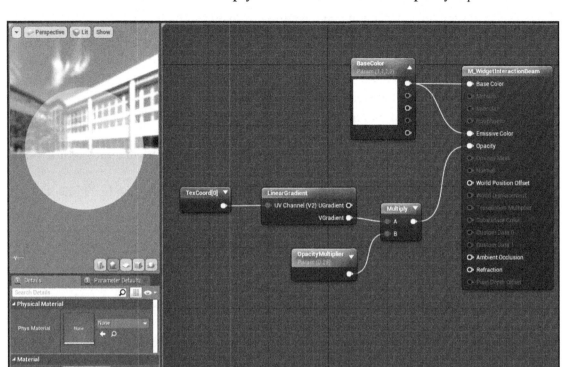

We're going to need to tune this material to work with our environment. We can make our life easier by creating a **material instance**. Material instances are derived from materials, but only those parameters that have been exposed in the parent material can be changed. Because material instances don't include any changes to the material graph, just value changes, they don't need to be recompiled when those changes are made. It's much faster to change values in a material instance than in a material.

15. Right-click M_WidgetInteractionBeam, and select **Material Actions | Create Material Instance**.

16. Name the new instance MI_WidgetInteractionBeam.

17. Assign `MI_WidgetInteractionBeam` to the `InteractionBeam` static mesh component on `BP_VRPawn`.

Run the map. It's still pretty bright.

18. Open `MI_WidgetInteractionBeam` and set its **OpacityMultiplier** to 0.01. (Put a checkmark beside a value you plan to change.)

Run it again. That's much better.

Creating an impact effect

Now we need an impact effect to show where the beam is intersecting a target.

1. Create a new **Static Mesh** component as a child of the `BP_VRPawn` player's root component (the `Capsule Component`).
2. Name it `InteractionBeamTarget`.
3. Set its **Static Mesh** property to `Engine/BasicShapes/Sphere`.
4. Set its **Scale** to (X=0.01, Y=0.01, Z=0.01).
5. Set its **Collision | Can Character Step Up On** to `No`, and its **Collision Presets** to `NoCollision`.

This target sphere needs a material too. For this, we'll create an emissive material with a dark outline so it shows up clearly on both light and dark backgrounds.

6. Create a new material named `M_WidgetInteractionTarget`.
7. Hold the *V* key and click to create a vector parameter. Name it `BaseColor` and set its default value to pure white.
8. Drag an output from `BaseColor` and click – to create a **Subtract** node.
9. Feed the result of the **Subtract** node into the material's **Base Color** and **Emissive** inputs.
10. Right-click and create a **Fresnel** node.
11. Hold the **1** key and click to create a **scalar material expression constant**. Set its value to **15**.
12. Feed it into the **Fresnel** node's **ExponentIn**.
13. Hit *Ctrl + W* to duplicate it, set the new constant's value to **0**, and feed it into the **Fresnel** node's **BaseReflectFractionIn**.
14. Hold *M* and click to create a **Multiply** node.

15. Feed the **Fresnel** node's result into the **Multiply** node's **A** input.
16. Hold *S* and click to create a scalar parameter. Name it `OutlineThickness` and set its default value to **10**.
17. Feed **OutlineThickness** into the **Multiply** node's **B** input.
18. Feed the **Multiply** node's result into the **Subtract** node's **B** input:

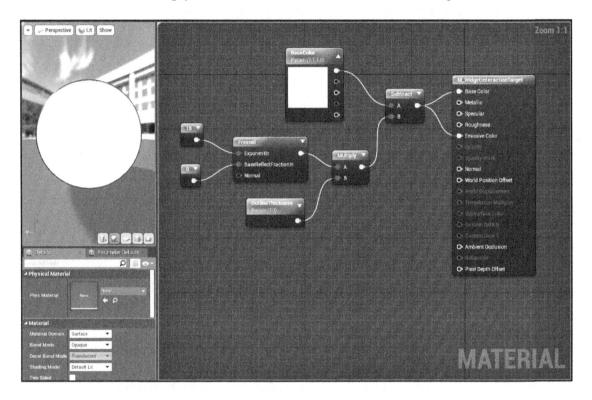

19. In your content browser, create a material instance from this material named `MI_WidgetInteractionTarget`.
20. Assign `MI_WidgetInteractionTarget` to the `InteractionBeamTarget` sphere we created on `BP_VRPawn`.

Finally, we need to set its position to the interaction component's impact location.

21. In `BP_VRPawn` player's event graph, find the `Event Tick` and create a **Sequence** node between `Event Tick` and the `UpdateTeleport_Implementation` collapsed graph.

22. Drag a reference to `WidgetInteraction` onto the graph, and call `Get Last Hit Result` on its output.

23. Right-click the **Return Value** and select **Split Struct Pin**.

24. Drag a reference to the `InteractionBeamTarget` static mesh component onto the graph.

25. Call `SetWorldLocation` on it, and feed the **Return Value Impact Point** from `Get Last Hit Result` into its new location.

26. Connect the **Sequence** node's **Then 1** output to the **SetWorldLocation** node's execution input.

27. Select these new nodes, right-click, and select **Collapse Nodes**. Name the collapsed graph `UpdateWidgetInteractionTarget_Implementation`:

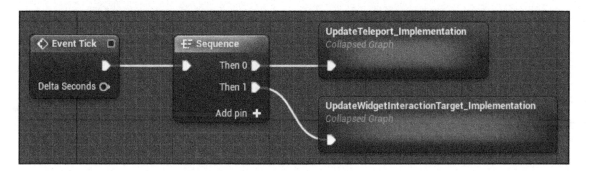

28. Open up the collapsed graph and clean it up.

The collapsed graph should look like this:

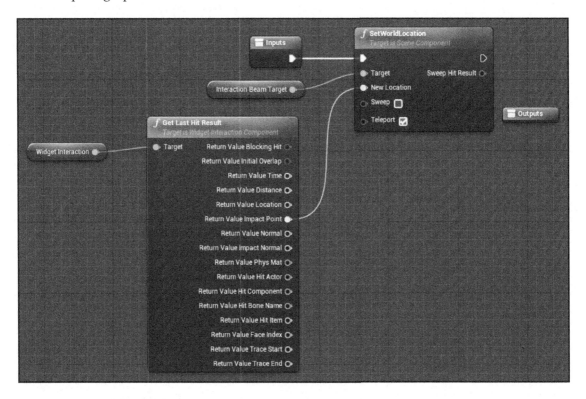

Test it out. The beam isn't bad, and the target point is fairly easy to spot:

There's quite a lot more we could do with this, like cutting off the beam where it hits a widget, and adjusting the target sphere's scale based on how close it is to the player's view, but what we have here is a very good starting ground. This system does a lot, and does it in ways that would be easy to extend and improve upon.

Explore the level and try out the companion controller. While what we've put together here is fairly streamlined, it contains the seeds for quite a lot of things we might want to do.

Summary

In this chapter, we added a major remaining piece to our development repertoire and added functional UI elements to our project.

In this chapter, we learned how to create a simple AI-controlled character and animate it, and we learned how to create a UI in 3D space using UMG, which also allowed us to change the character's AI state.

In the next chapter, we're going to move on from creating characters and interfaces, and begin to explore creating environments for use in VR.

8
Building the World and Optimizing for VR

Through the course of our work so far in this book, we've been focused for the most part on the player avatar. This makes sense—virtual reality dramatically changes the way the player engages with the world. We needed to learn new ways of enabling the player to get around, new ways of using their hands to interact with the world, and new ways of constructing user interfaces.

This is no small achievement, so congratulations for getting this far!

Now, we're going to shift our focus a bit and begin to look at the environment around us. Up to this point, we've been using existing environments, but now it's time to begin to build our own. As we do this, we are going to learn that environments in VR present challenges that we're going to need to address. Lighting, object scale, and sightlines all come into play to a greater degree than they do on the flat screen, and performance is a major consideration.

In this chapter, we're going to learn how to use the tools and techniques at our disposal to address these challenges as we build. We'll learn how to use the VR editor to lay out our environment from within the headset and see how it's actually going to appear in VR as we build it, and we'll learn how to profile and optimize these environments to make sure that we can meet our frame rate requirements.

In this chapter, we're going to explore the following topics:

- Building and lighting a scene using the VR editor
- Profiling the scene to identify performance bottlenecks
- Optimizing the scene using static mesh instancing, LODs, mesh combination, and lighting changes

- Project settings for optimization
- Special considerations and technical requirements for mobile VR

Let's get to it and give ourselves a place to play.

Setting up the project and collecting assets

For this chapter's work, let's create a new project with the following template options:

- A **Blank** Blueprint template
- **Targeting Mobile/Tablet hardware**
- **Scalable 2D or 3D**
- **No starter content**

Once the project has been created, open its **Project Settings** and set the following menu options:

- **Project | Description | Settings | Start in VR**: True
- **Engine | Rendering | Forward Renderer | Forward Shading**: True
- **Engine | Rendering | Default Settings | Ambient Occlusion Static Fraction**: False
- **Engine | Rendering | Default Settings | Anti-Aliasing Method**: MSAA
- **Engine | Rendering | VR | Instanced Stereo**: True
- **Engine | Rendering | VR | Round Robin Occlusion Queries**: True

Allow the project to restart once all these settings have been set.

Once the project has restarted, open the **File** menu and use it to load the previous chapter's project. Just as we did last time, we're going to grab elements that we previously created and carry them forward using the **Migrate** tool.

Migrating blueprints into the new project

From your previous project, select **BP_VRGameMode** from the content explorer, right-click it, and select **Asset Actions | Migrate**. Select your new project's `Content` directory as its destination content folder. Because the **GameMode** references **BP_VRPawn**, and **BP_VRPawn** references **BP_CompanionCharacter**, all of these objects and their required supporting assets should come across.

Once the migration is complete, there's one more thing we need to do. We have a few custom inputs set up for our previous project, and we'll need them for our new one as well. Navigate to last chapter's project directory and copy the `Config/DefaultInput.ini` file to your new project's config directory.

Verifying the migrated content

Re-open the new project. The first thing we're going to want to do here is verify that everything we've brought across is working correctly:

1. Let's select **File | New Level | VR Basic** to create a starting VR map.
2. Drop a **Nav Mesh Bounds Volume** onto the map and make sure it surrounds the floor. Setting its **Location** to (**X=0.0, Y=0.0, Z=0.0**) and **Scale** to (**X=10.0, Y=10.0, Z=2.0**) will take care of this. Remember to hit the *P* key to visualize your navmesh and make sure it's generating properly.
3. Save this level (we named ours **VRModePractice** and placed it in `Content/C07/Maps`).
4. Open **Settings | Project Settings | Maps & Modes | Default Modes**, and set your **Default GameMode** to the **BP_VRGameMode** we migrated from the other project. Set your **Editor Startup Map** and **Game Default Map** to this map, as well.
5. Drop an instance of **BP_CompanionCharacter** anywhere onto the level.

Test the map in a VR preview. You should be able to move and teleport, and your companion character should follow you:

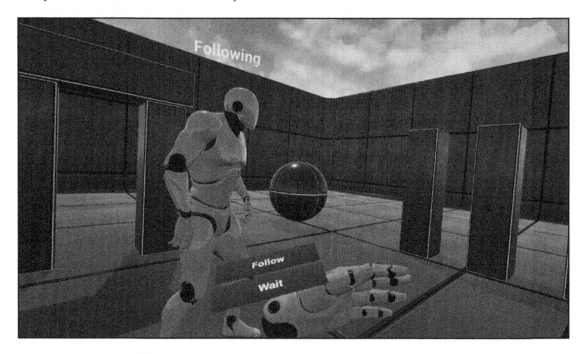

This map is a great map to use for learning the Unreal Editor's VR Mode—it's easy to get around, and gives us lots of pieces we can manipulate as we practice with the interface. Let's take advantage of this.

Using the VR editor

Unreal Engine comes equipped with a very capable virtual reality editor that allows you to build your scenes entirely from within the virtual environment. Nearly any editor operation you might need to perform can be done without leaving VR.

It may be tempting, though, to look at the VR Mode editor as a gimmick when you first encounter it. After all, what's wrong with the existing editor? Nothing, but here's the thing: virtual reality isn't a flat screen. Depth exists. Sightlines are different. Colors render differently. Developing for virtual reality by using a flat screen adds a layer of abstraction to your design process. You'll understand more and get better results by working directly in your target medium when you can.

In practice, you're likely to find both editing modes useful. Just as it's difficult to see what a scene is really going to look like in VR from the flat-screen editor view, it's difficult to achieve precision in placing objects in VR Mode. You'll discover your workflow as you get comfortable with the tools, and you'll discover which operations you prefer to do in which domains. The point here, though, is that it's worthwhile to think of VR Mode as an important part of your scene layout workflow for VR. Take the time to get comfortable with it so you can rely on it when it's warranted.

A good practice for VR editing is to do your initial block-out in VR. Place objects in ways that evoke the sense of space you want to convey, and then go to traditional flat-screen editing to refine your layout and populate it further. Finally, return to VR editing for your final refinements so you can see exactly what you're going to get.

Let's activate the VR editor and see what we can do with it. Since you won't be able to read this book while you're inside the headset, we'll go over a few basic principles, allow you to try them out, and then return here to explore a few more.

The first thing to know is how to enter and exit the VR editor.

Entering and exiting VR Mode

You can activate the VR editor by using the **VR Mode** toolbar button. To exit VR Mode, activate the radial menu (more on this later) and select **System | Exit**. It's easiest, though, to get used to using *Alt + V* to enter and exit **VR Mode**:

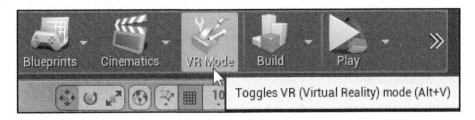

It's also possible to configure VR Mode to enter automatically when the headset is put on while the editor is running. To do this, select **Edit | Editor Preferences | General | VR Mode**, and set **Enable VR Mode Auto-Entry** to **True**. Whether you'd like to do this is your choice, but, in practice, it tends to have a difficult time figuring out when to turn itself back off, so using *Alt + V* to enter and exit is usually a better idea.

If you prefer to interact primarily using your left hand, you have the option here in the **VR Mode** preferences to switch your **Interactor Hand**:

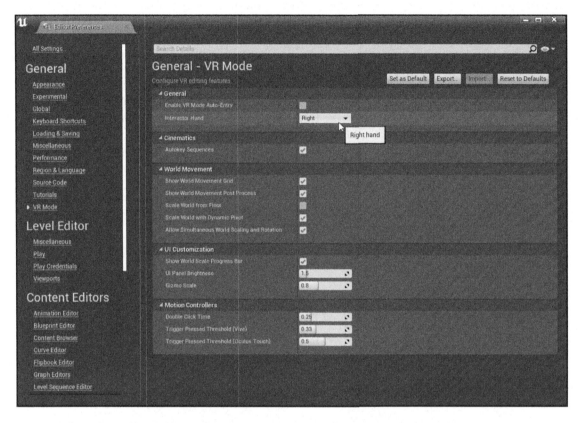

VR Mode settings are found under **Edit | Editor Preferences | General | VR Mode**.

Set either of these options if you'd like. We're going to leave the rest of these at their defaults for our work here.

The other thing we're going to need to address is how to move and look around.

Navigating in VR Mode

You activate movement mode in the VR editor by squeezing the grip buttons. When movement mode activates, the movement grid will appear and the interaction beam will turn green.

The interaction beam in the VR editor changes colors to indicate what mode it's in. Red indicates standard interaction mode, green indicates movement mode, yellow indicates that you currently have an actor selected, and blue indicates that you're in UI interaction mode.

The metaphor for movement in the VR editor is **pushing** and **pulling** the world. It's fairly intuitive. In most instances, the world will move in the way your hand is moving while your movement mode is active.

Moving through the world

If you move the controller while holding the grip, the world moves as though you're pulling it, or swimming through it:

If you release the grip while moving the controller, the movement continues for a bit, as though you'd pushed off of an object and were now floating away from it. This takes a bit of practice, but it becomes fairly intuitive once you get the hang of it. Squeezing the grip again stops your movement.

The movement grid displays the location of the floor in your real-world tracking volume. Align it with the floor in your scene to see what objects will really look like from the perspective of someone standing on the floor.

Teleporting through the world

To teleport through the world, squeeze the grip button on your dominant hand's controller and squeeze the trigger. Aim the controller at an object or destination, and you'll teleport there on release:

Using a combination of teleport and drag moves, you can get around the world pretty well.

Rotating the world

When you need to rotate your viewpoint, hold both controllers' grips and rotate the controllers around each other as though you were trying to spin the world:

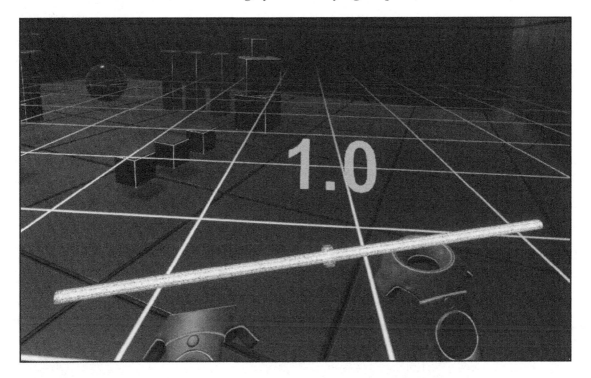

The number you see over the rotation axis is the world's current scale. We can manipulate that too.

Scaling the world

To scale the world, squeeze the grips and move the controllers toward each other to shrink the world, or away from each other to expand it:

It's weirdly satisfying to shrink your scene down until it looks like miniatures on a table.

Moving the controllers toward each other shrinks the world. Moving them away from each other grows the world. This can be useful for layout, as you can assemble the world in miniature, then teleport back to the ground and restore its normal scale to see what you've made.

One of the fastest ways to get around the world in VR Mode is to shrink the world, then use the teleport action (grip + trigger) to teleport to a new location on your map. The world will return to its default size when you teleport.

Practicing movement

Take some time now to practice navigating through the world using your controllers. Use *Alt* + *V* to enter VR Mode, and hit *Alt* + *V* again when you want to exit. Use the grip buttons to move through the world, teleport, rotate, and change its scale. Play with it until it feels natural. There's a bit of subtlety to getting this, but it's a very useful tool once you've made yourself comfortable.

Modifying the world in VR Mode

Now that you've practiced moving around the world a bit, let's start to learn some of the skills we'll need to do scene composition in VR.

Moving, rotating, and scaling objects

To select an object, just point at it and pull the trigger. Your interaction beam will turn yellow to indicate that you've entered selection mode. A gizmo will appear that allows you to move the object. By default, this will be a translate gizmo, which allows you to move the selected object around (we'll see in a moment how to switch to other types of gizmo):

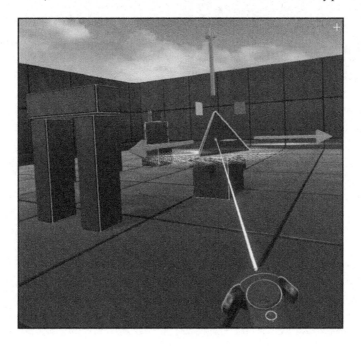

If you'd like to move the selected object, release the trigger and then pull it again while pointing at the object or at the transform gizmo. You can use the transform gizmo's arrows and planes to constrain your movement, or interact directly with the object to move it freely. When moving an object directly with the interaction beam, you can use the trackpad to move it closer or further from you.

Be aware that hidden objects with collision can sometimes interfere with selection in VR Mode. If your selection beam appears to pass through the object you want to select, move to a different vantage point to select it.

Usually it's a better idea to use the gizmo to move an object, as it's fairly difficult to move objects in depth with any precision.

The default transform gizmo can be switched to other modes using the radial menu interface. To activate the radial menu, touch the trackpad or thumbstick on your non-interactor hand and point at the menu option you'd like to select. Use the trigger to select it. Your controller's menu button takes you back out of sub-menus, or closes the radial menu if you're already at the top menu:

Selecting the **Gizmo** submenu allows you to switch between transform gizmo options:

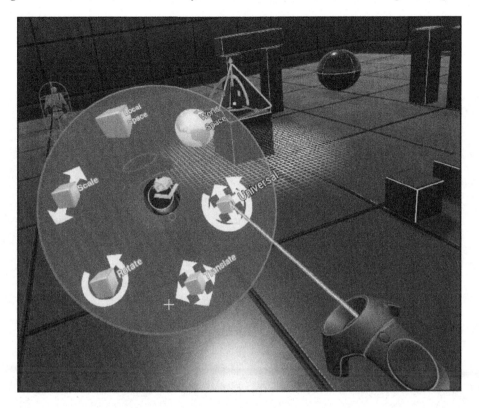

The **Universal** gizmo provides translation, rotation, and scale handles on a single gizmo. The **Translate**, **Rotate**, and **Scale** gizmos provide individual tools for those operations. Switching the transform mode to **Local Space** rotates, scales, and moves the object along its own axes, while the **World Space** mode transforms the object along the world axes.

Using both controllers to rotate and scale objects

You also may have noticed that, whenever you have an object selected and you're holding the trigger over the object itself (rather than a gizmo handle), a second interaction beam appears on your off-hand controller. If you aim that second interaction beam at the object and squeeze the trigger, you can use them both to tumble and stretch the object:

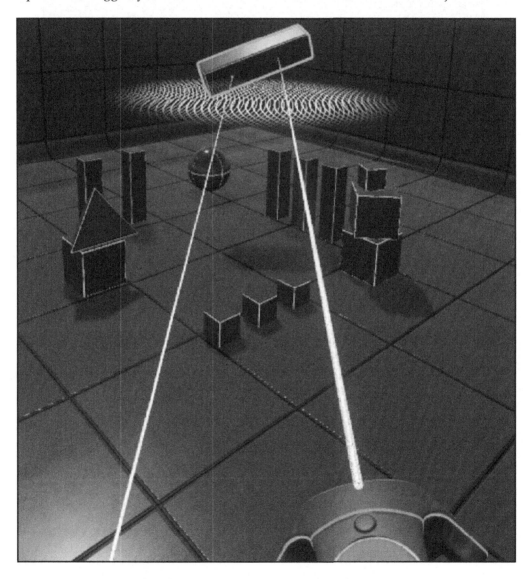

This is a great tool for exploring improvising rough layouts. It's intuitive and invites natural interaction with objects in your environment. This is a good tool to use for exploring and improvising layouts. You'll probably have a tough time getting things exactly where you want them, but if you use this tool for rough layouts and then clean them up in the flat-screen editor, you can achieve good results.

Practicing moving objects

Try it out now. Hit *Alt + V* to enter **VR Mode**, and, in addition to practicing moving around the world, practice using the transform gizmos and free movement to move objects around the world. Remember to use the radial menu to change movement modes, and use the **Menu** button to get back out to the Home menu. Take some time to practice this. The controls will probably feel unfamiliar at first, but once you get the hang of them, world-building in VR is a rewarding experience.

When you're done, hit *Alt + V* to exit **VR Mode** again, and, if you'd like, clean up your object alignments in flat-screen editing.

Now we're ready to begin composing a scene, and to do this, we'll be using the VR Mode menus.

Composing a new scene in VR Mode

Now that we've learned the basics of operating the VR Mode editor, let's go deeper and really see how we can use this as a scene composition tool. First, we're going to need some assets to work with. The free Infinity Blade: Grass Lands package will give us something to play with.

Open your Epic Games Launcher (it's fine to leave your existing project open as you do this), navigate to the **Unreal Engine** | **Marketplace** | **Free** tab, and search for **Infinity Blade: Grass Lands**. Hit **Add to Project** and select your new project as the target project:

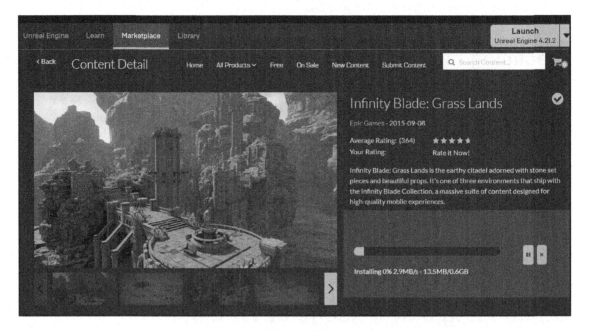

Once the assets have finished downloading and installing, let's force the new shaders to compile. Open up `Content/InfinityBladeGrassLands/Maps/Overview`, and let the shaders compile. While these shaders are compiling, feel free to enter **VR Mode** using *Alt + V* and navigate around the overview map to see what assets we have available to us.

After you've built your shaders, we can do some work composing a scene using these assets. For this exercise, we're going to start with an existing map and modify it.

First, we'll need to learn how to navigate the editor menus in VR.

Navigating the radial menu

Menu interaction in the VR editor, is for the most part, handled by a series of radial menus attached to the controller. In practice, these are fairly intuitive to use, as they map clearly to the touchpad or thumbstick inputs on the hand controllers. Let's look at how they work:

1. Select `Content/InfinityBladeGrassLands/Maps/ElvenRuins` and open it.
2. If you'd like, you can also change your **Project Settings** | **Maps & Modes** | **Default Maps** to open this map automatically.
3. Use *Alt + V* to enter **VR Mode**, and, while you're in this mode, touch the left trackpad or thumbstick to activate the radial menu.
4. To enter a menu, aim the interaction beam at it and squeeze the trigger or use the menu hand's trackpad to select options.
5. To back out of the submenus, use the non-dominant hand's menu button:

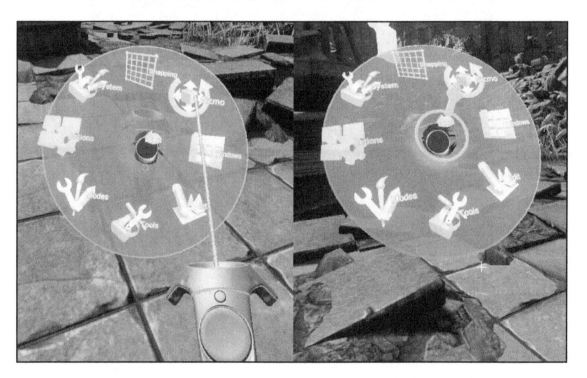

You can use the interaction beam or the menu hand's trackpad to navigate menus in VR Mode

Let's get into VR Mode and explore the menus. You have eight major menu categories available from the **Home** menu.

Gizmo

We've already explored the Gizmo menu, so we won't dive back into detail here. Remember that it's used to switch between behaviors of your in-editor movement tools.

Snapping

The **Snapping** menu is a close partner to the Gizmo menu. Most of these behave as you're used to in the flat-screen editor, but the **Smart Snapping** option is especially worth knowing about:

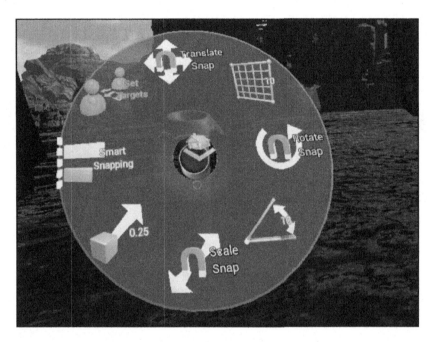

With **Smart Snapping** active, objects you move in-scene will attempt to align themselves to other objects as you move them. Since precise placement can be challenging to achieve in VR Mode, this is a big help.

Use the **Set Targets** option to select a specific object you'd like other objects to snap to, and use the **Reset Targets** option to clear it.

Windows

The Windows submenu provides access to the individual palettes and menus you'll be using as you compose your scene:

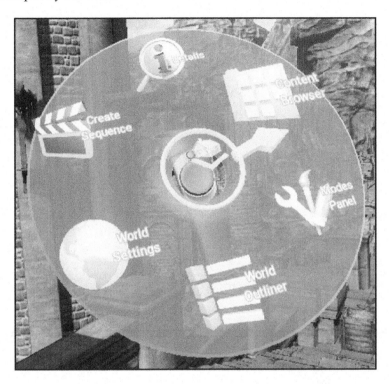

Each button opens its associated panel. These are the same panels you're used to from the flat-screen editor:

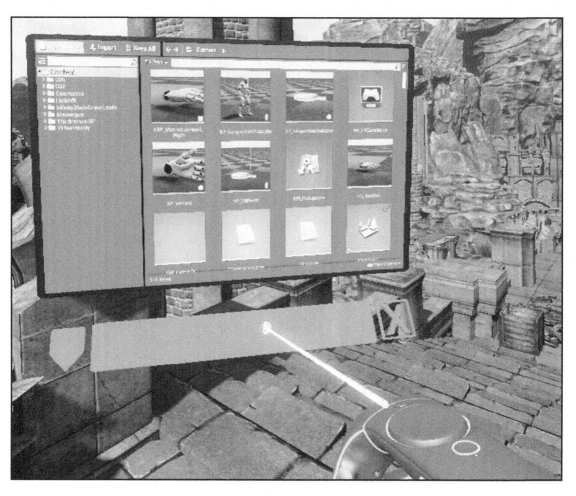

The Content Browser as seen in the editor's VR Mode

To move a window, aim the interaction beam at the large bar beneath it. You can place and angle it any way you want. The downward-facing arrow to the left of the move bar pins the window in place. When it's activated, the window will stay where you place it, regardless of how you move through the world. When it's un pinned, the window will move with you when you move. The X-shaped button to the right of the bar closes the window:

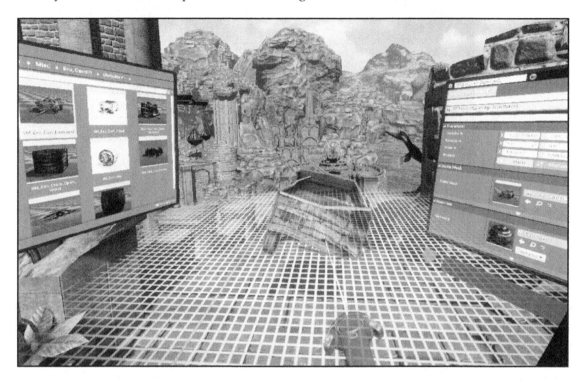

You can move your active windows around to create a virtual workspace from which to work

These windows work just as they do in the flat-screen editor. An effective practice in using them is to open only the windows that you need, and arrange them around yourself in a virtual workspace for the task you're doing.

In practice, much of the time, you'll find it useful to leave your content browser open to your side along with the details pane.

Edit

The **Edit** menu allows you to duplicate, delete, and snap objects in your scene:

Most of these options should be pretty self-explanatory and what you'd expect an edit menu to contain. **Snap to Floor** is a bit of an outlier, so it's worth remembering that it's in here. You'll use it often.

Tools

The **Tools** menu is primarily geared toward managing simulations in the editor. Here, you can start, pause, and resume simulations, and save their results back to the editor:

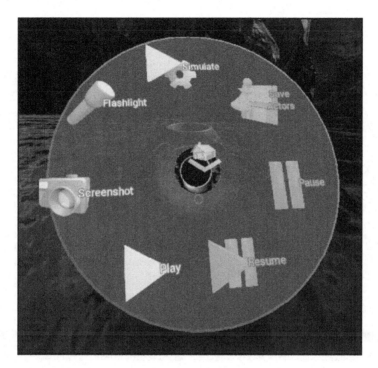

Two options that aren't related to simulations are also contained here. The **Screenshot** tool snaps a standard-resolution screenshot, but be aware that the screenshot will include the menu, so move it out of sight if you want a clean shot. The **Flashlight** tool is useful for finding your way around dark scenes, especially if you're midway through composing your scene lighting.

Modes

The **Modes** panel allows you to place actors such as lights, volumes, and primitives; manage foliage; enter landscape sculpting mode; and paint textures and vertex colors, just as it does in the flat-screen editor:

Selecting one of these options will bring up a **Modes** panel that can then be placed in the world and used in the same way as the other panels available from the **Windows** menu.

Actions and System

At present, the **System** menu just gives you a way to exit VR Mode. At the time of writing, it doesn't do anything else. The **Actions** menu's behavior varies depending on context.

Making changes to our scene

Now that we've learned how to get around in VR Mode, let's put some of this learning into practice. We're going to modify the Elven Ruins map from within VR Mode.

The first thing we're going to do is change the time of day. Let's see how these ruins would look at dawn.

Use *Alt + V* to enter VR Mode and touch your non-interaction hand's trackpad or thumbstick to bring up the radial menu. Use the menu button to navigate back up to home if you're currently in a submenu. Select the Windows menu and, from there, activate the **World Outliner**.

Use the interaction beam to drag the movement box at the base of the menu. Put it to your side and a bit below you.

We're going to look for the directional light that's acting as our sun in this scene. To find it, click the **Type** column's header to sort your actor list by type, and then use the trackpad to scroll through the list and find the **Directional Light** named **Light Source**:

Unfortunately, you don't have an easy way to enter text in **VR Mode**. The radial menu offers a number pad that you can use when setting values, but if you wanted to search for light, you'd have to type it using a conventional keyboard. Sorting, scrolling, and selecting works pretty well for this sort of work.

Once you've selected the directional light, use the radial menu to activate the **Details** panel. Use the bar beneath it to drag it to a location where you can read it and interact with it, but can still see the sky:

In this shot taken from within the VR headset, you can see how we've been able to create a virtual workspace by manipulating the panels in 3D space.

Point the interaction beam at the light's **Rotation Y** value and drag it back and forth over the box to change its value. You'll see the sun changing overhead. It starts out at around -48. Drag it to around 210 (or wherever you like, really) to create some nice dramatic shadows.

Now, select **BP_SkySphere**. From its **Details** panel, turn on **Colors Determined by Sun Position**, and check the **Refresh Material** checkbox to change the sky's color:

That's kind of nice, right? Lighting changes like this are often best made inside the **VR Mode** editor, as light and colors render very differently in the headset than they do on the flat screen.

Building new elements in your map is generally best done in the flat-screen editor. **VR Mode** is excellent for checking sightlines and adjusting object positions, but, in practice, it still suffers from some growing pains that can make object selection difficult:

Here are a few effective ways to work within VR Mode, benefit from its strengths, and work around its weaknesses:

- Get around by scaling the world down, then use teleport to land where you want to go
- Do rough lighting adjustments inside VR Mode where you can see what their effects on the world will really be
- Build geometry in the traditional editor, but use VR Mode to experiment with its placement

Get into the habit of using *Alt + V* frequently to check your environment in VR as you build it. You'll get a sense of which adjustments make sense to do in **VR Mode** and which work best in the traditional editor.

Most importantly, what we wanted to communicate in this section is that **VR Mode**, far from being a luxury or a gimmick, should be considered an essential tool for your scene construction workflow in VR.

Optimizing scenes for VR

Now that we've spoken a fair bit about editing scenes using VR Mode, let's talk about an absolutely crucial topic in VR development – maintaining an acceptable frame rate.

We've discussed the paramount importance of maintaining frame rate in virtual reality several times before. It's critical, and it's challenging to do. In the remainder of this chapter, we're going to talk about things that you can do to speed up your scenes and to find out what's preventing them from running faster.

Testing your current performance

The first thing you need to do when assessing your scene's performance is to find out how fast you're currently running. We're going to look at a few commands we can use for this.

From within the editor, click on the ` (backtick) key. It's to the left of the *1* key on your keyboard, above the **Tab** key. A console entry box will appear:

A wide range of console commands can be entered here. We're going to talk about those you're most likely to use as you optimize your scenes.

Stat FPS

Enter stat fps into the console command line. A frame rate counter will appear in your editor window, displaying two values:

The first is your **frames per second (FPS)**. The second value tells you how many milliseconds it took to draw the frame, and this is the value you should train yourself to focus on. Frame rate is what your player perceives, but, as you're developing and trying to solve problems that impact your frame rate, you're going to have a much easier time thinking about how the changes you make affect your performance if you train yourself to think in milliseconds. The frame rate describes your desired result, but the milliseconds you're spending on each part of getting the frame rendered are the cause. When fixing your scene, you need to look at the individual costs of each operation that's contributing to your frame time, and these are expressed in milliseconds.

Determining your frame time budget

If we're going to think in terms of milliseconds, the first thing we need to do is establish how many milliseconds we can spend drawing our frame and still hit our target frame rate. Figuring this out is simple.

 To find your application's frame time budget, divide 1,000 by your target frame rate.

This gives you the number of milliseconds in which you have to draw your frame to achieve this frame rate. So, for example, if you're targeting a headset that refreshes at 90 FPS (which describes most of them), we find our frame budget like this:

1000 / 90 = 11.11

This gives us a frame budget of around 11 milliseconds. Your VR application will refresh at 90 FPS if it takes you 11 milliseconds or less to deliver the frame. That's not a lot of time, so we're going to have to do some work with most scenes to achieve this.

Warnings about performance profiling

Before we dive too deep down the performance optimization rabbit hole, let's keep a few important things in mind.

First, the frame time reported on a flat screen isn't going to be accurate for VR. It's a good baseline value that you can use to see roughly how you're doing, but when you activate VR, your frame rate is going to drop.

If you see a really substantial drop in frame rate between your flat-screen values and your VR values, check your **Project Settings** and make sure you have **Instanced Stereo** turned on. If it's off, which is its default setting, you'll be paying the full cost of rendering your entire scene twice, which you definitely don't want to do.

Be sure you're not just checking your values on flat-screen. Test in VR often. A quick way of checking your VR performance is to read your **stat fps** values from within VR Mode.

- Activate VR Mode with **stat fps** visible. The text will probably be too small to read from within the headset, but you can read it from the flat-screen output.

Use this method to spot-check your environment. Move through the map and check for problem areas using VR Mode.

Another important thing to consider is that, because we're testing in-editor, our numbers are affected by the editor itself. We're paying to render all those windows that your editor displays along with the in-game scene. For accurate values, we have to run the game in a stand alone session. Checking your numbers in-editor is a good practice to see whether changes you're making are making things better or worse, but you should remember that they don't accurately describe what your packaged application will do.

We also need to remember that, when we test frame time in-editor, we're really just looking at rendering performance, but we're not getting any information about what the rest of our application is costing us. This is fine much of the time, since the bulk of your problems are likely to be in rendering, but you should still make sure you're testing the running application to make sure you don't have a runaway Blueprint or too many animated characters bringing you down.

Finally, we should talk about system specifications. Different hardware configurations will perform in different ways. If you're planning to release an application to the public, you should be sure that you're testing it on your minimum spec hardware, as well as on your development machines. Just because your application is running fine on a beast with a brand-new high-end video card doesn't mean it's going to run so well on older hardware. If you can test on your min-spec target, do so. If you can't, be conscious of how far your development machine is from your min-spec and make sure you leave a decent amount of headroom in your frame time budget to accommodate this.

Now that we've talked a bit about the things that can affect our measurements, let's dive in deeper and learn how to get better information than we can get with **stat fps** alone.

Stat unit

Checking our frame rate is useful and it's an important thing to do frequently, but on it's own it doesn't tell us much. It may tell us that we have a problem, but it won't give us much guidance in finding what's wrong or how to fix it. For this, we have a few more useful commands at our disposal.

The **stat unit** command breaks down the frame's cost in milliseconds and shows us which parts of that cost are coming from the scene we're rendering and which parts are coming from other things going on in our application, such as animations and AI.

Try it now. Click on the ` (backtick) key to bring up your console command window, and type **stat unit** to add this additional information below your frame rate information:

```
Frame:   10.75 ms
Game:    10.74 ms
Draw:    7.62 ms
GPU:     10.99 ms
RHIT:    10.76 ms
DynRes: Unsupported
```

The **stat unit** command displays four primary pieces of information:

- **Frame**: This is the total time it took to draw the frame. This is the same value we saw in the **stat fps** results.
- **Game**: This tells you how long your game thread is taking on your CPU. This covers things such as animation updates, AI, and anything else your CPU has to figure out in order to update the frame. If you have Blueprints doing inefficient things on the **Tick** event, that will drive this value up.
- **Draw**: This tells you how long your CPU spent preparing the scene for rendering. High values here may mean that you're doing too much occlusion culling or spending too much on lights or shadows.
- **GPU**: This value tells you how long the **GPU** took to draw the frame. High values here may mean that you're drawing too many polygons, using too many materials, or that your materials are too complex. Most of the time, your problems will be here.

These values are not additive. Your game thread will wait for the rendering thread to complete, so, if the **Game** timing matches your **GPU** timing, what that's really telling you is that your CPU isn't holding you up, and that your frame time is being driven by rendering.

In addition to these four base values, we also have two advanced pieces of information that you don't need to worry about right now:

- **RHIT**: This is your rendering hardware interface thread. Realistically, you won't be seeing values here that differ much from your **GPU** values unless you're working with advanced rendering hardware or a video game console, and you're running your rendering hardware interface calls on a dedicated thread. Until you're working on an advanced project with a dedicated team of engineers, this probably doesn't apply to you.
- **DynRes**: This indicates whether dynamic resolution is supported or being used by your application. In practice, this is only supported on video game consoles, so you don't need to worry about it here. If you're curious, further information can be found at `https://docs.unrealengine.com/en-us/Engine/Rendering/DynamicResolution`.

What we're interested in finding from our **stat unit** information is whether we're spending most of our time on our **Game** CPU, our **Game** rendering operations, or on our **GPU**. We're looking for the largest number, because this is going to tell us what we need to fix.

You should make it a habit to leave **stat fps** and **stat unit** on nearly all the time as you develop. If you introduce something new to the scene that is going to hammer your frame rate, the best time to discover this is when you put it in. If you go a long time before you discover a problem, you're going to have to do a lot more work to find out what caused it.

It's often worth it to see how your stat unit values are changing over time, either as things happen in your application (this is useful for finding hitches) or as you move through the scene. To get this information, use **stat unitgraph** to display a graph over time of your scene's performance metrics:

You'll see that your stat unit values have now been color-coded to correspond with lines on the graph.

As mentioned previously, most of the time, your problems will be with the **GPU** art that's just too heavy to fit within your scene.

Of course, if you're doing ridiculous things on your Tick, you may be getting killed on your CPU, in which case you're going to want to look for Blueprints that could be refactored to act in response to events or changes in data instead of using the tick. But, most of the time, **GPU** is where you're going to run into trouble.

Profiling the GPU

The first tool you should learn to use in optimizing your scene is the GPU profiler. You can activate this by typing **profilegpu** in the console, but since you're going to use it so often, it's a better idea to memorize the hotkey: *Ctrl + Shift + ,* (comma). Hit it now and let's look at the numbers:

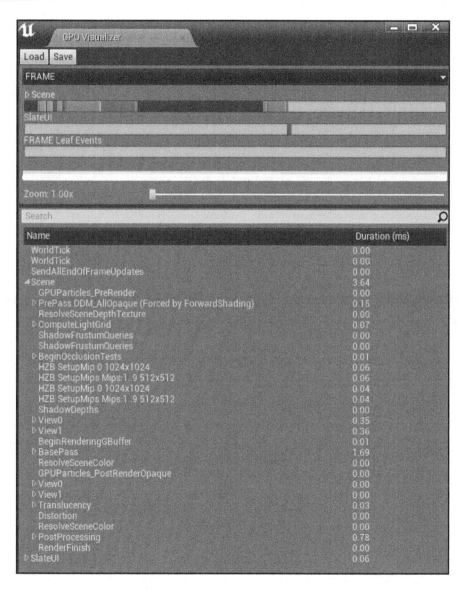

The most important part of this profile report is the graph under the **Scene** heading. Roll over the graph, and you'll see that tooltips tell you what each block represents. The two biggest blocks will usually be your **BasePass** and your **PostProcessing** pass. The base pass represents the act of drawing everything in the scene. Post processing handles anything that's taken care of after the scene has been drawn, such as screen-space ambient occlusion, color correction, and other effects.

Hit the expander to the left of the **Scene** heading to drill down for more detail into your scene rendering:

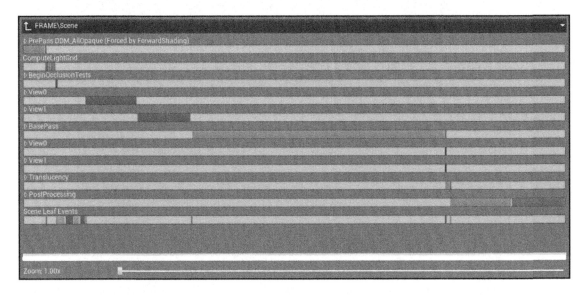

Here, we can see a more detailed breakdown of what's costing us time in drawing our frame. Lighting looks good here, as does translucency. Our **BasePass** is fairly sizeable, but that's to be expected.

You're not going to get too much more information by drilling down into your **BasePass**, but you can learn some useful stuff by drilling into your **PostProcessing** operations. Use the triangle beside your **PostProcessing** header to drill into it, and then click on large chunks in your **PostProcessing** operations to see what they are:

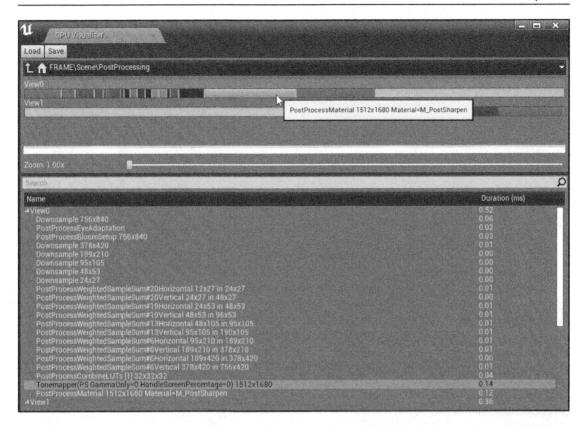

In this instance, these post numbers look pretty good. We don't have anything returning an unreasonably high duration.

Make sure you profile with the game running, or you'll see a lot of operations coming from the editor.

We're not going to have the space here to dig into everything involved in the rendering process and what it means, but in general, what you're looking for are large items that may be unnecessarily impacting your frame rate. When you find something that looks suspicious, search for it on the Unreal forums, and you'll likely find a discussion of what it means and what to do about it.

As you use this tool more and more, you'll develop a sense for what looks healthy and what problem areas look like. Use it often to get a clear handle on what your application is doing.

Now, let's look at a few other useful commands we can use to debug our scene.

Stat scenerendering

Behind the GPU profiler, your next most useful command is likely to be **stat scenerendering**. This command gives you a detailed list of the steps your system is taking to render the scene with their associated timings:

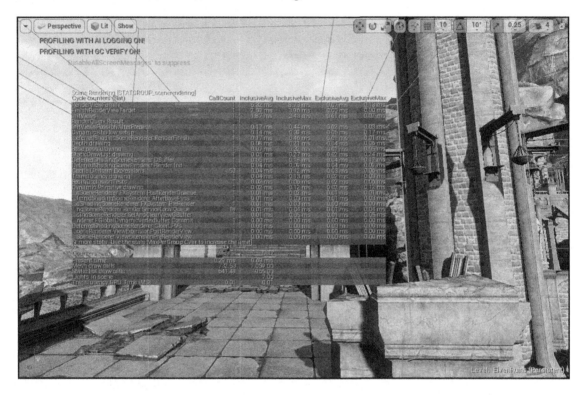

It's especially worthwhile in here to look at your **Dynamic shadow setup** and your **Translucency drawing**.

If you're seeing high values in your shadow setup, see whether one or more of your lights is doing too many shadow cascades or has a shadow distance that's too long. You can find more information on this topic at `https://docs.unrealengine.com/en-us/Platforms/Mobile/Lighting/HowTo/CascadedShadow`.

If your **Translucency drawing** is high, activate your editor's **Quad Overdraw** optimization viewmode, and look for translucent objects stacking over one another. If you have a problem here, you might be able to solve it by using masked rather than translucent materials, or by being careful about how they overlap in views:

At the bottom of this list are some very important numbers: Mesh draw calls and Static List draw calls. We should talk about these.

Draw calls

One of the biggest factors that will impact your scene performance is the number of **draw calls** required to get its information onto the GPU. What are we talking about here? It breaks down like this: everything you want the video card to draw has to be copied onto that card's memory. The act of sending a set of instructions to the card is called a draw call, or a **draw primitive call** (sometimes abbreviated to **DPC**). Let's say you have a static mesh appearing in your scene that has three materials on it. That's going to take four draw calls to set it up on the card: one for the mesh, and one for each material. You should endeavor to keep the number of draw calls in your scene as low as you can get it. Realistically, 2,000 draw calls is probably your limit for a VR scene. On mobile VR, like the Oculus Go or Quest, that number is lower.

What does this mean for you? First, put as few materials on your objects as you can get away with; ideally, one material per object. By adding just one more material slot, you've literally added one-third more to the cost of loading that object onto the video hardware, and if that object appears frequently in your scene, that's going to add up in a hurry.

We're going to talk shortly about what you can do about high draw call counts, but for now what you need to know about them is that, if these numbers are high, you're sending too many separate instructions to the video card, and that's going to slow you down. Maybe you have too many material slots on your objects, or too many individual objects being sent separately, but in all cases, it's a thing you'll need to fix.

Stat RHI

Another closely related command you'll use often is **stat rhi**. **RHI** stands for **rendering hardware interface**, and it tells you specifically what's impacting your rendering performance:

The two values you'll care most about here are **Triangles drawn** and your **DrawPrimitive** calls. Make it a habit to look through your scene with these values displayed, and look for views with unreasonably high triangle counts or draw call counts. For a VR scene on a desktop VR headset, you want to keep the number of triangles drawn below 2 million, and you want to keep your draw calls under 2,000.

The other value you should care about here is your memory consumption. Another way to get a scene running really slowly in real time is to use textures that are unreasonably large. Don't put a 4K texture on a pebble. We've seen it happen.

Stat rhi is one of the most useful commands overall for getting a general sense of how well your scene is fitting within its budget.

Stat memory

When you need more information about what's blowing your memory budget, you can use stat memory:

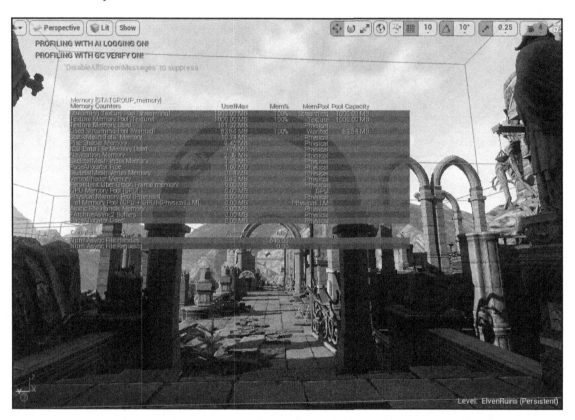

Most of the time, if you're consuming too much memory, the culprit will be textures. Be on the lookout for textures that are too large for what they're being used for. A huge object or a hero character might warrant a 2048x2048 texture. Anything else should be 1024x1024 or smaller. A 4K texture is probably not reasonable under any circumstances in VR. As you consider where to cut your textures down, look at the object in scene. How big is it? How close can the player get to it? Is it something the player really cares about looking at? It's awfully easy to spend way too much on an object the player can barely see. Start to think in terms of spending your texture and polycount budgets where they matter, and economizing where you can get away with it.

Optimization view modes

In addition to the stat commands, we also have a few optimization view modes that can be used to find problems in your scene. These are each accessed from the editor viewport's view mode menu. We're just going to talk about two of them here.

The **Shader Complexity** view shows you where your materials may be slowing you down. When you find a suspect object, select it, and see what's going on in its materials. Is your material too complicated or doing expensive math? Consider the following screenshot:

In the case of the preceding screenshot, the grass and tree are registering as expensive materials. When we select their objects and look at those materials, we can see that what's driving up their cost is that they use their **World Position Offset** input to simulate wind. That's expensive, but it's a nice effect and the player would notice if we turned it off, so we can leave it alone since the rest of our scene is running pretty efficiently.

Use this view to search for materials that may be costing you a lot without adding much value to the scene.

The **Light Complexity** view comes into play if you're using dynamic lights under the deferred shading model. Because we're using forward rendering and static lights here, it won't show us anything on this scene. When you are using dynamic lights and deferred shading, this view can show you where your lights are causing problems.

CPU profiling

If you're having trouble with your CPU times, you can use CPU profiling to find out where the problems are, just as we did earlier with the GPU profiler.

To activate CPU profiling, while the game is running, open a console command and type **stat startfile** to begin profiling. Profiling generates a lot of data, so you don't want to run your profiler over an entire session – just capture things you're interested in, such as, *why does the game slow down so much when that character alerts to an enemy?*

After you've captured whatever you're looking for, type `stat stopfile` to turn profiling back off. The profiler will save the captured data to a `.ue4stats` file in your project's `\Saved\Profiling\UnrealStats\` directory.

Now, open your Unreal Engine's install directory, and, inside its `Binaries\Win64` folder, look for the `UnrealFrontend.exe` application. Launch it and use the tabs to select **Session | Frontend | Profiler**. Use the profiler's **Load** button to open the `.ue4stats` file you just generated:

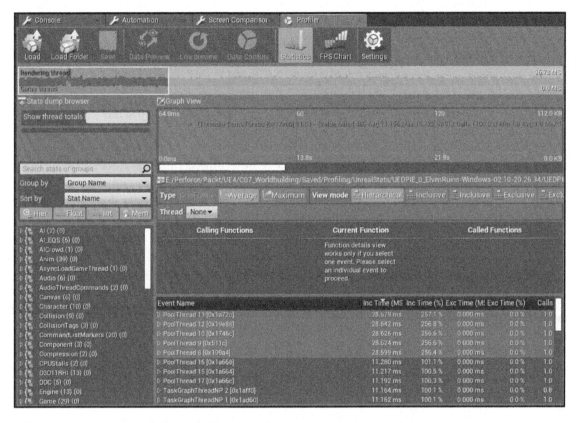

The CPU Profiler shows you how much time each operation called during a frame takes.

Just as we did with the GPU profiler, you can use this tool to burrow through expensive-looking function calls and see what's going on. It would take us beyond the scope of this book to go deeply into using the CPU profiler here—it's an extremely useful and powerful tool, but it does take some time to learn how to get good information from it. We recommend that you explore the write-up on the topic to go further, which can be found at `https://www.unrealengine.com/en-US/blog/how-to-improve-game-thread-cpu-performance`.

Turning things on and off

As primitive as it may sound, one of the most effective ways to find out what's costing you frame rate is simply to turn features on and off with the relevant stat information displayed (usually, stat unit is what you want for this). Use the viewport's **Show** menu to turn individual elements on and off, especially if you've determined through your GPU profiling or your stat information that the thing in question might be causing a problem. It can also be helpful to start deleting objects from your level (as long as you have a backup or it's under source control), and see whether a particular object makes a big change.

Addressing frame rate problems

Now that we've learned a bit about how to find problems in your scene, let's talk a bit about what to do about them.

Cleaning up Blueprint Tick events

If you're seeing high numbers on your CPU, one of the first culprits you want to look for is any Blueprint doing operations on the Tick event. This is an extremely common culprit. Remember that Tick events happen every single frame, so if you're doing a lot of work on your Tick, you're impacting every single frame you need to draw. Look for ways to spread this work out over multiple frames, or to avoid using the Tick altogether and use events to make objects change their state only when something changes.

Managing skeletal animations

If you have a lot of skeletal meshes animating, make sure they don't have a ridiculous number of bones in their skeletons, and make sure they're not using a ton of blend space animations. It's a much better practice to use skeletal mesh **Level of Detail** (**LOD**) to include fine details only when the player can see them, or to use separate skeletal meshes for cinematics, where highly-detailed facial animations matter, and for in-game meshes, use skeletons with lower bone counts. For more information on setting up skeletal mesh LODs, begin by looking at `https://docs.unrealengine.com/en-US/Engine/Content/ImportingContent/ImportingSkeletalLODs`.

Merging actors

This is a big one. Remember a short while ago when we mentioned that draw call counts have a big impact on your frame rate? One of the cheapest and easiest ways to drop your draw call counts is to merge multiple meshes into a single mesh. This will not only create a single mesh out of the multiple individual meshes you've selected, but it will also create a combined material for that mesh out of each child mesh's materials. This is a big deal.

Let's say you have a bunch of debris in a corner of a room; maybe 25 objects or so, and each of them uses one material slot. You're looking at 50 draw calls right there, out of a total of maybe 2,000 that you have available for your entire scene. That's a big hit. By merging these into a single object, you can drop 50 draw calls down to two. This is one of the fastest and most effective ways you can bring down your draw call count.

One caveat about this though: remember earlier in this book when we talked about Kent Beck's advice to *make it work, make it right, make it fast*? This is one of those areas where that wisdom applies. Once you bake all these objects into a single object, you no longer have the freedom to rearrange the individual components, so get the scene looking the way you want it, and then merge your actors to bring things under control.

Here's how to do it:

Select **Window** I **Developer Tools** I **Merge Actors**. The **Merge Actors** window will appear. Select the actors you want to merge. In general, it's a good idea to merge actors that are close together and likely to be in the same view. Once they're merged, all of them will be drawn even if only one of them is on camera, so merge items that are all going to be on camera simultaneously most of the time:

The Merge Actors dialog seen with multiple selected actors in the viewport behind it

If you select **Replace Source Actors**, the actors you've selected in-scene will be replaced by the merged model. For more information about merging actors, begin with `https://docs.` `unrealengine.com/en-us/Engine/Actors/Merging`.

Using mesh LODs

The number of triangles you're drawing in a scene (usually called the **polycount**) is another huge factor in determining your scene's rendering speed.

Of course, your first line of defense against high polycounts is in modeling. Use an application such as Pixologic's ZBrush to bake normal maps from a high-detail model, and apply them to a lower-detail mesh that you import into the game engine. Much of the time, your players will never notice the difference. VR is less forgiving of using normal maps to simulate geometric detail than the flat screen is, because players can sometimes see that the depth isn't real, but you should still make use of this technique anywhere you can get away with it.

Once you have a mesh in-game, however, you have a powerful LOD tool available to you to manage how many triangles you're drawing. LODs work like this: they store several versions of the same model, with increasingly small polycounts. As the model gets smaller on screen, the system switches out the high-detail mesh for a lower-detail mesh, since the player won't be able to see the detail anyway, now that it's further away.

Here's how to set up an LOD:

1. Select a static mesh and open the **Static Mesh** editor from the content browser.
2. Under its **Details**, look for the **LOD Settings** section.
3. Find the **Number of LODs** entry, and set it to a value greater than **1.** (For this test, just set it to **2** to create 2 LODs.)
4. Click on **Apply Changes**. One or more additional LOD models will now be created and added to the static mesh asset.
5. Under the **LOD Picker** section, find the LOD entry, and use it to select one of the new LODs.

   LOD 0 is the original model. Most of the time you'll leave this unchanged. **LOD 1** is the first LOD after **LOD 0**.

6. With the new LOD, such as **LOD 1**, selected, open the **Reduction Settings** entry from its LOD detail section and modify it.

You have a number of options available here, but most of the time, you'll be managing the **Percent Triangles** value. If you make changes here, click on **Apply Changes** to see the result:

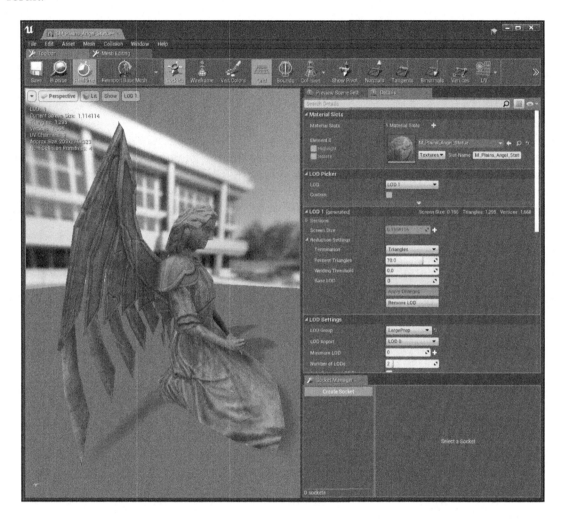

You'll see the modified mesh in your viewport. To see what it will look like at the real view distance, switch your LOD Picker back to LOD Auto and move your view around to see how the object changes as it switches between LODs. The LOD generator is surprisingly good.

For more information about creating and using LODs, start by looking at https://docs. unrealengine.com/en-us/Engine/Content/Types/StaticMeshes/HowTo/LODs.

Static mesh instancing

Remember those draw calls we were so concerned about a moment ago? There's another powerful way to reduce their count and dramatically speed up your rendering.

Say you have a big collection of mostly the same assets, such as a forest that reuses the same tree mesh hundreds of times. If you simply place those meshes in the environment individually, every single one of them is going to generate a minimum of two draw calls, and even more if it uses more materials. That's a recipe for a slide show. What you want to do instead is **instance** this geometry. Instancing is a way of telling your GPU that, even though it's about to draw a few hundred meshes, they're really all just the same mesh with different transforms. So, instead of making a separate draw call for each tree, the system makes one set of draw calls and gives the video hardware a list of locations, orientations, and scales at which to draw them. This is wildly faster than passing each item as a separate item.

By default in Unreal, the easiest way to instance objects is to use the foliage tool. While it's most commonly used for foliage, as the name suggests, you can also use it for repeated objects in lots of other contexts, like streetlamps on city streets. You can find more information on foliage instancing at `https://docs.unrealengine.com/en-us/Engine/ Foliage`.

Instancing static meshes outside the foliage tool is a bit more of a complex topic, but it can be done and can be a good idea if you're procedurally generating an actor that contains a large array of individual static meshes. Most of the time, however, when you're instancing objects in scenes, use the foliage tool to do it.

Nativizing Blueprints

Blueprints are already interpreted amazingly fast, but they can be made even faster by translating them automatically into C++ and then allowing the system to compile them.

To turn this on, open **Project Settings** | **Project** | **Packaging** | **Blueprints**, and use the **Blueprint Nativization Method** selector to select **inclusive** or **exclusive** nativization.

- **Inclusive** nativization will convert all your Blueprints to C++ when they compile.
- **Exclusive** nativization will convert only those Blueprints for which you set the nativize flag.

If you're using exclusive nativization, select the Blueprints you want to nativize by opening their **Class Settings**, and turn on the **Nativize** option in their **Details | Packaging** panel. Again, you don't need to do this if you're using inclusive nativization. In that case, every Blueprint is **nativized**:

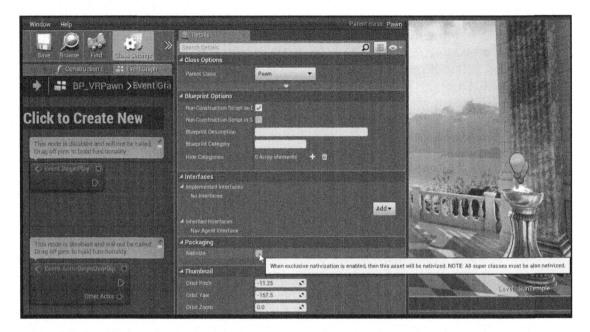

If you're planning to ship your application on desktop VR, inclusive nativization may be fine, but if you're planning to deploy to mobile VR, such as the Oculus Go or Quest, it's probably smarter to use exclusive nativization to choose which Blueprints you want to nativize, since including them all can increase your executable size.

This is a bit of an advanced topic. In general, you'll see a benefit if you nativize Blueprints that do a lot of work on the Tick event, or that just do a lot of work in general. If your Blueprints are fairly simple, you won't really see a difference either way. Because speed is so critical to VR development, it's good to know that this option is available to you.

If you do plan to do this, turn nativization on early in your project's development, and test on cooked builds frequently. Nativization is extremely good, but it can sometimes still cause unexpected side effects.

Summary

In this chapter, we learned quite a lot about how to use Unreal's VR Mode editor to compose environments from within VR, and we learned how to analyze and optimize scenes to see where our performance bottlenecks are.

In the next chapter, we're going to take a detour from building real-time 3D worlds in VR and look at another common application – movies and immersive photography.

Displaying Media in VR

9

In the previous chapters, we focused on creating real-time 3D media for VR, and spent a lot of time looking at player characters, interface elements, and building the world. Now, we're going to shift gears a bit and explore another important application for VR—displaying movies both on flat screens and in immersive environments.

VR is very good at this. Because it's possible to create a nearly infinite space within the headset, users can experience movies and media on enormous virtual screens with no distractions to take them out of the experience. These screens can take any shape as well. In addition to flat and curved screens, photos and movies of entire environments can be presented in a sphere surrounding the player so that they feel totally immersed in the space. In this chapter, we're going to learn how to create these things.

In particular, we will cover the following topics:

- Displaying video on a virtual screen
- Displaying video with stereo depth from side-to-side and over/under video sources
- Displaying media in 360-degree spherical environments
- Displaying 360-degree media in stereo
- Creating interactive controls to allow the player to start, stop, and rewind their media

Let's get to it and learn how to play movies!

Setting up the project

For this chapter's project, we don't need anything from our previous work, so we're going to begin simply by creating a new project with the following settings:

- **Blank** Blueprint template
- **Mobile / Tablet** hardware target
- **Scalable 3D or 2D** graphics target
- **With Starter Content** (we'll use some of the starter content in this one)

We still need to set our settings appropriately for VR, as we do with each project. Here's the cheat sheet:

- **Project | Description | Settings | Start in VR**: True
- **Engine | Rendering | Forward Renderer | Forward Shading**: True
- **Engine | Rendering | Default Settings | Ambient Occlusion Static Fraction**: False
- **Engine | Rendering | Default Settings | Anti-Aliasing Method**: MSAA
- **Engine | Rendering | VR | Instanced Stereo**: True
- **Engine | Rendering | VR | Round Robin Occlusion Queries**: True

Allow the project to restart once all of these settings have been set. Once your project has reopened, you'll be ready to begin learning about how media works in Unreal Engine.

Playing movies in Unreal Engine

We're going to begin by learning how we can play movies and other media in Unreal Engine in general. Of course, to get started, we're going to need a movie to play.

Video files come in a confusing array of configurations, and there are a few things you should know about them.

Understanding containers and codecs

The first point of confusion most people run into when they start learning about video files is not understanding that the container that a video file is wrapped in doesn't necessarily tell you much about how it was encoded. Let's take a moment to talk about this.

Video files consist of a lot of information, all packed into one file. There's the stream of images representing the video track. Often, there's audio, sometimes there are subtitles, and sometimes there's other additional information as well. All of this information gets bundled together inside a wrapping format called a **container**. You've no doubt seen video files with the `.mp4` extension. That's the extension used by the MPEG-4 container format. AVI is Microsoft's standard container format, and there are many others.

Here's the thing to remember, though: the container format specifies how these different parts of information are held together in the file, but it doesn't tell us how the video and audio streams were actually made. Just because you see the `.mp4` extension on a file doesn't necessarily mean it's going to work for what you're trying to use it for. There's another factor you need to take into consideration: the **codec**.

The word **codec** is a shortened combination of the words **compressor** and **decompressor**. Video files in their raw state can become huge. How big? Let's run some numbers. Say we have a 1080p video file. Its dimensions are 1920 x 1080 pixels. That's 2,073,600 pixels per frame. Let's say that we're displaying this video file in 24-bit color (8 bits per channel), which allows us to display a little over 16 million colors, which comes out to about 50 MB per frame. If we're running at 30 frames per second, that's going to eat up around 1.49 gigabytes per second. You're going to run out of space in a big hurry doing that.

We deal with this by compressing video files heavily when we store them, and then decompressing them in real time when it's time to stream them to the screen. This work is handled by the codec. Its compressor component is responsible for taking the raw source video and packing it into a format that can fit on disc, and its decompressor component handles unpacking it so that it can be displayed. Discussions of how video codecs work fill entire books of their own, so we're not going to get into the weeds on this, but the part that you do need to know is that while many codecs exist, not all of them work with all software solutions, and not all of them work on all hardware configurations. The most commonly used codec, and the most broadly compatible, is called **H.264**, but many codecs exist. Some are designed to be broadly used and some are very specifically made for certain applications, such as video editing. It's worthwhile spending a bit of time learning about these.

So, now you know a secret about video files. The container doesn't necessarily tell you about the codec, and you need to know about both to know whether the file will work. (So the next time you ask someone what kind of video file they've given you, and they answer that they've given you an `.mp4`, you'll know they haven't really answered your question.) Some container formats only work on specific operating systems or hardware, while others, such as `.mp4`, will work nearly anywhere.

For video files you intend to use with Unreal Engine, you should generally choose to wrap them in the `.mp4` container and compress them using the **H.264** codec. For more information on supported codecs, check out the following link: `https://docs.`
`unrealengine.com/en-US/Engine/MediaFramework/TechReference`.

We're not going to cover the topic of compressing your own video files here in this book – there's quite a lot to say about that, and quite a lot of information available online about how to do it. If you have access to the Adobe Creative Suite, the included Adobe Media Encoder application is an excellent tool for converting video into nearly any format you need. If you need a free video encoder, AVC Free is excellent and commonly used. You can find it at the following link: `https://www.any-video-converter.`
`com/products/for_video_free/`.

Finding a video file to test with

Let's find a file that meets these standards. If we navigate to the **"Video For Everybody"**
Test Page, we can find a suitable video for testing. Go to `http://camendesign.com/code/`
`video_for_everybody/test.html` and find the **Download Video** link for the `.mp4`
container format. Right-click the link and select **Save Link As...** to save the
`big_buck_bunny.mp4` video file to your hard drive.

If you don't already have the VLC Media Player installed on your system, download and install it from: `https://www.videolan.org/vlc/index.html`. In practice, you could use any video player to check your files, but VLC is a good tool to know about. It'll play nearly anything and gives you good information about the file you're playing. Refer to the following steps:

1. Open the video file you just downloaded in VLC and play it.
2. Pause the video somewhere and hit *Ctrl + J* to open its **Codec** information:

You can see here that this file has been encoded using H.264, and we can see from its file extension that it's using an .mp4 container. This file should work correctly for us on any platform in Unreal.

Adding a video file to an Unreal project

Let's add this file to our Unreal project.

For other asset types, you use the Import method from within Unreal Editor to add them to your project, but video files are different. To add a video file to an Unreal project, you must manually place it in a subdirectory of the Content folder named Movies.

TIP

The name and location are important. The engine will look for movies in `Content/Movies` by default, and your movies may not package correctly if you put them in another location.

1. From your **Content Browser**, make sure you're at the root `Content` folder and right-click to create a new folder.
2. Name it `Movies`, as shown in the following screenshot:

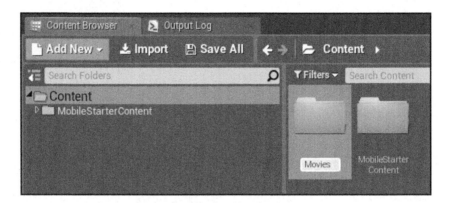

3. From your Windows Explorer, find the `.mp4` file you downloaded, and move it to your project's `Content\Movies` directory. (You can right-click this directory in your Content Browser and select **Show in Explorer** to navigate to the directory.)

Creating a File Media Source asset

Now, return to the Unreal Editor, and in your `Content/Movies` directory, right-click and select **Create Advanced Asset** | **Media** | **File Media Source** to create a new file media source asset. It's often easier to name file media sources using the same names as their source assets, so it makes sense to name it `big_buck_bunny` since that's the name of the file we're about to attach:

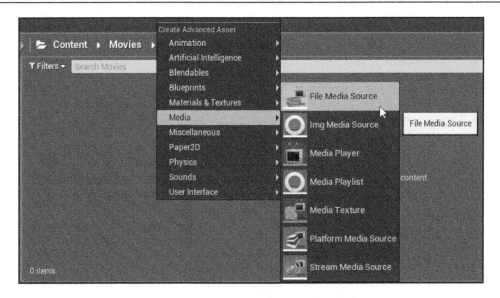

Open it up and use the ellipsis (...) button to select the video file you placed in your
Content/Movies directory as its **File Path**:

A File Media Source asset is simply a resolver that allows a media player to find a movie on disk. Media players point to file media sources, and those file media sources point to the actual file in the `Movies` directory.

File media sources also provide a few additional options:

- The advanced **Precache File** option can be used to force the entire media file into memory and play from there.
- The **Player Overrides** list allows you to force a specific player to decode the media on a specific platform. Leave these alone unless you're sure you need to override the automatic choice.

Three other media source types exist, and while we're not going to dive into them in depth here, you should know about them:

- **Img** Media Sources are used to display image sequences – individual images intended to be streamed in series as a movie. For detailed information on playing image sequences, check out the following link: `https://api.unrealengine.com/INT/Engine/MediaFramework/HowTo/ImgMediaSource/index.html`.
- **Stream** Media Sources allow you to specify a video file hosted at a specific URL for playback. For more information, check out the following link: `https://api.unrealengine.com/INT/Engine/MediaFramework/HowTo/StreamMediaSource/index.html`.
- **Platform** Media Sources allow you to specify different media to play on different hardware platforms. Check out the following link for details: `https://api.unrealengine.com/INT/Engine/MediaFramework/HowTo/PlatformMedia/index.html`.

Creating a Media Player

Now that we have a media source set up, let's create a **Media Player** to play it:

1. Right-click in your `Content/Movies` directory and select **Create Advanced Asset** | **Media** | **Media Player**. We'll be using the same media player for all of our media sources, so a general name such as `MediaPlayer` is fine. Refer to the following screenshot:

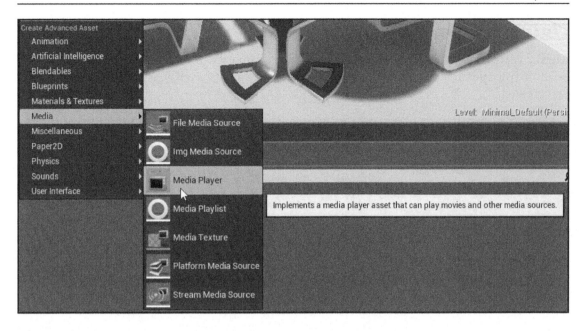

When you create it, a new dialog will appear, asking whether you whether you'd like to create a **Media Texture** asset to handle the video output. Let's allow it to do so, as shown in the following screenshot:

We could just as well have created it by creating a **Media/Media Texture** asset from our content browser, but this saved us a step.

Using Media Textures

Media Texture assets display the streamed video or images from their bound **Media Player** asset. If you open the one we just created, you'll see that it's bound to the **Media Player** we just created:

Don't worry if your media texture looks blank. It won't display anything until you've played something on its associated **Media Player**.

In general, you're going to want to leave your properties of **Media Texture** alone. Make sure it's bound to your **Media Player**, but you're unlikely to need to change any of its other properties.

Testing your Media Player

Open up the new **Media Player** asset you just created. You should see the file media source we set up a moment ago in its list of available media sources. Select it and play it to verify that it's playable in Unreal:

Ensure that **Play on Open** is selected for this file source, and turn on the **Loop** option as well.

Once we've verified that the video file plays in our media player, let's add it to an object in the world.

Adding video to an object in the world

Since we included Starter Content in this project, instead of launching with a blank map, our project launches with a simple map named **Minimal Default** by default, which contains a pair of chairs and a table. We can use this as a starting point for our movie playback map. Save the map by selecting **File | Save Current As...** and save it as Content/Chapter08/Maps/MoviePlayback2D. (Remember, it's a good idea to put your work into a subdirectory of your Content directory for your project. Otherwise, you're going to have a mess when you migrate something else in.)

If you'd like, feel free to use the starter content to arrange a more comfortable theater or viewing room set. We're not going to cover that here, but if you're up for it, create a living room or movie theater set, or anything that sparks your imagination.

What we do need in our scene is a screen to display our media. Follow these steps to create one:

1. From the **Modes** panel, select **Place | Basic | Plane**, and drag a plane onto the scene.
2. Set its **Location** to (X=-730.0, Y=0.0, Z=210.0) (or wherever fits the environment you've built).
3. Set its **Rotation** to (Pitch=0.0, Yaw=-90, Roll=90) (in the editor, this reads as X=90.0, Y=0.0, Z=-90.0).
4. Set its **Scale** to (X=8.0, Y=4.5, Z=1.0). By doing this, we've matched the shape of the screen to the 16:9 aspect ratio of the video we intend to play.

Now, we're going to assign our **Media Texture** to this plane:

1. Drag the **Media Texture** we created for our **Media Player** onto the plane.
2. A material will automatically be created to display the texture.

This is how you get media into a 3D scene. Assign a material or a material instance that uses a **Media Texture** as a source, and make sure that the **Media Texture** points back at a Media Player.

Using a media playback material

We should look at this material for a moment. Open it up. If you look at its material properties, you can see that it's an ordinary Surface material using the Default Lit shading model. There's nothing special here.

The Texture Sample, on the other hand, is interesting:

The important details here are that its **Texture** source has been set to our media texture, and its **Sampler Type** has been set to `External`. This is what will allow it to display our media in real time. We're going to do more work with this material shortly, but for now you can close it.

Adding sound to our media playback

We also want to be able to play sound in our scene. Follow these steps to do so:

1. With our screen actor still selected, click the **Add Component** button in its details panel.

2. Add a **Media Sound** component and set its **Media Player** property to our media player:

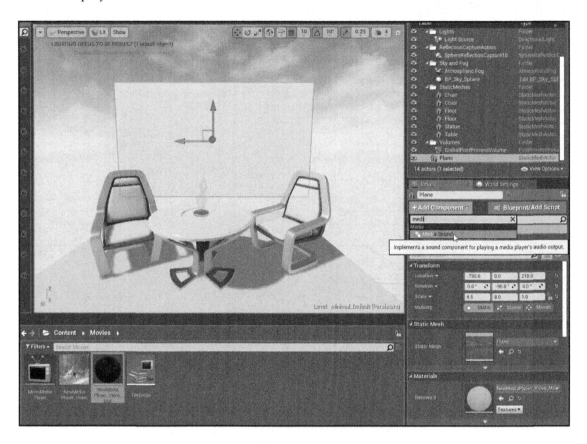

This **Media Sound** component will play whatever audio the associated media player is streaming. By default, it handles stereo audio, but it can be used for mono or surround audio sources as well.

Now that we've set everything up and placed an object in the world with video material and a sound component, let's get our media player playing our test video.

Playing media

We're going to start simply here, and just make the movie play when the level starts. Later on, we're going to do more to control our media player. Follow these steps to get started:

1. Click on **Open Level Blueprint**, as shown in the following screenshot:

2. Create a new variable and set its type to **Media Player** | **Object Reference**:

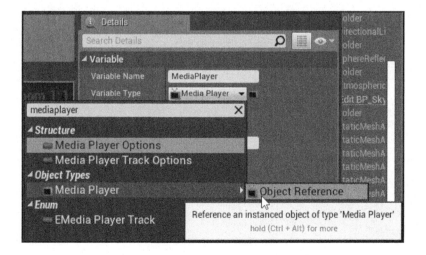

3. Compile the blueprint and change the variable's default value from None to the media player we created a moment ago.
4. *Ctrl* + drag the media player variable onto your event graph.
5. Find or create the **Event BeginPlay** node.
6. Drag a connector from your Media Player variable and call **Open Source** on it.
7. Set the call's **Media Source** to the file media source we created from our movie:

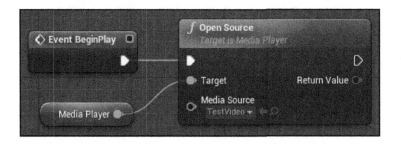

Launch it in your **VR Preview**, and let's see what happens:

Nice. The video is playing. We'll take a moment to review what we did to set this up, and then we're going to look at ways to improve it. Refer to the following screenshot:

Media playback works as follows:

1. Any media you want to play in engine begins as a file in `Content/Movies`. The source movie isn't imported into the engine and doesn't appear in your content browser.
2. To access it in the engine, you create a **File Media Source** asset that points to the media file on disk.
3. Media is played through a **Media Player** object that you can control through Blueprint calls.
4. **Media Texture** assets sample the video from their associated **Media Player**. These are included in materials.
5. **MediaSound** components on objects play audio from their associated **Media Player**. These are usually added to the object acting as a screen in your scene.

Going deeper with the playback material

Let's take a look at a few things we can do with our media playback materials. The right choices to make here entirely depend on what effect you're trying to create, so we'll talk about a few things you might want to do, but you'll want to decide on your own whether they fit what you're going for.

The first thing we need to talk about is how the screen responds to light. The material we created for our **Media Texture** uses the **Default Lit** shading model. What this means is that lights in the environment that fall on this material will affect it as they normally would. If the aesthetic effect you're going for is that this is a physical screen in the space, this may be exactly what you want, but if the purpose of your application is to show the media itself, you may not want any stray light falling on the screen and changing the way its colors appear to the viewer.

Let's take a look at what we're talking about. From your **Modes** panel, drag a Point Light onto the scene and put it right in front of your screen:

You'll see that the light creates a specular highlight on the screen, just as it would for any other surface in the scene. Things get worse if we turn off the rest of the lights in the scene. Now, parts of our screen are going dark, while others are obscured by the highlights from our remaining lights.

If this is how we want it, that's fine, but if it isn't, we can correct this by changing our material to use an unlit shading model and feeding the video signal into its emissive channel. Let's give it a try:

1. Open your media material.
2. With the output node selected, change the material's **Details** | **Material** | **Shading Model** from **Default Lit** to **Unlit**:

3. You'll see that its **Base Color** input becomes disabled. *Alt* + click that input to disconnect your **Texture Sample** from it.
4. Feed the results of your texture sample into the material's **Emissive Color** input instead.

Save the material and return to your scene. Now, because your material uses the **Unlit** model, it's no longer affected by lights in the world. The media appears exactly as it does in its source:

Adding additional controls to our video appearance

We can also use our material graph to exercise a lot of additional control over how the video signal appears. Let's take a look at this:

1. Return to your material.
2. Hold down the *S* key and click in the workspace to create a scalar parameter. Name it `Brightness` and set its default value to `1.0`.
3. Hold the *M* key and click to create a multiplier node.
4. Multiply your output of **Texture Sample** by the `Brightness` parameter you just made.
5. Hold the *S* key and click to create another scalar parameter. Name this one `Contrast` and leave its default at `0.0`.
6. Right-click in the graph and create a `CheapContrast_RGB` node.
7. Connect the result of the **Multiply** node to its **In (V3)** input, and feed your `Contrast` parameter into its **Contrast** input.
8. Feed the result into the material's **Emissive Color** input:

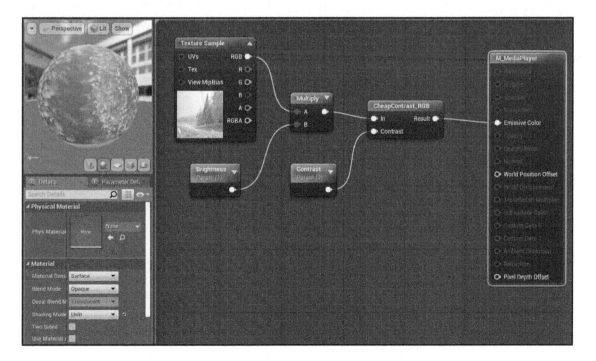

As you can see, we've now created a simple material that uses two scalar parameters to allow our user to control the image's brightness and contrast.

Let's create a material instance from this material so that we can see the effect of these parameters in real time:

1. Right-click your material in the Content Browser and select **Material Instance Actions | Create Material Instance**.
2. Drag the material instance onto your screen to assign it to the object.
3. Open the material instance and try changing the `Brightness` and `Contrast` values you just created. (Remember that you need to check the box beside a parameter to enable modification.)
4. Switch the material's preview mesh to a cube primitive so that you can see what you're doing more easily:

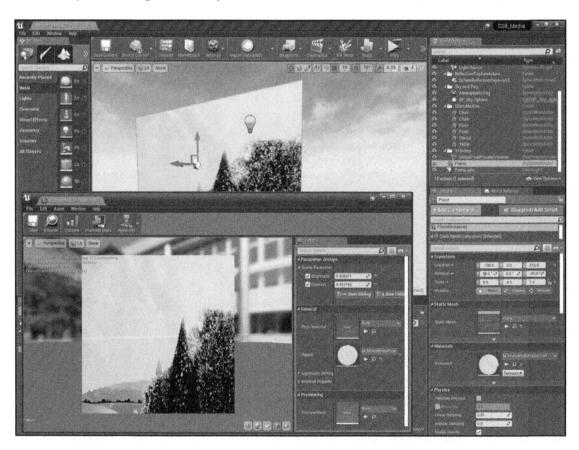

There's quite a lot we can do here, and we encourage you to explore and learn more about what you can do.

Now that you know the basics of playing video in Unreal Engine, let's start diving into some VR-specific work and learn how to display video in stereo 3D.

Displaying stereo video

Let's begin by creating another map to hold our stereo video screen. With your `MoviePlayback2D` scene open, hit **File | Save Current As...** and save the map as `MoviePlayback3D`.

Now, we need to find a stereo video file to test with. They're out there on the web, but they can be challenging to find since we need to download ours. stereomaker.net has a few example files here: `http://stereomaker.net/sample/`. Let's pull down the **Cycling in Hibaya Park** video from here. We can also find more example files here: `http://photocreations.ca/3D/index.html`. Download the **Bellagio Fountains, Las Vegas, Nevada** 3D 2048 x 2048 clip. This will give us a side-by-side stereo clip and an over/under stereo clip that we can use for our experiments. The Hibaya clip is wrapped in an `.AVI` container, but as long as we're running the clip on Windows, that will work. To run it on another platform, we'd have to use an application such as Adobe Media Encoder or AVC to convert it:

1. Place each of these files in your `Content/Movies` directory.
2. Create a **File Media Source** asset for each of your new video files. Again, it's often easier to use a name for the file media source that matches the movie clip on disk.

Now, open up your media player. You should see these new clips in its available file list, and you should be able to play them. You should see two frames side-by-side, representing the left and right stereo images (make sure you do this first test with a side-by-side stereo video – we'll handle over/under later on):

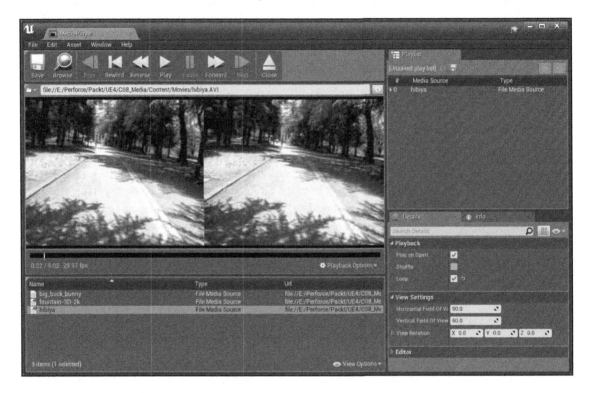

The trick now will be to interpret the side-by side or over/under images as stereo images and feed one frame to the left eye while we feed the other to the right.

We're going to handle that in our material. Specifically, what we want to do is modify the texture coordinates we feed to the texture's UV map.

A UV map determines the way a texture aligns itself on a mesh in a 3D space. By manipulating the texture coordinates we're using to apply textures in our material, we can choose to display only parts of the texture at a time.

Open up your media player material.

Since we want this material to be able to handle mono video sources as well, we're going to use a Static Switch Parameter to switch between mono and stereo modes. This will allow us to use this material as a master material but set up individual material instances that handle whatever specific settings we want.

> Static Switch Parameters are valuable tools that you can use to build a lot of behavior into a master material, and derive material instances from it that handle specific cases. As an added benefit, when those materials are compiled, anything that's turned off by your static switches simply doesn't even compile into the material instance, so you get it essentially for free. What this means is that you can make fairly complex master materials and only pay for the parts you use by using static switches to turn off functionality that you're not using.

Let's add a switch to our material so that we can create a stereo path without messing up our mono display:

1. Right-click in the material editing graph and create a **Static Switch Parameter**. Name it `SplitStereoMedia`.
2. Right-click and create a **Texture Coordinate** node, and feed its output into the switch parameter's False input. This will display in the graph as a **TexCoord** node.

Now, it's time to split the image. When images are rendered to the VR headset, they're rendered in two separate passes, and we can use this information to determine which side of the image to display.

Displaying half of the video

To split the image, we first need to get access to the two separate axes of our texture coordinates so that we can manipulate them individually:

1. Drag the output from the **Texture Coordinate** input and create a **BreakOutFloat2Components** node from it.
2. Hold down the *M* key and click to create a **Multiply** node.
3. Connect the Break node's **R** output to the **Multiply** node's **A** input and set its **Const B** parameter to 0.5.

4. Create an **Append Vector** node and connect the multiplier's output to the **A** input, and the **G** output from the Break node to its **B** input.

5. Feed the result of the **Append** node into the Split Stereo Media switch's **True** input.

6. Feed the result of the **Switch** node into the **UVs** input of **Texture Sample**:

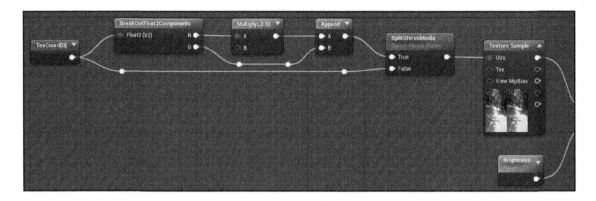

What we've just done here is split our texture coordinates into two channels, labeled **R** and **G**. We then cut the **R** channel in half while leaving the **G** channel alone, and then reassembled the vector and told our texture sample to use the result to map the image to the object it's applied to.

Let's test this to see what it does:

1. Open your scene's **Level Blueprint**. It should still contain the **Open Source** call to the Media Player.

2. Switch its **Media Source** to your side-by-side video. Since we need a place to set our Static Switch parameter, we need a new material instance to display our side-by-side image.

3. Duplicate the material instance we made a moment ago when we adjusted our contrast and brightness.

4. Name this one `MI_MediaPlayer_SBS` or something similar to remind us that it's intended to display side-by-side stereo media.

5. Open it up and set its **SplitStereoMedia** switch parameter to true.

6. Assign it to your screen object.

Test it out. You should now see only the video's left frame displayed on the screen. You won't see any stereo depth yet since we're still displaying the same image to each eye.

Displaying a different half of the video to each eye

Now, let's get the right frame to display in the right eye:

1. Return to your material.
2. Right-click in the material graph and create a **Custom** node.
3. In its **Code** property, enter the following: `return ResolvedView.StereoPassIndex;`.
4. Set its **Output Type** to **CMOT Float 1**.
5. Set its **Description** to **StereoPassIndex**.

   This creates a **Material Expression Custom** node that will return a 0 when we're rendering the left eye, and a 1 when we're rendering the right eye. We can use this information to choose which half of the frame we display for each eye.

6. Hold down the *M* key and click to create a **Multiply** node.
7. Pass the output from **StereoPassIndex** into its **A** input, and set its **Const B** parameter to 0.5:

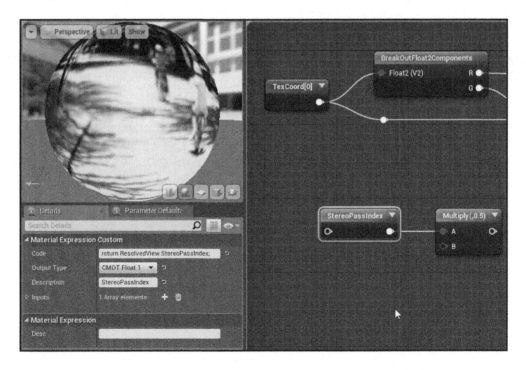

8. Now, hold down the *A* key and click to create an **Add** node.
9. Feed the result of the multiplied **R** channel from the texture coordinates into its **A** input.
10. Feed the result of the multiplied stereo pass index into its **B** input.
11. Feed the result of the **Add** node into the **Append** node's **A** input:

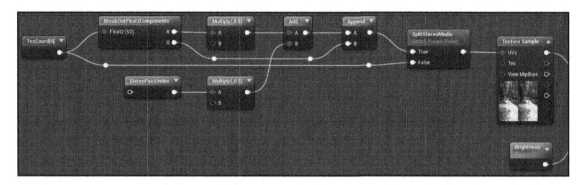

Test it again. You should now see stereo depth in the video image when you view it in your VR headset.

Let's take a moment to make sense of what we just created here.

When we break our texture coordinates and modify the **R** value, we're modifying the horizontal axis of the texture mapping. By multiplying it by 0.5, we're splashing half of the texture over the entire surface of the mesh. The Stereo Pass Index node we made returns a value of 0 for the left stereo pass, and 1 for the right stereo pass, so when we multiply this value by 0.5, we get either a 0 for the left eye or an 0.5 for the right eye. When we then add this value to our texture coordinate's **R** component, we're offsetting it by half its width. So, when the left eye is rendered, it simply divides the texture space in half, and when the right eye is rendered, it divides it in half and offsets it by half, displaying the right frame. This is how we're getting our stereo image.

Displaying over/under stereo video

Modifying our material to handle over/under stereo video is fairly easy. We just need to do our operation on the **G** channel instead of the **R** channel. Follow these steps to get started:

1. Reopen your media player material.
2. Create a new **Static Switch Parameter** node. Name it `OverUnderStereo`.
3. *Ctrl* + drag the **SplitStereoMedia** switch's **True** input to move it into the **OverUnderStereo** switch's **False** input.
4. Connect the output from the **OverUnderStereo** switch to the **SplitStereoMedia** switch's **True** input:

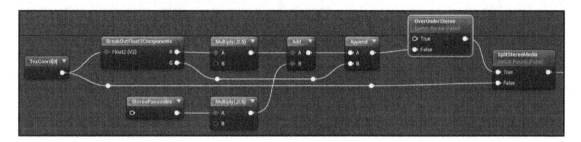

> If **OverUnderStereo** is set to False, our material continues to use the side-by-side split we set up a moment ago. Now, let's set up its behavior when this is set to True.

5. Select the chain of nodes that includes the **BreakOutFloat2Components** node, all the way to the **Append** node, and hit *Ctrl* + *W* to duplicate them.
6. Connect the **R** output from the BreakOut node directly to the **Append** node's **A** input.
7. Connect the **G** output from the BreakOut node to the **Multiply** node's **A** input.
8. Connect the output from the **Add** node to the **Append** node's **B** input.

> We've just swapped things, so we're now performing the same operation on the vertical axis as we'd previously performed on the horizontal axis.

9. Feed the output of the **Multiply** node from your Stereo Pass Index into the new **Add** node's **B** input.
10. Feed the **Texture Coordinates** into your BreakOut node's input.

11. Feed the output of the **Append** node into your **OverUnderStereo** switch's **True** input:

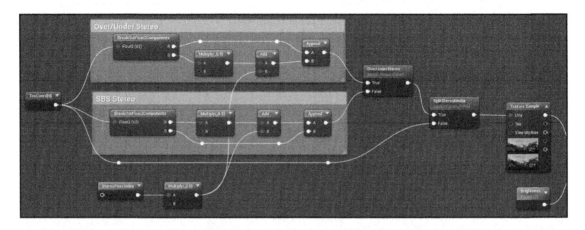

This material can now handle mono, side-by-side stereo, and over/under stereo sources.

Now, let's test this out:

1. Close your material and in your **Content Browser**, duplicate one of the material instances you've already made from it.
2. Ensure that its **SplitStereoMedia** parameter is set to **True**, and set its **OverUnderStereo** parameter to **True**.
3. Assign it to your screen object in your scene.
4. Open your scene's Level Blueprint and switch the Media Source on your Open Source node to your over/under stereo video.

Launch it into VR preview mode. We should now see our over/under stereo video playing correctly.

Displaying 360 degree spherical media in VR

So far, we've done a decent job of reproducing 2D and 3D traditional screens in VR, but let's take things a step further and do something we can't easily do in the outside world. One of the most compelling and common uses of VR is to display immersive 360 degree video that surrounds the viewer. Even in mono, this can create a fairly deep sense of presence in users, and can be produced fairly easily using an ordinary camera and stitching software, or a dedicated camera that's been purpose-built to create spherical images.

Displaying spherical media, for the most part, works exactly as it does on the flat screen, but of course we'll need new geometry for our screen.

Finding 360 degree video

First, let's find a video to play. A few good options live here: `https://www.mettle.com/360vr-master-series-free-360-downloads-page/`.

The Crystal Shower Falls link takes us to a Vimeo page that allows us to download the video. For our test here, the 1080p version should be fine:

1. Download the video and place it in your `Content/Movies` directory.
2. Create a **File Media Source** for your video.
3. Check it in your **Media Player** to be sure it plays.

   Now, we need an environment to display it.

4. Create a new empty level and name it `MoviePlayback2DSpherical` (or anything you like, really – it's your map).

Creating a spherical movie screen

Now, we're going to take an ordinary sphere and modify it to flip its normals inward so that we can see our material while we're inside the sphere:

1. From your **Modes** panel, grab a **Basic | Sphere** actor and place it in your scene.
2. Look at its **Details** panel, and under **Static Mesh**, hit the **Browse to Asset** button (the magnifier) to navigate the **Content Browser** to the sphere's static mesh. We're going to make a copy of it.
3. Drag the Sphere static mesh from `Engine Content/BasicShapes` into your project's `Content` directory (`Content/Chapter08/Environments` would be a good choice). Select **Copy Here** to make a copy of the sphere.
4. Rename it `MovieSphere`.
5. Open it up.
6. From your **Static Mesh** editor, select the **Mesh Editing** tab.
7. Activate **Edit Mode** by hitting the toolbar button.
8. Drag to select all of the mesh's faces.

9. Hit the **Flip** button to invert their normals:

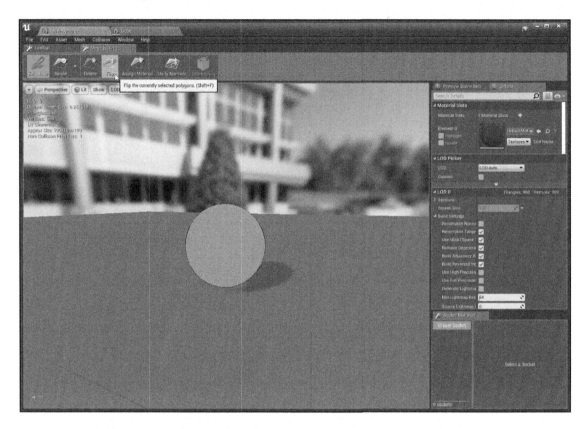

10. Save it and close the Static Mesh editor.
11. Place an instance of your MovieSphere mesh in your level and delete the old Sphere.
12. Set its **Location** to (X=0.0, Y=0.0, Z=0.0) and its **Scale** to (X=200.0, Y=200.0, Z=200.0).
13. With the MovieSphere selected, set its **Materials_Element** 0 to your **MI_MediaPlayer_Mono** material instance.
14. Hit **Add Component**, add a **MediaSound** component, and set its associated **Media Player** to your media player.

Now, just as we did with our previous scenes, we need to tell the media player to load our media.

15. In your map's **Level Blueprint**, create a variable named `MediaPlayer`, set its **Type** to **Media Player | Object Reference**, compile it, and set its **Default Value** to your Media Player.
16. Call **Open Source** on your Media Player variable with your new 360 video as its **Media Source**.
17. Execute this call from your **Event BeginPlay**.

Test your scene. You should now see the movie playing all around you.

Playing stereoscopic 360 degree video

Now, we're going to do the same thing for stereoscopic 360 degree video. At the time of writing, stereoscopic 360 degree video is much less common than its 2D counterpart, in part because it consumes so much more disk space, and also because it's significantly more difficult to produce, but it's reasonable to expect that things will continue to evolve.

In the meantime, we can find a viable test file here: `https://www.dareful.com/products/` `free-virtual-reality-video-sequoia-national-park-vr-360-stereoscopic`.

As always, download the file, put it in your **Content/Movies** directory, create a **File Media Source** asset that points to it, and test it in your Media Player to ensure that it plays on your system.

Next, let's make a copy of our 2D spherical test map to use for our 3D test:

1. Take the **MoviePlayback2DSpherical** map and hit **File | Save Current As...** to **MoviePlayback3DSpherical**.
2. Select the **MovieSphere** asset and change its assigned material to your **OverUnder** material instance.
3. Open the level blueprint and change the **Open Source** node to point to our new file.

Let's test it. We have spherical 3D, but our stereo is flipped (on this file, at least). Everything that should be close looks far away. We can correct this by adding another option to our master material:

1. Open your media master material.
2. Add a new **Static Switch Parameter** and name it **FlipStereo**.
3. Drag the output from your **StereoPassIndex** node into the **FlipStereo** switch's **False** input.

4. Create a **OneMinus** node, drag the output from **StereoPassIndex** into its input, and connect its output to the **FlipStereo** switch's **True** input.

5. Connect the **FlipStereo** switch's output to the **Multiply** node:

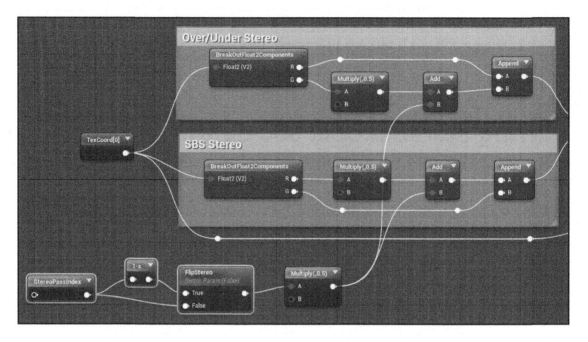

What we've done here is simply set up an option so that if FlipStereo is true, we'll receive a 1 for the left eye and a 0 for the right eye instead of the other way around.

Now, let's create another material instance to hold this option setting and apply it to our sphere:

1. Duplicate your **OverUnder** material instance and name it something like **MI_MediaPlayer_OverUnderFlipped**.

2. Open up the new material instance and set its **FlipStereo** parameter to **True**.

3. Apply it to your movie sphere:

Test the map – you should now be seeing the stereo imagery sorted correctly.

Spend some time looking around. This video runs at a fairly high bitrate, so you may experience occasional frame drops and there are a few perspective glitches, but the stereo effect is pretty compelling. It's clear that we're going to be able to do some astonishing work as this tech evolves.

Controlling your Media Player

Before we wrap things up for this chapter, let's give our players a few ways to control their Media Player.

We could do this work from within the level blueprint, and that's what we've been doing so far, but that's not an ideal solution if we're going to have multiple maps in our project. We're going to wind up copying and pasting Blueprint code from one level to another, and if we update one of them, we have to remember to update the rest. This is bad practice.

A much better idea is to create a manager actor that contains all the code we need to manage our media player, and that we can just drop into any level that needs to support it. This way, we're writing our code once, and as we update it, the effects are seen everywhere. Let's do this.

Creating a Media Manager

Let's create a new Blueprints subdirectory inside our project's content directory:

1. Right-click inside it and select **Create Basic Asset** | **Blueprint Class.**
2. For its **Parent Class**, select **Actor.**
3. Name it BP_MediaManager.

Up until this point, we've been using our level blueprints to open media on our media player. We're going to move that functionality into our media manager first:

1. Open up **BP_MediaManager.**
2. Create a new variable named MediaPlayer and set its **Type** to **Media Player** | **Object Reference**.
3. Compile it and set its default value to your media player.
4. Create another new variable named FileMediaSource and set its **Type** to **File Media Source** | **Object Reference**.
5. Set **Instance Editable** to **True** for this variable since we're going to need to set different values on it for each map.
6. Set its **Category** to **Config** so that it's clear to the user that they have to edit this value.

Now that we've set up our variables, let's use this actor's BeginPlay to load our media. To start with, we're just going to recreate what we've already been doing in our level Blueprints:

1. Open the Event Graph of **BP_MediaManager.**
2. *Ctrl* + drag the MediaPlayer variable onto the graph.
3. Call **Open Source** on it.
4. *Ctrl* + drag your File Media Source variable onto the graph.
5. Right-click it and select **Convert to Validated Get**. (We don't want to try and open a file media source if we haven't set it yet.)
6. Drag the execution line from **Event BeginPlay** into your File Media Source **Get**.

7. Drag the getter's **Is Valid** execution line into your **Open Source** call's execution input.

8. Drag the output of **GET** into your **Open Source** call's **Media Source** input.

9. Right-click and create a **Print String** node.

10. Set its **In String** value to **Media Manager's file media source is not set!**.

11. Drag the **Is Not Valid** execution line of **GET** to the **Print String** we just created:

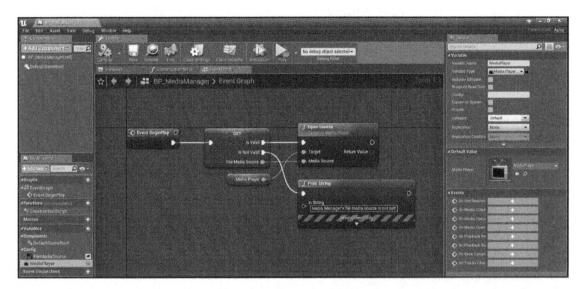

Now, if we place this actor in any level and set its File Media Source, it will start playing that source on the project's **Media Player**. If there's an object in that level with a material reading a Media Texture that points to this media player, whatever we're playing will show up there.

Whenever you set up a system that could fail if the developer or user fails to do something, as is the case here with our File Media Source variable, get in the habit of using validated gets and printing out warnings if the get fails. You'll save yourself a lot of debugging time if you train yourself to write code that tells you on its own when something is wrong.

Now, let's put a Media Manager in our current level and replace the work we're doing in the Level Blueprint:

1. Drag an instance of **BP_MediaManager** into your scene and zero out its **Location**.
2. Set its **Config | File Media Source** to whichever media source you were previously playing in the scene.
3. Open the scene's Level Blueprint and delete the code we previously put there on BeginPlay.
4. Test the scene. The media should still play, but now the Media Manager is handling opening the source.

Repeat this for your other test levels so that they're all using the Media Manager blueprint.

Now that each of our levels is using an instance of our Media Manager class to operate the Media Player, we can much more easily add functionality that will apply everywhere.

Let's do this now.

Adding a Pause and Resume function

Let's give our users a way to pause and play the video:

1. Open **BP_MediaManager**.
2. In its **Details** panel, set **Input | Auto Receive Input** to **Player 0** and **Block Input** to True.
3. Right-click in its **Event Graph** and select **Input | Keyboard Events | Space Bar** to create a new keyboard event.
4. Right-click again and select **Input | Gamepad Events | MotionController (R) Trigger** to create another input event.
5. *Ctrl* + drag your media player variable onto your graph.
6. Drag its output and create an **Is Playing** node.
7. Connect a **Branch** node to the **Is Playing** node's result.
8. Connect the **Pressed** execution line of **Space Bar** to the **Branch** node's execution input. Do the same for the **Trigger** input.
9. Drag another connector from your Media Player variable and create a **Pause** node for it.
10. Connect your **Branch** node's **True** execution line to the **Pause** node's execution input.

11. Drag another connector from the Media Player variable (or create a reroute node and branch from it) and create a **Play** call.

12. Connect the **Branch** node's **False** execution line to the **Play** node:

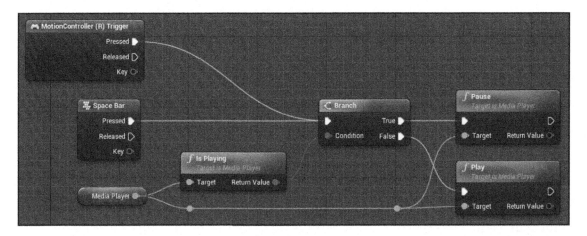

We've done a few things here that are worth talking about.

First, we're using a different means of capturing keyboard and motion controller input than we previously have. For everything we've done up until now, we've relied on the Project Settings and the `DefaultInput.ini` file to capture input from our hardware devices and remap it to named input events. In truth, this remains a better way to do it, but we wanted to show you another way it could be done. Very often, it can make sense to prototype your systems using input events mapped directly in your Blueprints like this one, and then once you've got your systems worked out, move them into your Project Settings so it's easier to remap them for different controllers.

It's important to note as well that this object is only able to hear input because we set its Auto Receive Input. Otherwise, it won't listen for input from other devices by default.

What we're doing here is querying the Media Player to see whether it's playing anything at present, pausing it if it is, and playing it if it isn't.

While we're not going to cover it here because it would become a project on its own, if you wanted to create a button-based user interface and use a widget interaction component to allow the user to interact with the controls, you could do so by having this Media Manager object own the interface and using the button events to manage the media player's behavior.

This is a fairly simple example, but it demonstrates a few ways you can interact with a media player. You can query its status, control playback, open new media, and even assign events to it so that it responds when it finishes loading media.

Assigning events to a media player

Let's demonstrate a way we can use an event on our media player. We're going to turn off our Media Player's **Play on Open** setting, and instead have our Media Manager play a file once it's finished opening. This is an important pattern to learn because large media files won't be ready to play immediately after you call Open Source. Depending on how big they are and how fast the hard drive they're stored on is, they're going to take a moment to open, so it's good practice after you open a file to instruct your media player to listen for when the file finishes loading, and to start playing it then.

In practice, the Play on Open setting already does this, but it's valuable for you to learn about this pattern so that you can use it when you need to do something more complex with your media player.

Let's set it up:

1. Open your media player asset and turn off its **Play on Open** setting.

    If you test one of your maps now, you'll see that the media no longer plays until you tap the *spacebar* or pull the trigger to start it.

2. Open **BP_MediaManager** and find the **Open Source** call you're making on **Event BeginPlay**.
3. Connect a **Branch** node to its **Return Value**.

    The Open Source call is going to return True if it found the file to open and is will opening it, and False if it couldn't. We only want our Media Player to wait for the file to open if we know it's actually opening it.

4. Drag a connector from your Media Player variable and select **Media | Media Player | Bind Event to OnMediaOpened**.
5. Drag a connector from the Bind node's **Event** input and select **Add Event | Add Custom Event**.
6. Name it `MediaOpened`.
7. Drag a connector from your Media Player variable and call **Play** on it.

8. Connect the execution output from your custom event to the **Play** call's input:

Test it. Your media should play when it finishes opening. In practice, it will behave exactly as it did when Play on Open was still true, but there's some important stuff to talk about here.

Most function calls will continue their execution only when they've finished whatever job it was they were supposed to do. **Open Source** is a little different. This is what's known as an **Async Task**. When you call **Open Source**, the execution will continue immediately, but the task itself will take an indeterminate amount of time to finish. You'll run into this a lot when opening large files, accessing URLs on the web, or doing any other task where you really don't know when you begin how long it's actually going to take. An **asynchronous** (**Async**) task starts up when you call it, and then finishes at some point in the future. The object that you call an Async task on is pretty much always going to have some sort of event it throws when the task finishes so that you can do whatever you need to do when it's done.

In the case of the **Open Source** task on a **Media Player** object, the **OnMediaOpened** event is called when the source finishes opening. By binding a custom event to this event, we're telling it to trigger that event in our blueprint when the media finishes opening, and call the `Play` method on the media player when this happens.

> When creating custom events for bindings, it's a good idea to create them by dragging out the event connector and creating the custom event from there, as we did in this example. This is because many bindings will require that their bound events include certain inputs (this is called a signature), and if you just create a basic custom event that doesn't match the required signature, it won't let you bind it. If you create your custom events directly from the event connector, it will automatically set up the correct signature for you. In this case, the bound event for **OnMediaOpened** is required to pass an Opened URL argument.

This is an important pattern and it's worth learning. Video files are big, and sometimes operations on them are going to take time. Get to know the events you can bind on your media player objects, and make sure you're doing whatever it is you're trying to do once you know the job has finished and succeeded.

> You will, at some point in your travels, come across a developer who handles asynchronous tasks by putting delays into their blueprints. They will discover through trial and error that the call they're trying to make works if they delay it and fails if they try to do it immediately, so they just stick a delay on there with some random duration and call the bug fixed. You, however, are not going to do this. It's amateur hour stuff, and will just fail later on if they try to open a larger file or something else changes. The correct way to deal with async tasks is always to find out what event gets called when they finish, and then bind whatever else you need to do to that event. Never use a delay to solve a problem unless you can describe in positive terms why you know the delay is the correct solution. The correct solution is almost always a bound event that will work no matter how long the task takes.

You've now seen examples of each of the ways you can interact with a media player object. We've polled its status, made calls to it, and bound additional code to its events so that we can respond when the media player tells us something has happened. There's more you can do with media players, and we encourage you to play with this. Try binding an event to its **OnEndReached**, or some other bindable event. Try using Get Time and Duration calls on the Media Player to create a progress bar. There's a lot you can do with this.

Summary

In this chapter, we learned a lot about how video files play in Unreal Engine. We learned a bit about containers and codecs and how to understand what a video file contains, and then we learned a variety of ways to play them back, both on flat screens and on spheres. We learned how we can create materials to display 3D video as well as 2D, and learned how to create a media manager class to manage their playback.

In the next chapter, we're going to learn about how multiplayer networking works in Unreal.

10
Creating a Multiplayer Experience in VR

In this chapter, we're going to move into some more advanced territory. Multiplayer software is significantly more complicated to write than single-player applications. There's no way around the reality that to write successful multiplayer code, you have to build a clear mental model of what's going on and how your data is getting from one computer to the other. The good news is that's what we're here to do. We're going to be dropping a lot more theory in this chapter than we usually do, and the reason for this is that if we simply walked you through the steps of setting up a networked application, that's really not going to help you. You have to understand how networking works to understand how you need to build your application. But don't worry—we'll try to alternate between theory and practical examples so you can build a hands-on understanding of how this stuff works.

We also need to be clear that networking is a big topic and it's fairly advanced. We're not going to have space in this chapter to go over every dark corner of the art, but we'll consider it a success if you finish this chapter with a good understanding of how networked applications fit together, what the major parts are, and how information most commonly moves around. If you come away with this understanding in a reasonably clear state, you'll be set up well to understand what you're seeing as you learn more about this topic.

In this chapter, we're going to learn to do the following:

- Work with Unreal's client-server model to ensure that important gameplay events happen on the server
- Replicate actors from the server to connected clients
- Replicate variables and call functions automatically when their values change
- Create a pawn that looks more different to the owning player than it does to other players
- Use remote procedure calls to call events on remote machines

Let's jump in!

Testing multiplayer sessions

Before we get into the weeds talking about how networking works, let's learn how to launch a multiplayer session. There are a number of ways you can do this. The easiest is to launch the multiplayer session directly from within your editor, and most of the time when you're testing network replication, this is going to be fine. For more comprehensive tests, or if you need one of the sessions to run in VR, you can launch two separate game sessions and connect them to each other. We'll show examples of how to do this a little later on when we discuss session types.

Testing multiplayer from the editor

Fortunately, the Unreal editor makes it fairly easy to set up a multiplayer session from within the editor on a single machine. To perform this test, we're going to use the **Content Examples** project:

If you haven't already downloaded the Content Examples project, do so now by selecting **Content Examples** | **Create Project** from the **Unreal Engine** | **Learn** tab in your Epic Games Launcher. You should get into the habit of always keeping a current version of Content Examples installed on your system and using it for reference.

1. Open the Content Examples project and open the **Network_Features** level.

2. Select the dropdown beside your toolbar's **Play** button and set the **Multiplayer Options** | **Number of Players** to **2**. Refer to the following screenshot:

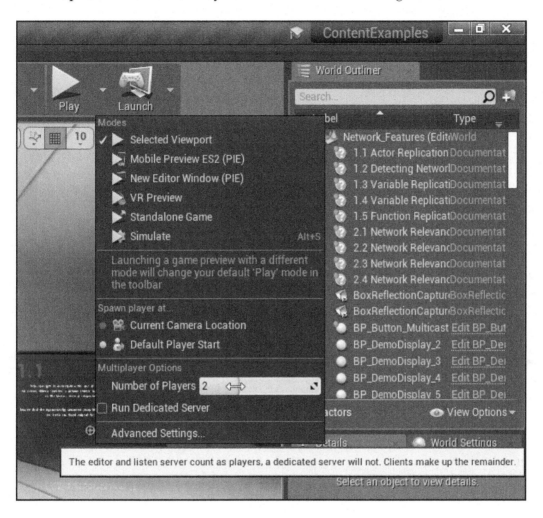

3. Select **New Editor Window (PIE)** to launch a multiplayer session as shown in the following screenshot (unfortunately, we can't use the multiplayer options to support a multiplayer VR session on a single machine):

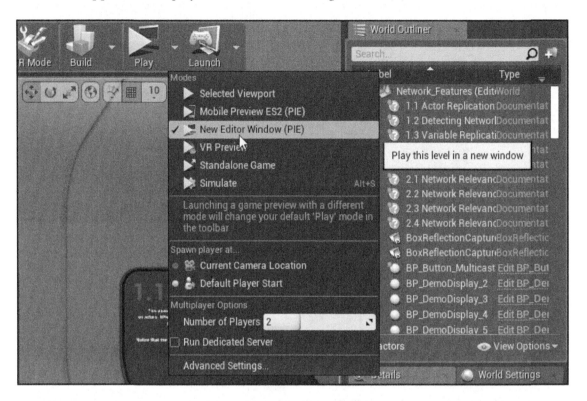

Explore the scene playing as both server and client. Notice the differences between what appears on the server and what appears on the client. We're going to look at these things in greater depth shortly:

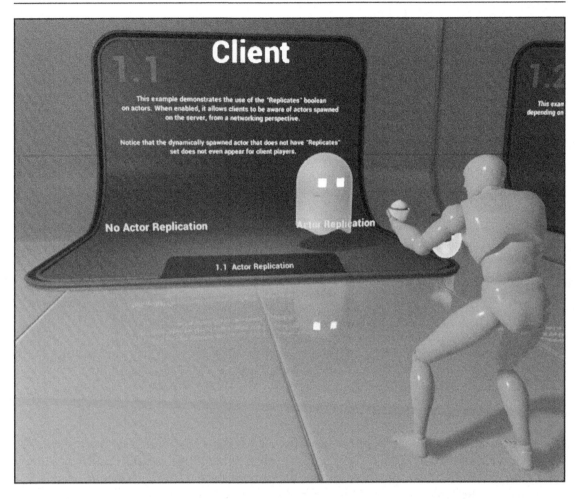

In this example, the ghost on the left is visible on the server but not on the client because it has not been set to replicate to clients.

Take some time to understand what each of these displays is telling you in the context of what we've described so far, but don't worry if some things are still fuzzy—we're going to make more use of these ideas in our upcoming exercises.

For additional information about multiplayer-testing options in-editor, refer to the documentation here: `https://docs.unrealengine.com/en-us/Gameplay/HowTo/Networking/TestMultiplayer`.

Understanding the client-server model

Now that we have a running test we can play with, let's get a bit of theory out of the way. It wouldn't be a bad idea to leave this test level open and explore it while we talk about this next concept.

To understand how multiplayer gameplay works in Unreal, you first need to understand how information moves between the connected game sessions and how changes are made to the game environment. There's no way around this. To write multiplayer code successfully, you have to build a clear mental model of what's going on, or you'll wind up hitting a lot of walls. Multiplayer is challenging to debug—if something doesn't work, you can't simply set a breakpoint in your blueprint and trace through to see what happened. Very often, all you'll know is that a bit of information you thought should have gone to the other machine never got there. If you take the time to understand how networking works, you'll have a much easier time figuring out what's gone wrong when something doesn't work as you expected it to. Multiplayer is absolutely not something you can debug by stabbing in the dark.

So, let's learn how networking in Unreal works.

To begin thinking about this, let's imagine a scenario. Let's say you've created a multiplayer shooter, and two players have joined a session and are both playing. One of the players aims and fires, and now we need to show both players what happened.

Sounds simple enough at first, but it isn't.

Player A is aiming, but this is happening on player A's game instance. How does player B's game instance know where player A is at all, let alone where they're aiming? Player A fires. How does player B's game instance find out that this happened? Now, someone needs to figure out whether player A's shot hit player B's avatar. Who figures out whether the shot hit? What if player B is on a slow network connection and the information about where player A was aiming hasn't gotten there yet? If both game instances were allowed to decide whether the shot hit, they wouldn't agree. Whose opinion would win?

The answer to the first question—how does player B's game instance know about player A's movements and actions—is handled through a process called **replication**. When player A moves, their avatar's movement is **replicated** to player B's game instance, and when player B moves, their movement is replicated to player A's game instance.

The answer to the last question—who decides whether the shot hit—is handled by the **server**, and it's worth taking some time to understand this.

Unreal Engine uses a **client-server** model of network management. What this means is that only one of the game instances connected to a game session is actually allowed to make important decisions about what's really happening. The server is **authoritative**, and the clients are not. If the server and a client come to two different conclusions about a thing that just happened, the server's opinion is the one that gets used.

In a **peer-to-peer** model, everybody would be equal. Peer-to-peer network architectures are relatively easy to set up, but they come at a high cost: when one of the connected peers gets out of sync with the other, nobody knows which one's state is actually true. That may be fine for a demo or a class project but would be absolutely unacceptable in an environment where players actually cared about the outcomes. We need to know without question what the actual state of the game and all its players is, and the client-server model gives us a reliable way to do this.

Here's what actually happens:

1. Player A moves, and their movement is replicated to the server, which replicates their movement to all the other connected game instances.
2. Player B and any other connected players see a **proxy** in their game sessions, which shows them where the server says player A's avatar is.
3. When player A aims and fires, player A's client actually sends a request to the server telling it that it wants to fire, and the server makes the actual determination of whether it can.
4. If the server determines that player A has ammo, is in the right state, or whatever the game rules specify, it fires the weapon and tells all the connected game instances that it did.
5. The server has also been receiving player B's replicated movement, so it has the information it needs to figure out whether player A's shot hit.
6. If it determines that it did, it decreases player B's health or does whatever it needs to do to respond to this event and tells all the connected clients that player B was hit.

7. Each client then updates its local state information, plays hit animations and effects, and updates its UI:

The top panel represents the server's view, while the bottom panel is the client's view. Lines have been added to indicate objects whose states can change and need to be replicated to clients.

Unreal's network architecture is astonishingly efficient, which is why a game such as *Fortnite* can run in real-time even when a large number of players are simultaneously connected. There are a number of reasons for this, and many of them are under your control as a developer. We'll cover a few of the important ones in depth later on in the chapter.

Now, let's take a closer look at a few important concepts.

The server

The term **server** refers to the **network authority** in a multiplayer environment. You'll hear these terms used interchangeably. Technical documentation will tend to use the term *network authority*, as that describes more precisely what it really is, while most of the other material you read will call it the *server*. Both refer to the same thing.

 A great deal of the time, when something goes wrong in your networked application, it's going to be because you allowed a client to try to change the game state when instead it needed to ask the network authority to make the change.

The architecture works like this: the server *hosts* the game and allows multiple clients to connect to it and communicate data back and forth. Communication happens between clients and the server, and clients almost never communicate directly with one another:

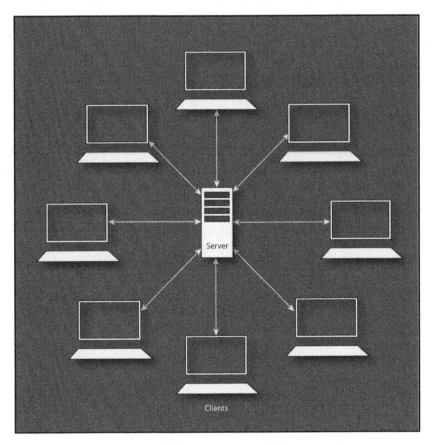

When a player performs an action, information about what the player is doing or wants to do is sent from that player's client to the server. The server validates this information and responds, telling the connected clients what it decided.

If, for example, you move your player avatar in a multiplayer game, you're not really moving your avatar locally at all. Instead, your client will tell the server that you want to move, and the server will then determine how you've moved and replicate your new position back to your client and to the other connected clients.

This is true for seemingly-direct messages between clients as well. If you send a chat message to another client, you're actually sending it to the server, and then the server decides which client or group of clients should receive it.

The server, as we mentioned previously, is the network authority responsible for maintaining the actual **authoritative state** of the multiplayer session. This idea of **authority** is one of the most important concepts to grok about networking and you're going to see when we get to the practical examples that we check for authority with almost everything we do. If you keep clear in your mind who should be allowed to make a change and you check to make sure that any change really is being made by the entity allowed to make it, you'll be ahead of the game.

A good rule of thumb to follow is this: if any other player would care about this change, it belongs on the server. If nobody else would care, do it locally. So, if you're playing a visual effect that doesn't matter to the game, don't bother running it on the server, but if you're changing a player's health or moving them around, do that on the server, since everybody else is going to need to agree on it.

In addition to ensuring that there's only one description at a time of anything important to the game, there's another reason why it's important to maintain a single network authority, and that is to ensure that a player can't easily cheat by modifying their client. When important decisions are left to the server, the server can fairly easily override results on a hacked client. If the player wants to fire a weapon, make sure their client tells the server about it, and let the server decide whether they have enough ammo and are allowed to take the shot. Never process an important gameplay event directly on the client. Only let them happen once the server allows it. Never trust the client.

Listen servers, dedicated dervers, and clients

There are three fundamental types of game session that can be running in an Unreal networked environment: two types of servers and one client type.

Listen servers

When you run a **listen server**, your machine is acting as the host for the game session and as the authority over that game session, but it is also running a client. If you've ever set up a networked game in Unreal, it may have looked as though you were running a peer-to-peer session, but this is what was really going on. The listen server is pretty much invisible to the local player—it doesn't look like a separate running process, but it actually is separate from the local client exactly as it would be if it were on another machine.

The following command-line arguments will launch a listen server using uncooked editor data:

```
UE4Editor.exe ProjectName MapName?Listen -game
```

Often, your easiest way to use these commands will be to create shortcuts containing the arguments, or to write a simple .bat file.

The following .bat file will launch a listen server using the Content Examples project's **Network_Features** map:

```
set editor_executable="C:\Program Files\Epic
Games\UE_4.21\Engine\Binaries\Win64\UE4Editor.exe"
set
project_path="D:\Reference\UE4_Examples\ContentExamples\ContentExamples.upr
oject"
set map_name="Network_Features"

%editor_executable% %project_path% %map_name%?listen -game -log -WINDOWED -
ResX=1280 -ResY=720 -WinX=32 -WinY=32 -ConsoleX=32 -ConsoleY=752
```

In this example, we're setting variables for our executable location, project path, and map name just to make the file easier to read and edit. We're also turning on the log and setting the window sizes and locations explicitly to make it easier to see what's going on and fit other sessions on the screen.

Dedicated servers

A **dedicated server** does not have a client running in the same session. It doesn't accept input or render output, and because of this it can be optimized to run less expensively than a listen server. Because dedicated servers are so much smaller than full game clients since they don't need to include anything that's going to be rendered to the player, you can fit many of them on a single machine for hosting. Your existing game executable can be told to run itself as a dedicated server, or developers have the option to compile a separate executable for dedicated servers, which can further deter cheating and can make the executable's footprint on the disk much smaller.

This command will launch a dedicated server using editor data:

```
UE4Editor.exe ProjectName MapName -server -game -log
```

Note that we've chosen to turn on the log for this session. This is because dedicated servers don't open a rendering window, so a visible log becomes essential for knowing what it's doing.

We could modify the preceding `.bat` file to launch a dedicated server:

```
set editor_executable="C:\Program Files\Epic
Games\UE_4.21\Engine\Binaries\Win64\UE4Editor.exe"
set
project_path="D:\Reference\UE4_Examples\ContentExamples\ContentExamples.upr
oject"
set map_name="Network_Features"

%editor_executable% %project_path% %map_name% -server -game -log
```

In this example, we replaced the `?listen` directive with a `-server` argument, and of course we didn't need any of the window placement specifications, since a dedicated server won't open a game window.

Clients

A **client** is the point of contact between a networked application and the player. The client may be running on the same system as the server if we're using a listen server, or it may stand entirely on its own if it's connected to a remote host or to a dedicated server. The client is responsible for accepting input from the player, communicating that input to the server via **remote procedure calls** (RPC), and receiving new information about the gamestate from the server via replication.

The following command will launch a client:

```
UE4Editor.exe ProjectName ServerIP -game
```

Note that in the preceding example, `ServerIP` is the IP address of the server to which you're trying to connect. If you're connecting to a server running on your own machine for testing, the default home address of `127.0.0.1` will connect to a server running on the local machine.

This `.bat` file will launch a client that connects to a server running on the same machine:

```
set editor_executable="C:\Program Files\Epic
Games\UE_4.21\Engine\Binaries\Win64\UE4Editor.exe"
set
project_path="D:\Reference\UE4_Examples\ContentExamples\ContentExamples.upr
oject"

%editor_executable% %project_path% -game 127.0.0.1 -log -WINDOWED -
ResX=1280 -ResY=720 -WinX=1632 -WinY=32 -ConsoleX=1632 -ConsoleY=752
```

Again, the `-log` and window size arguments are entirely optional—it just makes it easier to test multiplayer sessions if you set up your shortcuts to place your windows out of each other's way when they start up.

Now that we've done a bit of preliminary experimentation and talked about a few fundamental ideas, let's set up our own test project so we can perform our own experiments.

Testing multiplayer VR

To test multiplayer in VR, you're generally going to need two separate PCs on the network. It is sometimes possible to test multiplayer VR on a single machine, but some VR headset drivers will automatically send a quit signal to a running 3D application when a second one starts up.

 As of Unreal 4.21, the HTC Vive plugin automatically shuts down an existing Unreal session if a second one starts up. (The code that does this lives in `FSteamVRHMD::OnStartGameFrame()`, but unfortunately there's no easy way for users of the installed binaries to change this behavior.) The Oculus HMD plugin does not automatically quit existing sessions, so if you're using an Oculus Rift, you'll likely be able to test multiplayer on a single machine, but if you're using a Vive, you'll need two PCs.

If you'd like to give it a shot, simply add the `-vr` keyword to any launch string.

A server launch string would look something like this:

```
%editor_executable% %project_path% %map_name%?listen -game -vr -log -
WINDOWED -ResX=1280 -ResY=720 -WinX=32 -WinY=32 -ConsoleX=32 -ConsoleY=752
```

And, a client launch string would look something like this:

```
%editor_executable% %project_path% -game -vr 127.0.0.1 -log -WINDOWED -
ResX=1280 -ResY=720 -WinX=1632 -WinY=32 -ConsoleX=1632 -ConsoleY=752
```

Of course, if you're trying to test on a single machine, only set one session to use VR at a time.

Because it's going to be impractical for many users to test multiplayer VR with a single machine, we're going to run through our multiplayer examples in 2D for the most part so you can learn the concepts in an environment that can reasonably support testing. We will, however, still go through certain specific things you'll need to do to make a player character's animations respond appropriately to headset and motion controller movements, so you'll exit this chapter with a good foundation from which to get started in multiplayer VR.

Setting up our own test project

As we did with our last chapter, we're going to start out simply by creating a clean project with the following settings:

1. **Blank** blueprint template
2. **Mobile/tablet** hardware target
3. **Scalable 3D or 2D** graphics target
4. **No Starter Content**

As usual, here's our project settings cheat sheet:

1. **Engine | Rendering | Forward Renderer | Forward Shading**: True
2. **Engine | Rendering | Default Settings | Ambient Occlusion Static Fraction**: False
3. **Engine | Rendering | Default Settings | Anti-Aliasing Method**: MSAA
4. **Engine | Rendering | VR | Instanced Stereo**: True
5. **Engine | Rendering | VR | Round Robin Occlusion Queries**: True

We're going to set one value differently, however, for this test because we're going to be working mostly in the flat screen to simplify learning this challenging topic:

- **Project** | **Description** | **Settings** | **Start in VR**: False

Allow the project to restart once all these settings have been set.

Adding an environment

Let's give ourselves some environment assets to play with so we're not stuck looking at an empty level.

Open your Epic Games Launcher and find the **Infinity Blade: Ice Lands** pack. Add it to your project.

If you're unable to add a content pack to a project because it says it's not compatible with your current project version, you can very often get around this just by adding the content pack to a project built with the highest version the content pack allows, and then migrating its assets to your new project. So, for example, if I'm trying to add Ice Lands to a 4.21 project, and the launcher tells me I can't because Ice Lands has only been flagged as compatible with 4.20, I can add the content to a 4.20 project and then migrate it to a 4.21 project. Most of the time, this will work.

This may take a while. Once these assets have been added, open up your project. We're going to begin by creating a new Game Mode to get ourselves set up for a multiplayer session.

Creating a network Game Mode

Remember when we mentioned a long time ago that the Game Mode is responsible for the rules of a game? In a multiplayer game, this takes on additional significance because, as we've mentioned, important gameplay events should only ever happen on the server. If you put these two considerations together, then it shouldn't surprise you to learn that when a multiplayer game is underway, there's only one Game Mode, and it lives on the server.

What this means for you as a developer is if you write code that talks directly to the Game Mode, it's going to run fine when you test in a single-player session, but will fail when you try to test it in multiplayer because the game mode isn't going to be there on the client. This confuses many new multiplayer developers, so this would be a good time to take a quick look at Unreal's network framework and understand where different objects live.

Objects on the network

When thinking about objects in the multiplayer framework, you can think of them as occupying four different domains:

- **Server Only:** Objects exist only on the server.
- **Server & Clients:** Objects exist on the server and on every client.
- **Server & Owning Client:** Objects exist on the server and the client that owns them, but they do not exist on any other client.
- **Owning Client Only:** Objects exist only on the client that owns them.

Refer to the following screenshot:

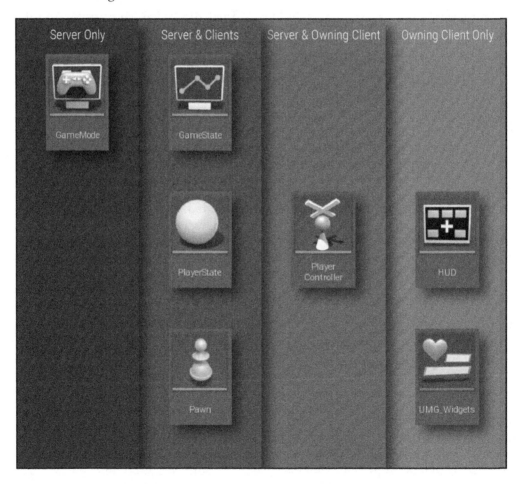

While this may seem at first like an academic point, you're really going to need to understand this. More than once in your early networking career, you're going to try to communicate with an object that doesn't live where you think it does because in a single-player session you never needed to think about this. Everything lives in the same space in a single-player game. In multiplayer, they don't, and you need to learn where they are.

Let's look at this another way:

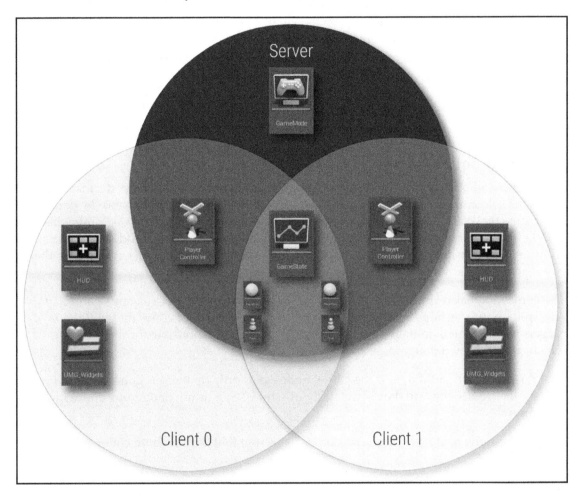

Diagram based on Cedric Neukirchen's excellent Multiplayer Network Compendium, found here: http://cedric-neukirchen.net/2017/02/14/multiplayer-network-compendium/

In the preceding diagram, you can see the following:

- The server owns the **GameMode**, and no client has access to it.
- The server and each connected client can see the Game State. There's only one of these.
- The server and each connected client can see a Player State for each client.
- The server and each connected client can see each client's pawn.
- The server can see each connected client's player controller, but clients can't see other clients' player controllers.
- The HUD and UI elements only exist on clients, and nobody else knows about them.

Let's talk briefly about what each of these objects does with regard to multiplayer gameplay.

Server-only objects

The Game Mode, as we mentioned a moment ago, lives on the server only. It runs the game and is the sole authority on what's going on. Clients, by design, cannot access the game mode directly. We've seen already that the game mode is responsible for deciding what object classes are created for a game. In a multiplayer game, the game mode often takes on additional responsibilities, such as choosing which team a player spawns into, where their pawn appears, and whether a match is ready to begin or ready to end.

The game mode also applies and enforces the rules of the game. Let's say our game's map was split up into sections and these sections can turn into danger zones that will damage players if they remain in them. The game mode would be responsible for determining which section turned dangerous, and when it happened.

This raises a question though. If the game mode exists only on the server and cannot be seen by the clients, how do the clients find out which sections are dangerous and which ones aren't?

This is where the next layer of objects comes in—those that exist on both client and server.

Server and client objects

When clients need to get information about the state of the game, they get it from the **Game State**, which is owned by the server but replicated to clients. We haven't really talked about replication yet, so for now you can think of it as a copy of an object that gets sent from the server to the connected clients. The game mode reads information from the game state and writes to it, and the server sends copies of the updated game state to all the connected clients through replication.

Returning to our previous example, if the game mode simply stored information about which zones were dangerous in a variable contained within itself, nobody is going to know about it. If the game mode instead stores this information on a game state that's replicated to the clients, they can read this information from the game state and respond to it.

What if our game mode is also updating scores for each player? Where should we put this information? We know of course that it shouldn't go on the game mode, since nobody can see it there. We could put it in the game state, and maintain an array of scores for each player, but there's a better place for this information. The game state maintains an array of **Player State** objects for each connected client. This is an ideal place to put information such as a player's score that applies to a single player, but that other players need to know about.

We're already familiar with the work that pawns do—these are players' avatars in the virtual world. They're maintained on the server and replicated to clients, so their movement and other state information can be seen by other players.

Server and owning client objects

We've seen previously that the player controller is responsible for managing input coming from the player and the output being displayed to the player. It owns the camera and the HUD, and it handles input events. Each connected client in a multiplayer game has a player controller associated with it, and can access it just as it would in a single-player session. The server is aware of what's going on with each client's player controller as well, but clients cannot see anything about each other's player controllers.

Owning client only objects

Finally, objects such as UI display widgets exist only on the clients to which they apply. The server doesn't know or care about them, and neither do any other clients. These are purely local objects.

That was quite a lot of of theory to dump on you, we know, but, as we mentioned, it's important. If you take a bit of time to internalize the structure described, you'll have a much less-confusing time writing multiplayer applications.

That having been said, let's get back to some hands-on work.

Creating our network game mode

We're going to use this login to spawn different players at different spawn points. Before we go on, let's jump into our map and add a second player start object:

1. From your **Modes** panel, select **Basic | Player Start**, and drag it on to your map somewhere, and save your map:

> Remember to use the *P* key to verify that your spawn point is on an area with a valid navmesh. (We don't actually need the navmesh yet, but this is a good way to verify that the floor collision is good in the location you've chosen and that it's inside the gameplay area.)

Here we've added a second player start at the other end of the map from the first.

Now, let's create a game mode to manage our network gameplay:

1. With your new project open, create a directory for it inside your **Content Browser**. Name it `Multiplayer` (or anything you like).

2. Create a blueprints subdirectory within this directory.

3. Right-click to create **Basic Asset | Blueprint Class | Game Mode Base**. Name it `BP_MultiplayerGameMode`.

If you look in the Content Examples project's **BP_GameMode_Network**, you'll see that it implements its own player start selection in **Event OnPostLogin**. You don't need to do this. The native **GameModeBase** class does it for you. If you did want to create special rules for selecting player starts (to select them by team, for example, the correct way to do this is to override the **ChoosePlayerStart** function. To do this, select **Functions | Override | Choose Player Start**, and put whatever logic you want in the resulting graph).

4. Open **Settings | Project Settings | Project | Maps & Modes**, and set the **Default GameMode** to our new game mode.

   Let's test it out:

5. Select the dropdown beside your toolbar's **Play** button and set the **Multiplayer Options | Number of Players** to 2.
6. Select **Play This Level in a New Window** from your **Play** button to launch a two-player test.

You should see one player spawning at the original spawn point and the other spawning at the new spawn point you just created.

Creating a network client HUD

Let's add a simple HUD to our clients so we can display information about the game to our user. Again, if we were planning this game to run exclusively in VR, we would not be using a HUD object, but rather building this in 3D as an attached widget. We're doing it this way here because we have quite a lot of ground to cover in this chapter and we want to keep it focused on networking.

While we're going to stay focused on creating a 2D HUD for this chapter, we can take this opportunity to add a bit of safety to ensure that we don't try to display 2D elements in 3D space.

Let's create a new HUD to work with:

1. From your project's blueprints directory, right-click on **Create Basic Asset | Blueprint Class**, and expand the **All Classes** expander and select **HUD** as your class. Refer to the following screenshot:

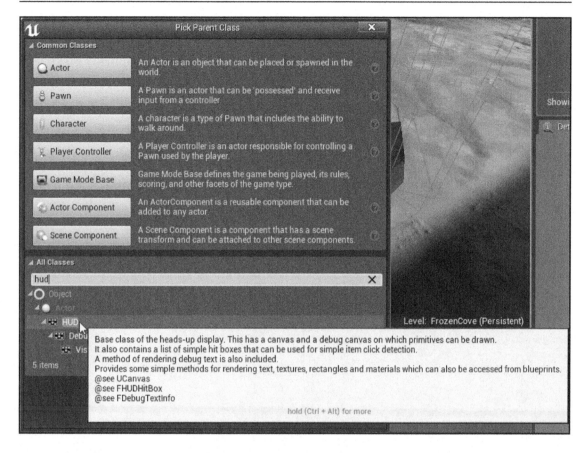

2. Hit the **Select** button to create it.
3. Name it BP_MultiplayerHUD.
4. Open our new game mode and set this **HUD** as its **HUD Class**.

Creating a widget for our HUD

Now, let's create a widget to display on our HUD:

1. Right-click or select **Add New** | **User Interface** | **Widget Blueprint**, and name the resulting widget WBP_NetworkStatus.
2. Open up its designer panel and drag a text block on to the lower-left corner of the panel.

Note that because we're creating a 2D interface in this case, we don't specify an explicit screen size; instead, we're allowing it to fill the screen. As you'll recall from our earlier UI work, when you're building a widget for 3D use, you'll want to specify its size.

3. Set the Text Block's **Anchor** to the lower-left corner.
4. Set its **Position X** to **64.0** and its **Position Y** to **-64.0**.
5. Set its **Alignment** to **X=0.0, Y=1.0**.
6. Name it `txt_ClientOrServer`.
7. Hit the **Bind** button beside its **Content | Text** entry to create a binding for it and select **Create Binding**:

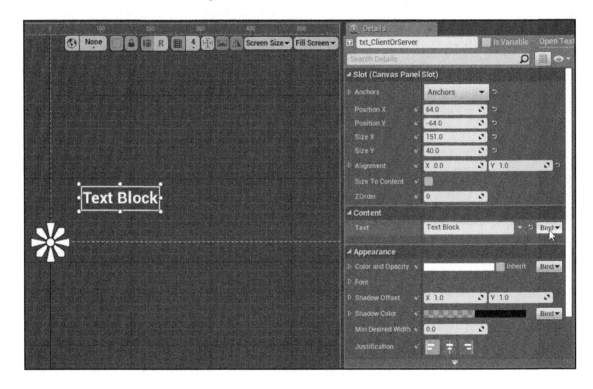

In the resulting function graph, we're going to check to see whether this widget's owning player controller is a client or a server and we'll set this widget's text accordingly:

1. Create a **Get Owning Player** node.
2. Drag the resulting player controller reference from its return value and call **Has Authority** on it.
3. Create a **Select** node from the **Has Authority** call's result.
4. Drag the **Select** node's return value into the function's **Return Value**.
5. Type Client into the **Select** node's **False** entry and **Server** into its **True** entry:

Let's talk about a few things here.

Remember how we we described the server as the *network authority*? This **Has Authority** check is now testing to see whether the owning player controller is resident on a server. You'll be testing for authority very frequently whenever you write network code, because you'll often have to do something different depending on whether your code is running on a client or a server. File this mentally as a very important concept to keep in mind. Checking for authority is how you're going to specify which behaviors happen on the server and which happen on the client.

Notice also the lightning-bolt and screen icon on the **Get Owning Player** node. In single-player applications, we didn't care about this icon, but it matters in a multiplayer setting. This icon is indicating that the call in question will only occur on a client and cannot be used on a server. In this case, this is fine. If you recall from the previous diagrams, the HUD and the widgets it owns exist on clients only, so this client-only call is going to work. The player controller reference it returns can exist on a client or on a server, which is why we're going to get a valid result from our **Has Authority** check.

Refer back to the network framework diagrams as you think this through.

Adding a widget to our HUD

Now, we're going to add this widget to our HUD:

1. Open the HUD's Event Graph and find or create an **Event BeginPlay** node.
2. Create an **Is Head Mounted Display Enabled** node.
3. Create a **Branch** using its result.
4. From the **Branch** node's **False** output, drag and create a **Create Widget** call.
5. Set its **Class** to the widget blueprint we just made.
6. Create a **Get Owning Player Controller** node and feed its result into the **Create Widget** node's **Owning Player** input.
7. Drag out the **Create Widget** node's **Return Value** and call **Add to Viewport** on it:

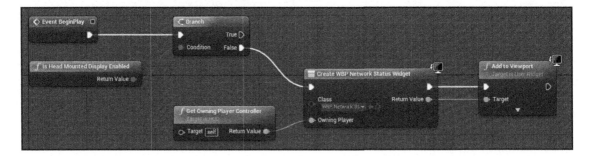

What we've just done here is check to see whether we're in VR, and if we're not, create an instance of our network status widget and add it to the HUD.

If you wanted to implement a 3D widget for use in VR, this would be a reasonable place to do it. You could create a 3D widget in much the same way we did before, and use a **Get Owning Pawn** call to grab the player pawn and attach the widget's containing actor to it. It would be equally reasonable to create a 3D widget on the pawn as we did earlier, and hide or destroy it if an **Is Head Mounted Display Enabled** check returned false.

Let's test it. You should see one session labeled **Server**, and the other session labeled **Client**.

Now, try checking the **Run Dedicated Server** checkbox on the **Play** menu and run it again:

This time, you'll see that both sessions indicate that they're clients. What's happened here is that a dedicated server has been spawned invisibly and both players have connected to it as clients. After you've run this test, uncheck **Run Dedicated Server** again. We're going to need a visible server and client for the next section.

Network replication

Now that we've talked a bit about servers and clients, let's learn more about how information moves between them.

The first and most important concept to talk about is **replication**. Replication is a process by which an actor or a variable value that exists on one system is communicated to another connected system so it can be used there as well.

This brings up an important point: only those items that you choose to replicate will be communicated to the other connected systems, and this is deliberate. Unreal's networking infrastructure is designed for efficiency, and a major way to maintain that efficiency, especially if you have a lot of players, is to send only the information you absolutely need to send over the network, and send it only to those who actually need to receive it. Think about a massively-scoped game such as *Fortnite*. It simply could not run if every single piece of data about every connected player was being sent to every other player. Unreal can handle very large player populations, and it does this by giving you as a developer complete control over exactly what gets replicated and to whom. With this power comes responsibility though. If you don't tell an actor or a variable to replicate, it won't, and you won't see it on a connected machine.

Let's start with a simple example to see how this works.

Creating a replicated actor

Let's say we wanted to use a flag to mark something in the game, and it was important that all players could see where it was.

We can begin by creating an actor for our flag, so let's do this first:

1. Inside your `Blueprints` folder, right-click to select **Create Basic Asset | Blueprint Class | Actor**. We can name our actor `BP_ReplicatedFlag`. Open it up.
2. Select **Add Component | Static Mesh**.
3. Set the component's **Static Mesh** property to `/Game/InfinityBladeIceLands/Environments/Ice/Env_Ice_Deco2/StaticMesh/SM_Env_Ice_Deco2_flag2`.
4. With the static mesh component selected, select **Add Component | Skeletal Mesh** to create a child skeletal mesh attached to the flagpole's static mesh.
5. Set the component's **Skeletal Mesh** property to `/Game/InfinityBladeIceLands/Environments/Ice/EX_EnvAssets/Meshes/SK_Env_Ice_Deco2_BlowingFlag3`.
6. Set the skeletal mesh component's **Location** to (**X=40.0, Y=0.0, Z=270.0**) and its **Scale** to (**X=1.8, Y=1.8, Z=1.8**).
7. Drag the static mesh component on to the root component and set it as the new root.
8. Add a **Point Light** component and set its Location to (X=40.0, Y=0.0, Z=270.0) so our flag stands out.

Spawning an actor on the server only

Now, let's spawn our flag into the level, but only on the server:

1. From your **Modes** panel, drag a **Target Point** somewhere on your map. Name it FlagSpawnPoint.
2. Open up your level blueprint, and with **FlagSpawnPoint** still selected, right-click in the event graph to create a reference to it.
3. Find or create an **Event BeginPlay** node.
4. Drag the execution line from this node and create a **Switch Has Authority** node.
5. Drag the execution line from the **Switch Has Authority** node's **Authority** output and create a **Spawn Actor from Class** node.
6. Set its **Class** to the **BP_ReplicatedFlag** actor we just created.
7. Drag an output from the reference to your flag spawn point in the level and call **Get Actor Transform** on it.
8. Feed the transform into the **Spawn** node's **Spawn Transform**:

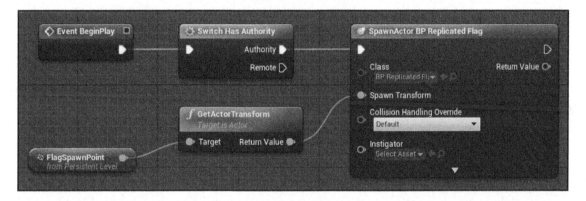

Run it. You'll see the flag spawned on your server, but you won't see it on the client. Let's talk this through to see why this is.

In the preceding screenshot, the first thing we did on BeginPlay was check to see whether we have authority. Again, *network authority* is simply another term for the server. If we have authority, meaning we're running on the server, we spawn the flag at the location we supplied. If we're not on the server, we don't spawn it, which is why we didn't see it in our client view.

This is an important pattern to remember. When we talk about making sure important gameplay events happen only on the server, this is how you do it. Check to see whether you have authority, and perform the action only if you do.

Replicating the actor to the client

Now of course in this instance, we want to see this actor on the client as well, but at present we can't because it exists only on the server. Let's change this by making it into a *replicated* actor:

1. Open our flag actor's blueprint, and in its **Details** | **Replication** section, set **Replicates** to true:

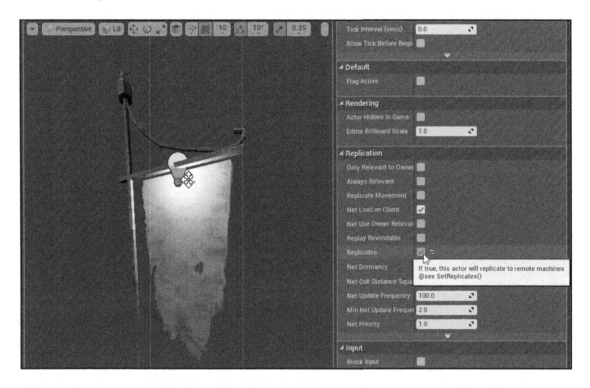

Test it again. Now, we see the flag on the client as well.

By indicating that this actor should replicate, we've now told the server to send the spawned object to all of the connected clients as well. You may have noticed as you were testing that you're able to see the other player's location represented as a gray sphere floating through space. This is because the default pawn class we're currently using is set to replicate as well. (If you're interested in seeing this in the source code, open `<Your Engine Install location|\Engine\Source\Runtime\Engine\Private\DefaultPawn.cpp>`, and you'll see that `bReplicates` is set to true in the constructor.)

Replicating a variable

Let's take this a step further and imagine that this point light we put on our flag is meaningful to our game. If that's the case, we need to be sure that only the server changes its value, and that all clients can see what that value is. That means that we need to ensure that we have authority before we change it, and then we need to replicate that change down to the connected clients.

1. Open the flag's blueprint and in the **Variables** section, and add a Boolean variable named `bFlagActive`.
2. Compile and save your blueprint.
3. In the event graph, on **Event BeginPlay**, add a **Switch Has Authority** node.
4. From the **Authority** execution line, *Alt* + drag a setter for `bFlagActive` and set it to **False**.
5. Create a **Set Timer by Event** node and connect it to your `bFlagActive` setter.
6. Set its **Time** to 3.0 and its **Looping** property to **True**.
7. Create a **Custom Event** and name it `ToggleFlagState`.
8. Connect the red connector (this is called an **Event Delegate** by the way) from your timer to your custom event.
9. *Alt* + drag another setter for `bFlagActive` on to the graph and connect it to your **ToggleFlagState** event.
10. *Ctrl* + drag a getter for `bFlagActive` on to the graph.
11. Create a **Not Boolean** node from its output and connect its result to the setter's input:

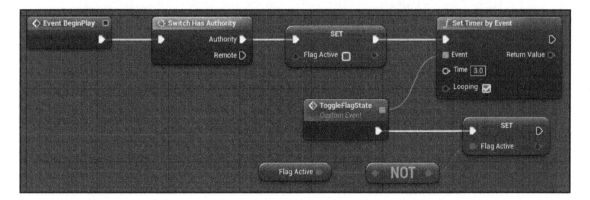

What we've just done here is, if we're on the server, initialize the `bFlagActive` variable, and then set up a looping timer that flips its value to the opposite value every three seconds.

> You have two **Set Timer** event types available to you. You can set timers to call functions by name when they trigger, or to call events. If you're working in the event graph, it's often more readable to connect an event directly to the timer's delegate connector. If you're working inside a function, where events are not available to you, call a function by name instead.

Now, we need to give ourselves a way to see the flag changing state:

1. Find or create the **Event Tick** node.
2. Drag a reference to your point light on to the graph.
3. Create a **Set Intensity** node and call it on the point light.
4. *Ctrl* + drag a getter for your `bFlagActive` variable on to the graph.
5. Drag out its result and create a **Select** node from it.
6. Connect the **Select** node's **Return Value** to the **Set Intensity** node's **New Intensity** input.
7. Set the Select node's **False** value to **0.0** and its **True** value to **5000.0**:

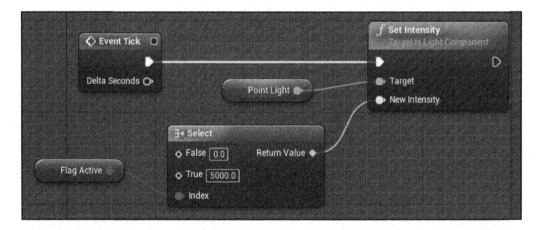

As you may recall, we're not fans of polling values on the tick event. It's a wasteful and generally sloppy technique. Don't worry—we're going to set up a better way to do this in just a moment.

In the meantime, though, let's test it.

We can see our light turning on and off on the server, but not on the client. You may be able to guess now why this is. Because of our authority check, we're only changing the value of bFlagActive on the server, and we're never telling any of the clients about this change. Fixing this is fairly straightforward:

1. Select the bFlagActive variable and, in its **Details** section, set **Variable |**
   Replication to **Replicated**:

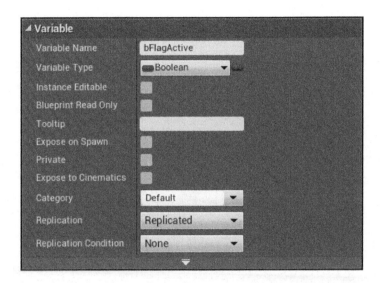

Run your test again. Now, you should see the flag's state changing on the client as well.

This brings up an important point. Just because an actor is replicated doesn't mean that any of its properties, other than their initial states, are replicated. Again, this is deliberate. You don't want to send anything over the network that you don't need to send. Every bit of traffic adds to the bandwidth load and adds to the cost of adding additional players. Unreal by default replicates only what you tell it to replicate.

Notifying clients that a value has changed using RepNotify

Now, we mentioned a moment ago that polling values on the tick is wasteful, since it performs an operation on every update even if there's no need to do it. It's nearly always a better idea to respond to events.

As it turns out, this is easy to do with replicated variables:

1. Select your `bFlagActive` variable and, in its **Details** | **Variable** block, set its **Replication** property to **RepNotify** instead of **Replicated**.
2. Take a look at your **Functions** list. A new function was just automatically added, called `OnRep_bFlagActive`.
3. Take everything you had on your **Event Tick**, select it, and *Ctrl* + *X* to cut it out.
4. Open up your new `OnRep_bFlagActive` function and paste everything into it, connecting the function's execution line to your **Set Intensity** node:

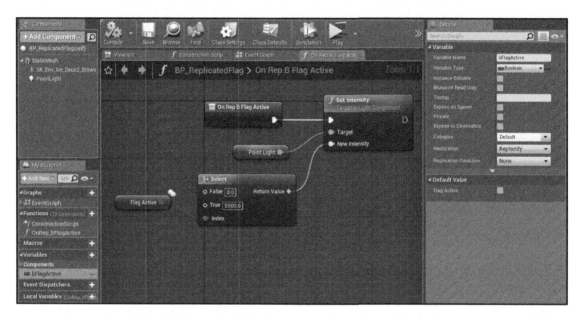

This is a more efficient way to respond to changes in the value. The `OnRep` function for a variable with its replication set to **RepNotify** will be called automatically every time that variable receives a new value from the server. This makes it easy and efficient to respond to those changes, and if we wanted to trigger an effect such as a particle system or perform some other operation when a new value arrived through replication, we now have a natural place to do this.

> If you need something to happen when a new value arrives on a client through replication, use **RepNotify** to create an **OnRep** function, and do the operation there.

The example we've built so far is fairly simple, but it actually illustrates a number of very important points. We've talked a bit about where objects live in the network framework, how to determine whether an action takes place on a network authority (server), or on a remote (client) session, how to determine whether an actor replicates from a server to clients, and how to replicate new values to clients and respond to their changes. Now, let's take things a step further and start to build something that looks a bit more like a game.

Creating network-aware pawns for multiplayer

Now that we've seen a bit about how information moves from the server to the clients, let's explore the ways player actions get communicated from the clients back to the server. To get ready for this, we're going to take a shortcut and add a pawn that can already perform a few basic actions, and we'll get right to the task of making these actions work in a multiplayer setting.

Adding a first-person pawn

We're going to set ourselves up by adding the pawn from the **First Person** template:

1. Create or open a project made using the **Blueprint | First Person** template.
2. Select **Content | FirstPersonBP | Blueprints | FirstPersonCharacter**, and migrate this character into our working project.

   Now, we need to tell our game mode to use it.

3. Open **BP_MultiplayerGameMode**, and set its **Default Pawn Class** to the **FirstPersonCharacter** we just migrated in.

Let's test it. We should see a number of problems here. Our projectiles are bouncing off invisible walls. When players fire, we can't see it happen from the other machine. The other player's representation just appears as a first-person weapon. We'll fix all of these.

Setting collision response presets

First, let's fix the collision problem. While it isn't directly network-related, it's distracting and not hard to correct:

1. Select one of the blocking volumes that's blocking our projectiles:

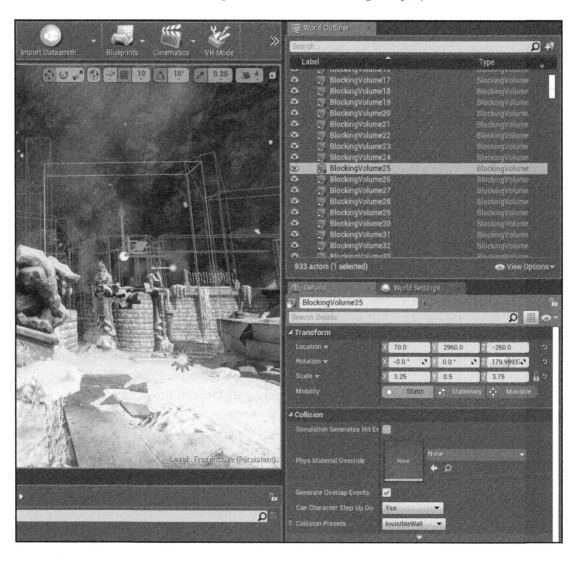

2. Take a look at its **Details** | **Collision** | **Collision Presets** to see what collision preset it's using.

   We can see that it's using the **Invisible Wall** preset. Probably, this preset is blocking a lot of things we don't want it to block. For our game, we really only want to stop pawns.

3. Open **Settings** | **Project Settings** | **Collision**, and expand the **Preset** section.
4. Find the **Invisible Wall** preset, and hit the **Edit** button:

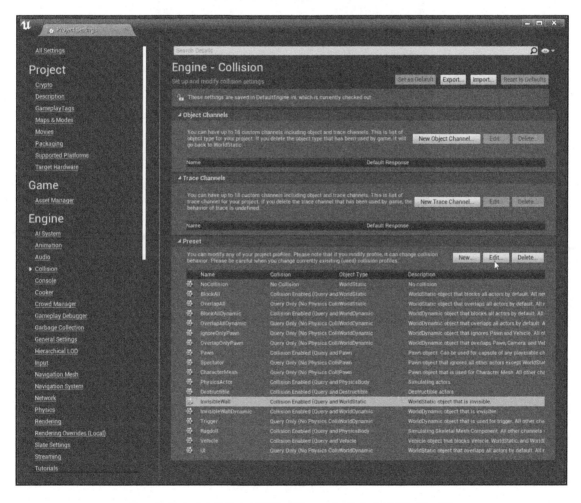

Here we've found and selected the InvisibleWall collision preset from the Engine | Collision | Preset list.

Sure enough, we can see that it's blocking everything except visibility. Let's change this. Set it to ignore everything except the **Pawn** in the **Trace Type**:

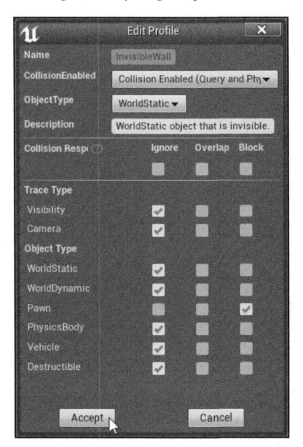

We also need to make a change to our projectile:

5. Open `Content/FirstPersonBP/Blueprints/FirstPersonProjectile`, and select its `CollisionComponent`.

6. Under **Details | Collision**, set its **Collision Presets** property to **OverlapAllDynamic**.

This will be good enough for now. The walls no longer block anything but pawns, and the projectiles no longer attempt to bounce off objects in the world.

With this out of the way, let's get back to setting up our networking.

Setting up a third-person character mesh

The first thing we want to do is get our remote pawn using a proper third-person mesh. Let's add the content we're going to need for this:

1. From your **Content Browser**, hit **Add New** | **Add Feature or Content Pack...**, and select **Blueprint Feature** | **Third Person**:

Here we're adding the Third Person content pack to our project.

2. Add it to your project.

   Now, we're going to modify our pawn to use the third-person mesh:

3. Open your **FirstPersonCharacter** blueprint, and hit **Add Component | Skeletal Mesh**. Make sure the actor or its **CapsuleComponent** is selected so this new component is created as a child of the **CapsuleComponent**.

4. Name the new component `ThirdPerson`.

5. Set its **Details | Mesh | Skeletal Mesh** to the **SK_Mannequin** mesh that just arrived with our third-person content.

6. Set its **Details | Animation | Anim Class** to use the **ThirdPerson_AnimBP_C** animation blueprint from our third-person pack.

7. Adjust its position so it lines up appropriately with the capsule (setting its **Location Z** value to **-90.0** and its **Rotation Z** (Yaw) value to **-90.0** works well enough):

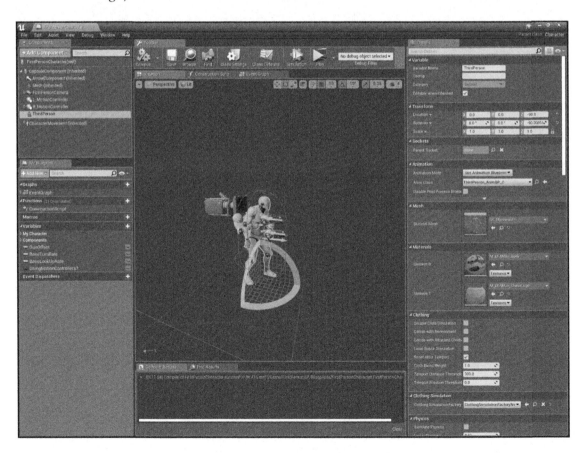

If we run it right now, we'll see that the third-person mesh is blocking our camera view. We want to display this mesh for other players, but hide it for ourselves:

1. Jump over to the **Event Graph** of **FirstPersonCharacter** and find its **Event BeginPlay** node.
2. Drag the **Event BeginPlay** node out a bit to give yourself some room to work.
3. Right-click and add an **Is Locally Controlled** node to the graph.
4. Create a **Branch** from your **Is Locally Controlled** node, and connect execution output of **Begin Play** to it.
5. Drag a reference to the `ThirdPerson` component on to your graph.
6. Call **Set Hidden in Game** on it, with **New Hidden** set to true.
7. Execute this **Set Hidden in Game** call from the **Branch** node's **True** output.
8. Connect execution output of **Set Hidden in Game** to the **Branch** node that **Event BeginPlay** used to feed into.
9. Connect your **Is Locally Controlled** branch's `False` output to the **Is Head Mounted Display Enabled** branch's input.

In an instance such as this, it's a good idea to double-click your execution lines to create reroute nodes to avoid crossing under other nodes, and to make it clear where the conditional part of an execution begins and ends. This has no effect on the behavior of the blueprint, but it can improve its readability.

Your graph should now look something like this screenshot:

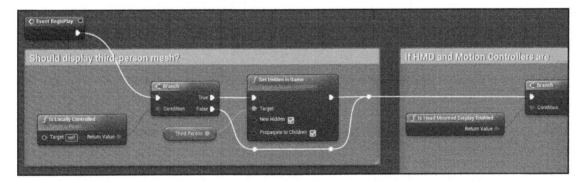

Checking whether an actor is locally controlled is a thing you'll do often in network development. In a single-player environment, of course, this isn't a consideration, everything is locally-controlled, but once you're dealing with objects that are arriving through replication, it can often be the case that you'll want to treat them differently if they belong to someone else.

You can also achieve this by setting the **ThirdPerson** component's **Details | Rendering | Owner No See** setting to **True**. This flag, and its companion, **Only Owner See**, can also be used to make certain things visible only to owners or invisible to them. You'll have to expand the **Advanced** area of the **Rendering** options to see it. For this example, we chose to use the **Is Locally Controlled** check because there are so many other cases in which it will be used, but it's worth it to know that these shortcuts exist.

Let's run it again, and you'll now see the third-person mesh for the remote character, and the first-person mesh for the locally-controlled character.

Adjusting the third-person weapon

The weapon is in a strange place for the third-person character. Let's fix that:

1. Open `Content/Mannequin/Character/Mesh/UE4_Mannequin_Skeleton` and find the **hand_r** bone in the skeleton tree.
2. Right-click the bone and select **Add Socket**:

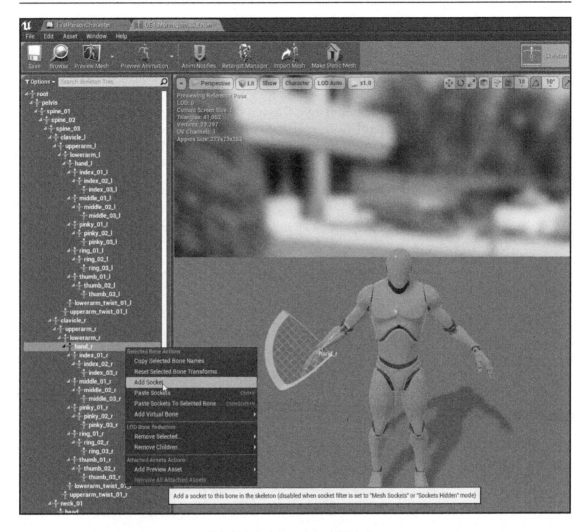

Right click the hand_r bone and select Add Socket here.

3. Name the new socket `Weapon`.

4. Right-click the socket and select **Add Preview Asset**, and select **SK_FPGun** as the preview.

5. Move the socket until the weapon appears to be lined up properly with the hand. (Setting **Relative Location** to **X=-12.5, Y=5.8, Z=0.2**, and setting the **Relative Rotation Z** (Yaw) value to **80.0** seems to work well enough.)

Now, we need to attach the weapon to the socket we just made, but only for remote players:

6. Jump back to our event graph of **FirstPersonCharacter** and find the **Event BeginPlay** node.

7. From the **Is Locally Controlled** branch's **False** output, connect an **AttachToComponent (FP_Gun)** node.

> We've seen this before, but again, as a reminder, there are two versions of **AttachToComponent**—one works on actors, while the other works on components. Select the one that's bound to your **FP_Gun** component.

8. Drag your third-person component into the **AttachToComponent** node's parent input.

9. Enter the name of the socket you created on your skeleton in **Socket Name**. (**Weapon**):

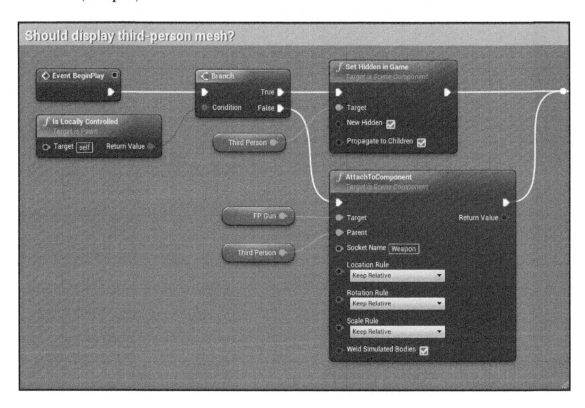

Run it again. The weapon should now be more reasonably-placed. It's not aiming where the other player is aiming because we haven't added anything to the third-person animation blueprint to handle this. Adding this capability falls outside the scope of this chapter, since it really takes us out of networking, so for the purposes of our game here, we're going to leave this as it is.

The next thing we need to do is make sure that when a player fires their weapon, the server handles the shot, and replicates it to the other clients.

Replicating player actions

As we saw earlier, in the current build players can't see it when other players fire their weapons. We'll begin simply enough, by making sure projectiles replicate from the server to the clients when they're spawned:

- Open up the **FirstPersonProjectile** blueprint, and in its **Details | Replication** section, set **Replicates** to true.

Run it now, and you'll see that if you fire the weapon on the server, the client can see the projectiles, but if you fire the weapon on the client, the server doesn't see it.

Take a moment to form a clear mental picture of why this is. Replication goes one way: from the server to the client. When we spawned the flag on the server in our earlier example, we saw it on the client because we'd told the server to replicate it. The same thing is now happening with the projectiles. So, the question, then, is how does a client tell the server that it needs to spawn a projectile?

Using remote procedure calls to talk to the server

The answer comes through a process called a **remote procedure** (RPC). A remote procedure call is a call made from one system that's intended to run on another system. In our case, when we want to fire the weapon, we'll have the client make an RPC to the server telling it that we want to fire, and the server will handle actually firing the weapon.

Let's change our pawn's firing method to use an RPC:

1. Open your **FirstPersonCharacter** blueprint's **Event Graph**, and look for **InputAction Fire**.
2. Somewhere nearby, create a custom event. Call it `ServerFire`.
3. In the custom event's **Details**, set its **Graph | Replicates** value to **Run on Server**:

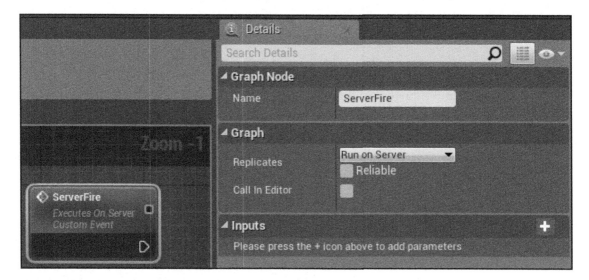

Now, let's get ready to use this call. The first thing we're going to want to do with our weapon firing is separate those things that are gameplay-relevant and should be run on the server, and those things that are purely cosmetic and can be run on the client.

Let's create an additional **Custom Event** to handle the non-essential client stuff.

1. Create a **Custom Event** and call it `SimulateWeaponFire`.

 Unreal developers commonly follow a naming convention whereby non-essential cosmetic aspects of a network action are named with the prefix *simulate*. This indicates to the reader that this function is safe to run on the client and contains only non-state-changing actions (sounds, animations, particles, those sorts of things). It also indicates to the reader that the function in question is safe to skip on a dedicated server.

2. Grab the **Play Sound at Location** call and the **GetActorLocation** call feeding it, disconnect them from the **SpawnActor FirstPersonProjectile** node, and connect them to your new **SimulateWeaponFire** event.

3. Get rid of the **Branch** feeding from the **InputTouch** node's **FingerIndex**. There's no execution line going into it, which means it's not doing anything. This is just clutter; someone didn't bother to clean out the graph.

The partially-updated graph should look something like this, so far:

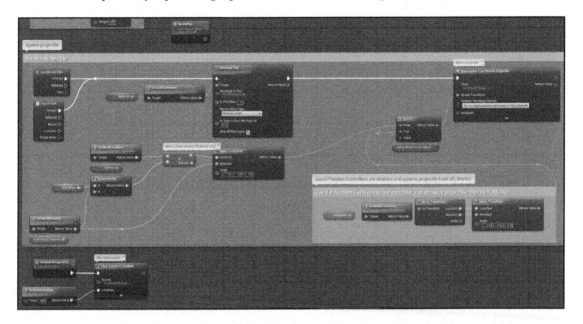

The Spawn Projectile method from the Third Person content pack we migrated into our project

4. Now, grab that **Montage Play** call, disconnect it from the execution line it's currently in, and put it on to the **SimulateWeaponFire** execution line.

What we've done now has been to take everything that's purely decorative and move it to its own event that can be called separately.

> This is a good convention to follow even when you're developing a single-player application because it makes it easy to see which chunks of code are actually changing things and which ones are cosmetic. It's a worthwhile practice to get into the habit of keeping them separate.

Now that we've created our SimulateWeaponFire event and populated it, we'll make sure it gets called on any system that receives the input:

1. Now, put a call to **SimulateWeaponFire** where the **Montage Play** node used to be, so it will get called any time this input event gets heard.

2. Add a **Switch Has Authority** node right after the **Simulate Weapon Fire** call.

3. Connect the **Switch** node's **Authority** output to the **SpawnActor First Person Projectile** call.

4. From its **Remote** branch, make a call to the **ServerFire** node we created earlier.

5. Feed the **ServerFire** node's execution output into the **SpawnActor First Person Projectile** node's input.

Your **SpawnProjectile** graph should now look something like this screenshot:

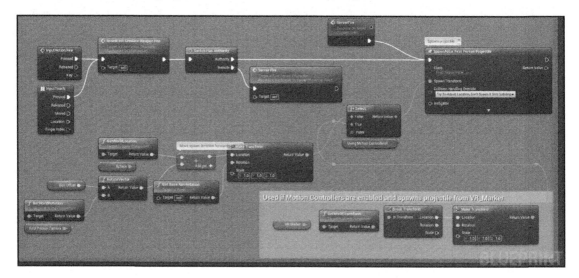

And, the **SimulateWeaponFire** graph should look like this screenshot:

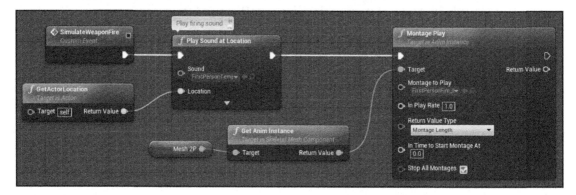

Try it out. Aiming is going to be incorrect for clients because we're not doing anything to send the client's weapon aiming to the server, but you should now see the projectile spawning and hear the fire sound in both directions.

Let's improve this.

At present, the projectile's spawn rotation is coming from the first-person camera. This isn't going to work when communicating from the client to the server, because the server doesn't know anything about that camera. Let's replace this with a value the server does know about:

- Right-click in the graph to create a **Get Base Aim Rotation** node, and feed it into the **Make Transform** node, replacing the input from the camera's **GetWorldRotation**:

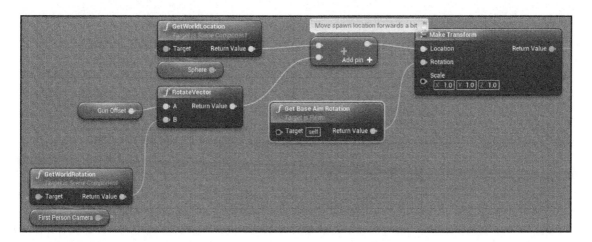

Test it again. The origin for the client's projectile when seen on the server is still going to be incorrect, but the aim rotation is now correct. (Fixing the origin would really require us to build a proper third-person animation blueprint, which takes us beyond the scope of this chapter.)

Let's talk about how this is working so far. There's an important pattern embedded here that's worth internalizing.

When the fire input event arrives, we check to see whether we have authority to spawn the particle. If we do, we just go ahead and spawn it. If we don't, however, we make a remote procedure call to the server to tell it to spawn it. It does, and then we see it here on our local client because it's been replicated.

Most gameplay events in multiplayer games will be written according to this pattern. Here's a simplified example for clarity:

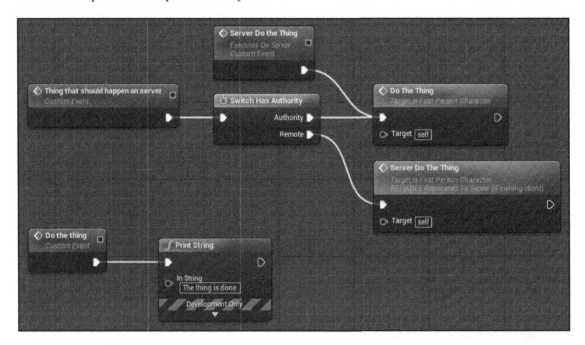

In the preceding screenshot, the **Do the thing** call will only ever run on the server. If the event that triggers it is happening on the server, it just runs, and if the event is happening on a client, the client calls the **Server Do the Thing** RPC, which then handles calling **Do the Thing**. This pattern is worth committing to memory. You'll use it a lot.

There's a common convention among Unreal developers whereby we prefix the names of the RPCs that run on the server with the prefix *Server*. You don't have to do this, but it's a good idea, and Unreal developers will cast disapproving glances your way if you don't. It makes it much easier to see which functions are RPCs and which ones run locally.

Using multicast RPCs to communicate to clients

There's another problem with what we've written that will be difficult to detect if you're testing on a single machine: the simulated sounds and animations only play on the owning client. If we were playing on two separate machines and the other player fired near us, we wouldn't hear it.

Why not?

In the previous screenshot, when the input event is received on the local client, it calls the `Simulate` method to play the sound and animation, and then checks to see whether it has authority to decide whether to spawn the projectile itself or ask the server to handle it. But, what if there's another player standing nearby?

Player A's client will send the RPC to the server to spawn the projectile, so everybody's going to see that, but the call to simulate the firing event only ever happened on player A's machine. The representation of player A's pawn over on player B's machine (we call this representation a *remote proxy*) was never told to play the animation, so it doesn't.

We can solve this using another type of RPC, called a **multicast event**.

You'll often hear developers referring to multicast events as **net multicast** events, or as **broadcast** events. These terms refer to the same thing. By convention, just as server RPC event names are prefixed with *server*, multicast events are often named with *broadcast* as a prefix. This is a less-commonly-followed convention than the *server* prefix and you don't have to do it, but you'll have an easier time following your blueprints later on if you make this a habit.

Since we've already abstracted our simulate methods to their own event, this isn't hard to do:

- Select your **SimulateWeaponFire** event, and in its **Details | Graph**, set its **Replicates** property to **Multicast**:

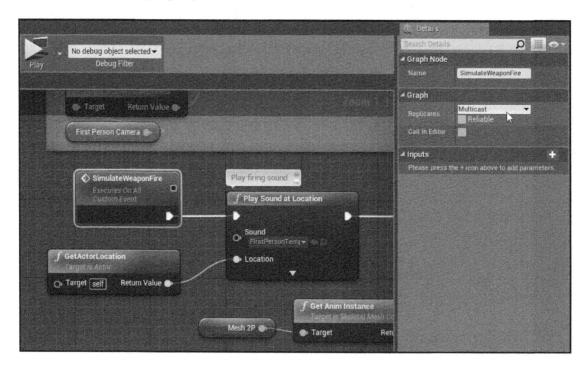

What this will do is send this event to the server and instruct it to send it down to all connected clients.

Now, when Player A fires, the call to spawn the projectile will happen only on the server, but the call to play the fire sound and animation will happen on every representation of player A's pawn across the network.

If you'd like, you can rename your `SimulateWeaponFire` event `BroadcastSimulateWeaponFire`. Some developers follow this convention, others don't. In general, though, the more information you give yourself and other developers about what you're doing, the easier a time you or they are going to have debugging or maintaining your code.

Client RPCs

There's one more type of RPC, which we're not going to demonstrate here, but that we should discuss for the sake of completeness. Let's say you were running an operation on the server and you needed to make a call specifically to the client that owns the object you were operating on. You can do this by setting the event to **Run on owning Client**.

Reliable RPCs

There's one final determination we have to make when we're deciding how to replicate a function call, and that's whether to make the call reliable.

To understand what this flag means, we need to understand something critical about networking. The internet is an unreliable thing. Just because you send an RPC to someone on the other side of the globe, there's absolutely no guarantee that it will get there. Packets get lost all the time. That's not an unreal thing; it's a reality-of-the-world thing. The choice you need to make as a developer is what to do about this.

If an RPC is important to the game, such as firing a weapon, make it reliable. What this will do is instruct the network interface to re-send it until it receives confirmation from the other system that the call was received. This adds traffic to your network, however, so do it only for those calls you care about. If you're just broadcasting a cosmetic call, such as a weapon sound, leave it unreliable, since your game isn't going to break if it doesn't arrive. The call to fire the weapon, however, should be reliable, since it matters to the player and to the game whether it happens.

Let's make this change now:

1. Find your **ServerFire** custom event, and in its **Details | Graph**, set its **Reliable** property to true.
2. Leave your **BroadcastSimulateWeaponFire** event unreliable, because it's just playing cosmetic events that aren't important enough to be worth clogging the network.

Going further

Networking is a substantial topic, and, to be honest, we've only scratched the surface here. Our purpose in writing this has been to give you a solid mental model from which you can understand what Unreal's network framework looks like, and what sorts of things you need to understand to work within it.

This is heady stuff, and it can get fairly confusing to new developers. The trick to network development is to create a clear mental model of what's going on. Take your time to understand these concepts, and you'll have a much easier time.

There are a few topics we didn't cover here, such as hosting sessions and making it possible for others to join them, and quite a lot of the finer points of how networking works, such as relevance. These things are worth understanding, and there are a few good resources available to you to take your understanding further.

First, check out the Network Examples map in your Content Examples project, and take some time to understand what they're showing. Next, Cedric Neukirchen's *Multiplayer Network Compendium*, `http://cedric-neukirchen.net/2017/02/14/multiplayer-network-compendium/`, is an outstanding resource for learning how Unreal's networking framework works. Unreal's documentation lives here: `https://docs.unrealengine.com/en-us/Gameplay/Networking`, and it's absolutely worthwhile to spend some time picking through its Multiplayer Shootout project in light of what you've learned here.

Summary

This chapter involved a bit more theory than other chapters have, and it's entirely fine if a good chunk of it is still sinking in.

In this chapter, we talked a fair bit about Unreal's client-server architecture, and which objects live in which domains. It's important to get a good working knowledge of this structure in place. We also learned a bit about how information and events move between machines via replication and remote procedure calls.

It's our hope that this chapter has given you a good foundation on which to stand as you dig into networking and really explore how it works. Be patient with yourself and take time to experiment.

We've now reached the point where we've covered a huge range of things you need to know to develop VR using Unreal Engine. Next, we're going to take a look at a few tools and plugins that can greatly accelerate your work in VR. With what you've learned so far in this book, you should be ready to dig through them and understand how they can help you develop and save you substantial amounts of time.

Taking VR Further - Extending Unreal Engine

11

One of the major factors that differentiates professional developers from the newbies is how they leverage existing tools and libraries to accelerate their work. Very often, new developers try to do everything themselves, either because they're unaware of resources that could help them or because they think that leaning on an existing library is somehow *cheating*. It isn't. If you're a photographer, you're not cheating if you didn't build your own camera in your garage—you're focusing on the part of your art that actually matters to you. Don't be afraid to make use of tools and libraries that can accelerate your development.

Here's the rub though: to make effective use of another developer's work, you need to put in the effort to understand what they're doing. Don't simply paste in someone else's code without really understanding why it works—you're just asking for difficult-to-find bugs if you do this. Do your homework and find code you can rely on, but consider it part of your homework to understand how it's built so you can make deliberate choices about how you use it.

Sooner or later in your development career, you'll encounter the phrase *cargo cult programming*. This term, commonly attributed to the physicist Richard Feynman, refers to aboriginal religious practices observed in some islands of the South Pacific after World War II, whereby the natives built replica airfields in an attempt to lure back the god-like cargo planes that had supplied the islands during the war. In doing this, they were reproducing the forms, but they didn't understand how those forms worked and didn't understand why they weren't working now. Don't let this describe how you develop software. For anything you include in the project you're building, you should be able to give a clear answer when another engineer points to any part of it and asks, *What is this doing*? This won't be possible in all cases, of course, but in general, consider that your work isn't finished until you've spent the time to understand how the library or plugin is doing what it's doing.

In this chapter, we're going to focus primarily on one of the most useful plugins available for VR Developers: Joshua (MordenTral) Statzer's **VRExpansion** plugin. It's licensed under the MIT license (we're going to talk about licenses shortly—they're important), which means that it can be used freely in both non-commercial and commercial software. It doesn't cost anything, but it represents absolutely outstanding professional-caliber work, so if you use it, seriously consider supporting his Patreon to allow the project to continue.

In this chapter, we're going to learn how to make effective use of an advanced plugin such as the VR Expansion plugin, and use the example Blueprints from its sample project to learn how it's intended to be used. We'll learn strategies for exploring and making sense of unfamiliar code, and ways of using debugging tools to show us how code runs.

Specifically, we'll learn to do the following:

- Install and build plugins to extend the capabilities of the engine
- Use documentation and sample projects to learn a plugin's capabilities and intended use
- Make use of new native classes provided by the plugin
- Use strategies to read complicated blueprints and make sense of their structure
- Use debugging tools to help us to explore unfamiliar blueprints and learn their execution flow

This chapter is going to involve less direct Blueprint-building than those that came before it, and that's deliberate. The real focus here is on helping you to develop strategies to learn how unfamiliar code works so you can leverage it for your own development and use it to learn advanced techniques. This is one of the most important skills you can cultivate as a developer. It's fairly easy to find tutorials for basic topics, but once you get into more advanced territory, you mostly need to learn by looking at other advanced work. It's not as daunting as it might seem at first. We're going to learn a number of strategies to do this effectively.

With that, let's add to the engine and learn how to make it do things it couldn't do before.

Creating a project to house our plugin

Let's begin by creating a new blank project:

1. Create a new **Blueprint** project using the **Blank** template, and set its hardware target to **Mobile / Tablet**, and its graphics target to **Scalable 3D or 2D**, **No starter content**.

Installing the VRExpansion plugin

Once we've created our project, we're going to add the VRExpansion plugin to it.

The first thing we need to do before we can install any plugin to our project is create a place to put it. Plugins must live in a directory named `Plugins` in your project directory or in the `Engine` directory:

1. Open the directory containing your new project file. You should see your `.uproject` file here, along with your `Config` and `Content` directories.
2. Create a new directory here named `Plugins`:

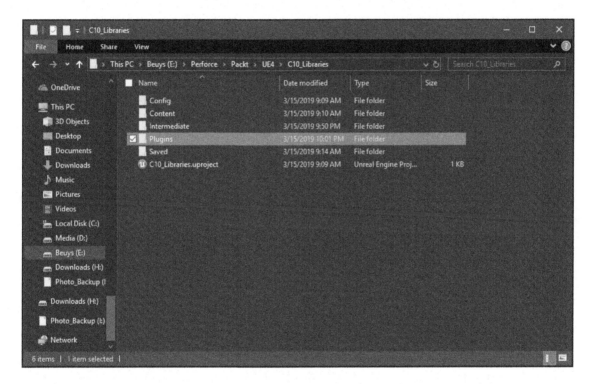

Now that we've created a `Plugins` directory for our project, let's add the VRExpansion plugin to it. There are a few ways we can do this.

Installing using precompiled binaries

The easiest way to get the plugin is to navigate to its forum discussion, `https://forums.unrealengine.com/development-discussion/vr-ar-development/89050-vr-expansion-plugin`, and use the **Plugin Pre-built Downloads** link for your engine version:

1. Hit the **Full Binaries and Source Package** link for your engine version and download the zipped plugin
2. Once the download has completed, open the `.zip` file and drag the `VRExpansionPlugin` directory contained within it into your `Plugins` directory

That's it. As long as you installed the plugin version that was built for your engine version, you're ready to go and can open up your project.

Compiling your own plugin binaries

If you need newer code for the plugin than what's included in the pre-built binaries (which you will if you're running a preview version of the engine), you're going to need to build your plugin binaries on their own. This isn't hard to do:

1. Navigate to the **VRExpansionPlugin** depot on BitBucket here: `https://bitbucket.org/mordentral/vrexpansionplugin`
2. Hit the **Downloads** link and hit the **Download repository** link to download a zipped version of the depot

> It's also possible to clone the plugin's Git depot directly into your project's plugins directory, but unless you're working on the bleeding edge and need absolutely up-to-date code, you don't really need to do this. You will want to do this if you're planning to contribute your own changes to the plugin. For most users, though, it's easier to download the zipped repository.

3. Now open up the `.zip` file you just downloaded.
4. You'll see a folder inside it named something like `mordentral-vrexpansionplugin-9c1737a17bef` (the hash at the end will be different)—drag this into your new `Plugins` directory.

5. Change the name of the directory you just extracted to `VRExpansionPlugin`:

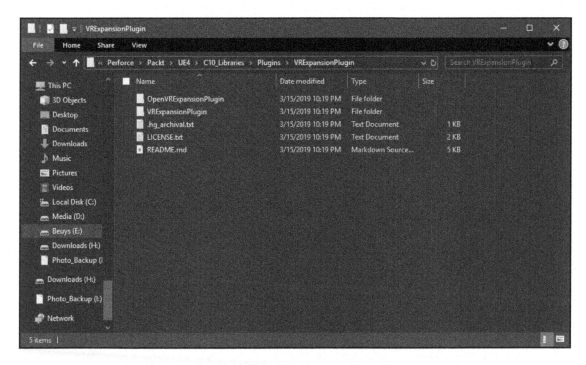

Now launch your project, or if it was already open, close it and re-open it.

A dialog should now appear indicating that you need to build your plugin binaries:

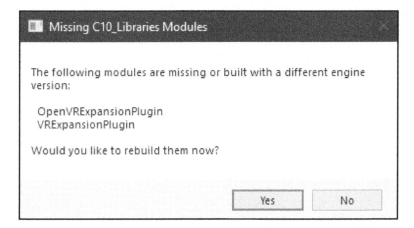

If you set up Visual Studio Community 2017 as directed in `Chapter 2`, *Setting Up Your Development Environment*, this isn't a problem. (If you didn't, jump back there now and follow the directions to set it up. It's always worth it to have a working compiler set up on your system because you will sometimes need it.) Say **Yes** and let Visual Studio build new binaries for you.

 Your plugin should build successfully, but if it doesn't, navigate to the plugin's home page at `https://bitbucket.org/mordentral/vrexpansionplugin` and follow the instructions under *Basic Installation Step-By-Step*, which will take you through the manual build process. As mentioned earlier, you also have the option to download pre-built binaries from here: `https://forums.unrealengine.com/development-discussion/vr-ar-development/89050-vr-expansion-plugin`.

If you hit **Show Log** on the build dialog, you should be able to see your build progress. Expect it to take a few minutes:

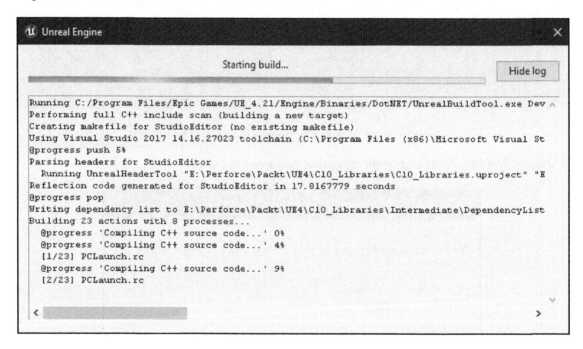

Once the build finishes, your project will open.

Verifying the plugins in your project

Regardless of how you downloaded and installed the plugin, it should now be available to you once you've opened the project.

On opening the project, you should see two indicators in the lower-right corner indicating that you have new plugins available and asking whether you want to update your project:

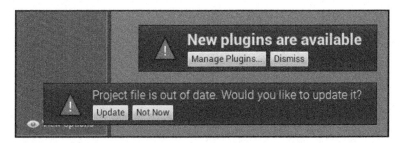

Hit **Manage Plugins...** to open the plugins list.

You should see two entries for the VRExpansion plugin, and they should both be enabled:

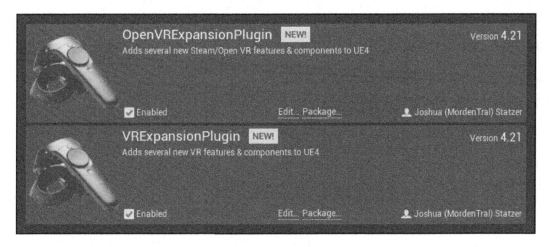

This is as it should be, so we can close this window.

Now, let's update our project file by hitting the **Update** button.

Remember that your `.uproject` file is really just a text file telling Unreal a few basic things about your project. If you open it up in a text editor, you'll see that new entries were added indicating that this project now relies on the VRExpansion plugin and its companion OpenVRExpansion plugin:

```
1  {                                          1  {
2      "FileVersion": 3,                      2      "FileVersion": 3,
3      "EngineAssociation": "4.21",           3      "EngineAssociation": "4.21",
4      "Category": "",                        4      "Category": "",
5      "Description": "",                     5      "Description": "",
6      "Enterprise": true                     6      "Enterprise": true,
7  }                                          7      "Plugins": [
8                                             8          {
                                              9              "Name": "OpenVRExpansionPlugin",
                                             10              "Enabled": true
                                             11          },
                                             12          {
                                             13              "Name": "VRExpansionPlugin",
                                             14              "Enabled": true
                                             15          }
                                             16      ]
                                             17  }
                                             18
```

This is a text comparison of the .uproject file before and after we added the VRExpansion plugin

That's it. We're ready to start developing using the plugin, but before we do, let's talk a little bit about what we just did.

Understanding plugins

Plugins are an important part of the Unreal ecosystem. They can contain content, blueprints, native code, and anything else that affects what Unreal Engine can do and how it does it. They can save you tremendous amounts of time and extend the engine's capabilities almost infinitely.

For the most part, you really don't need to know much about how Unreal handles plugins to use them—they pretty much just work, but if you want to be able to fix things if something goes wrong, or if you need to update a plugin to accommodate a new engine version, it is helpful to know a little bit about where they live and how they're put together. We're not going to go too deep into the weeds here, but there are a few quick things to point out that will help you in your future development. (If you do need to get deeper into how plugins are developed, begin with the documentation here: `https://docs.unrealengine.com/en-us/Programming/Plugin`)

Where plugins live

First, it's important to know where to put new plugins that you want to install to a project or the engine and to know where plugins downloaded from the Epic Games launcher will be placed.

Any plugin you install will live in one of two places: in a `Plugins` directory in your project for plugins that are installed just to that specific project or in an `Engine\Plugins` directory for plugins that are installed to the engine and apply to all projects.

Take a moment to look at your currently-installed engine plugins as given in the following step:

1. Open the directory where you installed Unreal Engine (by default, this will be in `C:\Program Files\Epic Games`), and open the `Engine\Plugins` subdirectory:

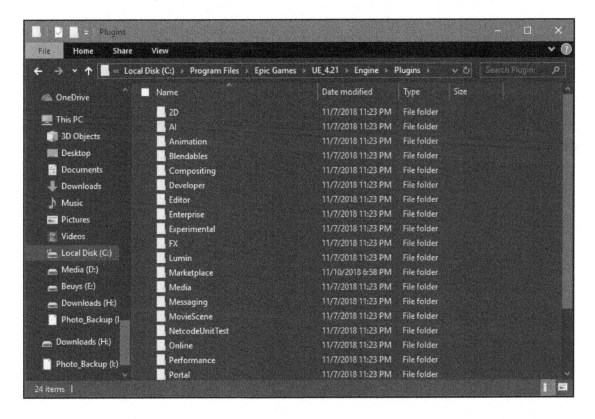

Here you'll notice something interesting: many features of the engine, even those we think of as core engine capabilities, such as effects editors, are really plugins living within the Unreal framework. That's worth remembering. Plugins aren't second-class citizens in Unreal Engine. Adding something to the engine through a plugin is really not meaningfully different than writing it directly into the engine code, except that it's easier to replace it or to turn it on or off if it's set up this way.

Plugins you download through the Epic Games launcher will appear in the **Marketplace** subdirectory of your `Engine\Plugins` directory. In general, the Epic Games launcher will alert you when a plugin you've installed from the launcher has an update available, and you can update it directly from within the launcher. You'll rarely, if ever, need to open your `Engine\Plugins` directory, but it's worth knowing that it's there.

Installing plugins from the Marketplace

To install a plugin using the Epic Games launcher, select the plugin you want from the **Marketplace** or from your **Library**, and hit the **Install to Engine** button, or if the plugin has been configured as an asset pack, hit the **Add to Project** button instead. **Install to Engine** will put the plugin in your engine install's `Engine\Plugins\Marketplace` directory, while **Add to Project** will put it in your project's `Plugins` directory:

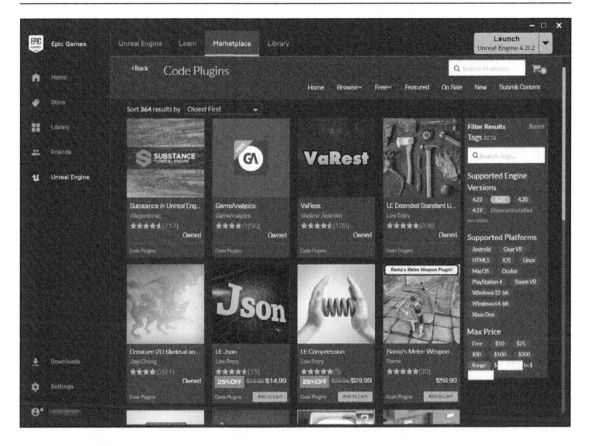

The Epic Games launcher will alert you automatically if a plugin you've installed using the tool has an update available.

What's inside a plugin?

Now that we know a bit about where plugins live in Unreal Engine, let's take a look at what they're made of.

To do this, we're going to do a quick exploration of the VRExpansion plugin we installed to our project's Plugins directory:

1. Open up your project's Plugins directory, and open up the
   VRExpansionPlugin directory within it

You'll see that VRExpansion actually consists of two separate plugins within this directory: `VRExpansionPlugin` and `OpenVRExpansionPlugin`. The latter exists to support Valve Software's OpenVR SDK. For our purposes here, we're not going to worry about it and we'll just focus on VRExpansion.

There are two files here that we should take a moment to mention.

The first is the `README.md` file. Take a moment to open it up. This is a markdown file containing some basic information about the plugin.

If you have Visual Studio Code installed on your system, you can use VSCode to open markdown files. Once the file is open, you can right-click on its tab in the viewing area and select **Open Preview**, or just hit *Ctrl + Shift + V* to view the markdown with formatting.

You'll see that this `readme` file basically recreates the text on the main BitBucket page here: `https://bitbucket.org/mordentral/vrexpansionplugin` and links to instruction and information pages. Many plugins will come with documentation or `readme` files that tell you where to find the documentation. It's worth it to take a look.

About licenses

The other file we should look at here is the `LICENSE.txt` file. If you're going to include a plugin in your project, it's important to know how you're allowed to use it.

If you've downloaded a plugin through the **Marketplace**, you don't need to worry about it. All plugins distributed through Epic's **Marketplace** are licensed for non-commercial or commercial use and don't place any additional restrictions on how they can be used.

If you need more information about licensing for plugins on the **Marketplace**, the details live here: `https://www.unrealengine.com/en-US/marketplace-distribution-agreement`.

If you're downloading a plugin directly from the net, as we did previously, you need to check the license and make sure the author allows you to use the plugin in the way you want to use it. Most plugin authors will not put restrictions on the way you use the software, but always read the license and make sure. You don't want to build a project with a plugin at its foundation only to discover when it's time to sell the software that you're not actually allowed to do so. Read the license first.

Be especially careful of software licensed under the GNU **General Public License (GPL)**—this license places significant restrictions on the software in which it can be used and isn't compatible with Unreal Engine's licensing terms. The much more permissive **MIT** and **Apache** licenses, however, are fine, and you'll encounter many Unreal plugins that use them.

In our case, the license for VRExpansion plugin allows you to do pretty much anything you want (other than removing the license file and trying to pretend that the work was your own), including modifying the plugin's code. It places no restrictions on the kind of project you use it for in terms of content or commercial versus non-commercial use. This is ideal. Whether we're making our project for sale as a commercial game, using it for live performance, just building as a hobby, or whatever, we're fine.

Inside a plugin directory

If we now open up the VRExpansionPlugin directory within the outer VRExpansionPlugin directory, we'll see a directory structure that looks a lot like the structure for an Unreal project. This isn't accidental. You can pretty much think of plugins almost as though they are mini projects being inserted into your project. They can contain code, blueprints, or assets and other content just as a project can.

We're not going to worry about the contents of this directory except to take a look at one thing:

1. Open up the VRExpansionPlugin.uplugin file in a text editor

You'll see that this file, just like your .uproject files, is just a text file containing information about your plugin. It's rare that you're ever going to need to open this file up, but just as with your .uproject files, you should know about it if you ever need to debug something or change something by hand:

```
{
    "FileVersion": 3,
    "Version": 4.21,
    "VersionName": "4.21",
    "FriendlyName": "VRExpansionPlugin",
    "Description": "Adds several new VR features & components to UE4",
    "Category": "VRExpansion",
    "CreatedBy": "Joshua (MordenTral) Statzer",
    "CreatedByURL": "",
    "DocsURL": "",
    "MarketplaceURL": "",
    "SupportURL": "",
```

```
    "EnabledByDefault": true,
    "CanContainContent": false,
    "IsBetaVersion": false,
    "Installed": true,
    "Modules": [
        {
            "Name": "VRExpansionPlugin",
            "Type": "RunTime",
            "LoadingPhase": "Default"
        }
    ],
    "Plugins": [
        {
            "Name": "PhysXVehicles",
            "Enabled": true
        }
    ]
}
```

Most of the information in here is just descriptive, but there's one important detail: the `Plugins` block is used to specify dependencies between a plugin and other plugins. In this case, we can see that the `VRExpansion` plugin requires the `PhysXVehicles` plugin to be enabled. This shouldn't be a problem because it's on by default, but if you ever run into an instance where a plugin isn't working, take a look at what it depends on and make sure those plugins are present as well.

There's one other property you'll sometimes run into. Some plugins specify an engine version that they're allowed to work with, using an `EngineVersion` entry that looks like this:

```
"EngineVersion" : "4.21.0",
```

If a plugin contains this entry, Unreal will only allow it to load with the engine version specified here. (You can *sometimes* get around this by modifying this value by hand in your `.uplugin` file, but whether the plugin will compile and work will depend entirely on what's in it and what's changed in the engine version for which you're trying to compile it.)

Finishing our brief tour

This has been a quick look at how Unreal plugins are installed and what's inside them. As we mentioned earlier, through most of your development, you won't need to mess with any of this, but when you do need to figure out what's going on with your software, it can be invaluable to know where to begin looking.

With this, then, let's move on and start working in VR.

Exploring the VRExpansion example project

Before we jump back into our own project, we're going to take one more detour to look at the example project maintained alongside the VRExpansion plugin, so we can see what sorts of things this plugin is going to let us do. We're also going to accelerate some of our development through this chapter by using blueprints from this project, so don't skip this step.

Let's begin by downloading it from here: `https://bitbucket.org/mordentral/vrexppluginexample/downloads/`. Follow the given steps:

1. Hit the **Download repository** link to download a zipped version of the project
2. Unzip the downloaded project to wherever you keep your Unreal example projects
3. Open up the project directory, right-click `VRExpPluginExample.uproject`, and from the context menu, select **Switch Unreal Engine version...**
4. Set it to your current Unreal Engine version

Because this project was created as a C++ project, a Visual Studio solution file will also be created for you when you set a new engine version association. You don't need to work in C++ to use this plugin. Everything in the project itself was created using blueprints on top of the plugin, and this is how we're going to build our project as well, but if you're interested in digging deeper into the C++ classes and seeing how the plugin was built, this solution file offers a good way to do this.

Try launching the project. It may ask you to build its included plugins. Let it. (Again, be sure you installed and set up Visual Studio according to the directions in `Chapter 2`, *Setting Up Your Development Environment*.)

Once the project launches, let it compile the shaders, and then explore a bit to see what it offers. It should become apparent fairly quickly that VRExpansion offers a tremendous leg-up to VR developers. It's a treasure trove of professionally-written code and Blueprint examples of things you can do in VR, and numerous professionally-made and released games have used this plugin or parts of it in their development:

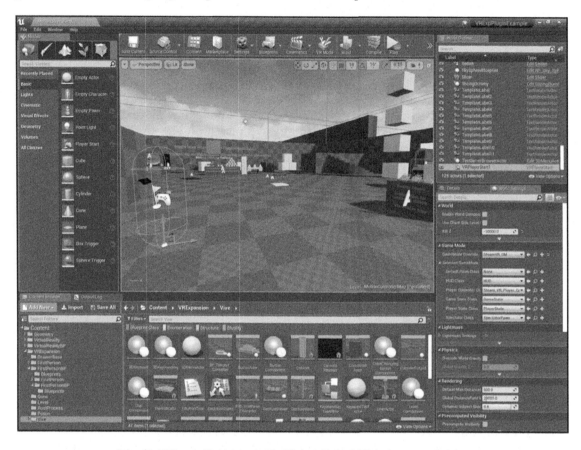

A view of the VR Expansion Plugin's test project. You'll find a wealth of useful VR development examples in here.

Play around in here. We're not going to cover everything in this example project, since we're about to begin building our own, but you won't be wasting your time to explore enough to come away with a good sense of what's included and what you could re-purpose for your own applications.

Here are a few tips to get you started:

- Your controller's D-Pad or thumbstick triggers teleport movement, just as it did in our own examples
- Squeezing the controller grips when you don't have an object in your hand changes your movement modes

We strongly encourage you now to spend some time experimenting with each movement mode. Teleportation and DPadPress-ControllerOrient modes will be familiar to you from the locomotion project we built earlier. Others will be new to you. Play with them and get ideas:

- Many objects can be gripped and used. Use the triggers to grip.
- White objects can be gripped and climbed.
- The player character does a nice job of handling cases where players shove their heads through walls. Try it.
- The Barf Platform lives up to its name. (If you recall our discussions from `Chapter 1`, *Thinking in VR*, you'll understand why.)

Consider this example project to be a major resource as you learn what this plugin allows you to do. As a result of the work you've done in this book, you should be set up well to understand what you're seeing in the blueprints and to use them as starting points to develop further.

Now, let's jump in and build our own project using this plugin as a basis for our own work.

Finishing our project setup

Now that we have our project set up, the VRExpansion plugin installed, and a basic understanding of what plugins are, let's jump back into building content.

First, of course, we need to set our project settings appropriately for VR:

- **Project | Description | Settings | Start in VR**: False
- **Engine | Rendering | Forward Renderer | Forward Shading**: True
- **Engine | Rendering | Default Settings | Ambient Occlusion Static Fraction**: False
- **Engine | Rendering | Default Settings | Anti-Aliasing Method**: MSAA
- **Engine | Rendering | VR | Instanced Stereo**: True
- **Engine | Rendering | VR | Round Robin Occlusion Queries**: True

Now let's give ourselves an environment to play in:

1. Find the soul: Cave environment pack in the marketplace and add it to your new project. (It's fine to do this while your project is open.)
2. Once the environment pack has finished downloading, open up your project if it wasn't already open.
3. Under `Content/SoulCave/Maps`, find the **LV_Soul_Cave_Mobile** level and open it. Let your shaders compile.

While this is happening, let's set this as your project's default level:

1. Open **Settings | Project Settings | Project | Maps & Modes**, and set **Editor Startup Map** and **Game Default Map** to **LV_Soul_Cave_Mobile**

Once your shaders have finished compiling, we can get down to work.

Using VRExpansion classes

We're going to use this project both as a review of the things we need to do when we set up a scene for VR and as an introduction to the VRExpansion classes.

Adding navigation

The first thing we're going to need to do, of course, now that we have our environment, is set it up with a nav mesh so we'll have the option to use teleport locomotion and so AI characters can navigate through it.

Begin by checking your collision environment:

1. Hit *Alt + C* (or the from the viewport, **Show | Collision**) to visualize your collision environment and make sure it looks sensible.

   The collision here looks good, so let's add a **Nav Mesh Bounds Volume** to the scene.

2. Drag a **Nav Mesh Bounds Volume** into the scene and scale it to encompass the areas where you want your player to be able to navigate.
3. The following values work reasonably well: **Location** (X= **-11420.0**, Y= **-3790.0**, Z= **-490.0**), and **Scale** (X= **100.0**, Y= **160.0**, Z= **20.0**).

Remember that you can make your life easier when setting up volumes by using the viewport's top and side views to make sense of what you're doing.

The resulting navmesh is going to cover a lot of spots where you're not going to want players to navigate, so remember to use **Nav Modifier Volumes** to block out undesirable teleport destinations.

Adding a game mode

As always, we're going to want to set up a game mode for our project to specify which classes to load and to handle any rules we want to apply to our game:

1. Create a directory for your project inside the Content directory, and then create a blueprints directory inside this.
2. Create a new **Blueprint Class** inside this directory and use **Game Mode Base** as its parent. Name it BP_VRExpansionGameMode.
3. Open **Settings | Project Settings | Project | Maps & Modes**, and set the **Default GameMode** to the new game mode you just created.
4. Open the **World Settings** for your map and reset **Game Mode | GameMode Override** to clear it.

We'll be revisiting our new game mode multiple times as we add new classes based on the VRExpansion classes.

Updating the PlayerStart class

The VRExpansion plugin provides a new player start class that's scaled more accurately for the VRCharacter we're going to spawn, so it represents more accurately where the player can fit. We're going to use it here:

1. Drag a VRPlayerStart into your scene near the existing PlayerStart actor.
2. From the old PlayerStart **Details**, right-click its **Transform | Location**, and copy the value.

3. Delete the old `PlayerStart`.
4. Select the VRPlayerStart and in its **Details**, right-click its **Transform** | **Location**, and paste in the value you copied from the old one.
5. Move it down a bit to place it on the floor. (**X= -20220.0, Y= -13080.0, Z= -2118.0**) works pretty well.

Adding a VR character

Now it's time to add a VR-enabled character to our project. The `VRExpansion` plugin gives us two new classes from which we can derive a character for use in VR:

- `VRSimpleCharacter` is a base class for VR-enabled characters that automatically sets up two `GripControllers`, a network-replicated VR camera, and implements a movement component specifically designed for use in VR.
- `VRCharacter` includes everything found in `VRSimpleCharacter`, but adds a few additional methods to offset the collision by neck location and support more significant re-scaling of the character's collision capsule.

In general, unless you're sure you need to use the neck collision offset or you're going to be radically changing the collision capsule size, use `VRSimpleCharacter`.

Let's do this now:

1. From within the blueprints directory where you placed your GameMode, right-click to create a new **Blueprint Class**.
2. Expand the **All Classes** expander, and in the search box, type `vr char`.

3. You'll see the `VRCharacter` and **VRSimpleCharacter** classes listed. Select **VRSimpleCharacter**. Name the new blueprint `BP_VRCharacter`:

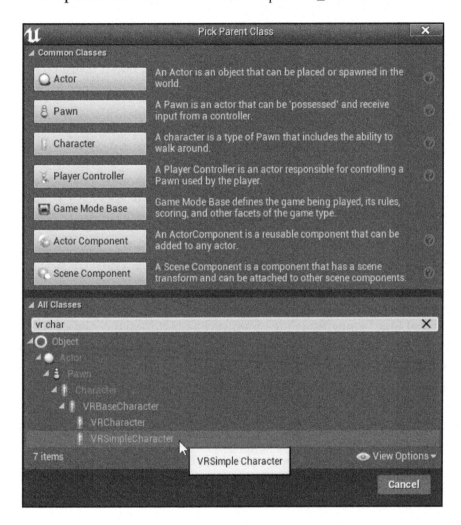

4. Now, open up your Game Mode and set `BP_VRCharacter` as its **Default Pawn Class**.

Run the map. You won't be able to move around yet, but you should be properly registered to the floor.

Setting up input

Now that our character is in place and our game mode has been told to spawn it, let's allow our player to control it.

First, we're going to need to map some inputs. If we wanted to do this by hand, we would do this through **Settings** | **Project Settings** | **Engine** | **Input**, but to save a bit of time here, let's just copy the `DefaultInput.ini` file from the VRExpansion sample project into ours:

1. Open the directory where you unzipped the VRExpansion example project, and copy the `DefaultInput.ini` file from its `Config` directory
2. Open your current project directory and paste `DefaultInput.ini` into it

Re-open your working project. Of course, if we were building our own game, we would design our own input scheme for it, but this gives us a quick way to have a few inputs already mapped and ready to go for testing.

Setting up your VR character using example assets

Now, ordinarily we would walk through the process of building this character from the ground up, but we have a lot of material to get through here, so we're going to save ourselves a bit of time by migrating the example character from the VRExpansion example project into our own, and then we're going to dig into how it works.

Making effective use of example assets

This brings up a point worth mentioning about using plugins and example assets and code. Very often, libraries and plugins will ship with example assets that have already been designed to work with them. It's always a good idea to get familiar with these, as they show you the author's intention for how they expect their code to be used. It's often the case, too, that these assets will be pretty close right out of the box to what you need them to be, though they'll rarely be exactly what you need.

There are two approaches you can take when making use of someone's example assets or code—you can incorporate the example wholesale, and then modify or remove anything that works differently than the way you want it to work, or you can build your own assets from scratch, using the example for guidance to see how the author recommends that you use their code. There are benefits and drawbacks to each approach. The first approach tends to get you working much earlier, but you'll often wind up with a lot of extra stuff that you don't need that then needs to be cleaned out. (Remember that we don't believe in cargo-cult programming here—you're not simply going to dump this code into your project and walk away without understanding it.) The second approach can take a more time, but gives you a clean class that does exactly what you need and only what you need, and that you understand fairly well because you wrote it.

There's a middle road too, which is the path we recommend. Remember Kent Beck's advice: *Make it work; make it right; make it fast*? Consider using an existing example asset or class as part of your *make it work* phase. During this phase, you're experimenting with the class as the author wrote it, and learning how it works and how it's meant to be used. Then, once you have a handle on things, start pulling out the stuff you now know you don't need, and changing things that need to work differently, until you have a version that does what you need it to do. Now, move into your *make it right* phase. Is it OK as it is? Could it be maintained easily? Would another engineer, or future-you, a year from now, be able to read this blueprint and understand what's going on? Consider in light of these questions whether you want to write a new, parallel version of the class now that you have a workable template for how it should be built.

Migrating the example pawn

In light of this approach, let's migrate the example project's VR character blueprint into our project so we can start experimenting with it and learn how it's built:

1. From the `VRExpPluginExample` project, find the `Vive_PawnCharacter` blueprint in `Content/VRExpansion/Vive`, and migrate it into your new project's `Content` folder

 Don't worry about the Vive-centric name. This character works fine with the Oculus Rift and Windows Mixed Reality headsets as well. When this plugin was first written, only the Vive supported room-scale VR. Once Oculus added this support, the plugin was updated to accommodate it, but the example names were never changed.

2. Return to your new project, and switch your Game Mode's **Default Pawn Class** to the `Vive_PawnCharacter` we just migrated in.

We wanted to create the other VR character as an example to demonstrate that new classes introduced in plugins can be used just like any other engine class, but for the work we're actually going to do here, we're going to use the migrated character.

Test it out. You should now be able to navigate through the environment using teleport, and you should be able to use the grip buttons to change your movement mode:

Play around a bit with this, and then we're going to take a look under the hood.

Making sense of complicated blueprints

Now that we have the basics working, let's do some digging and understand how this class was built. You should find, as we do this, that many of the techniques you'll see in this blueprint will make more sense as a result of the work you've done so far in this book.

The techniques we're going to explore here are valuable. If you work professionally in software development, or even if you work as a hobbyist, sooner or later, you're going to encounter an existing piece of code and you're going to need to figure out how it works. We're going to guide you through a few strategies to make this a far less-daunting task than it might at first seem.

Let's get to it:

1. Open `Content/VRExpansion/Vive`, and find the `Vive_PawnCharacter`
   blueprint. Open it up.
2. Open its **Event Graph**.

Yikes! There's a lot of stuff in here.

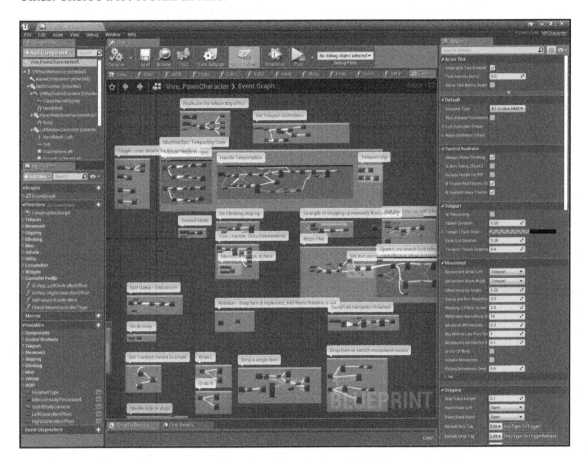

The example project's Vive_PawnCharacter Blueprint contains a lot of Blueprint code. Digging through it isn't as daunting as it may seem at first.

Here's the thing though: as daunting as this may seem at first, you're going to appreciate this soon enough. This class is an incredible compendium of useful techniques for developing VR characters. On its own, this would be a thing of beauty, but what makes it even more amazingly useful is that the blueprints written here and the underlying C++ code have been written with network replication in mind, so if you're planning to write a networked VR experience, this class will help you right out of the box.

To make use of it, however, you need some sense of where to begin. Let's learn how to approach a new class and figure it out.

Begin by checking the parent class

The first thing you want to do any time you're looking at a new blueprint is check the upper-right corner of the interface, and see what its parent class is.

In our case, we can see that this blueprint derives from `VRCharacter`. `VRCharacter` is a native class written in C++. If you follow the link provided by the parent class indicator, it will open Visual Studio to this class, and you can explore its native implementation to learn more about it. For our purposes here, we're going to stay in Blueprints, but it's worth knowing that this is a thing you can do.

(If we were to burrow through this class in its native implementation, we would see that it derives from a `VRBaseCharacter` class, which in turn derives from `Character`. So, this class is essentially an Unreal character as described here: `https://docs.unrealengine.com/en-US/Gameplay/Framework/Pawn/Character`. But it has additional VR-specific modifications to replicate the camera and hand-controller positions, and handle movement in ways that make sense for VR.)

Looking at the components to see what they're made of

The next thing to look at for any new class you're exploring is its **Components** list:

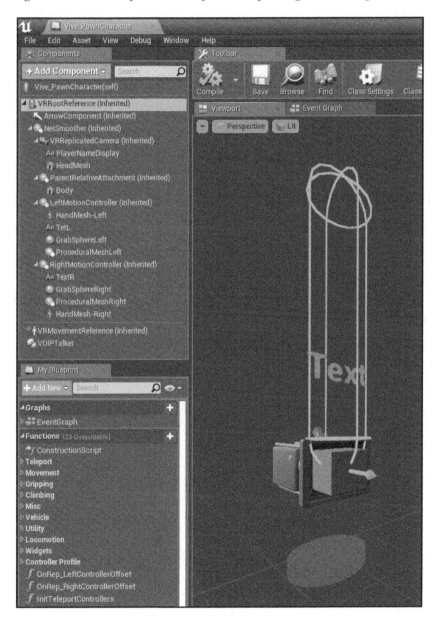

Looking at this components list tells us a lot about this character class and what it can do. It's worth doing this with the viewport active so you can see which components have visible representations. Roll over each component to see what type of component it is, and allow this to build an overall sense of the whole class in your mind.

We can see that the VRCharacter supports a static mesh for the head, a static mesh for the body, and two motion controllers with text renderers, grab-detection spheres, and skeletal meshes attached. (This motion controller setup should feel somewhat familiar to the work we did on grip interactions.) We can also see that it provides a character movement component and some support for VOIP communication.

You don't need to agonize over every detail when you're doing this. The point at this stage of the process is to build an overall mental model of what's in the class and how the parts fit together.

Look for known events and see what happens when they run

Another useful starting point for getting information about a blueprint is to begin with events we know are likely to be implemented and see what they do.

Most classes will do some sort of setup work on **Event BeginPlay**, and most will do some work on **Event Tick**, so these are generally smart starting points:

1. Hit *Ctrl + F* to activate the **Find Results** panel and type beginplay into the search bar.

2. Hit *Enter*, since we're just interested in searching inside this blueprint:

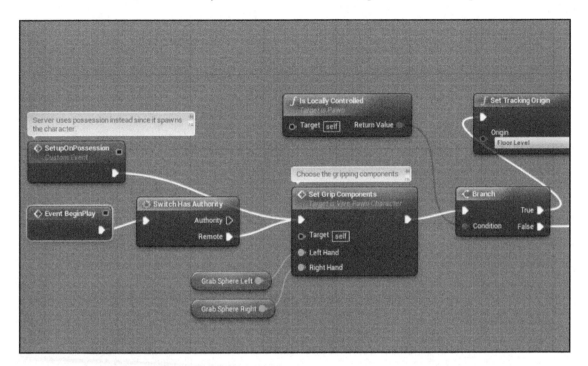

Event BeginPlay appears on the **Find Results** list. We can double-click it to jump to that event in the blueprint.

Looking at **BeginPlay**, we can see that it only handles this event on clients from the server; it uses a **SetupOnPossession** custom event instead. We can see that it's setting up grip components for the locally-controlled player; it's adjusting the tracking origin and spectator screen, and then for every body it's going to spawn and set up a pair of BP_Teleport_Controller actors, which get attached to the motion controllers.

We may not know everything yet about this pawn, but just from looking at its **BeginPlay**, we've learned a few things:

- This pawn has been set up to be used in network play—it's executing different paths depending on whether it has the authority
- The pawn handles some things differently depending on whether it's running locally or controlled by another player
- Teleport handling is managed by a separate class from the pawn. We'll want to look at this

Now let's do the same thing for **Event Tick**:

- Search for `Tick`, and double-click the **Event Tick** entry that comes up in the results:

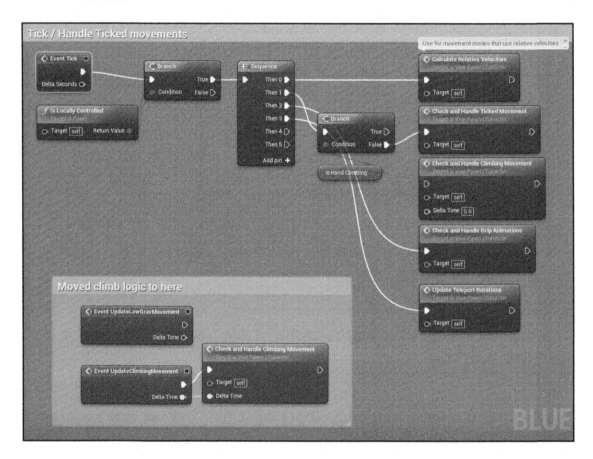

Again, this tells us a few things right off the bat:

- Remote pawns don't do anything on the tick at all. This is good.
- The tick is handling movement for the most part, but climbing movement was moved to a separate event.
- Grip animations and teleport rotations are being handled on the tick too.

It's not necessary to do a deep dig at this stage of the process yet. Your intention here is to give yourself a broad view of what parts this class contains and when and how they do their work. This way, when you're looking for details later on, you'll have a good sense of where to look.

This process has given us a bit of information so far. Just by knowing the parent class, the components it contains, and two of its known events, we can already intuit a fair bit about what this class can do. Now it's time to get more specific and begin with a simple question—what happens when the player tries to teleport?

Using inputs as a way to find a starting point in your blueprint

We could try to answer this question by looking through this huge event graph and trying to find what we're looking for (and in this instance, that would work out reasonably well for us because the graph is well-organized and the author has done a good job of documenting it), but there's an easier way.

Start with a thing you know, and follow the execution from there to see what happens.

In our case, we know that the player executes the teleport by hitting one of the Dpads or thumbsticks, depending on whether they're on a Vive, an Oculus, or some other device. That's going to be mapped as an input. Let's find it:

1. Open **Settings** | **Project Settings** | **Engine** | **Input**, and expand the **Action Mappings** expander.

There's an input here named **TeleportRight** that sounds promising. If we expand it, we can see that it's mapped to the right thumbstick, or **FaceButton 1** (which is on the Vive is the Dpad's top quadrant). That's the one:

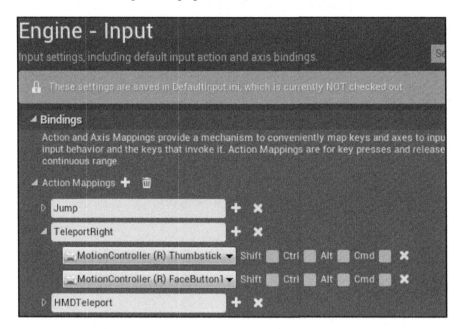

Now that we have an input name to look for, we'll search for **TeleportRight** in our blueprints, and we're probably going to find something. (Some projects handle their inputs in the native C++ environment, but it's much more common to do it in blueprints.)

2. Jump back to your event graph and hit *Ctrl + F* to bring up the **Find Results** panel.

3. Type `TeleportRight` in the search box and hit the binoculars symbol to the right of the box to run the search in all blueprints:

There it is. Our character is handling that input:

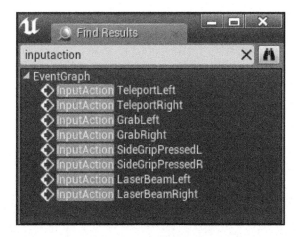

Another useful strategy when you're looking for inputs is simply to type inputaction into your search box. Any input that's been mapped using the project's Inputs settings (which are written to DefaultInput.ini) will begin with this prefix.

4. Double-click the entry for **InputAction TeleportRight**, and you'll be taken to that event handler in the event graph:

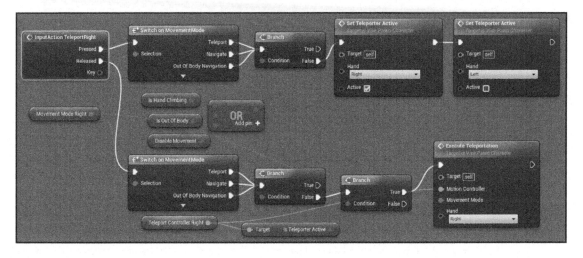

Now we have something to look at. We can use a breakpoint to confirm that we're looking at the right thing.

Setting breakpoints and tracing execution

We're going to use a breakpoint to verify that the code we think is going to execute when we trigger the input is really what executes. This is a common technique for understanding someone else's code. When you're not sure about its execution path, put breakpoints at locations you expect to be hit, and then see which ones really trip. This will give you a starting point from which to begin exploring the software:

1. Select the **InputAction TeleportRight** node, and hit *F9* to put a breakpoint on it, or right-click and select **Toggle breakpoint** from the context menu:

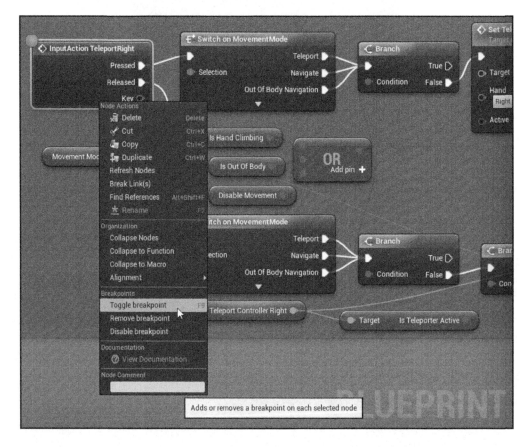

When a breakpoint is active on a blueprint node, it instructs the editor to pause the blueprint's execution when it reaches the node containing the breakpoint. You can then step through execution one action at a time and see what the blueprint is doing. Let's test this now.

2. With the breakpoint still set on **InputAction TeleportRight**, launch a **VR Preview** session (you don't really need to put on your headset for this—we're going to be back out of it in a second), and activate the right teleport input.

   The game should appear to freeze on you, and your VR headset will stop displaying the environment.

3. Take a look now at the **InputAction TeleportRight** node. You'll see a red arrow indicating that the blueprint simulation has paused at this node:

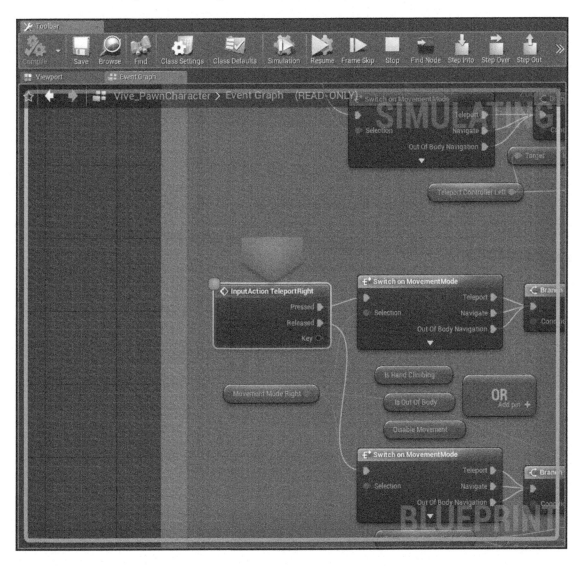

Let's take note of a few other things here too. You can see that the blueprint display is ringed with a yellow indicator to indicate that it's currently simulating, and you can see from the title line that the graph is currently in a read-only state. You're not allowed to change a blueprint while you're simulating it:

Let's also take a look at the execution controls that have appeared on our toolbar:

- The **Resume** button will resume normal execution. (This is dicey when running VR—your headset may not properly wake back up from the paused state.)
- The **Frame Skip** button allows a single frame to execute and returns to a paused state.
- The **Stop** button will shut down your **Play-in-Editor** (PIE) session and return to the editor.
- The **Find Node** button takes you back to the node at which execution is currently stopped.

These next three nodes are the important ones for stepping through code, and you should memorize their hotkeys because you'll use them all of the time:

- **Step Into** (*F11*) steps to the next executed node, and jumps into a function's implementation if the node represents a blueprint function call or a macro.

Let's see this in action before we move on.

Hit *F11* now. See how we've now jumped to the **Switch on MovementMode** node:

1. Roll over the selection input of **Switch on MovementMode** node. The rollover tooltip indicates the input's type and its current value:

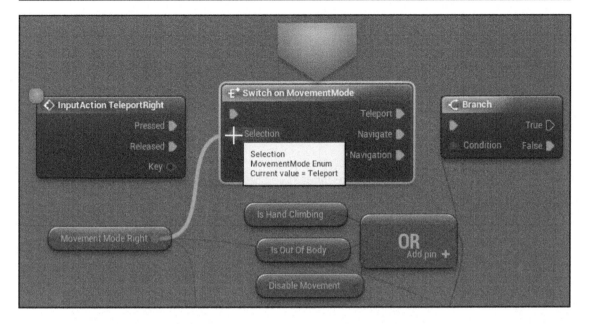

We can see that **Movement Mode Right** is currently set to **Teleport**, so the first branch of the switch statement is going to execute.

2. Hit *F11* again, and execution steps to the `Branch` statement.

   Rolling over its input value, we can see that, because we're not hand-climbing, out of body, or in a movement-disabled state, this value is false and the false branch is going to execute.

3. Hitting *F11* again takes us to the **SetTeleporterActive** node as we expected.
4. Hit *F11* again, and this time something interesting happened. Instead of jumping to the next node in the event graph, we jumped inside of the `Set Teleporter Active` function.

   This is the difference between **Step Into** (*F11*) and **Step Over** (*F10*). *Step into* will take you wherever execution goes, even into function calls or macros, while *F10* will step over a function call without taking us inside it.

5. Continue hitting *F11* until we step inside of the **Is Valid** macro.

   We're not actually interested in the contents of this macro, so we'd like to step back out so we can continue looking at our `SetTeleporterActive` function.

6. Hit *Alt + Shift + F11*, or the **Step Out** button to get back to the SetTeleporterActive graph.

Now you've seen each of these three navigation operations in action. Practice them and get used to using their hotkeys. Stepping through blueprints like this is one of the fastest and most effective ways of seeing how a complex blueprint runs.

Remember the following:

- *F11* (**Step Into**) steps to the next executed node, even if it's inside another function or macro.
- *F10* (**Step Over**) steps to the next executed node in the current context, but does not step inside functions or macros that get called from that context.
- *Alt + Shift + F11* (**Step Out**) steps back out of a function or macro to the context that called it.

Memorize these keys. You'll be happy you did.

These hotkeys—*F9* to toggle a breakpoint, *F10* to step over, and *F11* to step in, also work pretty much exactly the same way in Visual Studio when tracing through C++ code, and the same general techniques—find a known point in the code, set a breakpoint, and then step through to see how it works, and apply it there too. Use *Shift + F11* to step out of a method in Visual Studio.

7. Hit *F11* until execution jumps into the Activate Teleporter method.

Take a look at your tab bar and you'll see that you've now jumped into a different class altogether. The VRExpansion plugin's example project uses a separate Blueprint actor called BP_TeleportController to handle drawing the teleport beam and the target indicator. This is useful information.

This is also a smart way to design this system. Keeping a system such as this bundled together into its own object makes it easier in the long run to swap things out, to add it to a new character class, or to find what you're looking for if you need to debug. What you're seeing here is a more advanced organizational principle, but it's worth learning to think in these terms.

Viewing the execution trace

Let's say we were stepping through a blueprint and we realized we needed to jump back a few steps to see what values drove a branch or a switch. To do this, we can make use of the **Debug** panel's **Execution Trace**:

1. Select **Window** | **Debug** to bring up the **Debug** panel.
2. Expand the panel's **Execution Trace** section.
3. Continue stepping through your blueprint and watch what happens here:

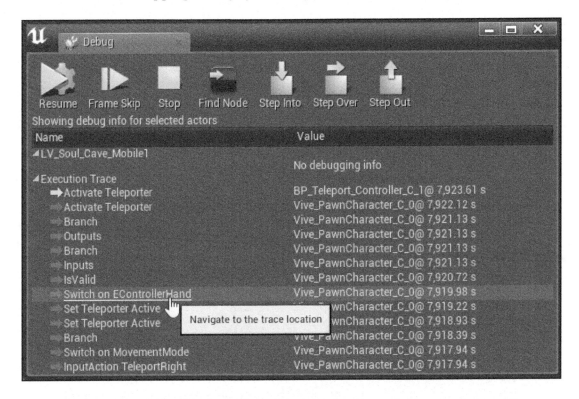

The execution trace will build a list of breadcrumbs showing where we've been so far as we step through execution. Any time you need to revisit a previous execution step, you can click it, and you'll be taken to that section of the graph, where you can see what inputs were driving it and what outputs it produced.

This is one of the most effective ways you can learn a new blueprint: set breakpoints and see how it runs. You'll develop a very clear sense of how the class is built this way.

As you progress through your development career and get good at figuring out and leveraging existing code, you're probably going to be surprised by how many developers you encounter who hold themselves back by failing to learn to do this effectively and wind up doing things the hard way, if they get anything done at all. Some of this, you'll find, is what developers call the *not-invented-here* syndrome (generally a fear of doing the work masked as an ego), and some of it is simply lack of knowledge. The time you spend doing your research and learning what's already been figured out about the problem you're trying to solve is never wasted time.

Managing breakpoints with the Debug window

We're going to do another exploration in a moment, but, first, we're going to clear our breakpoints out of the **Vive_PawnCharacter** blueprint:

1. Hit the **Stop** button to end the simulation and return to the editor.
2. Tab back to the **Vive_PawnCharacter** blueprint, and if it isn't still open, select **Window | Debug**.

This time, we're interested in the **Breakpoints** list displayed on this panel:

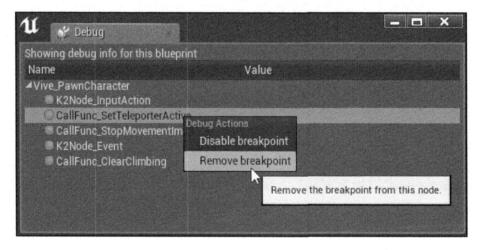

In this screenshot, I've added a few more breakpoints to make the example clearer.

You can click any breakpoint in the list to jump to its location in the blueprint, and you can right-click to disable or remove a breakpoint.

 Disabling a breakpoint turns the breakpoint off without removing it. This is useful if you want to omit a breakpoint temporarily but still want to be able to re-enable it later for further debugging.

You can also toggle any breakpoint on or off by selecting a blueprint node and hitting *F9*.

Let's clear them all out of our class for now:

- Hit **Debug** | **Delete All Breakpoints** (or use *Ctrl + Shift + F9*).

This will remove the breakpoint we set on the input action earlier, along with any other breakpoints we might have set in this blueprint. This menu also gives you the option to disable and enable all breakpoints in a class, as well.

Using the call stack

Let's do another experiment now. We've seen how we can begin stepping through execution at an input event to see what happens when the event gets called, but what if we're interested in a particular function, and we want to see when it gets called and who calls it? We have a few powerful tools to help us here too.

Let's say we were seeing a camera fade happen in-game and we wanted to find out who was calling it. Maybe we're not even sure what the name of the call is going to be, but we're guessing it might have the word *fade* in its name:

1. Hit *Ctrl + F* to activate the **Find Results** window, and type `fade` into the search bar.

2. Use the binoculars to find in all blueprints:

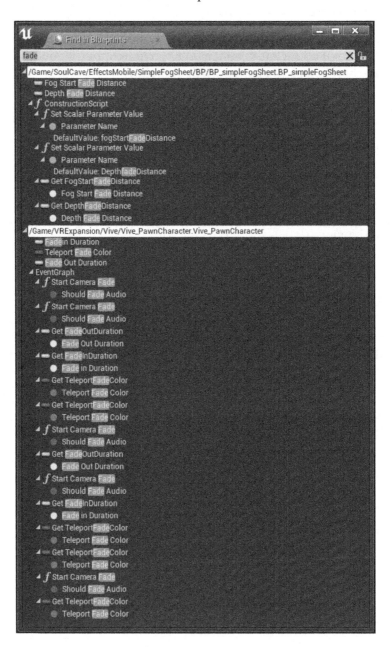

We can see a number of entries here, but most of them are variables. Clearly, the stuff in the fog sheet isn't what we're looking for, but these **Start Camera Fade** calls in **Vive_PawnCharacter** look promising.

3. Double-click the first **Start Camera Fade** entry to jump to its location in the graph, and hit *F9* to set a breakpoint on it.
4. Repeat this for the other three.
5. Launch a **VR Preview** session and activate a teleport.

Execution will stop at one of the **Start Camera Fade** nodes. This time, though, instead of stepping through the code to see what happens next, we want to see how we got here.

6. Hit **Window | Developer Tools | Blueprint Debugger** to open up **Blueprint Debugger**.

You'll see that the first of the three displayed tabs is labeled **Call Stack**:

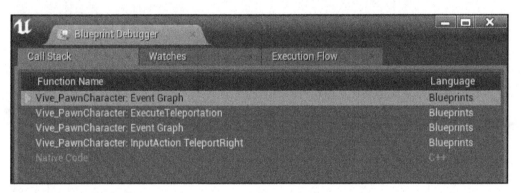

The **Call Stack** is a list of all of the events and functions that led to where the execution has currently been paused. This gives you an enormous amount of information. The top of a call stack represents where execution is currently paused, and the entry right below it is the function or event that called it. The entry below that one is whatever called that function, and so on.

Looking at this stack, we can see that a C++ routine detected the button-press and triggered **InputAction TeleportRight**. Then, a call was made from the event graph. Let's double-click this entry in the **Call Stack** to see it:

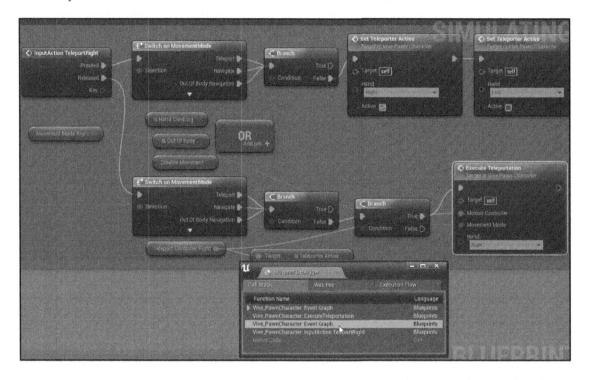

It's an **Execute Teleportation** call triggered by the input action's **Released** event.

We can double-click the next call—the ExecuteTeleportation event, and see the graph that leads to the camera fade we were looking for.

This is a powerful technique, and you should get into the habit of using it.

 For more information on using Unreal's blueprint debugging tools, look here: https://docs.unrealengine.com/en-us/Engine/Blueprints/ UserGuide/Debugging.

Do a bit of exploring through the blueprint using this tool, and then hit **Stop** to return to the editor.

Finding variable references

Going back to our teleport example, what if we wanted to know what changes that
`Movement Mode` variable that drives the `switch` statements from **InputAction
TeleportRight**?

This is easy to do:

1. Select the **Movement Mode Right** variable.
2. Right-click it and select **Find References**, or hit *Alt + Shift + F*:

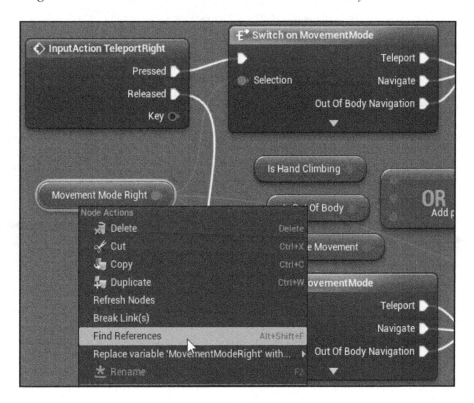

We can see that this variable is used in a number of places, but it's only set in two locations. This is what we're interested in:

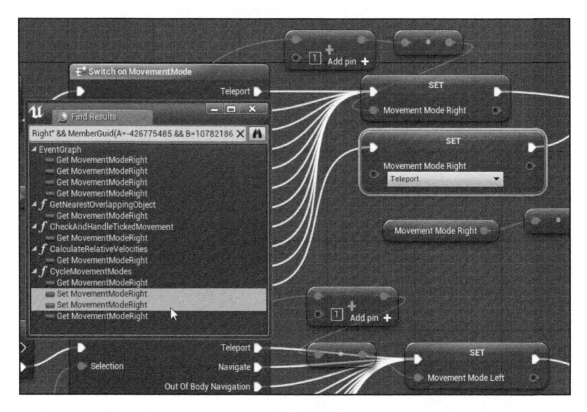

3. Double-click on of the **Set MovementModeRight** entries in your **Find Results**.

This takes us to the location where this variable is set, and we can see that this is taking place in a function called `Cycle Movement Modes`. We could then use the strategies we've learned to see when and how this function gets called, and what else happens along with it.

You can use *Alt* + Shift + *F* with functions as well as variables. Practice doing this.

Making sense of someone else's code is like untying a complicated knot. You'll discourage yourself if you try to make sense of it all at once. Instead, you find a single strand and start following it and pulling it apart, and the structure of it becomes clear as you go. These tools can help you to do this.

Using more of the VRExpansion plugin

VRExpansion is a large plugin, and it provides a great deal of functionality to VR developers. Now that you have some strategies in place for exploring it and figuring out how it works and how you can use it, you're going to be able to unlock enormous potential.

In addition to the character we've just explored, this plugin provides a VR-enabled player controller, an AI controller, stereo widgets, buttons, levers, and much more.

If you'd like to get a better sense of what this plugin includes (there's far too much to fit within this chapter), hit the **View Options** popout in your content browser, turn on **Show Plugin Content**, and make sure **Show C++ Classes** is visible:

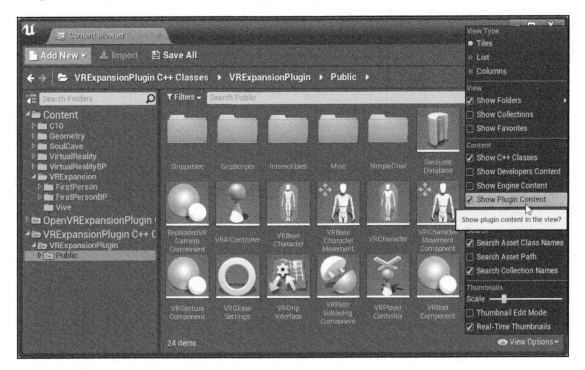

Browse through the class directory and see what's in there. If you double-click any of these classes, its native source will open in Visual Studio.

One of your best resources though is the VR Expansion Plugin forum at UnrealEngine.com, found here: https://forums.unrealengine.com/development-discussion/vr-ar-development/89050-vr-expansion-plugin.

The plugin's author, Joshua Statzer (mordentral) is very active on the forum and is surrounded by a community of helpful developers who are very willing to help new developers to get on their feet.

Summary

This chapter took a bit of a different turn from the tutorials we've done up to this point, as its intention really is to help you to get to a point where you can explore the numerous plugins, templates, examples, and other projects you find within the Unreal ecosystem and learn how to use them to accelerate your work and learn new techniques. This is one of the most valuable skills you can teach yourself as a developer. If you get comfortable exploring code you find in the wild, you'll develop much more powerful software in a much shorter time and learn more advanced techniques by seeing how experienced developers have approached the problem you're trying to solve. This will make you a better developer faster.

12
Where to Go from Here

Serious congratulations are in order.

By reaching this point, you've done more than many aspiring developers ever will, and that's no small achievement. The most valuable asset you can cultivate in your journey as a VR creator is your persistence and your willingness to do the work. By finishing this book, you've already shown dedication and a desire to see things through that will set you apart from the rest. Take a moment to recognize this quality in yourself.

You've probably spotted by now that our focus in writing this book differed from that of a lot of other tutorials. There's no shortage of material out there that will tell you what buttons to push, but here's the thing—knowing those things isn't how you become a good developer. You get good at this by learning how to think about the challenges you're trying to solve and how you can use the tools you have to solve them. To this end, we digressed multiple times into discussions of why something works the way it does or how else it could be used. Continue this thinking as you continue your own self-education. Taking the time to learn *why* will carry you much further than simply learning *what*. The latter could change with the next software update and usually won't apply to anything else. The underlying reasons we do things tend not to change. Train yourself to recognize that, to know a thing, you have to be able to describe why it is the way it is. We've tried throughout the course of this book to get you used to thinking about these *why* questions and to give you a number of tools to make more of these distinctions yourself.

We hope you've come away from this book with a lot that you can use as you develop VR, but, honestly, if you just came away with these two realizations alone, it would have been worth it:

- Success comes from persistence and willingness to do the work
- Focus on *why* rather than *what*

We also tried throughout the course of this book to demonstrate another important truth: **development is iterative**. Many of the examples we did together involved solving problems and changing our solutions as we discovered new problems or better ways of doing things. We tried, in doing this, to recreate the way developers really think as we solve problems. It's a process that happens one step at a time. By focusing on the next steps, doing whatever work is required to do the next step, and not giving up or surrendering to discouragement when it's not clear what those next steps should be, you can create nearly anything you imagine.

You will find yourself constantly asking yourself why you saw the results you did, or why a problem you need to fix might be happening. Becoming an effective developer isn't a matter of memorizing a lot of things—it's a matter of building effective ways of thinking so you can find your way through the problems you need to solve.

Take this to heart. You're embarking on a frontier, developing for a medium whose rules and vocabulary are still almost wholly unknown to us, and we're all in this together, learning what works and how we can help VR bloom into the art form we sense it's going to be. You'll be facing challenges that don't have known answers, because they simply haven't been solved yet. Maybe you'll be the first to discover them.

Final word

As we write this, VR is at a crossroads.

In the years immediately following the release of the Oculus Rift and the HTC Vive, there was a flurry of activity and interest around VR, and then as the years wore on, that interest leveled out. Many people brought out their VR headsets for parties or demos and then put them away again—why?

Well, it happened for a few reasons.

The first was a question of technology, and here we need to be honest with ourselves that this is first-generation tech. What's actually going on to make these headsets work is astonishing, but they have limitations. This first generation of the technology was too expensive and too difficult to set up for mainstream consumers. The headsets weren't comfortable to wear for long periods of time, and the limitations of the lenses and the screens combined to break presence by reminding users of the technology they were using. Fields of view were narrow, lenses blurred the image if they were even a little bit misaligned, and low-screen resolutions left pixel boundaries visible (the dreaded *screen door* effect). The hardware developers knew this, but they also knew that the only way past the growing pains of a newly-emerging technology is to work through them.

Think ahead a few years and you can see how these problems start going away in a big hurry. Screen resolutions are only going to keep improving, even as the screens get lighter and require less power. Optical waveguides are likely to replace the heavy Fresnel lenses we're using now and dramatically lighten the headsets and widen their field of view. External sensors are soon going to be a thing of the past, so setting up your VR headset won't require you to chew up three USB ports or mount base stations on your walls. Increasingly good standalone headsets and PC-based headsets that can communicate wirelessly with their base PCs will soon become the norm. These are very solvable problems, and it's reasonable to expect that they won't be significant concerns soon.

Then there's the question of simulator sickness. In the early years of the VR gold rush, developers tended to be utterly naive about this, or they became paranoid. Usually, the latter came as a response to the former. We all got our original DK1s and DK2s and immediately started making locomotion schemes just as we had on the flat screen, and we made ourselves sick. So, then we swung the pendulum in the other direction and teleported everywhere. Neither extreme is how it has to be. We're learning more about what we can do to move the player's view that works, and we encourage you to experiment with this as well. There are solutions that can work. The other reality is that people become acclimated to simulators, just as they do to being on a boat at sea. In the early 1990s, it was common for first-person shooters to induce motion sickness too. That doesn't happen anymore, in part because the rendering tech improved, but also in part because players got used to them. A similar effect is happening with VR. Be conscious of simulator sickness and design your software to mitigate the effect, but don't live in mortal fear of it: explore. Figure out what else can work. Early filmmakers had to figure out how they could get away with moving the camera and what cuts would work. This is the same thing. We'll solve this challenge through experimentation. Frontiers aren't places to be bound by rules. We don't know them yet.

The last challenge especially is where you come in. We really don't know what we can do with this technology. Anyone who tells you we *have* figured this out isn't using their imagination. We've barely gotten started.

In the gold rush that followed the first release of the Rift and the Vive, developers for the most part treated this medium as an updated version of whatever medium they already knew. Movie people saw this as a 3D movie device. Games people saw it as an immersive gaming device. Neither really had it right.

The language of this medium is mostly undiscovered, and that makes this an exciting place to play. We've advised you a few times to question those who try to tell you what you can't do in VR, and here we want to take this a step further. Break those boundaries on purpose. Try things you know aren't going to work, because one time in a hundred, they just might. Put active thought and imagination into the work you do in exploring VR. Let the medium show you how it works. We firmly believe that VR or some variant of it will be the defining medium of the 21st century. If you really think it through, it's hard to argue convincingly any other way. The benefits of immersion and presence are just too pronounced. But we need to figure out how these things really work. We know a few of the basics, but we are far from knowing the whole. Early film viewers watching the Lumière brothers' films of trains pulling into stations would have been hard-pressed to imagine anything even remotely approaching what films ultimately evolved into. Accept that this is the case here too. We've only begun to learn what we can do with this medium, and only barely begun to figure out how we can do it. The most exciting parts of this exploration lie ahead of us. Take a look at the following picture:

A frame from L'Arrivée d'un Train en Gare de la Ciotat (The Arrival of a Train at la Ciotat Station). by Auguste and Louis Lumière

In this book, we've really tried to give you a foundation from which to embark on this adventure. We wanted to give you a grounding in VR as a medium, but we also wanted to set you up to think about development and about Unreal Engine in ways that will empower you to do this exploration. We genuinely hope we've been able to be helpful regarding this. VR matters to us, as it obviously does to you too, or you wouldn't have made it through this book. Let's make some art.

Thank you, sincerely, for taking this journey with us.

Useful Mind Hacks

We've talked a lot throughout this book about ways to think about development, and we've suggested once or twice before that the factor that differentiates an effective developer from an amateur isn't so much what they know as how they think.

Effective thinking is a skill, and, like any other, it can be practiced. As we saw in the last chapter, you can simplify a complicated problem by breaking it down and finding a starting point. Let's take a moment now to explore a few more tricks that can help.

Rubber-duck debugging

You may have heard this phrase before: **rubber-duck debugging**. It's been around a long while and it's one of the most effective problem-solving tricks you can perform. The idea here is simple. Take anybody who will listen, and if there's nobody around, a rubber duck on your desk would do just as well (hence the name). Describe the problem you're trying to solve, out loud, and in simple terms. This forces you to organize your thoughts about the problem. If you find that you can't describe the problem in clear, simple terms, then you don't understand it yet. You're not ready to try to answer the question because you're not yet clear on what question you need to ask. Play with it and explore it until you really can phrase it in simple terms. Often, this process alone will suggest a clear solution to you, and if not, you now have a much better shot at finding a solution because you now know what question you're asking. Do this out loud or in writing. It's too easy to stay fuzzy and gloss over things when you let it tumble around in your mind. Force yourself to put the words in order. You'll be surprised by how powerful and effective this technique is.

Just the facts

When you realize something is going wrong in your software, write down what you see happening. Not what you think you see happening—just what you see. It's far too easy in debugging to jump to a conclusion about why something is happening and then dive into trying to solve that problem before you've really ascertained what problem you actually have. Take a step back and just look at what you can concretely observe.

Think like this: *That torch is appearing in the wrong position when it spawns*, as opposed to *The spawning routine is putting things in the wrong place*. You don't know that yet. You just know that one torch isn't where you expected it to be. Do an experiment. Spawn a different object. Does it appear in the right place? OK, then maybe there's a weird offset in your model. Another object is also out of position? OK, then, yes, it might be the routine that's spawning it. Or it might be some collision in your level that's keeping things from spawning where you want them and is shoving them to the closest available spot. Try moving the spawn point and see whether that changes things.

See what we're doing here? We're applying a basic scientific method to the problem we're solving. What do we see? What can we think of that might be causing that? How could we test it to see whether we're right? What new information did our test just give us? Do we know enough to work on a solution now?

It's very very easy to jump to a conclusion and burn a lot of time debugging the wrong problem. Taking the time to take a step back will help to keep you from doing this and keep you from a lot of frustrated stabbing in the dark. You'll solve problems this way.

Describing your solutions in positive terms

We talked a bit about *cargo-cult programming* in `Chapter 10`, *Creating a Multiplayer Experience in VR*, and made you promise not to do it. To take this idea further, let's look at a phrase we'd like you never to utter: *It works—don't touch it!*

This isn't how we describe a robust system. If you feel tempted to say this, congratulations! You're at step one of the *make it work; make it right; make it fast* process, and that means you're not done. What you've created is a successful example of what your ultimate solution may look like, but now it's time to start the *make it right* phase. You've met the requirements for this step of your development when you can give three answers about your solution in positive terms:

- It needs to solve X
- I know it solves X because....
- I know it's safe because....

Remember these three statements. Don't skip them. You should be able to describe in clear, simple terms what you're trying to do. (Your rubber duck is a good listener for this too.) You should be able to explain why the thing you just did takes care of the thing you're trying to do, and you should be able to do this in positive terms: *We needed to make sure the player can't fire their weapon while the pause menu is up. This takes care of it by having the input handler check for a paused state before it calls the fire function.* Finally, you should be able to explain why this thing is safe to do: *I know this is safe because we're ensuring that we clear any existing input when the pause state begins, and the input handler knows to allow only the unpause command through.*

Discipline yourself to do this, and use clear, positive terms. If you're being vague, you're hiding from a thing you need to solve. Make this a habit: describe what you're trying to do, why you know your solution does it, and why you know it's safe to do it. You'll head off a lot of bugs before they ever even have a chance to make it into your software this way.

Plan how you're going to maintain and debug your code when you write it

Technical debt is an insidious thing. This term describes the downstream cost of fixing a mess that was left in the code, usually as a result of rushed development. And it's a project-killer.

Let's say, for instance, that you needed to get something ready for a demo, and you ran out of time so you put in a hack solution. Then, you left it there and built a bunch of additional systems on top of it. Now, you're trying to get your game online, and the thing you did shows up incorrectly on the client, and you realize to your horror that you have to rewrite every one of those systems you built on top of that hack that went in for the demo, and, even worse, you realize it's going to take weeks of work to do this.

Or, let's say you were in a hurry building your blueprint, and it works but looks like a clump of hair in a drain. You move on to the next problem. Six months later, you're about to demo the game for your publisher and a weird bug keeps happening in your system. You haven't looked at it since you wrote it, and now you're forced to spend all day and all night untangling the mess you made so you can figure out where the bug is happening.

In both of these cases, you would have saved yourself a lot of time and heartache if you'd taken the time to clean up the work you did while it was fresh in your mind. If you absolutely have to hack, mark the hack as a hack, and if you know what the proper solution should really be, write it into a comment right next to the hack. And then fix it before you build anything else on top of it. If you've gotten a blueprint or a bit of code running, go straight into your *make it right* phase while everything you learned during your *make it work* phase is still fresh in your mind.

Remember this truth: *The vast majority of the life cycle of a piece of code is spent maintaining and debugging it*. Drill this into your head. It's much harder to debug code than it is to write it the first time, so give yourself every advantage you can. You are not saving yourself any time if you rush when you first write your solution. You're saving time on the small part of its life and creating a big headache that will haunt you during the long part of its life. Plan for your code to be debugged when you write it. You'll be happy you did.

Favor simple solutions

Sadly, you're going to run into developers who write complicated, impenetrable code or blueprints in a mistaken effort to impress everyone else with how smart they are. They're secretly fantasizing that someone else is going to look over their shoulder at their unreadable code and think, *Wow! They must be so smart! I can't read any of that*. Please, oh please, don't be this developer.

The experienced developers whose respect you really want won't be impressed by a shambolic blueprint or obfuscated code. They'll wonder why you left it in such a mess and assume that it's because you didn't know any better. Amateurs write unreadable code. Pros know they're going to have to maintain it a year from now when they've forgotten everything about it, and they don't want to make that job any harder than it has to be.

You'll know you're doing it well if your *make it right* draft is simpler and cleaner than your *make it work* draft was.

Look it up before you make it up

We mentioned this in `Chapter 10`, *Creating a Multiplayer Experience in VR*, and want to reiterate it here: one of the core mistakes new developers make is failing to do research before they dive into a problem, and they wind up rewriting code that's already been written.

Do your homework. When you're trying to solve a problem, before you start hacking away at it, see whether anybody else has tacked anything similar and left footprints behind. Is there already a tool in the engine that does this or does most of it? Are there examples in the templates or the sample projects that show how it can be solved? Has someone written a tutorial somewhere? Sometimes, the answer is going to be *no*, but far more often, you're going to find something that either points you directly toward a solution or gets you closer than you would have gotten without it.

We once saw a small team of engineers waste weeks of development budget on a problem that had already been solved with a single function in a freely-licensed plugin. That's time that didn't go into making the game better, and you don't need to fall into this trap. Research is part of your development process and should always happen before you start typing or dragging nodes.

This leads us right into our next topic of discussion where can you look when you need to find information?

Research and Further Reading

A browser and search engine are among your best friends when developing software. If you practice the art of effective searching and take note of a few useful starting places for your search, you're going to accelerate your learning enormously. Software development changes extremely quickly, and cutting-edge software development such as real-time VR changes even more so. The time you spend learning how to search for information effectively will serve you forever.

Let's talk about a few places to begin.

Unreal Engine resources

Of course, one of the first and most important places to look for information about Unreal Engine is at the source. `https://www.unrealengine.com` should be one of the first places you look any time you need new information. You can get there via a browser or find the information in your Epic Games launcher.

Here are a few essential Unreal Engine links:

- **Unreal Engine 4 Documentation**: `https://docs.unrealengine.com/en-us/` —Start here always. Any time you're working with something new, give its relevant page a read.
- **Unreal Engine Forums**: `https://forums.unrealengine.com/`—There is a lot of useful information here, along with a huge population of forum users willing to help out others with questions. Jump in here and contribute constructively. You'll grow as a developer much faster with a community around you.
- **UE4 AnswerHub**: `https://answers.unrealengine.com/index.html`—When you're facing a specific question, search for its answer here. If you can't find it, ask. The key word here is *specific*. If you ask, *How do I Unreal?* that question clearly demonstrates you haven't done your homework, so you'll be ignored. Good questions, though, get good answers. Be willing to return the favor, too. If you see a question you know the answer to, jump in and help out.

- **Unreal Academy**: `https://academy.unrealengine.com/`—This is a series of focused tutorials geared toward specific topics of interest, either within the engine or out in the professional world. They generally take the form of a series of video lessons, and the quality is consistently high. This is one of the best places to broaden and sharpen your skills.

- **Unreal Engine YouTube Channel:** `https://www.youtube.com/channel/UCBobmJyzsJ6Ll7UbfhI4iwQ`—This is another resource many new developers overlook, but you shouldn't; it's important. Here's the thing: Unreal Engine is absolutely huge, and with hundreds of engineers working on it, along with thousands more in the community, it evolves and grows fast. Because of this, there's a ton of amazingly useful stuff in the Engine that just hasn't been documented anywhere because it's too new or too niche. The secret to finding this stuff are the *Live Training* videos on the Unreal Engine channel. These are nearly always given by whatever engineer wrote the system they're talking about or by a trainer who knows it really well, and they're a fountain of useful information. If you really want to learn how to use this engine, this is the place to do it.

- **User Groups:** `https://www.unrealengine.com/en-US/user-groups`—Get involved in the community of real-life people in your area. Find meet-ups and events, and then go to them. This is one of the biggest secrets we see new developers overlook—they don't put themselves out in the world. Whether you're looking for collaborators, looking to get hired, or looking to hire someone, you're doing yourself a big service by getting out there and participating in the community.

For more general programming questions, one of the best resources out there is **Stack Overflow** (`https://stackoverflow.com/`). It's not Unreal-centric, but if you're looking for information on C++ development, this is where you'll find some of the most experienced developers on the web. Be warned though—the Stack community is notoriously intolerant of low-effort questions. Be respectful of everyone's time and come in with a question after you've gone as far as you can to find the answer to it on your own. Describe what you were trying to do, what you did, and what challenges you faced. Do this, and you'll get some of the most reliable expert advice you can get on the web.

VR resources

Getting good information on VR is tricky. Everyone's still figuring this medium out, and nearly anything you read will wind up being some combination of legitimate information and unfounded opinion and lore. That's nobody's fault—this medium is simply too new for us to understand fully.

We began this book by advising you to question any accepted wisdom about VR, and we want to repeat that here. Remember that the earliest surviving motion picture was made in 1888, and it wasn't until 1925 that Sergei Eisenstein really figured out the language of film editing. It took thirty-seven years to figure out one of the most fundamental aspects of the genre. *Citizen Kane* came sixteen years after that. Please remember this when somebody tells you what you can't do in VR. We haven't got the faintest inkling of a clue what the limits of this medium are. Dive in and play with it. You're working on a frontier. Don't be afraid to try weird things you think might not work. This is how discoveries are made.

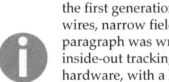

A quick word about the occasional bloggers who will crop up in your feed declaring VR *dead* because it hasn't yet erupted into a mass medium in the space of two years: that's not how new means of communication propagate through society. It took almost three decades for cellular phones to become common consumer devices and longer for personal computers. This is no different. At the time of this writing, we're still on the first generation of consumer VR headsets, with heavy lenses and wires, narrow fields of view, and external sensors. (On the morning this paragraph was written, Oculus announced its first desktop headset with inside-out tracking.) We're very, very early in the development of this hardware, with a lot of technical challenges still to overcome, but it's evident to anyone really paying attention that they are going to be overcome. We have no way of knowing whether, when you read this, we'll be in another *VR is dead* phase or another VR gold rush, or hopefully somewhere in the middle, but think about this from a standpoint of reality. When XR headsets are as comfortable to wear as glasses, don't require wires, have batteries that can last all day, and can offer immersive fields of view, we'll all be using them. This medium isn't going away. Work in it because you love it.

This advice aside, here are a few resources we recommend that you check out:

- **Oculus VR design resources**: https://developer.oculus.com/design/ —The Oculus *VR Best Practices* document, while a little dated at the time of this writing, remains one of the best overall guides for things to think about when designing for VR, and the *Developer Perspectives* collection should be considered essential reading for anyone designing for VR.
- **Road to VR**: https://www.roadtovr.com/—This is one of the longest-running and most expertly-edited news sources for VR. They're serious about this medium, and they know what they're talking about. Consider this essential regular reading.
- **Upload VR**: https://uploadvr.com/—This is another of the genuinely good sources of information on VR, and a great place to get information on the state of the VR hardware and software industry.

Here are a few people worth seeking out and listening to:

- **Jaron Lanier** is a computer scientist, author, and composer, and he was a crucial pioneer in the development of VR's first phase in the 1980s. He's the reason we call it *virtual reality*. You'd be hard-pressed to find anyone on Earth who's spent more time thinking about and working with this medium.
- **Michael Abrash** is chief scientist at Oculus and is a consistent voice for its future. Seek out his talks on YouTube, or wherever you find them.
- **John Carmack**, co-creator of *Doom* and *Quake*, now works for Oculus and is one of the foremost engineers pushing VR forward. If you want a good sense of where the tech is right now and where it's about to be, you can count on him to be a very candid and deeply informed source of information.
- **Marshall McLuhan** was one of the most influential thinkers in the 20th century about the ways media and communication shape our society. You've been swimming through an ocean of his ideas whether you've heard his name before or not. *The medium is the message*—that's him. *Global village*—also McCluhan. His central work, *Understanding Media*, is a sometimes-challenging read, but it quite literally changed how we viewed the role of electronic media in the world. We bring him up here because to work in VR is to work on a frontier of communication technology that, through its powers of immersion and presence, has the potential to shape us more dramatically than anything previously has. McCluhan would have been fascinated by VR and probably terrified of what it could do to us. Why not put some thought into what that might mean?

There are many, many others we could cite, but, in truth, it's fairly impossible to write an exhaustive list of resources on a topic as new and fluid as VR, and it's possibly futile given that this is a medium within which five-month-old information is considered woefully out-of-date. Consider these resources as starting points, but understand that they're far from complete. Let your own exploration take you where it will.

Other Books You May Enjoy

If you enjoyed this book, you may be interested in these other books by Packt:

Hands-On Data Science and Python Machine Learning
Frank Kane

ISBN: 978-1-78728-074-8

- Learn how to clean your data and ready it for analysis
- Implement the popular clustering and regression methods in Python
- Train efficient machine learning models using decision trees and random forests
- Visualize the results of your analysis using Python's Matplotlib library
- Use Apache Spark's MLlib package to perform machine learning on large datasets

Kali Linux Cookbook - Second Edition
Corey P. Schultz, Bob Perciaccante

ISBN: 978-1-78439-030-3

- Acquire the key skills of ethical hacking to perform penetration testing
- Learn how to perform network reconnaissance
- Discover vulnerabilities in hosts
- Attack vulnerabilities to take control of workstations and servers
- Understand password cracking to bypass security
- Learn how to hack into wireless networks
- Attack web and database servers to exfiltrate data
- Obfuscate your command and control connections to avoid firewall and IPS detection

Leave a review - let other readers know what you think

Please share your thoughts on this book with others by leaving a review on the site that you bought it from. If you purchased the book from Amazon, please leave us an honest review on this book's Amazon page. This is vital so that other potential readers can see and use your unbiased opinion to make purchasing decisions, we can understand what our customers think about our products, and our authors can see your feedback on the title that they have worked with Packt to create. It will only take a few minutes of your time, but is valuable to other potential customers, our authors, and Packt. Thank you!

Index

W

Y

Z